"If you are a science teacher or homeschool parent [ ] engaging approach to teaching science, this book prov[ ] students *experience* (not just learn about) science. This organized, research-based resource fits the title of a "toolbox." It can help anyone from the novice to veteran teacher plan and deliver lessons that will excite students about concepts in science (aligned to the Next Generation Science Standards)."

Dr. Amanda McAdams, Director of Curriculum in Wyoming's Lincoln County School District #2, 2010 Arizona Teacher of the Year

"This book contains valuable strategies for both new and veteran teachers. It is an organized and interesting compilation of ready to use tools that will engage students at all levels."

Robin Norwich, NBCT, math and physics teacher, 2019 recipient of the Sloan Award for Excellence in Teaching Science and Mathematics

"This book is a comprehensive collection of creative lesson plan strategies with detailed references and supplementary resources cited. Also, Part III provides many general strategies for effective teaching. Clearly written in both content and organization, it provides specific and detailed concrete examples for putting into practice the authors' Introduction: 'Not having heard something is not as good as having heard it, having heard it is not as good as having seen it, having seen it is not as good as knowing it, knowing it is not as good as putting it into practice' — attributed to Chinese Philosopher Xun Kuang.

I recommend it to any science teacher, and especially those new to teaching science or with minimal scientific knowledge. I think, with this book, even I, an engineer, could teach a quality science course."

Jon S. Wilson, BSME, MAE, MSIE; 25+ years practicing engineer and 25+ years training practicing engineers

"As a teacher, I have often heard professionals discuss the importance of 'soft skills' our students require upon graduation. The ideas in *The Science Teacher's Toolbox* successfully describe solid strategies for teachers to utilize in their classrooms to get kids experiencing science, producing thinking, problem-solving citizens that the world will need."

Connie Kennedy, K-12 Mathematics & Science Instructional Support Specialist, Bay City Public Schools

The Science Teacher's Toolbox

A winning educational formula of engaging lessons and powerful strategies for science teachers in numerous classroom settings

The *Teacher's Toolbox* series is an innovative, research-based resource providing teachers with instructional strategies for students of all levels and abilities. Each book in the collection focuses on a specific content area. Clear, concise guidance enables teachers to quickly integrate low-prep, high-value lessons and strategies in their middle school and high school classrooms. Every strategy follows a practical, how-to format established by the series editors.

The Science Teacher's Toolbox is a classroom-tested resource, offering hundreds of accessible, student-friendly lessons and strategies that can be implemented in a variety of educational settings. Concise chapters fully explain the research basis, necessary technology, Next Generation Science Standards correlation, and implementation of each lesson and strategy.

Favoring a hands-on approach, this book provides step-by-step instructions that help teachers to apply their new skills and knowledge in their classrooms immediately. Lessons cover topics such as setting up labs, conducting experiments, using graphs, analyzing data, writing lab reports, incorporating technology, assessing student learning, teaching all-ability students, and much more. This book enables science teachers to:

- Understand how each strategy works in the classroom and avoid common mistakes
- Promote culturally responsive classrooms
- Activate and enhance prior knowledge
- Bring fresh and engaging activities into the classroom and the science lab

Written by respected authors and educators, *The Science Teacher's Toolbox: Hundreds of Practical Ideas to Support Your Students* is an invaluable aid for upper elementary, middle school, and high school science educators as well as those in teacher education programs and staff development professionals.

Books in the *Teacher's Toolbox* series, published by Jossey-Bass:

The ELL Teacher's Toolbox, by Larry Ferlazzo and Katie Hull Sypnieski
The Math Teacher's Toolbox, by Bobson Wong, Larisa Bukalov, Larry Ferlazzo, and Katie Hull Sypnieski
The Science Teacher's Toolbox, by Tara C. Dale, Mandi S. White, Larry Ferlazzo, and Katie Hull Sypnieski
The Social Studies Teacher's Toolbox, by Elisabeth Johnson, Evelyn Ramos LaMarr, Larry Ferlazzo, and Katie Hull Sypnieski

The Science Teacher's Toolbox

Hundreds of Practical Ideas to Support Your Students

TARA C. DALE
MANDI S. WHITE
LARRY FERLAZZO
KATIE HULL SYPNIESKI

The Teacher's Toolbox Series

JB JOSSEY-BASS™
A Wiley Brand

Published by Jossey-Bass
A Wiley Brand
111 River Street, Hoboken NJ 07030—www.josseybass.com

Jossey-Bass books and products are available through most bookstores. To contact Jossey-Bass directly call our Customer Care Department within the U.S. at 800-956-7739, outside the U.S. at 317-572-3986, or fax 317-572-4002.

Wiley also publishes its books in a variety of electronic formats and by print-on-demand. Some material included with standard print versions of this book may not be included in e-books or in print-on-demand. For more information about Wiley products, visit www.wiley.com.

Library of Congress Cataloging-in-Publication Data is available:

ISBN 9781119570103 (Paperback)
ISBN 9781119570172 (ePDF)
ISBN 9781119570196 (epub)

Cover Design: Wiley
Cover Images: © GeorgePeters/Getty Images | © cnythzl/Getty Images

Printed in the United States of America

FIRST EDITION

PB Printing V10018158_031920

Clay Farrow has been a graphic artist since 2000, working in both print and digital media. He lives with his wife Terri and their two ill-behaved dogs in Phoenix, Arizona. Mr. Farrow designed the three icons that represent thinking critically, problem-solving creatively, and communicating effectively.

Contents

4. Strategies for Teaching the Inquiry Process 87

5. Strategies for Using Project-Based Learning 115

6. Strategies for Teaching the Engineering Process 133

II   Integration of ELA, Mathematics, and the Arts   159

7. Strategies for Teaching Vocabulary 161

8. Strategies for Teaching Reading Comprehension 181

9. Strategies for Teaching Writing 205

12. Strategies for Incorporating the Arts and Kinesthetic Movement 331

List of Tables

About the Authors

*T*ara C. Dale is a Nationally Board Certified Teacher (NBCT), currently teaching high school science, and is an instructional coach. Previously, she has taught middle school science and social studies in addition to the following high school classes: biology, ecology, earth and space science, AP psychology, and AP environmental science. She earned her Bachelors of Science degrees in psychology and biology from Arizona State University. She earned her Master's in Secondary Education from University of Phoenix. In 2014, she was an Arizona Teacher of the Year Finalist and in 2011 was honored as a STEM Innovation Hero by Science Foundation Arizona. She sits on the Board of Directors for the Arizona NBCT Network and is on the Superintendent Teacher Advisor Team for Maricopa County, Arizona. Her field work includes the effects of deforestation on biodiversity in the rainforests of Ecuador and the diurnal movement of plankton in the surface of the ocean as it relates to water temperature.

Tara has facilitated professional development classes and presented at conferences throughout the United States, most notably with ACT, the National Network of State Teachers of the Year, Student Achievement Partners, and Collaborative for Student Success. She and Mandi White have contributed to Larry Ferlazzo's *Education Week* Teacher blog and his BAM! Classroom Q&A radio show.

Tara was in the financial industry for 14 years prior to becoming a public school teacher. She is married with two children.

Mandi S. White has worked in education for 13 years and is currently an academic and behavior specialist at Kyrene del Pueblo Middle School in Chandler, Arizona, where she works with students and teachers across all settings to improve student success in school. Mandi began her career as a middle school special education resource teacher and later moved into a middle school English language arts teaching position. Mandi also has experience teaching middle school social studies and math. She earned her Bachelor of Science degree in Interdisciplinary Liberal Studies and her first Master's of Education degree in Special Education from James Madison University. In 2017, she earned her second Master's of Education degree in Educational Leadership from Arizona State University. Additionally, Mandi has earned a graduate certificate in Positive Behavior Support from Northern Arizona University.

Mandi has worked with Tara Dale on presenting professional development to educators on teaching for understanding both through their school district and at an ACT conference in 2018. She has also contributed to Larry Ferlazzo's *Education Week* Teacher blog and his BAM! Classroom Q&A radio show.

Mandi currently resides in Chandler, Arizona.

About the Editors of the Toolbox Series

Larry Ferlazzo and Katie Hull Sypnieski wrote *The ELL Teacher's Toolbox* and conceived of a series replicating the format of their popular book. They identified authors of all the books in the series and worked closely with them during their writing and publication.

Larry Ferlazzo teaches English, Social Studies, and International Baccalaureate classes to English Language Learners and others at Luther Burbank High School in Sacramento, California.

He has written nine books: *The ELL Teacher's Toolbox* (with co-author Katie Hull Sypnieski); *Navigating the Common Core with English Language Learners* (with co-author Katie Hull Sypnieski); *The ESL/ELL Teacher's Survival Guide* (with co-author Katie Hull Sypnieski); *Building a Community of Self-Motivated Learners: Strategies to Help Students Thrive in School and Beyond*; *Classroom Management Q&As: Expert Strategies for Teaching*; *Self-Driven Learning: Teaching Strategies for Student Motivation*; *Helping Students Motivate Themselves: Practical Answers to Classroom Challenges*; *English Language Learners: Teaching Strategies That Work*; and *Building Parent Engagement in Schools* (with co-author Lorie Hammond).

He has won several awards, including the Leadership for a Changing World Award from the Ford Foundation, and was the Grand Prize Winner of the International Reading Association Award for Technology and Reading.

He writes a popular education blog at http://larryferlazzo.edublogs.org/, a weekly teacher advice column for *Education Week* Teacher blog and posts for the *New York Times* and the *Washington Post*. He also hosts a weekly radio show on BAM! Education Radio.

He was a community organizer for 19 years prior to becoming a public school teacher.

Larry is married and has three children and two grandchildren.

A basketball team he played for came in last place every year from 2012 to 2017. He retired from league play after that year, and the team then played for the championship. These results might indicate that Larry made a wise career choice in not pursuing a basketball career.

Katie Hull Sypnieski has taught English language learners and others at the secondary level for over 20 years. She currently teaches middle school English Language Arts and Social Studies at Fern Bacon Middle School in Sacramento, California.

She leads professional development for educators as a teaching consultant with the Area 3 Writing Project at the University of California, Davis.

She is co-author (with Larry Ferlazzo) of *The ESL/ELL Teacher's Survival Guide, Navigating the Common Core with English Language Learners,* and *The ELL Teacher's Toolbox.* She has written articles for the *Washington Post, ASCD Educational Leadership,* and *Edutopia.* She and Larry have developed two video series with *Education Week* on differentiation and student motivation.

Katie lives in Sacramento with her husband and their three children.

Acknowledgments

Tara C. Dale: First and foremost, I want to thank my husband, Joe, and our children, Josh and Sami, who have been supportive and patient throughout this project. They knew this was important to me and because of that, it was important to them.

I'm forever grateful to Mandi White, who was thoughtful, honest in her feedback, and a cheerleader. I believe we spent more time together than we did with anyone else this past year, and my admiration for her has only grown. Working side-by-side for more than a decade has made me a better teacher and a better person.

Thank you also to Larry Ferlazzo and Katie Hull Sypnieski, our editors. I thought writing a book would be simple because I'm passionate about the content. After receiving the eighth edited version from them, I quickly realized there is much more to writing than I had ever imagined. They were patient in their explanations, decisive when we couldn't make decisions, and a guiding force throughout the project. Their suggestions, not just with editing but also with the writing process itself, were appreciated, effective, and appropriate. They were an integral part of this book!

I am most appreciative of Pete Gaughan and Amy Fandrei at Jossey-Bass. They were continually accessible, willing to answer all questions, and address any issues we had throughout the writing process. It always felt as though we were a team. Every time we had to reach out to Pete and Amy, they responded quickly and professionally. And, yes, Pete, I finally learned how to take a picture—add more light!

Last but not least, I want to thank the thousands of students who have gone through my classroom during my career. I often asked them to try new learning strategies that required them to trust me. They never faltered as we enjoyed the learning process together. I often share that I wake up before my alarm clock and it's because I can't wait to get to school. I love going every day because I get to spend my time with amazing young people.

Mandi S. White: I would like to start off by thanking my family and friends, who have given me so much love and support through this process. Additionally, I am so thankful for my co-author, Tara Dale, who was patient, encouraging, and kept me sane as we spent countless hours together. I could not imagine embarking on this book-writing journey with any other person. Thank you to Larry Ferlazzo and Katie Hull-Sypnieski for their guidance and continuous support. Also, a big thank you to Pete Gaughan and Amy Fandrei at Jossey-Bass for their patience, understanding, and assistance with all the many aspects of book writing that we, as first-time authors, were unaware of. Lastly, the biggest appreciation goes out to all of the students I have had the honor of calling "my kids" throughout the years. You all have made me a better teacher and human and I am ever so grateful for that.

Both of us would like to express our appreciation to the many educators who have shared their ideas with us throughout the years to use both in our classrooms and this book.

Letter from the Editors

"Science" comes from the Latin words *scientia*, meaning knowledge, and *scindere*, meaning "to divide."

Mandi White and Tara Dale have done an incredible job of doing just that in *The Science Teacher's Toolbox*: identifying the critical knowledge that science teachers need and dividing it up into exceptionally practical and accessible chapters.

Though we are not formal science teachers, we often do incorporate science as language learning opportunities with our English language learner students, and Larry teaches science units as part of his International Baccalaureate Theory of Knowledge classes.

We know just enough science, and know more than enough about the "science of teaching," to say with confidence that *The Science Teacher's Toolbox* will be an invaluable resource to educators everywhere, and not just those in the science classroom. Many of Tara's and Mandi's instructional strategies can be easily implemented in many different content classes.

We're proud to introduce their book as another member of the *Teacher's Toolbox* "family."

Larry Ferlazzo and Katie Hull Sypnieski

Introduction

Not having heard something is not as good as having heard it; having heard it is not as good as having seen it; having seen it is not as good as knowing it; knowing it is not as good as putting it into practice.—attributed to Chinese philosopher Xun Kuang.

(Knobloch, 1994, p. 81)

When people see a science classroom what do they expect to see? Is it a teacher in front of the class lecturing with a slideshow while the students diligently take notes? Or is it students forming hypotheses and creating experiments to solve a problem?

We firmly believe that regardless of the grade level or concept, students should be *experiencing* science. They should be provided with opportunities to be engaged beyond just hearing and reading about science. Yes, there is a time and place for direct instruction, but it should not be the primary focus of any science classroom. All of the strategies in this book focus on intellectually engaging *all* students to increase learning.

The learning activities in our book can be used to teach all science content. We focus on the four main disciplinary core ideas identified in the Next Generation Science Standards (NGSS): (1) physical sciences; (2) earth and space sciences; (3) life sciences; and (4) engineering, technology, and application of science. Each strategy, when applicable, will include the Science and Engineering Practices and/or Crosscutting Concepts, which are also found in the NGSS. When the NGSS were written, each performance expectation combined a relevant practice of science or engineering, with a core disciplinary idea and crosscutting concept (NGSS, 2013b, p. 382).

During Tara's second year as a seventh grade science teacher, a student asked, "When will we ever need to know the moon phases?" After reflecting on her response to this student, Tara felt as though she had failed to provide a valid answer. She realized that most of the content her state standards required her to teach would not be useful to the average student. As a result, she shifted her focus and made the content a vehicle through which to teach her students what we call the Skills for Intentional Scholars. We define an "intentional scholar" as one who is actively learning, engaged, and thinking while in school, not passively receiving information and spitting back facts on Friday's test. There are three skills we believe all intentional scholars should have: (1) to think critically; (2) to problem solve creatively; and (3) to communicate effectively. Each strategy in this book will address at least one of the Skills for Intentional Scholars, while also effectively supporting science learning in a classroom.

The NGSS highlight the need to incorporate Skills for Intentional Scholars. While answering a question on how critical thinking and communication skills are addressed in their standards, they state:

> It is important to understand that the scientific practices in the *Next Generation Science Standards* (NGSS), as defined by the National Research Council (NRC), include the critical thinking and communication skills that students need for postsecondary success and citizenship in a world fueled by innovations in science and technology. These science practices encompass the habits and skills that scientists and engineers use day in and day out. In the NGSS these practices are wedded to content. In other words, content and practice are intertwined in the standards, just as they are in the NRC *Framework* and in today's workplace. (NGSS, n.d., para. 2)

The NGSS support the idea that all science-related teaching strategies need to incorporate active learning and allow students to effectively demonstrate their understanding of scientific concepts while utilizing the three Skills for Intentional Scholars. Science classes must be more than simply requiring students to memorize facts.

The Teacher's Toolbox series consists of four books, including strategies for teaching English language learners, social studies, math, and science. The first book in the series, *The ELL Teacher's Toolbox* (2018) by Larry Ferlazzo and Katie Hull Sypnieski, uses an easy-to-read format that we've chosen to follow and modify slightly. This format breaks each strategy into the following sections:

- what the strategy is
- why we like the strategy
- research that supports the strategy

- which of the three Skills for Intentional Scholars is being taught while using this strategy, which will be indicated using an icon to help teachers quickly identify which of the three skills are being practiced. Where appropriate, we will also be listing the crosscutting concepts and science and engineering practices from the NGSS connected to each strategy.

- applications of the strategy (practical ideas for using it in the classroom)

- how to execute the strategy while differentiating for students with diverse needs, such as those with learning challenges, English language learners, and advanced students

- what could go wrong while using the strategy and how to proactively address those problems

- Technology Connections for the strategy (available online)

- attributions to recognize other educators who have contributed ideas to the strategy

- finally, each strategy ends with related figures (handouts and student examples). These are available online at http://www.wiley.com/go/scienceteacherstoolbox.

> A "bonus" chapter, "Strategies for Using Scientific Tools and Technology"—not in this version of this book—is also available at http://www.wiley.com/go/scienceteacherstoolbox.

This book is divided into three Parts. Part I highlights several lab formats, such as the scientific method, project-based learning, and engineering process. Part II focuses on strategies that integrate reading, writing, speaking and listening, mathematics, and the arts into science lessons. The final Part is entitled Additional Resources, which contains strategies that did not necessarily fit into the other sections, for example, methods for activating prior knowledge, reviewing content, and assessing student learning.

This science strategy book will enhance science classrooms from fourth to twelfth grade. Additionally, many of these strategies can be integrated into other curricular areas with great success. We hope you get as much use out of them as we have throughout the years!

PART 1

Science Labs

CHAPTER 1

Strategies for Teaching Lab Safety

What Is It?

Lab safety includes the behavioral expectations, rules, and procedures that students follow during an interactive lab.

Why We Like It

During the first week of school, teachers can focus on getting to know their students. In addition, they can provide opportunities for their students to learn about each other, the teacher, and the classroom. See Chapter 14: Strategies for Cultural Responsiveness for resources that help you to get to know your students.

We've found that lab safety is the logical first unit in a science class. Students need to know the teacher's expectations and have time to practice safe behavior prior to doing science labs. Lab safety, when implemented correctly, reduces the risk of injury to the teacher and their students while also minimizing damage to lab equipment. Most important of all, lab safety can enhance student engagement and learning in science.

Supporting Research

Every science class should be teeming with lab and fieldwork that requires students to behave in specific ways to avoid injury. The National Science Teachers Association (NSTA) declares that "inherent in conducting science activities, however, is the potential for injury" (NSTA, 2015). Students need to learn how to proactively avoid injury as well as how to appropriately react if an accident occurs.

Teaching students to follow lab safety rules provides them with an opportunity to practice taking personal responsibility. Some teachers believe punitive measures, such as receiving an F on a quiz, is an effective way to teach personal responsibility. However, simply receiving a bad grade does not teach students how to behave in a more responsible manner. Students are more likely to learn how to manage their behavior and attitudes when they receive guidance from an adult who takes the time to encourage students to reflect on their actions (Wormeli, 2016). Instruction on lab safety is a meaningful way to show students the bigger picture of a situation and, thus, enhance personal responsibility.

Skills for Intentional Scholars/NGSS Standards

The activities in this chapter require students to practice thinking critically as they apply their newly learned lab safety rules and procedures. Simply memorizing the rules won't suffice, especially in the case of an emergency. Students will not have time to read the lab safety rules when an emergency arises. They must know the rules well enough in order to instinctively react appropriately in a dangerous situation.

Application

There are multiple ways to introduce and teach lab safety in science classrooms. We will highlight the use of a contract and safety rule story, as well as list several other interactive methods that we use to reinforce appropriate lab behavior.

SCIENCE SAFETY CONTRACT

We use a Science Safety Contract to introduce the rules. It is important to read every rule with students before having them sign the bottom. Students then take the contract home to obtain a parent signature. Figure 1.1: Science Safety Contract English is an example of a lab safety form that can be adapted for all grade levels. A Spanish version of the contract is available in Figure 1.2: Science Safety Contract Spanish.

LAB SAFETY RULES STORY

This activity gives students an opportunity to interact with their new learning about lab safety. It can also be used as a formative assessment to determine how well students understand lab safety rules in context. See Chapter 17: Strategies for Assessing Student Learning for additional formative assessment resources.

To personalize the lesson for our students, we replace the student names in Figure 1.3: Identifying Broken Lab Safety Rules with our current students' names. Every class period receives a unique copy that includes four of the students from the respective class. We find that students tend to be more engaged when they find their names in the story, which helps us build a positive rapport with them. Figure 1.4: Identifying Broken Lab Safety Rules—Answer Key provides the answers, assuming a teacher is using Figure 1.1: Science Safety Contract.

OTHER INTERACTIVE WAYS TO TEACH LAB SAFETY

There are many fun and interactive ways to teach lab safety that require students to do more than memorize a list of rules. Here are some ideas for activities that students can do to demonstrate their understanding of lab safety:

- Draw a cartoon showing what happens when lab safety rules aren't followed.
- Produce a video explaining why it's important to follow lab safety rules.
- Write and act out a skit that demonstrates the lab safety rules. Have small groups create two skits each—one showing how to correctly follow lab rules and the other showing an example of not following them. Not only can students have fun with this juxtaposition, but showing "bad" examples is also an effective learning and teaching strategy (Taylor, Wirth, Olvina, & Alvero, 2016).
- Analyze a "lab scene." Before class begins, set up a lab scenario where several lab rules were broken and someone has fallen victim to the violations. To make this interactive, the victim can be a parent or student volunteer. Include props such as a broken beaker, a Bunsen burner that's been left unattended, and water on the floor. Students then analyze the scene to determine which rules were violated and what changes need to be made in the lab to avoid future accidents. Crime scene tape can be added and is available at most local dollar stores.
- Each student creates a poster that focuses on one rule; some rules may be duplicated, depending on class size. Students share their posters during a gallery walk during which they provide constructive ideas and feedback to their peers by applying a sticky note to other students' posters. (This is always the first student work we display, and it's available for students to add to their portfolios for parent/teacher conferences.)

Students must pass a test demonstrating their knowledge of lab safety rules and procedures. Figure 1.5: Science Lab Safety Quiz is our true/false test.

DIFFERENTIATION FOR DIVERSE LEARNERS

All lab safety activities can be modified by allowing students to have more time or to work with a partner.

When we watch online lab safety videos in class, English language learners and hearing-impaired students can benefit from closed captioning. In addition, consider playing the videos at a slower speed to make them more accessible to all.

Learning lab safety is usually easier for older students because they've experienced most, if not all of the rules, in previous classrooms. Younger students may require more instruction and practice. We sometimes use a reading strategy called Cloze, which is discussed in depth in Chapter 8: Strategies for Teaching Reading Comprehension. Cloze activities provide students with the lab safety rules contract with keywords missing. Students are challenged to use context clues and background knowledge to guess the word that best fits in the blank. For example, using Figure 1.1: Science Safety Contract, rule number 1 would read like this:

> Wear lab safety _____ when chemicals are used or something is being heated.

Students then work independently or in pairs to determine that the blank should be filled with the word "goggles." After providing ample time for students to fill each blank, we then provide them with a word bank so they can begin to check the validity of their answers. The word bank can also be shared at the beginning of the activity with students who may need extra scaffolding.

Differentiation can also occur when assessing students.

Instead of taking a traditional summative test, students can prove they've learned a concept using other formats. We provide a variety of options for students to review and ask them to select one. When students are given choices, they can perceive classroom activities as more important because they feel their choice is going to impact their grade so they must make a good one (Marzano, n.d.). Also, giving students choices can enhance a sense of autonomy and increase motivation (Ferlazzo, 2015). In our experience, students who are provided options also tend to complete more work.

Students can choose from any of the following to demonstrate their new learning:

- Take an oral test (particularly for students who have reading comprehension challenges).

- Create a lab safety hero. The student chooses five lab safety rules they think are the most important. The hero they create then "explains" why these five rules are the most important, including the consequences of not following these rules. After giving the hero a catchy name, the student then draws and colors a picture of his/her hero. Teachers can allow students the option of choosing how to present their heroes (PowerPoint, Google Slides, Prezi, a skit, or a poster).

- Find an online article dated within the last year where someone didn't follow lab safety rules. Students write a summary of the event including who, what, when, where, why, and how with an emphasis on the specific lab safety rule(s) that was broken and the consequence(s) that followed. Searching "lab accidents" followed by the year will generate many options.

- Write a letter to a younger student explaining the lab safety expectations of their future classroom. The student's letter must explain the lab safety rules in a meaningful way so the younger student understands the expectations of how to behave in a lab and why it is important to follow lab safety rules.

- Create a lab safety board game that includes three or four players. The student's board game must cover at least ten of the lab safety rules.

Differentiation can also be accomplished in how a teacher writes directions. For example, Figure 1.5: Science Lab Safety Quiz is a simple true-false quiz teachers can use to assess their students. The directions state, "Indicate if the following statements are true or false." This quiz can be made more difficult for advanced students by altering the directions. Here is one example of how the directions could read:

Answer the following true-false questions. If a statement is false, you must alter the statement so it is true.

See Chapter 17: Strategies for Assessing Student Learning, for more assessment strategies that can be utilized in a science classroom.

Student Handouts and Examples

Figure 1.1: Science Safety Contract English (Student Handout)
Figure 1.2: Science Safety Contract Spanish (Student Handout)
Figure 1.3: Identifying Broken Lab Safety Rules (Student Handout)
Figure 1.4: Identifying Broken Lab Safety Rules—Answer Key
Figure 1.5: Science Lab Safety Quiz (Student Handout)

What Could Go Wrong?

Students cannot participate in a lab until two things are complete. First, students must return their signed Science Safety Contracts. Second, they must prove they know the lab safety rules either by passing a lab safety test or accurately completing an alternate summative activity.

Some students struggle to obtain their parent's signature on the contract. To help these students, we email the Science Safety Contract to the parents and ask them to respond to the email. If a parent doesn't have email, we make a phone call and ensure the child has a copy of the contract to take home that afternoon. We also work with our administration and district to develop translated versions of the contract based on student and family needs. Figure 1.2: Science Safety Contract is a Spanish-language version of our contract.

Some students don't pass a lab safety test the first time or complete an alternate summative activity accurately. To ensure they know safety rules and procedures prior to participating in science labs, these students must retake the original test, retake a different version of the test, or redo their summative activity. Their new grade replaces the original grade. They should be allowed to test and redo their activities until they earn at least 90% on the assessment. We let English language learners use online translators while taking the safety test.

Technology Connections

There are many YouTube lab safety videos that are appropriate for all ages. They are usually made by secondary teachers or their students and include humor. Some are parodies, some are cartoons, and yet others are raps. Simply search for "lab safety videos."

Attribution

Many thanks to Monica Valera for translating our Science Safety Contract from English into Spanish.

Figures

Student Name_____

Science Safety Contract

Safety is the number one priority in our classroom. The following rules will be strictly enforced. If you choose to violate a lab safety rule, you will be removed from the current lab and possibly future labs.

Dress Code

1. Wear lab safety goggles when chemicals are used or something is being heated. Know where the eye wash station is. If something gets into your eye, go directly to the eye wash and start rinsing your eye. I will come to you at the eye wash station and help you.

Figure 1.1 Science Safety Contract English (Student Handout)

2. Tie back long hair to avoid it accidentally mixing with chemicals or catching on fire. To avoid contamination, don't apply make-up in the classroom and don't comb your hair here either.
3. Remove loose jewelry and secure loose clothing to ensure these items do not catch on fire, causes spills, or contaminate chemicals.

General Safety Rules

4. Come into our classroom quietly and go directly to your desk. Do not interact with lab materials until you have been instructed to do so. It is very common for you to come into our room and find lab materials on counters and tables. Exercise self-control and avoid them until you receive directions for how to use them properly and safely.
5. Read and listen to all directions. Start with step number 1 and when you're done with #1, go on to #2. If you aren't sure about something, then ask! It's better to be safe than sorry!
6. To ensure your safety and the safety of those around you, horseplay will NOT be tolerated during a lab. If you don't keep your hands to yourself, then you will be asked to leave for the rest of the period and you may be excluded from future labs.
7. Do NOT eat in our classroom. This room has been used for mixing chemicals, dissecting specimens, and other science projects. I don't want you to consume something that will make you sick. You can drink water but it needs to be clear and in a closed container. It also needs to be kept at your desk. Do not take your water to your lab table.
8. When your lab is complete, clean up your lab station. Clean all materials, dry the space, and return all materials to their original location. Also, push in your chair so there is a clear area for us to walk.
9. Complete every chemical lab by washing your hands with warm water and soap. Hand sanitizer is not soap!

First Aid

10. REPORT ALL ACCIDENTS TO ME IMMEDIATELY! It does not matter how small (or big).
11. Know where all of the safety equipment is in our classroom. Where is the eye wash? Lab shower? Phone? Lab safety goggles? Exit? Fire extinguisher? Fire blanket?

Chemical Safety

12. NEVER touch, taste, or smell a chemical. If you need to smell a chemical, then hold it six inches away from you and gently wave your hand over the substance towards your nose. This action will "waft" some of the fumes toward your nose without exposing you to a large dose.

Figure 1.1 (Continued)

13. NEVER MIX CHEMICALS FOR THE "FUN OF IT"! The result may be disastrous.

14. Keep lids closed on all containers when they are not being used. This will help you avoid accidental spills. Be sure all materials are kept at the back end of the lab table so they aren't easily knocked to the floor.

15. Rinse off any chemicals that have spilled or splashed onto your skin. DO THIS IMMEDIATELY! Do not come to me first. Take care of yourself first! I will come to you to help you with the spill.

I understand and agree to follow all of the safety rules discussed in class and within this contract. I accept the consequences for not following all of the safety rules discussed in class and within this contract.

Student Signature: _____ Date: _____

Parent/Guardian Signature: _____ Date: _____

Figure 1.1 (Continued)

Nombre del estudiante_____

Contracto De Seguridad para la Clase de Ciencias

La seguridad es la mayor prioridad en nuestra clase. Las siguientes reglas serán estrictamente aplicadas. Al violar algunas de estas normas de seguridad del laboratorio, usted será destituido del laboratorio y posiblemente de otros laboratorios en el futuro.

Código de Vestimenta

1. Utilice gafas de seguridad cuando use químicos o cuando algo se está calentando. Debe saber dónde está la estación de lavatorio de ojos. Si ocurre un accidente y tiene algo en el ojo, vaya inmediatamente al lavatorio de ojos y empiece a lavarse los ojos. Yo iré rápidamente al lavatorio de ojos para ayudarle.
2. El pelo largo debe ser atado para evitar un accidente con los químicos o el fuego. Para no contaminar, no se maquille, ni se peine el pelo en el laboratorio.
3. Quítese joyas colgantes y no use ropa suelta, si lo hace, asegúresela para evitar fuego, contaminación, o tumbar algo.

Las Reglas Generales

4. Llegue al salón de clase silenciosamente y vaya directamente a su escritorio. No toque los materiales del laboratorio hasta que reciba las instrucciones. Sería muy común llegar a clase y encontrar los materiales del laboratorio en las mesas y mostradores. Debe controlarse y evitar tocarlas.
5. Lea y siga todas las instrucciones. Empiece con el paso número 1 y cuando termine con el número 1 siga con el número 2. Si no entiende algo, pregúnteme. ¡Es mejor prevenir que lamentar!
6. El mal comportamiento NUNCA será permitido en el laboratorio. Si no mantiene las manos en su persona, usted tendrá que salir del laboratorio y no podrá participar en la clase y posiblemente en futuros laboratorios.
7. NUNCA coma en el salón de clase. En este salón hemos mezclado químicos, disecado especímenes y otros experimentos de ciencias. No quiero que usted consuma algo que lo enferme. Sí puede tomar agua, pero tiene que estar en una botella tapada. Su botella de agua tiene que quedarse en su escritorio. No lleve el agua a la mesa del laboratorio.
8. Cuando haya terminado con su trabajo, limpie su estación de laboratorio. Limpie, seque y regrese todos los materiales a su lugar. También empuje su silla para mantener espacio para caminar en el salón.

Figure 1.2 Science Safety Contract Spanish (Student Handout)

9. Termine cada experimento de química lavándose las manos con agua tibia y jabón. El gel antibacterial no es jabón.

Los Primeros Auxilios

10. ¡INFÓRMEME DE CUALQUIER ACCIDENTE INMEDIATAMENTE! No importa si sea un accidente pequeño o grande, yo necesito saber.

11. Aprenda dónde está localizado todo el equipo de seguridad. ¿Dónde está el lavatorio de ojos? ¿Dónde está el teléfono? ¿Dónde está la ducha del laboratorio? ¿Dónde están las gafas de seguridad? ¿Dónde está la salida de emergencia? ¿Dónde está el extinguidor de incendios? ¿Dónde está la manta del fuego?

La Seguridad de los Químicos

12. NUNCA toque, pruebe o huela un químico. Si necesita oler un químico, mantenga el químico por lo menos seis pulgadas de su persona y suavemente mueva la mano arriba de la substancia hacía la nariz. Esto dirigirá el humo hacía la nariz sin exponerlo a una dosis grande.

13. ¡NUNCA MEZCLE QUÍMICOS POR GUSTO! El resultado puede ser desastroso.

14. Mantenga los frascos cerrados cuando no los está usando. Esto ayuda evitar accidentes. Asegure que todos los materiales estén en el fondo de la mesa del laboratorio para evitar tumbarlos al piso.

15. Enjuague cualquier químico que ha tumbado o que ha tocado su piel. ¡HÁGALO INMEDIATAMENTE! No venga a informarme primero. ¡Cuídese primero! Yo iré a ayudarle con el derrame.

Yo entiendo y estoy de acuerdo en seguir todas las reglas de seguridad mencionadas en clase y en este contrato. Yo acepto las consecuencias al no seguir estas reglas de seguridad.

Firma del estudiante: _____   Fecha: _____

Firma del padre/guardián: _____   Fecha: _____

Figure 1.2 (Continued)

Name _____

Period _____ Date _____

Identifying Broken Lab Safety Rules

Directions: The following story includes many broken lab safety rules. Using the safety rules outlined in the Science Safety Contract, identify when someone breaks a lab safety rule in the story. Underline when a rule is broken and next to it, write the rule number that was broken. The first one was done for you.

Jalen, Mateo, Lily, and Emma were excited to begin their lab. Their teacher had been talking about burning rocks with acid since the first day of school. Lily and Emma placed a sample of the first acid in a test tube. Emma <u>stuck her nose directly into the test tube</u> *(rule number 12)* to smell the acid. Meanwhile, Jalen obtained 15 mL of the second acid. It seemed to have an unusual odor that made his nose feel funny, so he put a drop of it on his finger and tasted it.

Mateo mentioned to everyone that they should wear safety goggles but Lily made a good point that you look like a dork with lab goggles so they decided to bypass the goggles.

Emma and Jalen had a great time sword fighting with pipettes! What fun science lab can be!

By this time, Lily was growing bored, so she started to mix the two acids even though the lab's instructions didn't say anything about mixing them.

Emma was distracted by her friends who were in a different lab group. She never did any of the work but instead focused on getting ready for her next class. She brushed her hair, applied lipstick, and started eating a granola bar.

As Mateo performed his experiment, Lily followed directions. She started the lab by placing five drops of the first acid onto the first rock sample. While holding the pipette in one hand and the test tube in the other, she tripped! She caught herself so she didn't fall but she did splash some of the acid on her thumb, then splashed a little more on her shirt sleeve. Then, without putting the top back onto the bottle of acid, Lily went to test something else. When the group was finished working, they left the remaining acids in the test tubes and put the test tubes away in the rack.

As she was leaving the lab, Emma noticed she had a small cut on her hand. She decided it was not important because it didn't hurt. She chose not to mention it to her teacher.

Figure 1.3 Identifying Broken Lab Safety Rules (Student Handout)

Name _____ **Answer Key** _____

Period _____

Identifying Broken Lab Safety Rules–Answer Key

Directions: The following story includes many broken lab safety rules. Using the safety rules outlined in the Science Safety Contract, identify when someone breaks a lab safety rule in the story. Underline when a rule is broken and next to it, write the rule number that was broken. The first one was done for you.

Jalen, Mateo, Lily, and Emma were excited to begin their lab. Their teacher had been talking about burning rocks with acid since the first day of school. Lily and Emma placed a sample of the first acid in a test tube. Emma <u>stuck her nose directly into the test tube</u> *(rule number 12)* to smell the acid. Meanwhile, Jalen obtained 15 mL of the second acid. It seemed to have an unusual odor that made his nose feel funny, so <u>he put a drop of it on his finger and tasted it</u>. *(rule number 12)*

Mateo mentioned to everyone that they should wear safety goggles but Lily made a good point that you look like a dork with lab goggles so the students <u>decided to bypass the goggles</u>. *(rule number 1)*

Emma and Jalen had a great time <u>sword fighting</u> with pipettes! What fun science lab can be! *(rule number 6)*

By this time, Lily was growing bored, so she started to <u>mix the two acids even though the lab's instructions didn't say anything about mixing them</u>. *(rule numbers 5 and 13)*

Emma was distracted by her friends who were in a different lab group. She never did any of the work but instead focused on getting ready for her next class. <u>She brushed her hair, applied lipstick, and started eating a granola bar.</u> *(rule numbers 2 and 7)*

As Mateo performed his experiment, Lily followed directions. She started to observe the lab by placing five drops of the first acid onto the first rock sample. While holding the pipette in one hand and the test tube in the other, she tripped! She caught herself so she didn't fall but she did splash some of the acid on her thumb, then splashed a little more on her shirt sleeve. Then, <u>without putting the top back onto the bottle of acid</u> *(rule number 14)*, Lily went to test something else. When the group was finished working, they <u>left the remaining acids in the test tubes</u> and put the test tubes away in the rack. *(rule number 8)*

As she was leaving the lab, Emma noticed she had a small cut on her hand. She decided it was not important because it didn't hurt. <u>She chose not to mention it to her teacher.</u> *(rule number 10)*

(And the students didn't wash their hands with soap and water so they also violated rule number 9).

Figure 1.4 Identifying Broken Lab Safety Rules—Answer Key

Name: _____

Period: _____ **Date:** _____

Science Lab Safety Quiz

Directions: Indicate if the following statements are true or false. You must receive an A before you can participate in a lab. Retakes will be offered for anyone who receives less than 90%.

_____ 1. In a lab setting, it is appropriate to wear loose-fitting clothing.

_____ 2. When you sit down at your lab station, make sure you start the lab immediately so there is enough time to complete it.

_____ 3. If you have questions, or are not sure how to handle a particular chemical, procedure, or part of an activity, you should always ask for help.

_____ 4. Be sure to clean up your lab area when you are instructed to do so.

_____ 5. Always use goggles, tie back your hair, and cover clothing when working with candles and burners.

_____ 6. Point test tubes and other containers that are being heated toward you.

_____ 7. Don't tell the teacher if you are hurt, but instead report directly to the nurse.

_____ 8. Notify your teacher immediately if a chemical is spilled.

_____ 9. You should wash your hands only after investigations involving chemicals.

_____ 10. Clean up your lab area completely before you leave.

Figure 1.5 Science Lab Safety Quiz (Student Handout)

CHAPTER 2

Strategies for Teaching Lab Procedures

What Is It?

Teaching lab procedures is explicit instruction on how to productively and safely complete labs. In addition, some of these procedures are useful in the traditional classroom setting when students are working at their desks.

Why We Like It

The best part of a science classroom is labs. The most stressful part of a science classroom is labs.

At the end of the school year, when we ask our students what was the best part about their science classes, they almost always respond that the labs were the most fun and memorable.

Teachers, however, may have a different perspective because we know all about the preparation, stress, and clean-up that accompany a successful lab experience. Teaching lab procedures at the beginning of the year is one of the most powerful tools teachers have to proactively ensure students are safe, on task, and learning.

Procedures are different from rules. Rules communicate a teacher's expectations, and there are consequences associated with breaking the rules. One rule in science could be "clean up after the lab or you do not get to participate in future labs." This only tells students they need to clean up, but does not explain how to properly clean up or allow for practice cleaning up. It also adds a punitive component. Procedures, on the other hand, are used to communicate the "how" to students. For example, we teach our students how to clean up after labs. If students don't follow procedures, they are not assigned a consequence. Instead, students *practice* the procedures until they demonstrate understanding.

Another example of a rule versus a procedure relates to student communication in class. A rule would be "don't talk when the teacher is talking" and if students do, there is a consequence assigned. However, there are times in class when students should be communicating with each other. In this scenario, the teacher uses a procedure to get students' attention so they do not chat while the teacher is talking. If we take time to teach procedures, the class will be much easier to manage, there will be more instructional time, and both the teacher and students will find the class more enjoyable.

Supporting Research

There is substantial research that supports teaching students classroom procedures. Teachers who maintain a classroom with order can enhance the ability of students to regulate their own behavior during activities (Blazar & Kraft, 2017).

Procedures are especially imperative in the science classroom because labs can be dangerous and students are responsible for learning independently. When procedures are not in place, there can be more off-task behavior and discipline issues. To optimize learning time during science activities, classrooms should have more procedures and less rules (NGSS Life Science, 2018).

Skills for Intentional Scholars/NGSS Standards

Teaching procedures is a part of classroom management and helps establish a safe environment where students maximize their learning experiences. When students are on task and actively learning during labs, they are enhancing their abilities to communicate effectively and problem solve creatively. Science labs provide opportunities for students to build these skills when they use teamwork to conduct experiments and draw conclusions. Group dynamics will be discussed in later chapters when we introduce strategies for specific labs and other activities.

Application

This section describes five important procedural sets we teach our students before performing the school year's first lab: moving students, obtaining student attention, cleaning up, time management, and keeping students on task.

MOVING STUDENTS

There are many different types of classroom and lab environments. Some teachers have very large classrooms where students sit at desks in one half of the classroom and work at lab stations in the other half of the room. Other teachers work in traditional classrooms with a separate lab room located somewhere else on campus.

Many science teachers leverage the outdoors as a lab site. Teachers who don't have lab space often pull student desks together to create a makeshift lab table.

Regardless of a teacher's physical situation, moving students from one location to another one can be challenging. Students often begin to move before the teacher is done giving directions.

To address this issue, we teach our students a procedure for moving from their seats to the next location. Students remain in their seats while we give directions and explain the lab safety procedures. When we are finished, we say the cue words, "get to work." We practice this procedure during the first week of school. When students hear the verbal cue, "get to work," they can move from their seats and go to the next location. Do all students correctly follow this procedure every time? Of course not, but pre-teaching it increases the odds that the majority will do so.

OBTAINING STUDENTS' ATTENTION DURING LABS AND OTHER ACTIVITIES

During a lab or other activity, we may need to regain our students' attention. Although it doesn't happen too often because we don't want to interrupt learning, there are times when it's necessary. For example, we may have forgotten to tell them a detail about lab safety or the lab directions. Or it may be that a student asked a great question or discovered a creative way to accomplish the goal and we want to share it with the entire class. At that moment, we must obtain everyone's attention so we can provide further instruction.

To maintain a good relationship with our students, we never want to yell at them. So, how can a teacher obtain students' attention while they are fully engaged in a lab or other activity?

Some teachers ring bells while others use call and response procedures. Regardless of which strategy a teacher uses, the best results occur when the procedure is taught and practiced during the first weeks of school. And, if later in the school year, students forget how to respond appropriately and in a timely manner, the class simply practices it again so they remember the expectation.

In Tara's science classroom, she teaches her students Harry Wong's call and response procedure called SALAME, which stands for Stop And Look At ME (Wong & Wong, 2018). During the first week of school, she explains the meaning and procedure of SALAME and then asks all students to stand. She calls out a color. Students walk to a wall and touch an item that was the color Tara called out. Randomly, Tara will say, "SALAME" and students are expected to immediately stop what they are doing and look at her. Students, without fail, don't stop when first learning the procedure because they are too focused on searching for an item of the assigned color. This provides an opportunity for Tara to reteach the procedure. Students practice through the first week of school. And, if students forget the procedure later in the year, she reteaches it and students practice again.

At one of Mandi's previous schools, every teacher followed the same call and response procedure, which provided consistency for students across the entire campus. The school mascot was a rattlesnake so the teachers would say, "WE ARE..." and the students would respond, "RATTLERS!" and were then expected to wait silently for the next set of instructions. Students were taught this procedure in every classroom the first week of school so they knew exactly how to stop what they were doing and pay attention to their teacher.

Other call and response ideas are available in the Technology Connections section.

Again, as we've said before, does this mean that *every* student pays attention *every* time? No. But, consistently reinforcing the procedure can improve its odds of success.

CLEANING UP AFTER LABS AND OTHER ACTIVITIES

Cleaning up after labs and activities should not and, from a logistical perspective, *cannot* be the teacher's responsibility.

Cleaning up is a type of transition. Primary teachers have more transitions than secondary teachers because elementary students must transition from one subject to another multiple times throughout the day in the same classroom. There is a potential loss of 15 instructional minutes every day in an elementary classroom if transitions aren't executed efficiently (Stacho, 2013). This totals 45 instructional hours throughout a school year. As teachers, we are always looking for extra teaching minutes. Having well-planned and well-executed cleaning strategies is an easy means to increase instructional time in an elementary setting.

As secondary teachers, we only have a few precious minutes between classes. Many teachers use these transition minutes greeting students at the door because this simple task can increase student engagement and decrease disruptive behavior (Allday & Pakurar, 2007; Cook et al., 2018). This time pressure means that passing periods for secondary teachers should not be used to clean up after one class and set up for the next. Of course, sometimes we can't avoid doing these tasks ourselves. However, teaching and reinforcing cleaning procedures should reduce the number of times that is necessary.

While planning a lab or other activity, we also consider how students will be responsible for cleaning their areas and, if necessary, to set up for the next class period. Here is a list of questions we ask ourselves while planning:

- Where will students obtain required resources?
- How will those resources be allocated among student groups?

- How will students clean the resources so they are reusable?
- Where will students return the resources?
- How will students clean their general working area? This is especially tricky if the resources include such things as water, dirt, glue, glitter, and paint.
- Which resources will be thrown in the recycle garbage and which will be thrown into the regular garbage?

We've found that the most successful cleaning strategy is to assign a number to each student in the group. Then we assign a different task to each number. Table 2.1: Clean-Up Responsibilities provides an example of how we communicate responsibilities to students. These responsibilities can easily be consolidated or divided if there aren't four students in a lab group.

To communicate these responsibilities to students, we introduce most labs with both verbal and written directions, explaining how to perform the lab. We've found that students do a better job cleaning up if the clean-up procedures are provided orally before the lab begins and in writing on the board or on the lab worksheet. This can be accomplished by sharing Table 2.1: Clean-Up Responsibilities with students.

While students are cleaning, it's fun to have background music playing. In our secondary rooms, we've found that kids love the Barney clean-up song, which is available on YouTube. The first time we play the song, we receive looks of "Are you kidding me?" but soon students are singing along and being silly. It's fun to have high school seniors singing and dancing with Barney!

One minute before the bell rings, we begin to walk through the lab area to check students' clean-up status. Teachers can use this time to positively reinforce student behavior. For example, teachers can say, "Group number 1, your lab station is perfect. Thank you." If a lab station isn't up to par, the teacher can ask that group to return to their station to finish their cleaning responsibilities. Once the group is done, they too can receive a positive comment.

Table 2.1 Clean-Up Responsibilities

Student number	Student clean-up responsibility
1	Wash out test tubes and return to test tube rack on the teacher's demonstration table.
2	Return test tube clamp, tongs, and pipette to the teacher's demonstration table.
3	Using paper towels, wipe down the lab table and throw the paper towels into the regular trash can.
4	Double check that students 1–3 have completed their work and grabbed all of their personal materials, including pencils and lab worksheets. Remind them to return to their seats to begin the lab report.

TIME MANAGEMENT

Students need to make the most of their time in science class, especially on lab days, because most labs can't be completed at home. And if students don't finish collecting their data in class, then they can't complete the lab write-up.

Planning a Lab or Activity

Time management begins in the planning stage and is critical if you are trying a new lab that you haven't experienced with students. You don't want students to finish early and have nothing to do because bored kids can be the ones who "get into trouble." You also don't want students to rush at the end because it impedes their learning. Teachers can find a balance by planning class time purposefully.

When planning a lab or activity, create a schedule for the lesson plan. The schedule is then posted on the board for the students and the teacher. Students should be moving along at that pace or as close to it as possible. Here are the guiding questions we ask ourselves when creating a schedule:

1. How long will it take me to get class started (attendance, pass out papers, collect homework)?
2. How much time will students need to complete a warm-up?
3. How long will it take me to introduce the activity to the students?
4. How long will it take for students to move into their groups and obtain resources?
5. How long will it take for students to perform each section of the lab or activity?
6. How much time needs to be set aside for cleaning?
7. Do I need more than 1 minute to check lab stations?

We make cleaning up a priority and provide ample time for doing so. Secondary students have another class and they need to arrive on time. No one likes to feel rushed and no one does a thorough job when they are hurried.

Once these timeframes have been determined, we establish the schedule for the class period. Often, what we thought could be accomplished in one class period actually takes more time. This is why planning is essential for teacher and student success. We can either alter the lab or activity so it requires less time or we can change the number of days dedicated to this particular lesson plan.

Here are some tricks for shortening labs and activities:

- Complete a quick mock lab or activity yourself to determine all of the resources students will need for the lesson. Then, have those resources on hand for student use. This kind of preparation will prevent you from running around during the lab looking for a class set of calculators because you didn't realize students needed calculators.

- Set out resources at each lab station before class. This decreases the amount of time that students need to obtain supplies and put them away.

- Have extra resources readily available, just in case. It requires precious time to track down another teacher to ask for extra masking tape in the middle of class.

- If it's financially feasible, each group should have their own resources. The bottleneck to most lab work is when the entire classroom has access to only one scale or only one microscope. There are a few options if a teacher is in search of additional resources, such as borrowing from other teachers, contacting the district's science liaison, or writing a grant requesting funds to purchase more resources. See the Technology Connections section for additional suggestions.

- Cut all material beforehand. When we first began our teaching careers we were shocked at how long it took middle school students to cut paper. When Tara transitioned into the high school, she was even more shocked to find that cutting takes just as long for high school seniors. Parent and/or student volunteers/TAs are a great way to get cutting done before class begins. If push comes to shove, teachers cutting resources while binge-watching television is not ideal, but it's better than classroom chaos!

- Have liquid resources premeasured. This type of preparation is not a shortcut we suggest for every lab because students need practice measuring volume and using lab supplies, such as graduated cylinders. But, every so often, it can cut several minutes from lab time.

Communicating Time to Students

Students stay more focused during labs and activities if they can visually see there is a finite amount of time to complete the task. At the beginning of the lab, we post a timer on our projection screen. If you search for "timer," there are plenty of free ones available online. Other teachers who don't have screens can write the time left on the board and update it every 5 or 10 minutes. We've also seen other teachers use egg timers. Regardless of the tool used to track time, the goal is to keep students on task by communicating the amount of time they have to complete their work.

KEEPING STUDENTS ON TASK

Monitoring

Monitor, monitor, monitor. We can't say this enough.

In Robert Marzano's five-point scale for teacher evaluation, he differentiates a teacher with a 3 rating (referred to as a "developing teacher") and a teacher with a 4 rating (referred to as an "applying teacher") by how much monitoring the teacher performs. An applying teacher is one who monitors "the majority of the students" (Marzano, Carbaugh, Rutherford, & Toth, 2013, p. 19).

Monitoring achieves two goals. First, teachers can monitor for on-task behavior to ensure students are using lab time as a learning opportunity, not a social opportunity. Second, and more importantly, teachers can monitor for student understanding. There have been numerous occasions when we tried a new lab or activity and, while walking around monitoring student work, we realized we had written unclear directions. We've also discovered that questions we wrote on lab write-ups were confusing. Because we were monitoring, we were able to stop the class, clarify the errors we had made, and get our students back on the right track. If we hadn't been monitoring, we wouldn't have realized that students did not have an accurate understanding until we graded the assignment. This late realization would have required that we reteach the content on a future day.

Here is a list of meaningful monitoring strategies:

- Walk around to make your presence known. Teacher proximity has been proven to increase on-task student behavior (Allday, 2011).

- Ask individual groups and students, "What questions do you have for me?" We've noticed that students are more likely to ask questions when we initiate the conversation.

- In addition to the Technology Use Agreements that most districts have, some districts also have online monitoring tools, such as Hapara or GoGuardian. These systems can help teachers monitor the websites that students are accessing real time. They also allow teachers to monitor the quality of the work students are completing so that real-time feedback can be provided. Some systems allow the teacher to close inappropriate websites that students are using (such as online gaming). If students are working in Google Classroom, teachers can log on and watch them in real time. Teachers can also add supportive comments and other feedback, including suggestions. For example, while Tara's students walked the school courtyard searching for examples of ecosystems and communities, she was monitoring the accuracy of their answers from her laptop. She knew who was actively working and who was not and she knew who understood the concepts and who required further instruction. This helped her to identify which students would benefit from some type of intervention and which students required an enrichment lesson. There are examples of enrichment activities in the Differentiation for Diverse Learners section. See Chapter 17: Strategies for Assessing Student Learning for additional intervention and enrichment resources.

- Of course, the monitoring strategy that we think works best, and which we generally use, is actually walking around, looking at screens, and talking to students individually about their work.

Grouping Strategies

The first question we ask ourselves when planning for group work is, "How many students should be in a group?"

The University of Leicester published the results of an experiment conducted in 2010 where students were in groups of two, three, and four. The experiment concluded that, "gains gradually exceeded losses in groups of two but not in three-person and larger groups" (University of Leicester, 2010). The researchers hypothesized that when two students work together, they can intuitively learn to communicate; however, when the group is larger, communication becomes more difficult.

Nevertheless, some science activities logistically require more than two students in a group. Based on our experience, one important criterion for determining the number of students in a group is the number of individual jobs required by the activity. If a lab only calls for two jobs, then there should only be two students in a group. And if a lab has five jobs, then there can be as many as five students in a group. Table 2.2: Lab Jobs and Responsibilities lists the most common jobs we assign students during a lab.

This can also be a classroom management tool. Students are more likely to stay on task when they have been given a specific responsibility.

You'll notice that Table 2.2: Lab Jobs and Responsibilities doesn't assign cleaning to any one student. When every student is responsible for cleaning, it maximizes the amount of class time allocated for learning.

Table 2.2 Lab Jobs and Responsibilities

Job title	Job responsibility
Artist	Drawing and sketching, such as documentation of microscope slides
Supply manager	Obtaining and calibrating lab supplies
Scientist	Managing the experiment
Recorder	Recording observations and data
Time manager	Ensuring all other jobs are being completed in a timely manner and keeping peers on task
Safety engineer	Ensuring all lab safety rules are being followed; is the first to respond to a spill or accident

There are several ways to determine which students will work together. Students can be grouped by their abilities, interests, behavior, proximity, or random selection. Another option is for students to choose their own groups.

As secondary teachers, we generally allow our students to choose their own groups, but there are times when we select them. Two grouping strategies involve pairing students based on ability. Students can be in homogeneous groups where they have the same ability. Or students can be in heterogeneous groups where students have a range of abilities. Research shows that sometimes homogeneous groups are more effective and other times heterogeneous groups are more effective for student learning (Pare, 2017). To leverage the benefits of each grouping strategy, we use both throughout the year.

When students are grouped based on same-ability (homogeneous grouping), it becomes easier to keep differentiation inconspicuous. For example, one student group may have a simpler article to read or their lab write-up directions may include more detail.

When students are grouped based on their differences (heterogeneous grouping), the students' diversity can improve the end product because research has shown that "diversity enhances creativity" (Phillips, 2014, para. 3). Diversity can include such things as race, ethnicity, gender, religious beliefs, ability, sexual orientation, and background knowledge. The most common use of heterogeneous groups in our classrooms is when students must use their imagination, such as creating rockets, producing dioramas, or solving problems.

Grouping can be a classroom management tool also. For example, if Student A and Student B routinely behave inappropriately when they are together, they can be assigned to two different lab groups. At the same time, if Student C and Student D consistently work well together, we might group them together more often.

Other ideas regarding how to group students are available in the Differentiation for Diverse Learners and Technology Connections sections.

DIFFERENTIATION FOR DIVERSE LEARNERS

Moving Students

Students with physical disabilities appreciate when teachers subtly differentiate for them. For example, we've had students in walkers and wheelchairs who needed to have the classroom rearranged so they could perform labs. To minimize the amount of attention they received when we moved from one location to another, we allowed these students to sit closest to the door and use alternate entrances into the classroom. Tara's classroom has chairs in the front and lab stations in the back. She allows her students with physical disabilities to begin and end lab days at their assigned lab stations so they don't have to move.

Obtaining Students' Attention

Some sources suggest that flashing classroom lights on and off is an effective method of obtaining student attention. We strongly disagree. As explained by Veronica Lewis (2017), a college student who has Chiari Malformation, students with light sensitivity disorders find flashing lights disorienting and sometimes even painful. Please don't flash your classroom lights as a means to get your students' attention.

Veronica has a blog (https://veroniiiica.com/2017/08/07/photosensitivity-in-the-classroom) about her Chiari Malformation, which is when brain tissue grows into the spinal column and sometimes causes visual disturbances. She provides a unique and powerful insight into how classroom lights affect students who are sensitive to light and how her teachers successfully differentiated for her. Flashing lights can originate from surprising places, such as videos, UV overhead lights, and slideshows.

Time Management

The length or complexity of an assignment can cause an automatic stress response in some students. We chunk the assignment to help manage these students' stress levels by giving them only a portion of the assignment at a time. When students complete the first portion (maybe questions 1 and 2), we then give them the next portion (questions 3 and 4). They continue to receive the assignment in small chunks until they've completed the entire assignment. Chunking is especially useful for students who have anxiety disorders or trouble remaining focused for long periods of time. When they are able to focus on the small portion they've been assigned, they are more likely to stay on task and get more work done in the allotted time (Minahan, 2017).

We also chunk time. Some students are more successful when they have smaller goals. Again, we've found this type of differentiation most useful for students with anxiety disorders and those who have difficulty focusing. We give these students personal timers for their desk or we set an alarm on our phone. When the timer goes off, we check in with the students and ask how they are doing. If they seem anxious, we provide them with a 1-minute break. This resting period helps students get back on task so they can complete more work during the class period.

In our experience, there are often two types of students who complete work very quickly: advanced students with a large amount of background knowledge and students who may not be particularly conscientious about their work. Both kinds of students require an enrichment opportunity because they are done with the work they've been assigned and may claim they have nothing to do. To engage these students until the bell rings (we very much believe in bell-to-bell instruction) and to get the most out of a class period, we plan enrichment activities that enhance student learning of the current content. Teachers can give students the choice to complete a myriad of tasks (some of these require classroom technology that may or may not be available), such as

- Completing a webquest or an online scavenger hunt. While scavenger hunts generally require students to perform online searches for answers to a series of questions, webquests promote higher-order thinking by challenging students to perform authentic tasks. See the Technology Connections section for resources teachers can use to search for and create scavenger hunts and webquests.

- Making a test that can be given to their peers.

- Practicing on Kahoot, Quizizz, or Quizlet (online educational gaming platforms that include games that have already been created and allow students to create their own). See Chapter 16: Strategies for Reviewing Content for more detail about using these and other online games.

- Watching videos and answering comprehension questions. A free resource of online videos that are embedded with questions is www.edpuzzle.com. See the Technology Connections section for other online tools.

- Reading a current article and determining how it could be used in class.

- Reading "Folder Activities" and answering comprehension questions. We created this strategy while attending a class that emphasized best practices for teaching English language learners (ELLs). It does require a significant amount of planning prior to teaching a unit. We start by finding articles that are fun to read, applicable to our content, and appropriate for students with diverse interests and reading comprehension skills. The articles are attached to the front of a manila folder. On the inside of the folder there are Who, What, When, Where, Why, and How questions whose answers can easily be found in the article. Additionally, there are three questions written on sticky notes that require students to participate in higher-level thinking skills. An example of a Folder Activity is shown in Figure 2.1: Folder Activity—Outside and Inside—Thermal Power Plant. Students have the choice to read any of the Folder Activities that interest them as long as it pertains to the current unit. They then answer the comprehension questions on their own paper. Many of our folders use articles and pictures found in magazines such as *Smithsonian*, *National Geographic Kids*, *Reader's Digest*, *Highlights*, and *Sports Illustrated Kids*. And, while on vacation, we pick up pamphlets and brochures at the museums we visit or travel guides from the cities we tour. Any reading material, including recipes, bus schedules, and historical diary entries, can be made into a Folder Activity. However, sometimes we need a specific article with a specific picture. In those cases, we write our own article and take an appropriate picture, which is what Tara did to make Figure 2.1: Folder Activity—Outside and Inside—Thermal Power Plant.

The enrichment activity shouldn't be busy work, but instead should be an additional learning opportunity. Those students who finished early because they have strong background knowledge appreciate the extra opportunity to advance their knowledge and experience. The students who rushed through their work may not have acquired the new learning they were responsible for so they require another learning opportunity.

Keeping Students on Task

When monitoring, the teacher walks from group to group, checking for understanding by reading what students wrote, listening to their conversations, and watching them perform a lab. This is the easiest technique to determine who needs differentiation and what type of differentiation they need. Students are more likely to stay on task when you are in close proximity. We've both had students who stop working the moment we turn our backs, so to keep those students on task, we spend more time with them. We also chunk work for them and tell them that we'll return in two minutes to check on their progress. By following up with the students later, they are held accountable for their work and are more likely to complete their work.

Grouping Strategies

A teacher can strategically assign a job to a student based on the student's individual needs, interests, and capabilities. For example, Tara assigned a specific student the job of safety manager in most labs because the student had aspirations to be a police officer.

Asking an English-language proficient student to be a "buddy" for an ELL and assigning them to the same group can often be a very effective source of support to the ELL *and* a good learning strategy for the "buddy," as well. When students peer tutor, their math and science scores tend to increase (Sparks, 2015).

Student Handouts and Examples

Figure 2.1: Folder Activity—Outside and Inside—Thermal Power Plant

What Could Go Wrong?

The aim of this chapter is to avoid things that can go wrong. However, it's an unrealistic expectation to believe that explicitly teaching procedures will result in every student making good decisions every time. There are always instances when our students choose not to actively participate in work. When these situations occur—and they will—we first reteach the procedures that students have forgotten. While these instances may happen all year long, it is important to never give up on the procedures.

To proactively help students make good decisions, we walk around, monitoring their choices. As Doug Lemov says, we need to "break the plane" by not just staying in front of the classroom but, instead, monitor the class by walking around

(Lemov, 2015a, 2015b). Whenever possible, as hard as it may be, we try to resist the temptation to spend class time grading papers or answering emails. Our students need us to be readily available if they have questions or begin to veer from lab directions.

Technology Connections

More call and response ideas to obtain student attention can be found at "27 Good Attention Getters for Quieting a Noisy Classroom" (https://www.weareteachers.com/good-attention-getters-grabbers-to-quiet-noisy-classroom) and "50 Fun Call-and-Response Ideas to get Students' Attention" (https://thecornerstoneforteachers.com/50-fun-call-and-response-ideas-to-get-students-attention).

Here is a link to the Barney clean-up song on YouTube: "Barney – Clean-Up Song 2" (https://www.youtube.com/watch?v=whrNJH8S-Ys).

Dr. Thomas Stacho has discussed ways to gain 45 instructional hours in a classroom. His main focus is on how to use the PBIS (Positive Behavior Intervention and Supports) network. He offers many examples of how to establish procedures with students so they behave in a positive manner, thereby increasing your time as a teacher and decreasing your time as a disciplinarian. His published work is "My Students Have Trouble with Transitions. . . What Can I Do?" (http://www.behaviorinschools.com/My_Students_Have_a_Hard_Time_with_Transitions.pdf).

Larry Ferlazzo's blog includes additional information about the difference between online scavenger hunts and webquests. His blog also provides online resources for finding and making webquests, which can be found at "The Best Places to Create (and Find) Internet Scavenger Hunts & Webquests" (http://larryferlazzo.edublogs.org/2009/02/15/the-best-sources-for-internet-scavenger-hunts-webquests).

For the best and most popular online video resources, see Larry Ferlazzo's "A Potpourri of the Best & Most Useful Video Sites" (http://larryferlazzo.edublogs.org/2012/11/06/a-potpourri-of-the-best-most-useful-video-sites).

More ideas for grouping students both purposefully and randomly can be found at "30 Ways to Arrange Students for Group Work" (http://www.teachhub.com/30-ways-arrange-students-group-work).

Larry Ferlazzo's blog has a list of websites to help teachers obtain donations for their classrooms. This can be found at "The Best Resources on—& Advice for Using—Donors Choose (Please Share Your Experiences!)" (http://larryferlazzo.edublogs.org/2015/04/05/the-best-resources-on-advice-for-using-donors-choose-please-share-your-experiences).

Attributions

Harry and Rosemary Wong, in their book, *The First Days of School* (Wong and Wong, 2018) outline how to use procedures to establish a well-run classroom. This is where we found the idea of SALAME.

Figures

Thermal Power Plants
by Mrs. Dale
(article and photo)

Coal is made up of mostly carbon (C), which came from producers that died millions of years ago. Coal is made up of chemical energy that turns into heat energy when it is burned. The heat energy boils water, causing evaporation. The steam then causes a turbine to spin, making electrical energy, which is called electricity.

Thermal power plants offer many benefits. Thermal power plants require much less land than hydropower plants (dams) so less of the natural environment is harmed when a thermal power plant is constructed. This conserves the natural biodiversity, erosion prevention, and balance of the local ecosystem. There are economic benefits as well. The cost to build thermal power plants is relatively cheap when you compare it to nuclear power plants. Finally, thermal power plants are powered by coal, which is very inexpensive to mine and haul to the plant. Thermal power plants offer a cheap and potentially environmentally healthy means to obtain electricity.

Unfortunately, thermal power plants also have potential environmental drawbacks. The environment is harmed because although scrub brushes remove the ash from the coal's smoke, they cannot remove single atoms of pollution. Nitrogen and sulfur are in coal smoke that when released into the air eventually lead to acid rain, changes in soil chemistry, and a loss of forests. Coal is mined out of the ground, which requires mining companies to clear-cut forests, which in turn increases the chance of erosion. Using coal as an energy source is potentially very negative on the environment.

Thermal power plants can cause health issues in many animal populations, including humans. When coal is burned, it releases pollutants, such as carbon (C) that is so small the scrub brushes miss them. This carbon (C) mixes with oxygen (O_2) to make carbon monoxide (CO2). People who are exposed to too much CO2 experience headaches, vomiting, and eventually death. Burning coal also releases carbon dioxide (CO_2). Making electrical energy via the burning of coal causes 25% of all CO_2 that is released into the atmosphere. The average _____ CO_2 is one of the major greenhouse gases that accelerates global warming. The average _____ that is released by thermal power

Figure 2.1   Folder Activity—Outside and Inside—Thermal Power Plant

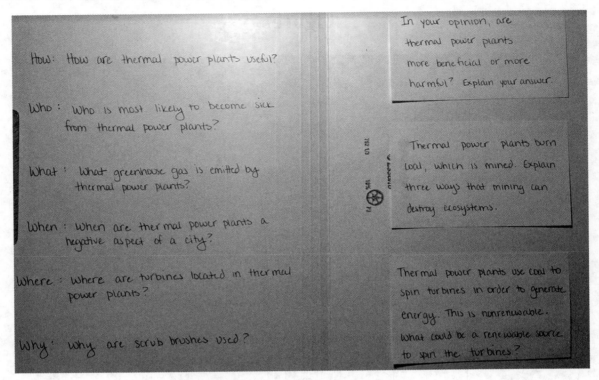

How: How are thermal power plants useful?

Who: Who is most likely to become sick from thermal power plants?

What: What greenhouse gas is emitted by thermal power plants?

When: When are thermal power plants a negative aspect of a city?

Where: Where are turbines located in thermal power plants?

Why: Why are scrub brushes used?

In your opinion, are thermal power plants more beneficial or more harmful? Explain your answer.

Thermal power plants burn coal, which is mined. Explain three ways that mining can destroy ecosystems.

Thermal power plants use coal to spin turbines in order to generate energy. This is nonrenewable. What could be a renewable source to spin the turbines?

Figure 2.1   (Continued)

CHAPTER 3

Strategies for Teaching the Scientific Method and Its Components

What Is It?

The scientific method and its components are the backbone of all sciences, so it is emphasized in nearly every science curriculum. The most detailed version of the scientific method includes the seven steps listed here. Many educators teach students all seven steps; however, some prefer to combine steps 5 and 6.

1. Ask a question.
2. Perform research.
3. Write a hypothesis.
4. Set up and perform an experiment.
5. Analyze results.
6. Write a conclusion.
7. Publish results.

The scientific method is used when a question can be answered through data collection via an experiment. If a question can't be answered with an experiment but, instead, requires additional research or observation, then the inquiry process is used. See Chapter 4: Strategies for Teaching the Inquiry Process for resources to teach this process. If a question can be answered through the design of a new technology or process, then it's more appropriate to use the engineering process, which is discussed in Chapter 6: Strategies for Teaching the Engineering Process.

Why We Like It

The scientific method is used to learn many topics, including some that go beyond the field of science. Its purpose is to organize information to solve problems in a manner that minimizes bias and prejudice (Harris, n.d.). The scientific method's basic components (asking a question, creating a hypothesis, testing the hypothesis, and drawing a conclusion) are not limited to science classrooms. Examples include students so_____ _____blems through trial and error, performing historical research, ar_____ _____

Student_____ _____method are better prepared for future sci_____ _____form well on college entrance exams tha_____ _____e ACT and SAT Subject Tests (ACT, 201_____ _____mponent that requires students to have b_____ _____arth/space sciences, and physics, and emp_____ _____d such as analyzing and evaluat-ing dat_____ _____ogy, chemistry, and physics. The three ex_____ _____d analyze data, draw conclusions, and m_____ _____n the scientific method (College Board,_____

[handwritten note: Helps students excel more than peers and score higher on tests since they can participate in active learning]

_____search

Research shows that students who participate in active learning, including the use of the scientific method, tend to outperform their peers who are taught using tradi-tional lecture-based learning. These studies indicate that when students are taught science through active learning, failure rates can decrease significantly, while test performance increases (Wieman, 2014, p. 8319).

In addition, using hands-on learning through the scientific method has been shown to increase motivation and learning in science (Dhanapal & Shan, 2014, pp. 34–38).

The scientific method can also be used to teach scientific literacy, the ability to ask and answer questions about everyday life, describe and predict natural phenom-ena, read and understand scientific articles, participate in arguments regarding the validity of conclusions, and analyze data validity and reliability based on how it was obtained (National Research Council, 1996, p. 22).

By learning the scientific method, students are practicing many skills that increase their scientific literacy, such as asking questions, reading scientific articles for research, describing observations after experimentation, and identifying errors in experimental designs to determine if data is valid and reliable.

Skills for Intentional Scholars/NGSS Connections

All three Skills for Intentional Scholars are practiced while students use the scientific method. For example, students are using critical thinking skills when performing research and writing their hypotheses. They are creatively problem solving while designing experiments. And, students are effectively communicating during the data analysis and conclusion steps.

Components of the scientific method are integrated throughout the Science and Engineering Practices and Crosscutting Concepts that are intertwined in Next Generation Science Standards (NGSS) (National Research Council, 2012, p. 85). The NGSS advise science teachers to integrate required science content, the scientific method, the inquiry process, and the seven crosscutting concepts into their lessons (NGSS, 2013c, p.3). The activities in this chapter will include several of these requirements.

Application

In this section, we walk through the seven steps of the scientific method and provide specific activities that can be used in any experimental situation. Depending on the age of the students, it has been our experience that teaching these seven steps requires three to four 1-hour instructional periods, in addition to the time needed to perform the experiment. Since we don't always know how much experience high school students may already have using the scientific method, we include an activity to assess their background knowledge later in the chapter.

We begin teaching the scientific method by explaining that it is the process used in many authentic science labs and out in the field. It is used by many scientists such as biologists, oceanographers, physicists, chemists, and engineers.

When we first introduce the scientific method in class, we describe its step-by-step process. Obviously, less scaffolding is required after students become more familiar with the steps.

STEP 1: ASK A QUESTION

We begin by explaining that the scientific method starts with a question because it provides the focus for a scientist's research and experimentation. The question keeps scientists focused and prevents them from steering off topic.

Often, we generate the question and not our students. This is because we want all students focused on a specific concept. There are times when it's appropriate to have students generate questions, which is discussed in Chapter 4: Strategies for Teaching the Inquiry Process.

Table 3.1 Connecting Content with Experimental Questions

Content being taught	Question generated
Biomimicry requires scientists to understand structural and functional properties of nature	How strong is human hair?
Heat denatures enzymes and enzymes break down proteins	What happens when fresh pineapple is added to gelatin?
The difference between hydrophobic and hydrophilic	What is the most efficient process to clean birds after an oil spill?
Osmosis is an example of diffusion, a process of passive transport	What happens to gummy candy when left in water overnight?
Newton's third law of motion	Why do balloons move away when the air inside is released?

To generate experimental questions, we begin with the content we want students to learn. Table 3.1 depicts five examples of how we connect content to the first step of the scientific method: Ask a Question.

When we are creating a new unit, we make a concerted effort to generate questions that can be leveraged in teaching multiple concepts. For example, after cleaning oily duck feathers to teach the difference between hydrophobic and hydrophilic liquids, the same feather experiment can be used to teach the difference between polar and nonpolar molecules or it can be used to teach the effects of water pollution on aquatic wildlife.

Students don't perform these experiments a second time, but, instead, use their data later in the school year when they are learning other content. The benefit is that this data will now function as the required background knowledge for future lessons. See Chapter 13: Strategies for Activating Prior Knowledge for resources that help students identify and use their background knowledge.

STEP 2: PERFORM RESEARCH

After we've written the scientific question, we then decide what information our students need to know so they can perform their experiment. To help students understand why it's important to do research, we explain that step 3 will require them to write a hypothesis, which includes a justification for the anticipated results of their experiment. The research they do in this step will help them justify the hypothesis they will be writing.

There are two possible methods to direct student research. One method involves teaching the content beforehand and then requiring students to research only the information that is needed to answer the experimental question. We choose this format when the science content is difficult to understand or when students have very little background knowledge. When we work with middle school students, we use the gummy candy example in Table 3.1 to teach the concept of osmosis. Students do a lab where they leave the gummy candy in water overnight. Osmosis is a new concept for many students and it's difficult to understand by simply reading about it.

Other times, we require our students to research a broader scientific concept we want them to learn, in addition to the information that is needed to answer the experimental question. We choose this format when students have some background knowledge about the topic or the topic is simple to understand. Using the Newton's third law of motion example in Table 3.1, many high school students have been exposed to Newton and his laws in previous classes. In this case, students are required to research all of the following: Newton's third law of motion, the concept of air pressure, and how balloons function.

We also take the age of our students into account when we determine what they should research. In our experience, younger students become overwhelmed if they are exploring too many topics. Given this challenge, we tend to reserve the research of multiple topics for advanced middle school and high school students.

Determining where students will find their research is another decision we make when we plan an experiment. When we work with younger students, we typically provide resources for them, such as library books or a list of websites. We often require students at the higher grades and advanced students to find the resources themselves. Students can obtain information from books, online resources, and articles. Research can also be accomplished by watching videos, performing interviews, and observing phenomena. See the Technology Connections section for student-friendly, online research resources.

We've found that students who struggle with reading comprehension may benefit from a structured note-taking process when they perform research. We use Figure 3.1: Student Research Organizer to assist these students. It requires them to document three main points from each source, which tends to increase student comprehension and retention of the material (Naidu, Briewin, & Embi, 2013, pp. 62–63).

Another benefit of using Figure 3.1 is that plagiarism tends to occur less often, but only when students fill it out by hand. When students are allowed to document their research electronically, many tend to copy-and-paste entire passages with no modifications or attributions. Additionally, having hard copies for students limits the amount of space they have to take notes because, unlike in an electronic format, the size of the boxes doesn't expand as students write. By minimizing the amount of space students have to write, students are challenged to summarize, which is an effective strategy for increasing reading comprehension (Janzen & Stoller, 1998, pp. 254–259).

One struggle we experience every year is that many students have difficulty discerning fact from fiction when they perform online research. In Chapter 4: Strategies for Teaching the Inquiry Process, we provide strategies that help students develop information literacy skills.

STEP 3: WRITE A HYPOTHESIS

We first explain that a hypothesis is a proposed outcome of an experiment that includes a justification for the proposal. For example, if a hypothesis proposes that cats always land on their feet if they fall from a minimum height of 12 in., then the hypothesis must also include the reason why cats can do so (they have advanced righting reflexes).

Before writing a hypothesis, students must first identify the independent and dependent variables. Note that some state standards refer to these variables as the manipulated and responding variables.

Prior to sixth grade, most teachers identify the variables for their students. However, starting in sixth grade, the NGSS require that students begin to independently identify the variables and controls (NGSS, 2013b, p. 1). This practice continues throughout high school as students are exposed to more complicated concepts and advanced experimental designs.

We use Figure 3.2: Identifying Independent and Dependent Variables to introduce students to the concept of variables. This worksheet requires students to become familiar with the new vocabulary terms and then teaches them the differences between the two variables. Students complete the worksheet in partners because, as we discussed in Chapter 2: Strategies for Teaching Lab Procedures, research concludes that student groups of two tend to promote better communication (University of Leicester, 2010).

The first practice problem in Figure 3.2 includes the answer, so students have a model. There are five additional practice problems and three challenge problems. Some students who struggle to remain focused during class may need shortened assignments. In this case, we only require them to complete three of the additional practice problems and one of the challenge problems.

The teacher answer key can be found in Figure 3.3: Identifying Independent and Dependent Variables—Answer Key.

Once students are familiar with identifying variables in hypothetical experiments, their next challenge is to identify the independent and dependent variables in the class experiment. For example, if the experimental question is "What happens to gummy candy when left in water overnight?," they first need to determine that the independent variable is whether or not the candy is left in water. Then, they need to identify if the dependent variable is the mass, height, length, width, density, and/or color of the candy before and after it's placed in water.

Depending on the purpose of the lesson and the age of the students, the teacher can either dictate the dependent variable(s) or the students can choose their dependent variable(s). When using this experiment to teach about osmosis, we give our middle and high school students the option of choosing two or more dependent variables because any of the variables in this experiment will demonstrate that osmosis has or has not occurred overnight.

Once students identify their variables, they can write their hypotheses. One format for writing a hypothesis is "If. . .then. . .because. . ." where the *if* statement holds the independent variable, the *then* statement holds the dependent variable, and the *because* statement explains the research that justifies the expected results.

For those students new to writing hypotheses, we use Figure 3.4: How to Write a Hypothesis. Each student receives a copy of the worksheet, but they work together in pairs. We begin by asking for volunteers to take turns reading the directions aloud so the class can hear the definition and purpose of a hypothesis. Then we explain the format of writing a hypothesis.

We want students to understand why the scientific method requires scientists to perform research prior to writing their hypothesis. To initiate this connection, the worksheet instructs students to talk to their partners and discuss the order of performing research and writing hypotheses. As students have their discussion, we walk around the room and listen to their conversations. We may ask struggling students a guiding question, such as, "What three things are required to write a hypothesis?" Students can reference their worksheet and may answer, "The two variables and the research," at which time we reply, "So why should the research be completed before writing the hypothesis? Why can't we write the hypothesis first and then perform the research?" Students might respond, "Because we need the research to write the hypothesis."

Our goal in this lesson, and in most lessons, is that students use their critical thinking skills to answer the questions on their own. We try to avoid simply giving them the answers. Instead, we provide resources they can use to determine the answers, including a learning partner and a guiding question.

Once the class understands that research is a critical component of forming a hypothesis, students continue to read the worksheet. They read the two methods that will help them remember which variable goes into each part of the hypothesis. The first method involves using the letters I and D. We explain that the word *independent* begins with the letter I and it is *I*, the scientist, who determines the independent variable. The word *dependent* begins with the letter D and it is the *Data* that is collected *During* the experiment and recorded in a *Data* table. By using the first letters of the words *independent* and *dependent*, students are less likely to confuse the two.

The second method uses the definition of the two terms. *Independent* means that an event occurred without help from other events. *Dependent* means that an event occurred because of another event. After reviewing the definition of the words with students, we further explain that independent variables occur without the help of other variables, but dependent variables occur because they require the help of the independent variable. Students are instructed to choose whichever method helps them to properly differentiate between independent and dependent variables.

As a class, we go over the first problem on the worksheet. We walk the students through the example, challenging them to identify the independent and dependent variables. Once every student has documented the correct variables, we challenge them to write the hypothesis using the "If. . .then. . .because. . ." format.

We ask them to fill in the *because* statement of the hypothesis with any facts they may already know. After all, the purpose of the worksheet is to learn the format of hypothesis writing so, while completing this worksheet, it's less important what students write in the *because* statement.

Students are then instructed to work with their partner to complete the worksheet. Afterwards, groups of two are paired with other groups of two to compare answers. Students must then debate any differing answers to determine whose answer is correct. We provide the class with sentence starters (see Table 3.2) in order to help students build their academic vocabulary and discourse skills. Table 3.2 can be projected onto a screen or printed and distributed to students. We explain that these sentence starters are intended to begin and maintain respectful conversations.

As we mentioned earlier, some students may benefit from shortened assignments. They could be given the option of completing half of the practice problems. This modification provides students with some practice and is not as overwhelming as having to complete the entire worksheet.

After students complete Figure 3.4: How to Write a Hypothesis, we choose random students using popsicle sticks, index cards, or an online tool such as Class Dojo, to share their answers with the class. Sometimes, we are more strategic in choosing students. For example, we may practice in advance with an English language learner so he or she can develop more confidence when participating in class. Or, perhaps, we'll choose a student who has been struggling but has a good response for this assignment. Students can either read their answers or project them onto the board using a document camera. We provide students with an opportunity to ask questions after each response is revealed. The teacher answer key is found in Figure 3.5: How to Write a Hypothesis—Answer Key.

Table 3.2 Debate Sentence Starters

Agreement statements	Disagreement statements
"I agree with you because. . ."	"I like what you were thinking but I was thinking. . ."
"I like what you wrote here. I also wrote. . ."	"Can you explain this answer to me because I wrote something different?"
"I agree that. . ."	"Have you considered. . .?"
"We agree with each other on this question because. . ."	"I notice. . ."
"You made me realize that. . ."	"I wonder. . ."

Once students can identify variables and plug them into the "If. . .then. . . because. . ." format, they are ready to write a hypothesis for the class experiment.

We connect the experimental question, variables, and research in order to write the hypothesis. For example, in grades 7–12, an appropriate experimental question about osmosis would be, "What happens to gummy candy when left in water overnight?" A student's hypothesis could state, "If gummy candies are placed in water overnight, then their mass will increase because osmosis causes water to passively move across the candy's membrane." Elementary students would not necessarily study osmosis but could study the movement of water in plants. If their experimental question was, "Does the color of the water affect the color of a flower?," then their hypothesis would be, "If a white carnation plant is given colored water, then its petals will match the water's color because water moves through the plant's petals."

Before moving to the next step of the scientific method, we require every group to turn in their hypothesis so we can review it for accuracy. The hypothesis is the experiment's backbone because it drives the experimental design, data collection, and lab report. Their hypothesis must be written correctly if they are going to be successful in the remaining steps of the lab.

If a group's hypothesis does not use the correct format, we meet with the group members and ask guiding questions so they can identify what is incorrect and how to make improvements. Research shows that if teachers want their feedback to impact learning, students must be allowed to use that input immediately to improve their work (Irons, 2010, p. 148).

After we verify that a group has written a hypothesis that follows the format, they are then free to begin setting up their experiment.

STEP 4: SET UP AND PERFORM AN EXPERIMENT

Prior to performing an experiment, we require students to complete the following:

- Write a materials list.
- Document the step-by-step procedures.
- Make a list of the controls.
- Create the data table.

We begin teaching Step 4: Set up and Perform an Experiment by explaining the purpose of identifying materials, procedures, and controls: that experiments must be completed multiple times with similar results to be considered reliable. This means that other scientists need to know precisely how the first scientist conducted the experiment so they can duplicate the experimental design.

Materials List

As students design their experiment, they need to create a materials list. This includes the materials used and the required quantity of each material. Older students typically don't struggle with this task. However, since younger students may require more structure, we provide them with Figure 3.6: Student Materials List.

Step-by-Step Procedures

Using their materials list, students then write their step-by-step procedures.

To achieve reliability in an authentic science lab, scientists perform multiple trials. According to Science Buddies, a popular online resource for science fairs, school-based experiments should have at least three trials (see Technology Connections). Students' step-by-step procedures should reflect the number of trials they will have in their experiment.

The traditional lesson plan for teaching students how to write step-by-step procedures is to have them write the directions for making a peanut butter and jelly sandwich. Although we could not determine who first created this lesson plan, we confidently assume it's popular because many students have background knowledge about how to make a peanut butter and jelly sandwich. However, with the rise in peanut allergies, we've replaced this lesson with a list of activities that students can choose from when they practice writing their procedures. Here is the list we provide our students:

1. How to brush your teeth.
2. How to make your bed.
3. How to charge your cell phone.
4. How to read a book.
5. How to catch a football.
6. Come up with your own idea and have it approved by your teacher.

Students first write their practice step-by-step procedures using one of the options from the above list. They then have a family member follow the procedures at home or have a fellow student follow them in class. We emphasize that the person following the procedures should *literally* do each step as written. Students use that person's interpretation as feedback to edit their procedures. We only ask classes to practice using non-experimental scenarios, such as the ones listed above, at the beginning of the year when the scientific method is first introduced. After this practice is complete, all future step-by-step procedures are written for authentic science experiments.

Once students have practiced writing their step-by-step procedures using something familiar to them, they then write the procedures for the class experiment. We remind students that the procedures must include any applicable lab safety requirements, everything in their materials list, and clean-up directions. Note that the lab safety rules we use are in Figure 1.1: Science Safety Contract English in Chapter 1: Strategies for Teaching Lab Safety. We tell students ahead of time that the lab's required materials will be at the lab stations on the day of the lab so they do not have to write a procedure for how and where to obtain lab materials.

Controls and Data Tables

Prior to performing an experiment, we also have our students list their controls, which sometimes are referred to as constants, and make their data table. We first explain that controls are the things that must remain the same between the experimental and control groups. To provide an example, we describe a hypothetical experiment, such as determining if plants grow taller if they are given fertilizer. We draw two pots on the board and ask students to first identify the independent variable (whether the plant receives fertilizer) and the dependent variable (how tall the plant grows). Then we explain that controls are all the characteristics that must be the same between the two pots. Students are asked to brainstorm the controls with a partner. We then hand markers to several random students and ask them to write one control on the board, around the pots. This continues until we have about 10 controls, which may include the size of the pot, the amount of soil in each pot, the amount of water given to each plant, and the species of plant.

To engage the students in critical thinking, we ask them, "Why are controls important?" They discuss this question with a partner and then share out their answers. We want students to understand that when an experiment has too few controls, there is no way of knowing if the results occurred because of the independent variable or the lack of a control. For example, did the fertilized plant grow taller because it received fertilizer or because it was watered more often than the non-fertilized plant? We can't determine what caused the plant growth because there were two differences between the two pots.

To teach students the concept of controls and how to make data tables, we use the worksheet in Figure 3.7: Finding Controls and Making Data Tables. We created this worksheet for younger students (fourth through eighth grade) but have also found it useful at the high school level because it's a good review for identifying independent and dependent variables. As we stated earlier, we provide some students with shortened assignments as a differentiation strategy. We may only require them to complete two of the four practice problems, which gives them more time to complete the assignment accurately. The answer key can be found in Figure 3.8: Finding Controls and Making Data Tables—Answer Key.

When we introduce this worksheet to our younger students, they are challenged to identify the dependent and independent variables. After a class discussion of the correct answers, we model how to use the variables to make a data table with an appropriate title and measurements, along with a list of controls. The students then work with their learning partner to complete the same tasks for the other scenarios.

Once students have completed the worksheet, we provide the correct answers and respond to any questions that arise. Some students may finish earlier than others. Those students who complete the worksheet prior to their classmates are instructed to create their own experimental scenario, identify the variables and controls, and make the data table. We encourage students to write their scenarios about something they find interesting, such as a sport, a hobby, or a musical instrument.

When using this worksheet with high school students, we model the first scenario and then allow them to answer the remaining questions independently. Students compare answers with a partner and then we review the answers as a class. During this activity, as usual, we walk around the classroom so we can assist students who require more instruction and support.

Once students are familiar with identifying controls and making data tables, we ask them to make a list of the controls in their class experiment and create a data table using their independent and dependent variables.

Performing the Experiment

Prior to performing any experiment, we tell students that their grade is not based on whether their data does or does not support their hypothesis. Instead, it is based on how they *interpret* their data. We tell them that when scientists obtain data they are not expecting, it indicates that they have learned something, which is the purpose of science!

Students are now finally ready to begin experimenting and collecting their data. As they perform the class experiment, we remind students to record their data in their data tables. See Chapter 2: Strategies for Teaching Lab Procedures for strategies on grouping students, monitoring for on-task behavior, and ensuring thorough clean-up after a lab is complete.

STEP 5: ANALYSIS

The analysis step of the scientific method includes making a graph and writing a Discussion of Results. We explain to students that scientists use data analysis to identify patterns and outliers, which allows them to draw conclusions.

Making a Graph

After students complete their experiment and clean their lab area, they use their data to make a graph. The NGSS require second-grade students to learn how to make bar graphs and fifth grade students must learn how to make line graphs (NGSS, 2013a, p. 2). Because it is likely that fourth and fifth grade students are familiar with bar graphs but not line graphs, we provide them with a premade graph so all they need to do is plot their data. Their premade graphs include a title, x- and y-axis titles, units of measurement, and a key, if necessary. Beginning in sixth grade, students are provided with blank graph paper and we make the graphs together as a class. In seventh grade and above, we provide students with blank graph paper, an example of a well-made graph, and a checklist, which can be found in Figure 3.9: Example and Checklist—Making Graphs.

Of course, it is a mistake to assume that all students have learned the science concepts required by the NGSS at each prior grade level. Not all states have adopted the NGSS and some students may have moved from different countries. Even if you are in a state that has adopted the NGSS, there is no guarantee that prior teachers have followed the standards in their teaching or, even if they have, that students remember what they were taught. Ultimately, we must meet students where they are and provide any needed scaffolding.

We teach a step-by-step process for making graphs, both with traditional graph paper and in Microsoft Excel. This strategy can be found in Chapter 11: Strategies for Incorporating Math, which also includes information on teaching students how to interpret data in charts and graphs.

Writing the Discussion of Results

In our experience, writing lab reports can be challenging for students. To help students of all ages, we use lab report "starters," also known as paragraph frames. Figure 3.10: Discussion of Results guides them through the process of writing a full analysis. Students are instructed to complete the sentence starters and deepen their answers where space allows. Younger students are allowed to complete the Discussion of Results in small groups, but starting in seventh grade, we require each student to complete his/her own analysis.

We explain to students that scientists write a Discussion of Results to present the data in written form and to interpret the data's meaning, including possible experimental errors and suggested improvements for future experiments.

STEP 6: CONCLUSION

Before students write their Conclusion, we explain that scientists write Conclusions because they must now connect their hypothesis to the data they collected. Scientists use Conclusions to summarize the meaning of their data as it pertains to the hypothesis.

Students whose data didn't support their hypotheses still have valuable data. Prior to students beginning their experiments, we explain that when a scientist's data is unexpected, the scientist learned something and can use that knowledge in future experiments. We assure students that scientists often have data that doesn't support their hypotheses and it's okay for them to be in the same situation.

We've also found that many students struggle to write Conclusions, so we created Figure 3.11: Conclusion, another lab report starter that follows the same pattern as Figure 3.10: Discussion of Results. And, just as with the previous lab write-up, younger students can write their Conclusion in small groups. However, in our experience, it's appropriate to expect seventh graders and above to write their Conclusions independently (obviously, there will be exceptions to support differentiated instruction).

STEP 7: PUBLISH RESULTS

We explain to our students that Step 7: Publish Results is possibly the most important step in the scientific method. We ask them, "Can you imagine if a scientist found a cure for a disease but then never told anyone?" After a class discussion about the ramifications of not sharing scientific discoveries, we offer students options for publishing their data. They can:

- Share their results with a parent and then obtain their parent's signature.
- Place their lab reports in a portfolio. Some schools have student-led conferences instead of traditional parent/teacher conferences. Students create a portfolio, which is a collection of the work they feel best represents their learning. They then share the portfolio with their families.
- Make a Prezi at www.prezi.com or a slideshow outlining their experiment and its results. Both are then published online automatically.
- Share their lab report with another student whose class is doing the same project. We've arranged class meetings with other teachers on our campus, allowing students to share results with their peers. Students have also shared their results with other students via email or Google Drive.
- Participate in a science fair.
- Publish the results in a class blog and share them with a "sister class." See the Technology Connections section for further information on this option.

DIFFERENTIATION FOR DIVERSE LEARNERS

In addition to the differentiation ideas we mentioned throughout the Application section, here are more specific strategies for some steps in the scientific method.

Step 2: Perform Research

We require our advanced and older students to find research independently and provide them with only a few resources or guidelines. For example, Tara's AP Environmental Science students are required to find their research using at least one Internet site, two scholarly articles, an interview, and one library book.

English language learners can be shown a closed-captioned English video that provides information on the topic being researched. Many videos on YouTube have the option of closed-captioning. We allow them to watch videos as many times as they need. Or, students can watch videos or read articles in their home language on the same topic. See the Technology Connections section for more bilingual resources.

These resources can be provided to students prior to the lesson being taught in class. This strategy is a modification of the Preview-View-Review sequence often used in bilingual classes where the lesson is previewed in the home language, taught in English, and then reviewed in the home language (see Larry Ferlazzo's blog titled "The Best Resources Explaining Why We Need to Support the Home Language of ELLs," details in Technology Connections).

Students with focus issues or high anxiety can be provided with a list of specific questions they need to answer while they perform their research. Students are then able to focus on the specific questions they've been assigned so they can accomplish more in the allotted time (Minahan, 2017, pp. 2–3). For example, if the experimental question was, "What is the most efficient process to clean birds after an oil spill?" students would be provided with the following list of research questions:

1. What are the physical characteristics of oil?
2. Why can't birds wash the oil out of their own feathers?
3. How do people help birds who are covered in oil? How well do these processes work?
4. How does oil negatively affect birds?

Table 3.3 Scientific Method Pretest Skills

Station number	Scientific method skill being tested
1	Identifying independent and dependent variables
2	Identifying experimental controls
3	Making data tables
4	Writing a hypothesis using "If. . .then. . .because. . ." format
5	Making graphs

Step 3: Write a Hypothesis

When we teach the scientific method to younger students, we have all lab groups perform the same experiment with the same variables. We tell the students what their variables are and we work as a class to write the hypothesis. In order to prevent preconceived ideas of what the results should be, the teacher doesn't model the experiment first. However, the teacher needs to have previously provided various examples of other experiments on different topics.

Steps 6 and 7: Analysis and Conclusion

Some students' IEPs (Individualized Educational Plans) have an accommodation that requires teachers to minimize the amount of writing requirements. In that case, we don't require students to write both a Discussion of Results and a Conclusion. Instead, they write one document that covers both steps. We provide a structured lab report with sentence starters for these students, which is Figure 3.12: Discussion of Results and Conclusion Modified Version.

High School Students

If we assume all of our high school students have the same background knowledge about the scientific method, we may not be providing equitable instruction. Therefore, we give high school students a pretest, which consists of five lab stations. Each station tests a student's ability to use the various skills required by the scientific method. Table 3.3: Scientific Method Pretest Skills lists the scientific method skill for each of the five stations.

The stations are provided in Figure 3.13: Scientific Method Pretest Stations. We print each station on a separate sheet of paper and post them around our classroom. Students are allowed to move freely from station to station, in no particular order. To maximize on-task behavior, we have two of every station around our room. We've found that it typically requires approximately 45–60 minutes to complete all five stations.

Prior to beginning the pretest, we explain to students that this is a non-graded activity and their results will indicate what aspects of the scientific method we need to teach prior to performing experiments. We ask them, "Please help us become better teachers." We emphasize that we need students to complete the tasks individually so that we can get a clear picture of individual student needs. We also monitor during the activity to ensure students are working independently. Students are provided with Figure 3.14: Scientific Method Pretest—Student Answer Sheet.

The answer key for each station is provided in Figure 3.15: Scientific Method Pretest—Answer Key.

As we grade the students' answer sheets, we note which students need more practice in the various scientific method concepts. The next several days are then used to provide more practice and instruction in the areas that students struggled with the most. For example, students who cannot accurately identify independent and dependent variables are placed in a small group and challenged to work together to complete Figure 3.2: Identifying Independent and Dependent Variables. Table 3.4 lists the scientific method skills and the coordinating activities that can be used to help students practice them. Students who perform all five stations correctly are asked to help their peers. They are instructed not to give the answers to their classmates but instead to explain the process they used to complete the tasks.

Students who need more practice making graphs are provided with Figure 3.9: Example and Checklist—Making Graphs. They create a graph using provided data like that found in Table 3.5: Data for Graph Practice.

Table 3.4 Scientific Method Skill and Coordinating Learning Activity

Scientific method skill	Coordinating learning activity
Identifying independent and dependent variables	Figure 3.2: Identifying independent and dependent variables
Identifying experimental controls	Figure 3.7: Finding controls and making data tables
Making data tables	Figure 3.7: Finding controls and making data tables
Writing a hypothesis using "If. . .then. . .because. . ." format	Figure 3.4: How to write a hypothesis
Making graphs	Figure 3.9: Example and checklist—making graphs

Table 3.5 Data for Graph Practice

Car color	Internal temperature (°C)	External temperature (°C)
Red	25.5	18.3
Blue	25	18.3
White	21.7	18.3
Black	27.8	18.3

Student Handouts and Examples

Figure 3.1: Student Research Organizer (Student Handout)

Figure 3.2: Identifying Independent and Dependent Variables (Student Handout)

Figure 3.3: Identifying Independent and Dependent Variables—Answer Key

Figure 3.4: How to Write a Hypothesis (Student Handout)

Figure 3.5: How to Write a Hypothesis—Answer Key

Figure 3.6: Student Materials List (Student Handout)

Figure 3.7: Finding Controls and Making Data Tables (Student Handout)

Figure 3.8: Finding Controls and Making Data Tables—Answer Key

Figure 3.9: Example and Checklist—Making Graphs (Student Handout)

Figure 3.10: Discussion of Results (Student Handout)

Figure 3.11: Conclusion (Student Handout)

Figure 3.12: Discussion of Results and Conclusion Modified Version (Student Handout)

Figure 3.13: Scientific Method Pretest Stations

Figure 3.14: Scientific Method Pretest—Student Answer Sheet (Student Handout)

Figure 3.15: Scientific Method Pretest—Answer Key

What Could Go Wrong?

The most common incident that causes student anxiety is when they don't get data that supports their hypothesis. When this happens, students believe they are going to fail the lab. We've learned through the years that the best way to combat this is to be proactive. As mentioned earlier, prior to performing any experiment, we explain to students that their grade is based on how they interpret their data and not on the data itself. We tell them that when scientists obtain data they are not expecting, it indicates that they learned something, which is the purpose of doing science!

We share examples of how scientists didn't obtain the data they were expecting, which led to major scientific advances, including the invention of the microwave, Super Glue, the Slinky, and pacemakers (Biddle, 2012). We make a point of highlighting people of color and women who have found success through failure. Here are a few of our favorites, some of which can be found in the *Business Insider* article "These 10 Inventions Were Made by Mistake" (Krueger, 2010).

- American chef Ruth Wakefield ran out of baker's chocolate while making chocolate cookies. She attempted to solve the problem by adding small sweetened chocolate pieces to the cookie dough, hypothesizing that the chocolate would melt and make chocolate cookies. However, the small pieces stuck together and the first chocolate chip cookie was invented.

- Chef George Crum, who had an African-American father and a Native-American mother, served a customer a side dish of potatoes. The customer sent the plate of potatoes back to the kitchen multiple times demanding the potatoes be cut thinner and fried again. Crum hypothesized that if he cut the potatoes thinner than he had ever cut potatoes and fried them until they had a very crunchy texture, then the customer would finally be satisfied. The customer loved his thin crunchy potatoes and Crum soon opened his own restaurant that included a basket of potato chips on every table.

- American chemist, Patsy Sherman, accidentally invented Scotchgard with her partner, Sam Smith. She was experimenting on a rubber material that would not deteriorate when it was exposed to jet aircraft fuels. During the experiment, an assistant unintentionally dropped the rubber material and some of it landed on Sherman's white canvas tennis shoes. Her shoes' structure didn't change but it repelled water and oil. Three years later, Sherman and Smith developed the stain repellent, Scotchgard, all due to an error made during an experiment.

Of course, this is just a very tiny effort at being culturally responsive. We share many more substantial strategies in Chapter 14: Strategies for Cultural Responsiveness.

The most common incident that causes *us* anxiety is when one or two lab groups gets grossly behind in the experimental process. When we were new teachers, this was the most challenging part of labs. Over the years we've found that keeping the lab groups on the same schedule is logistically imperative because otherwise we are challenged with finding something for the rest of the class to do while the remaining lab groups complete their experiments.

To keep all groups on the same schedule, we provide enough time for students to complete every step of the scientific method in class. We find that the groups who fall behind are typically the ones who do not complete their homework. To address this issue, we don't assign homework and instead use class time to complete all necessary work, including the preparation, data collection, and conclusion. This process also allows us to provide support and ensure students are on task, which is something that can't be done when they take work home.

Another challenge relates to the scientific method itself. There are inherent problems with the scientific method; for example, it is impossible to always control every variable and to eliminate scientists' biases. When these situations arise in our classrooms, we use them to teach our students about the struggles of real scientists. We teach students that when an experiment isn't completed perfectly, it's acceptable, but they must describe the errors in their lab reports. There is an area for students to communicate their errors in Figure 3.10: Discussion of Results when they complete Step 5: Analyze Results.

Technology Connections

GENERAL SCIENTIFIC METHOD RESOURCES

There are many entertaining and educational videos on YouTube that walk students through the scientific method steps. Be careful, though, because many of them don't include Step 7: Publish Results. Larry Ferlazzo's Edublog includes a list of online videos that teach the scientific method. The list can be found at "The Best Videos for Learning About the Scientific Method" (http://larryferlazzo.edublogs. org/2017/03/10/the-best-videos-for-learning-about-the-scientific-method).

Teachers can search "scientific method" in any of these educational sites to find activities other teachers have already created:

- Quizlet www.quizlet.com
- Quizizz www.quizizz.com
- Kahoot https://kahoot.com

Students can be assigned online activities to complete as a class (such as Quizlet Live) or individually (such as Quizlet Match). Additional ways to leverage these sites in a classroom can be found in Chapter 16: Strategies for Reviewing Content.

There are many online science resources available in multiple languages. See Larry Ferlazzo's blog at "The Best Multilingual and Bilingual Sites for Math, Social Studies, & Science," which can be found at http://larryferlazzo.edublogs.org/2008/10/03/the-best-multilingual-bilingual-sites-for-math-social-studies-science.

We use Science Buddies (www.sciencebuddies.org) for experiment ideas and supporting documentation, such as a sample materials lists and step-by-step procedures.

RESEARCH RESOURCES

When we provide research for our students, we begin searching online by adding the phrase "for kids." For example, if we were going to search for sites that teach students about osmosis, we would search for "osmosis for kids." We've found that student-friendly results are more common using this trick.

When we want to provide our students with articles that are about current events or real-life applications of a concept, our favorite source is Newsela (https://newsela.com). This website has thousands of articles that are offered in five different lexile levels ranging from 690 L to more than 1,230 L. And, some of the articles are offered in both English and Spanish. For schools that don't provide students with online access, there is a printer-friendly version of each article so teachers can provide their students with a hard copy.

There are additional websites that offer articles. Larry Ferlazzo's Websites of the Day, "The Best Places to get the 'Same' Text Written for Different 'Levels'" contains a list of great sources (http://larryferlazzo.edublogs.org/2014/11/16/the-best-places-to-get-the-same-text-written-for-different-levels).

When performing research, ELL students can be given the topic prior to the lesson being taught in class. This strategy is a modification of the Preview-View-Review sequence often used in bilingual classes where the lesson is previewed in the home language, taught in English, and then reviewed in the home language. See Larry Ferlazzo's blog titled "The Best Resources Explaining Why We Need to Support the Home Language of ELLs" for more online resources to support ELL students (http://larryferlazzo.edublogs.org/2017/04/10/the-best-resources-explaining-why-we-need-to-support-the-home-language-of-ells).

PUBLISH RESULTS RESOURCES

There are many organizations designed to assist teachers in connecting with other classes around the world. These "sister classes" can provide an "authentic audience" where students can share the results of their experiments. See "The Best Ways to Find Other Classes for Joint Online Projects" for more information (http://larryferlazzo.edublogs.org/2009/05/30/the-best-ways-to-find-other-classes-for-joint-online-projects).

Figures

Name: _____

My Research—Organized

Directions: Use this graphic organizer to record the information you obtain during your research. First, complete the left column. Then read the resource. Finally, determine what the three most important points are in that resource and document them in the boxes.

Title of Each Resource, Author, Date, Publisher, Page Number(s), URL	Important Points Found Using This Resource
	1.
	2.
	3.
	1.
	2.
	3.
	1.
	2.
	3.
	1.
	2.
	3.

Figure 3.1   Student Research Organizer (Student Handout)

Name: _____

Identifying Independent and Dependent Variables

What does the word "vary" mean? _____

When a scientist sets up an experiment, only one thing can vary. Everything else must stay the same. For example, if an entomologist (a scientist who studies insects) wants to know which insect can jump the highest, she would make sure there is only one difference when studying the insects. With a partner, brainstorm what should be the same and what is the one thing that should be different. Record your ideas:

Six things that should be the same when determining which insect can jump the highest:

1.

2.

3.

4.

5.

6.

The one thing that is different, which in this experiment is the species of the insects, is called the **independent variable** and it must be identified while the scientist is designing their experiment. Scientists attempt to control as much as they can so there is only one independent variable. Why is it bad to have many independent variables? Make a guess and record it here:

As an example, let's say the scientist changed the type of insect (ants, grasshoppers, and crickets) and the surface they were jumping on (cotton, wood, and water). Her data reveals that crickets on cotton jump higher than grasshoppers on water. Why can't she say that crickets jump higher than grasshoppers? Talk to your partner and jot down your ideas:

Figure 3.2 Identifying Independent and Dependent Variables (Student Handout)

During the experiment, data is collected. Each set of data is called the **dependent variable**. An experiment can have as many dependent variables as the scientist desires. What data will the entomologist collect during her experiment with ants, grasshoppers, and crickets? Write it here:

She could also collect the number of times they jump, how fast they jump, or the distance they jump. If she collected all of this data, plus the height they jump, she would have four dependent variables.

To remember the difference between independent and dependent variables, use their first letters. Independent begins with the letter I and it is *I*, the scientist, who determines the independent variable. Dependent begins with the letter D and it is the *Data* that is collected *During* the experiment and recorded in a *Data* table. If that doesn't help you, maybe it is easier to remember that the independent variable changes first and it causes the dependent variable to change. In other words, the dependent variable *depends* on the independent variable.

Identify the independent and dependent variables in each of the following investigations. The first one has been done for you.

1. Problem: Is the inside of a car cooler if you put up a windshield sunshade?

   Independent Variable: *whether or not there's a windshield sunshade*

   Dependent Variable: *the inside temperature of the car*

2. Problem: How long do you have to shake a can of soda before it explodes when you open it?

   Independent Variable: _____

   Dependent Variable: _____

3. Problem: What kind of exercise is best when trying to avoid heart disease?

   Independent Variable: _____

   Dependent Variable: _____

4. Problem: Does studying help you perform better on a test?

   Independent Variable: _____

   Dependent Variable: _____

Figure 3.2 (Continued)

5. Problem: How many selfies do you have to post to become an Internet star?

Independent Variable: _____

Dependent Variable: _____

6. Problem: Are some dog breeds smarter than others?

Independent Variable: _____

Dependent Variable: _____

Challenge: Read the following investigations and answer the questions.

1. A group of students chose to investigate the relationship between the amount of tree movement and wind strength. They used rulers to measure the distance that tree branches moved, and a wind gauge to measure the wind speed. They concluded that their data supported their hypothesis, which was "If there is more wind speed, then tree branches will move more because the wind is a force acting upon the branches."
What is the independent variable?

What is the dependent variable?

2. Botanists (scientists that study plants) want to know if tomato plants grow taller in sunlight or artificial light. Their hypothesis says, "If you grow tomato plants in sunlight, then they will grow taller because sunlight offers nutrients that artificial light does not offer."
What is the independent variable?

What is the dependent variable?

3. Now create your own experiment. . . be creative and have fun! Choose something you are interested in, such as an extracurricular activity. Explain the experiment thoroughly and identify the independent and dependent variables.

Figure 3.2 (Continued)

Name: _____ *Answer Key*_____

Identifying Independent and Dependent Variables

What does the word "vary" mean? *to change, to be different*

When a scientist sets up an experiment, only one thing can vary. Everything else must stay the same. For example, if an entomologist (a scientist who studies insects) wants to know which insect can jump the highest, she would make sure there is only one difference when studying the insects. With a partner, brainstorm what should be the same and what is the one thing that should be different. Record your ideas:

Six things that should be the same when determining which insect can jump the highest:

1. *Answers will vary*
2. *The medium the insect is perched upon*
3. *The process of measuring jumped distance*
4.
5.
6.

What is the one thing that should be different in this experiment? *different insect species*

The one thing that is different, which in this experiment is the species of the insects, is called the **independent variable** and it must be identified while the scientist is designing their experiment. Scientists attempt to control as much as they can so there is only one independent variable. Why is it bad to have many independent variables? Make a guess and record it here:

When there are two or more independent variables, the scientist doesn't know which variable caused the results.

As an example, let's say the scientist changed the type of insect (ants, grasshoppers, and crickets) and the surface they were jumping on (cotton, wood, and water). Her data reveals that crickets on cotton jump higher than grasshoppers on water. Why can't she say that crickets jump higher than grasshoppers? Talk to your partner and jot down your ideas:

There are two independent variables: the insect species and the type of surface they are jumping on. We don't know if the crickets are jumping higher because they are on cotton or if it's because they are crickets.

During the experiment, data is collected. Each set of data is called the **dependent variable**. An experiment can have as many dependent variables as the

Figure 3.3 Identifying Independent and Dependent Variables—Answer Key scientist desires. What data will the entomologist collect during her experiment with ants, grasshoppers, and crickets? Write it here:

The height the insects jump.

She could also collect the number of times they jump, how fast they jump, or the distance they jump. If she collected all of this data, plus the height they jump, she would have four dependent variables.

To remember the difference between independent and dependent variables, use their first letters. Independent begins with the letter I and it is *I*, the scientist, who determines the independent variable. Dependent begins with the letter D and it is the *Data* that is collected *During* the experiment and recorded in a *Data* table. If that doesn't help you, maybe it is easier to remember that the independent variable changes first and it causes the dependent variable to change. In other words, the dependent variable *depends* on the independent variable.

Identify the independent and dependent variables in each of the following investigations. The first one has been done for you.

1. Problem: Is the inside of a car cooler if you put up a windshield sunshade?

Independent Variable: *whether or not there's a windshield sunshade*

Dependent Variable: *the inside temperature of the car*

2. Problem: How long do you have to shake a can of soda before it explodes when you open it?

Independent Variable: *the amount of time you shake the can of soda*

Dependent Variable: *whether or not the soda explodes when you open the can*

3. Problem: What kind of exercise is best when trying to avoid heart disease?

Independent Variable: *type of exercise a patient participates in*

Dependent Variable: *whether or not the patient gets heart disease*

4. Problem: Does studying actually help you perform better on a test?

Independent Variable: *whether or not a student studies for a test*

Dependent Variable: *the test score*

Figure 3.3 (Continued)

5. Problem: How many selfies do you have to post to become an Internet star?

Independent Variable: *the number of selfies a person takes*

Dependent Variable: *whether or not the person becomes an Internet star*

6. Problem: Are some dog breeds smarter than others?

Independent Variable: *different dog breeds*

Dependent Variable: *how smart the dogs are, determined by how quickly they learn a trick*

Challenge: Read the following investigations and answer the questions.

1. A group of students chose to investigate the relationship between the amount of tree movement and wind strength. They used rulers to measure the distance that tree branches moved, and a wind gauge to measure the wind speed. They concluded that their data supported their hypothesis, which was "If there is more wind speed, then tree branches will move more because the wind is a force acting upon the branches."

What is the independent variable? *The speed of the wind*

What is the dependent variable? *The distance the tree branches moved*

2. Botanists (scientists that study plants) want to know if tomato plants grow taller in sunlight or artificial light. Their hypothesis says, "If you grow tomato plants in sunlight, then they will grow taller because sunlight offers nutrients that artificial light does not offer."

What is the independent variable? *Whether the plants are grown in sunlight or artificial light*

What is the dependent variable? *The height of the plant*

3. Now create your own experiment. . .be creative and have fun! Choose something you are interested in, such as an extracurricular activity. Explain the experiment thoroughly and identify the independent and dependent variables.

Answers will vary.

Figure 3.3   (Continued)

Name: _____

How to Write a Hypothesis

A hypothesis is a tentative prediction (a possible prediction) for an observation or scientific problem written in a special way that leads to further investigation and explains why phenomena occur. Keep in mind these important points about hypotheses:

- The results of an experiment cannot prove that a hypothesis is correct because a hypothesis must be tested in every possible environment by multiple scientists before it is considered to be correct or incorrect. For this reason, instead of saying that a hypothesis is correct or incorrect, we say that the results either support or do not support the hypothesis and refer to the hypothesis as valid or null.

- You can gain valuable information even when your results do not support your hypothesis. There is no pressure to have a valid hypothesis.

- In science, a hypothesis is supported only after many scientists have conducted many experiments and produced consistent results. This helps a hypothesis's reliability.

- Science does not deal in opinions. . . only facts.

When you write a hypothesis, use this format:

If _____**independent variable**_____, then ____**dependent variable**_____, because ____**research**____.

Talk to your partner about why the scientific method requires us to perform research before we write hypotheses. Write your answer here:

To remember that the independent variable goes into the *If* statement of the hypothesis, use the first letter of the words as a reminder: the *If* statement starts with the letter *I* and the independent variable starts with the letter I. Another way to remember the order of the variables is to remember that the independent variable must come first because it causes the dependent variable to change. And in a hypothesis, the independent variable is the first variable.

Below are practice problems that require you to identify the variables and then write an accurate hypothesis. The first one has been done for you.

Figure 3.4   How to Write a Hypothesis (Student Handout)

1. Experimental Question: Which dog breed runs the fastest?

    Independent Variable: *the different dog breeds*

    Dependent Variable: *how fast the dogs run*

    Hypothesis: *If different dog breeds race, then the greyhound will run the fastest because they are bred for racing.*

2. Experimental Question: Do plants grow taller with water or milk?

    Independent Variable:

    Dependent Variable:

    Hypothesis:

3. Experimental Question: Can wet or dry snow make a taller snowman?

    Independent Variable:

    Dependent Variable:

    Hypothesis:

4. Experimental Question: Do violent video games cause students to have violent behaviors?

    Independent Variable:

    Dependent Variable:

    Hypothesis:

5. Experimental Question: Which sport is the most dangerous?

    Independent Variable:

    Dependent Variable:

    Hypothesis:

Figure 3.4 (Continued)

6. Directions: Decide which of the following hypotheses are written in the correct format. Identify the dependent and independent variables first. Then if the hypothesis is written correctly, just say so. If it's incorrectly written, then write it so it is correctly written.

a. Problem: Which cell phone chargers work?

Hypothesis: If a cell phone is charged using the charger that came with the phone, then the phone will charge better, because the charger was made by the same manufacturer as the phone.

Independent Variable:

Dependent Variable:

Hypothesis:

b. Problem: Which are better, skateboards or bicycles?

Hypothesis: If you ask 100 students at an elementary school whether they prefer skateboards or bicycles, then more will answer skateboards, because skateboards are more fun.

Independent Variable:

Dependent Variable:

Hypothesis:

c. Problem: Which invention keeps food cold longer?

Hypothesis: If you place food in a plastic cooler, then it will keep food cooler than 5°C for a longer period of time, because plastic coolers have more insulation than Styrofoam coolers.

Independent Variable:

Dependent Variable:

Hypothesis:

Figure 3.4 (Continued)

Name: _____Answer Key_____

How to Write a Hypothesis

A hypothesis is a tentative prediction (a possible prediction) for an observation or scientific problem written in a special way that leads to further investigation and explains why phenomena occur. Keep in mind these important points about hypotheses:

- The results of an experiment cannot prove that a hypothesis is correct because a hypothesis must be tested in every possible environment, by multiple scientists before it is considered to be correct or incorrect. For this reason, instead of saying that a hypothesis is correct or incorrect, we say that the results either support or do not support the hypothesis and refer to the hypothesis as valid or null.

- You can gain valuable information even when your results do not support your hypothesis. There is no pressure to have a valid hypothesis.

- In science, a hypothesis is supported only after many scientists have conducted many experiments and produced consistent results. This helps a hypothesis's reliability.

Science does not deal in opinions. . .only facts.

When you write a hypothesis, use this format:

If _____**independent variable**_____, then ____**dependent variable**_____, because ____**research**____.

Talk to your partner about why the scientific method requires us to perform research before we write hypotheses. Write your answer here:

The research is used to write the hypothesis so we must perform research before writing our hypotheses.

To remember that the independent variable goes into the *If* statement of the hypothesis, use the first letter of the words as a reminder: the *If* statement starts with the letter *I* and the independent variable starts with the letter *I*. Another way to remember the order of the variables is to remember that the independent variable must come first because it causes the dependent variable to change. And in a hypothesis, the independent variable is the first variable.

Below are practice problems that require you to identify the variables and then write an accurate hypothesis. The first one has been done for you.

Figure 3.5 How to Write a Hypothesis—Answer Key

1. Experimental Question: Which dog breed runs the fastest?

Independent Variable: *the different dog breeds*

Dependent Variable: *how fast the dogs run*

Hypothesis: *If different dog breeds race, then the greyhound will run the fastest because they are bred for racing.*

2. Experimental Question: Do plants grow taller with water or milk?

Independent Variable: *whether the plant is given water or milk*

Dependent Variable: *the height of the plant*

Hypothesis: *Answers will vary but here is an example—If a plant is given water, then it will grow taller because milk includes ingredients that plants don't need.*

3. Experimental Question: Can wet or dry snow make a taller snowman?

Independent Variable: *whether the snow is wet or dry*

Dependent Variable: *the height of the snowman*

Hypothesis: *Answers will vary but here is an example—If a snowman is built using dry snow, it will be taller because dry snow isn't as heavy as wet snow.*

4. Experimental Question: Do violent video games cause students to have violent behaviors?

Independent Variable: *the amount of violence in video games*

Dependent Variable: *the number of violent behaviors in students*

Hypothesis: *Answers will vary but here is an example—If a child plays a video game with more than average violent scenes, then the child will have more than average violent behaviors because children mimic the behavior they witness.*

5. Experimental Question: Which sport is the most dangerous?

Independent Variable: *different sports*

Dependent Variable: *the amount of injuries athletes experience while playing*

Figure 3.5 (Continued)

Hypothesis: *Answers will vary but here is an example. If a person plays basketball then they will experience more injuries because basketball is a contact sport that doesn't require athletes to wear safety gear.*

6. Directions: Decide which of the following hypotheses are written in the correct format. Identify the dependent and independent variables first. Then if the hypothesis is written correctly, just say so. If it's incorrectly written, then write it so it is correctly written.

a. Problem: Which cell phone chargers work?

Hypothesis: If a cell phone is charged using the charger that came with the phone, then the phone will charge better, because the charger was made by the same manufacturer as the phone.

Independent Variable: *the type of charger used to charge the cell phone*

Dependent Variable: *how fast it takes to charge the phone from 0–100%*

Hypothesis: *This hypothesis is incorrect because the term "better" is an opinion, not data that can be collected. Answers will vary but here is an example of a properly written hypothesis: If a cell phone is charged using the charger that came with the phone, then the phone will be charged faster from 0–100% because the charger was made by the same manufacturer as the phone.*

b. Problem: Which are better, skateboards or bicycles?

Hypothesis: If you ask 100 students at an elementary school whether they prefer skateboards or bicycles, then more will answer skateboards, because skateboards are more fun.

Independent Variable: *skateboards or bicycles*

Dependent Variable: *number of students who prefer to ride one over the other*

Hypothesis: *This hypothesis is written incorrectly because the research is an opinion, not a fact. Answers will vary but here is an example of a properly written hypothesis: If you ask 100 students at an elementary school whether they prefer skateboards or bicycles, then more will answer skateboards because skateboards are cheaper so more students have experience with skateboards than bicycles.*

Figure 3.5 (Continued)

c. Problem: Which invention keeps food cold longer?

Hypothesis: If you place food in a plastic cooler, then it will keep food cooler than 5°C for a longer period of time, because plastic coolers have more insulation than Styrofoam coolers.

Independent Variable: *the type of cooler the food is stored in*

Dependent Variable: *how long the food stays below 5°C*

Hypothesis: *This is a well-written hypothesis.*

Figure 3.5 (Continued)

Directions: Use this table to document the materials you'll be using in your experiment. An example is included on the first line.

Material name	Detailed description	Quantity
Example: Beaker	*250 mL, glass*	*2*

Figure 3.6 Student Materials List (Student Handout)

Finding Controls and Making Data Tables   Name: _____

Ally wanted to know if one brand of microwave popcorn would pop more popcorn than other brands. She went to the store and purchased three brands of microwave popcorn: PopALot, Popcorn Galore, and Butter Me a Dream.

1. What is her dependent variable?

2. What is her independent variable?

3. What would her data table look like during the experiment while she was collecting the data?

4. What are the six controls in her experiment?

Austin asked himself, "Can dogs see color?" He decided to find out with his three dogs, all of whom were female Chihuahuas. He bought three different colors of dog food. He hypothesized that if his dogs always chose one color of food over the others, it would indicate they could see color.

1. What is his dependent variable?

2. What is his independent variable?

3. What would his data table look like during the experiment while he was collecting the data?

4. What are the six controls in his experiment?

Figure 3.7 Finding Controls and Making Data Tables (Student Handout)

Samantha was at gymnastics one day and asked her coach, "Can boys or girls climb the rope faster?" Her coach wasn't sure, so they decided to do a test. Samantha and four of her female friends met up with five other male gymnasts. They each climbed the rope, timing how long it took to get from the floor to the ceiling.

1. What is her dependent variable?
2. What is her independent variable?
3. What would her data table look like during the experiment while she was collecting the data?

4. What are the six controls in her experiment?

A dentist was told by a sales representative that his company's teeth whitening gel, called WhiteMore, would work faster than all other whiteners on the market. The dentist didn't believe it because the gel was so inexpensive. In addition, he already had a favorite whitener called ToothFairy. The sales rep offered to conduct a scientific experiment to prove that WhiteMore was the superior product. The dentist chose six patients, three of whom used ToothFairy and three of whom used WhiteMore.

1. What is his dependent variable?
2. What is his independent variable?
3. What would his data table look like during the experiment while he was collecting the data?

4. What are the six controls in his experiment?

Figure 3.7 (Continued)

Finding Controls and Making Data Tables Name: _____ Answer Key____

Ally wanted to know if one brand of microwave popcorn would pop more popcorn than other brands. She went to the store and purchased three brands of microwave popcorn: PopALot, Popcorn Galore, and Butter Me a Dream.

1. What is her dependent variable? *The amount of kernels that pop*
2. What is her independent variable? *The brand of microwave popcorn*
3. What would her data table look like during the experiment while she was collecting the data?

Number of Popped Kernels Based on the Microwave Popcorn Brand

Microwave Popcorn Brand	Number of Popped Kernels
PopALot	
Popcorn Galore	
Butter Me a Dream	

4. What are six controls in her experiment? *Answers will vary but acceptable answers include the microwave used, the amount of time the popcorn is popped, the flavor of the popcorn (buttered, reduced fat), the volume of popcorn in the bag, the manufacture date of the popcorn, how a kernel is defined during the counting process*

Austin asked himself, "Can dogs see color?" He decided to find out with his three dogs, all of whom were female Chihuahuas. He bought three different colors of dog food. He hypothesized that if his dogs always chose one color of food over the others, it would indicate they could see color.

1. What is his dependent variable? *The color of the dog food*
2. What is his independent variable? *Which dog food color the dogs chose*
3. What would his data table look like during the experiment while he was collecting the data?

Food Color That Dogs Choose

Dog	Dog Food Color	Number of Times Chosen
Max	brown	
	red	
	pink	
Rover	brown	
	red	
	pink	
Pipsqueak	brown	
	red	
	pink	

Figure 3.8 Finding Controls and Making Data Tables—Answer Key

4. What are six controls in his experiment? *Answers will vary but acceptable answers include the brand of the dog food, the flavor of the dog food, the amount of dog food, the distance the dog is from the dog foods, the same type/shape/color of bowl that holds the dog food, the last time the dog ate a meal*

Samantha was at gymnastics one day and asked her coach, "Can boys or girls climb the rope faster?" Her coach wasn't sure, so they decided to do a test. Samantha and four of her female friends met up with five other male gymnasts. They each climbed the rope, timing how long it took to get from the floor to the ceiling.

1. What is her dependent variable? *The gender of the gymnast*
2. What is her independent variable? *The time it takes for the gymnast to climb the rope*
3. What would her data table look like during the experiment while she was collecting the data?

Which Gender Climbs Ropes Faster?

Gymnast Gender	Time to Climb the Rope (seconds)
Male	
Male	
Male	
Female	
Female	
Female	

4. What are six controls in her experiment? *Answers will vary but acceptable answers include the age of the gymnasts, the time the gymnast spent warming up and training that day, the height of the gymnasts, the rope they climb, the temperature in the gym, the material their clothes are made of*

A dentist was told by a sales representative that his company's teeth whitening gel, called WhiteMore, would work faster than all other whiteners on the market. The dentist didn't believe it because the gel was so inexpensive. In addition, he already had a favorite whitener called ToothFairy. The sales rep offered to conduct a scientific experiment to prove that WhiteMore was the superior product. The dentist chose six patients, three of whom used ToothFairy and three of whom used WhiteMore.

1. What is his dependent variable? *The different brands of whitening gel*
2. What is his independent variable? *How much whiter the patients' teeth became*
3. What would his data table look like during the experiment while he was collecting the data?

Figure 3.8 (Continued)

Brand of Teeth Whitener vs. How Much Whiter Teeth Become

Patient Number	Teeth Whitener Brand	On a Scale of 1-10, Whiteness Rating Before	On a Scale of 1-10, Whiteness Rating After
1	ToothFairy		
2			
3			
4	WhiteMore		
5			
6			

4. What are six controls in his experiment? *Answers will vary but acceptable answers include the dietary habits of the patients, the type and number of beverages the patients drink, how often they brush their teeth, how long they brush their teeth for, whether or not they smoke*

Figure 3.8 (Continued)

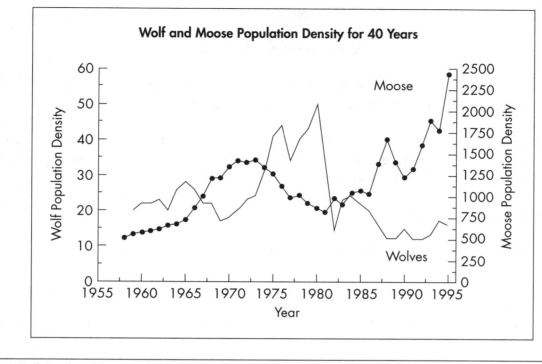

Use this checklist and the example of a line graph to ensure **your** graph has all of the necessary components.

_____ Graph's title—includes both variables

_____ Independent variable on the x-axis; Dependent variable on the y-axis; both axes have titles

_____ Units of measurement are included in the x- and y-axis titles

_____ Use of a line graph if the independent variable is a number; use of a bar graph if the independent variable is not a number

_____ A consistent increment for the x-axis

_____ A consistent increment for the y-axis

_____ Key (if necessary)

_____ If you have a broken graph, be sure to explain to your reader that it's broken and how you did it.

Figure 3.9   Example and Checklist—Making Graphs (Student Handout)

Name: _____

Discussion of Results

To write your Discussion of Results, complete the sentence starters. The more space there is for you to write, the more writing you'll need to do.

The Discussion of Results includes an explanation of what your results mean in relation to your question, research, and hypothesis. It should also include any limitations and/or errors in your experiment.

Writing the first paragraph:

The problem being studied in this experiment was _____

_____

It was proposed that (*hypothesis*) if _____

_____

_____

The data showed that (*include important data points, not all of them*) _____

_____

_____

_____

This was measured and calculated by (*explain the experiment briefly*) _____

_____

_____

_____

These results are believed to have occurred because (*cite your research*) _____

_____

Figure 3.10   Discussion of Results (Student Handout)

_____

_____

More research or study is needed regarding (*explain the topics that need further research or experimentation in order to further describe the meaning of your results*)

_____

_____

_____

_____

Writing the second paragraph:

Although the experiment was controlled, there were still some possible sources of error. Sources of error in this experiment include (*what couldn't you control during your experiment?*) _____

_____

_____

_____

_____

These errors could be avoided in the future by (*how can you improve your procedure so that you don't make the same mistakes?*) _____

_____

_____

_____

_____

Figure 3.10 (Continued)

Name: _____

Conclusion

To write your Conclusion, complete the sentence starters. The more space there is for you to write, the more writing you'll need to do.

The Conclusion is a summary. It outlines your hypothesis, most important results, and suggested future studies. It should also paraphrase the most important results that either supported your hypothesis or were a surprise. If you found your hypothesis was null, this is where you rewrite your hypothesis based on your new data.

Writing the Conclusion paragraph:

Analysis of the results revealed that (*summarize data here **including important data points** and what they mean in relation to your hypothesis and research*)

_____

_____

_____

_____

_____

The data proves that the hypothesis was (*null or valid*) _____.
(*If your hypothesis was null, then rewrite the hypothesis and state here why it was null and how you know it was null. If the hypothesis was valid, then explain how you know it was valid by tying your results to the hypothesis and research*).

_____

_____

_____

The experiment proved that (*state what you learned*) _____

_____

_____

Figure 3.11 Conclusion (Student Handout)

A future experiment that would be an extension of this experiment includes

_____

_____

_____

Figure 3.11 (Continued)

Name: _____

Discussion of Results and Conclusion

To write your Discussion of Results and Conclusion, complete the sentence starters. The more space there is for you to write, the more writing you'll need to do.

The Discussion of Results explains what your data (numbers) means. It also includes any errors in your experiment. The Conclusion is a summary of how your hypothesis and results are connected.

Analysis: Discussion of Results

The question I asked was _____

_____

My hypothesis stated if _____

_____

My most important data points were _____

_____

These data points prove that _____

_____

This is how I set up my experiment. First, I _____

_____

_____

_____

During the experiment, I made a mistake. I should have _____

_____

Figure 3.12 Discussion of Results and Conclusion Modified Version (Student Handout)

Conclusion

My research and data points prove that _____

_____

_____

_____

My hypothesis was _____ *(null or valid)*. This experiment
makes me want to know more about _____

_____

Figure 3.12 (Continued)

Station 1

Answer these questions on your answer sheet:

1. I wanted to know if boys or girls receive higher grades in math. What is the independent variable?
2. Using the experimental question in #1, what is the dependent variable?
3. It has been stated that third-grade students whose parents began to read to them while they were in preschool can read higher-level books than their peers who weren't read to until they were in first grade. What is the independent variable?
4. Using the experimental question in #3, what is the dependent variable?
5. A math teacher and a science teacher were having a conversation about students making healthy choices at lunch. The math teacher believes that if students have an earlier lunch, they would be less hungry and would be more likely to choose fruits and vegetables. The science teacher disagreed, stating that she believes students will choose junk food all the time. What is their independent variable?
6. Using the experimental question in #5, what is the dependent variable?

Station 2

Answer these questions on your answer sheet:

1. I wanted to know if boys or girls receive higher grades in math. What are three controls for this experiment?
2. It has been stated that third-grade students whose parents began to read to them while they were in preschool can read higher-level books than their peers who weren't read to until they were in first grade. What are three controls for this experiment?
3. A math teacher and a science teacher were having a conversation about students making healthy choices at lunch. The math teacher believes that if students have an earlier lunch, they would be less hungry and would be more likely to choose fruits and vegetables. The science teacher disagreed, stating that she believes students will choose junk food all the time. What are three controls for this experiment?

Figure 3.13 Scientific Method Pretest Stations

Station 3

Answer these questions on your answer sheet:

1. I wanted to know if boys or girls receive higher grades in math. Make a data table for this experiment.
2. It has been stated that third-grade students whose parents began to read to them while they were in preschool can read higher-level books than their peers who weren't read to until they were in first grade. Make a data table for this experiment.
3. A math teacher and a science teacher were having a conversation about students making healthy choices at lunch. The math teacher believes that if students have an earlier lunch, they would be less hungry and would be more likely to choose fruits and vegetables. The science teacher disagreed, stating that she believes students will choose junk food all the time. Make a data table for this experiment.

Station 4

Answer these questions on your answer sheet:

1. I believe girls receive higher math grades than boys. What is my hypothesis?
2. It has been stated that third-grade students whose parents began to read to them while they were in preschool can read higher-level books than their peers who weren't read to until they were in first grade. What is my hypothesis?
3. A math teacher and a science teacher were having a conversation about students making healthy choices at lunch. The math teacher believes that if students have an earlier lunch, they would be less hungry and would be more likely to choose fruits and vegetables. The science teacher disagreed, stating that she believes students will choose junk food all the time. What is the math teacher's hypothesis?

Station 5

On your answer sheet, make a graph using these data:

Age of Driver vs. Number of Speeding Tickets

Driver's Age	Number of Speeding Tickets
15	1
16	3
20	2
27	1
34	0
48	4
62	1

Figure 3.13 (Continued)

Name: _____

Scientific Method Stations – Show Me What You Know

Directions: Around the classroom you'll find five stations. You can complete the stations in any order, but you must be working at a station at all times. This is a pretest so it will not be graded.

Station 1 Answers

1.

2.

3.

4.

5.

6.

Station 2 Answers

1.

2.

3.

Station 3 Answers

1.

2.

3.

Figure 3.14 Scientific Method Pretest—Student Answer Sheet (Student Handout)

Station 4 Answers

1.

2.

3.

Station 5 Answer

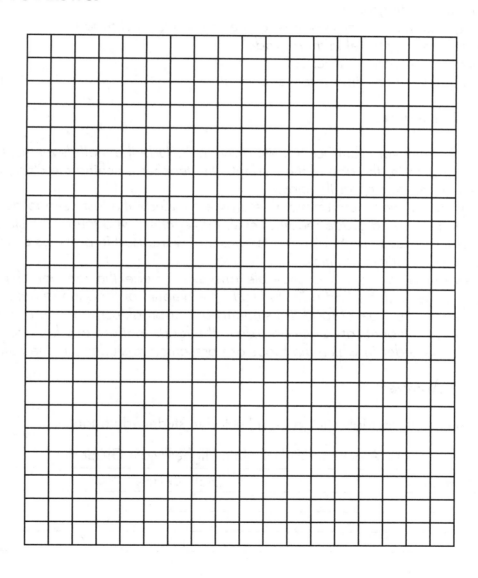

Figure 3.14   (Continued)

Name: _____*Answer Key*_____

Scientific Method Stations – Show Me What You Know

Directions: Around the classroom you'll find five stations. You can begin at any station. There is no order you need to follow, but you must be working at a station at all times. Your results will tell me how I can be a better teacher for you.

Station 1 Answers

1. *Student gender*
2. *Students' math grades*
3. *The grade the student was in when he or she was first read to*
4. *Student reading level in third grade*
5. *Time lunch is served at school*
6. *Food the students choose to eat at lunch*

Station 2 Answers

1. *Answers will vary, but acceptable answers include the math level the students are enrolled in, the age of the students, the teacher teaching the class, the curriculum and pacing of the class*
2. *Answers will vary, but acceptable answers include the test used to determine the student's third grade reading level, the teachers who taught the students in previous grades, the books and lessons that were used in previous grades, the students' cognitive abilities*
3. *Answers will vary, but acceptable answers include the amount of physical activity the students had prior to lunch, the amount of food the students ate for breakfast, the type of food the students ate at breakfast, amount and type of snacks the students ate since breakfast, the foods that are available for sale at lunch, the order in which the foods are presented to students in the cafeteria*

Station 3 Answers

NOTE: At least three trials should be reflected in student data tables.

1. A Boys or Girls Obtain Higher Math Grades?

Student Gender	Math Grade
Male	
Male	
Male	
Female	
Female	
Female	

Figure 3.15 Scientific Method Pretest—Answer Key

2.   Grade Student was First Read to vs. Student Reading Level in the Third Grade

Grade Level the Student was First Read To	Student Reading Level in the Third Grade
Preschool	
Preschool	
Preschool	
First Grade	
First Grade	
First Grade	

3.   Do Students Who are Served Lunch at an Earlier Time Choose Healthier Foods?

Lunch Time	Student Food Choice
10:30am	
10:30am	
10:30am	
11:30am	
11:30am	
11:30am	

Station 4 Answers

*Note: although the "if" and "then" statements should be as they appear below, the "because" statements will vary.

1.   *If boys and girls take a math class, then the girls will have higher math grades because, in general, girls' brains develop faster than boys' brains.*
2.   *If parents read to their preschool-aged children, then the children will read at a higher reading level in third grade because they have a larger vocabulary that is naturally developed at a young age.*
3.   *If students eat lunch earlier, then they will choose healthier food options because when teens aren't in starvation mode, they make healthier choices for themselves.*

Figure 3.15   (Continued)

Station 5 Answer

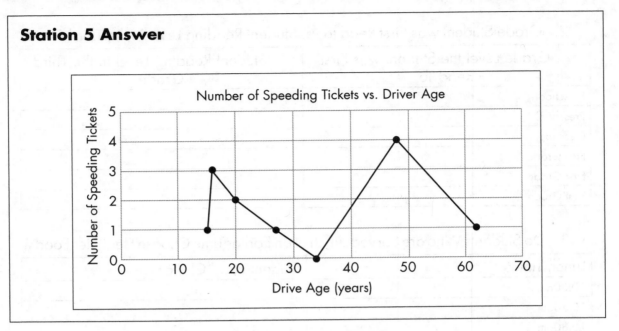

Figure 3.15 (Continued)

CHAPTER 4

Strategies for Teaching the Inquiry Process

What Is It?

In Chapter 3: Strategies for Teaching the Scientific Method and Its Components, we provide resources for teaching students the scientific method. However, with the implementation of the NGSS, many classrooms are using the scientific method less often. Teachers are now focused on teaching science and engineering practices, which are as follows:

diff. ways to do experiments

- Asking questions and defining problems.
- Developing and using models.
- Planning and carrying out investigations.
- Analyzing and interpreting data.
- Using mathematics and computational thinking.
- Constructing explanations and designing solutions.
- Engaging in argument from evidence.
- Obtaining, evaluating, and communicating information.

The scientific method includes several of these practices, with a focus on *planning and carrying out investigations* (performing an experiment). However, not every question can be answered through experimentation. Here are examples of questions whose answers *can't* be determined by using an experiment:

1. When will Mount St. Helens erupt next?
2. How did rattlesnake venom evolve?
3. Is there life on other planets?
4. How fast will the world's fastest car go?
5. How does a frog's abdomen differ from a human's?

To answer these types of questions, scientists use the inquiry process, which replaces experimentation with the science and engineering practice of *obtaining, evaluating, and communicating information.*

When the inquiry process is written in a linear format, like that of the scientific method, it replaces Step 4 in the scientific method: *Set up and Perform an Experiment* with a new Step 4: *Perform More Research and/or Complete Observations.* Here are the linear steps for the inquiry process:

1. Ask a question.
2. Perform research.
3. Write a hypothesis.
4. Perform more research and/or complete observations.
5. Analyze results.
6. Write a conclusion.
7. Publish results.

While this chapter focuses on the inquiry process and Chapter 3 provides strategies for teaching the scientific method, there are two other processes that expose students to the science and engineering practices. See Chapter 5 for resources that support project-based learning and Chapter 6 for resources that teach the engineering process.

Why We Like It

The inquiry process can provide students an opportunity to choose a topic of study. When students are given a choice of work, their intrinsic motivation tends to be enhanced, which increases their engagement level. And, students can learn more when they are intellectually engaged (Patall, Cooper, & Wynn, 2010).

The inquiry process may also contribute toward creating a more culturally responsive learning environment. Culturally responsive teaching can occur when teachers acknowledge and use students' cultural backgrounds and experiences to ensure learning is student-centered and accessible to all (The Education Alliance, Brown University, n.d.). See Chapter 14: Strategies for Cultural Responsiveness for additional resources to foster a culturally responsive environment in your classroom.

Supporting Research

The inquiry process is a tool that science teachers can use to engage students because it feeds their natural curiosity. Many teachers use the inquiry process for student-directed research activities. Students choose their topic of interest, follow the inquiry process to learn more about their topic, and complete a lab report. By allowing students to declare their topic of interest, teachers are tapping into their students' curiosity (von Stumm, Hell, & Chamorro-Premuzic, 2011).

Curiosity may be a predictor of academic success. A meta-analysis of over 200 studies was performed by von Stumm et al. (2011). Their conclusion suggests that, in addition to intelligence and conscientiousness, a third predictor of success is a student's curiosity. In fact, they found that it was as much a predictor of school success as was conscientiousness (von Stumm et al., 2011).

Skills for Intentional Scholars/NGSS Connections

All three Skills for Intentional Scholars are practiced while students use the inquiry process. For example, students creatively problem solve when they are making decisions regarding the resources they'll use when they perform their research and observations. Critical thinking occurs when students perform their research and observations. And students must communicate effectively when writing and publishing a lab report.

Components of the inquiry process are integrated throughout the science and engineering practices, crosscutting concepts, and NGSS (National Research Council, 2012, p. 85). The NGSS advise teachers to integrate the required science content, the scientific method, the inquiry process, and the seven crosscutting concepts into their lessons (NGSS, 2013c, p. 3). The activities in this chapter cover many of these requirements.

Application

How do we decide when to use the scientific method and when to use the inquiry process?

During a unit's planning stage, we determine if student learning can be accomplished with data gathered from an experiment. We use the scientific method if there is an experiment available and we have access to all of its required supplies (see

Chapter 3: Strategies for Teaching the Scientific Method and Its Components for resources in teaching the scientific method). If student learning cannot be accomplished through experimentation, we default to the inquiry process.

For example, when we wanted our students to identify the drivers of evolution, we couldn't fabricate a lab that would teach this concept. We decided to forego the scientific method and, instead, use the inquiry process.

We will describe how to apply the inquiry process in this chapter as we use it for the first time in our classes. Obviously, less scaffolding is required after students become more familiar with the steps.

The first step of the inquiry process is to ask a question. There are two ways to move forward with this activity. One way is to have the teacher write a question that focuses student learning on a *specific* concept. For example, when exploring tides, we wrote the specific question, "What causes spring and neap tides?" A second way is to have students ask their own questions based on a *broad* concept the teacher wants them to learn. For example, when we wanted students to study how Earth is a unique planet, one student wrote, "How is the earth different from other planets in our solar system?" and a second student asked, "How is Earth different from other terrestrial planets?"

If our students are writing their own questions, we require them to obtain our approval prior to beginning step 2 of the inquiry process, which requires them to perform research. We review each student's question to ensure it cannot be answered through experimentation (because then it's a scientific method question) and to confirm that it is school-appropriate.

Some students may struggle to understand the difference between a question appropriate for the scientific method and one appropriate for the inquiry process. To teach students the difference, we first explain how the scientific method (an experiment) differs from the inquiry process (more research and/or observation). We begin by providing students with an example of a scientific method question, such as "How many pennies can one strand of hair hold before it breaks?" and ask them to brainstorm an experiment that would provide data to answer the question. After the class creates the hypothetical experiment, we explain that because an experiment can answer the question, we would use the scientific method.

Then we provide an example of an inquiry process question, such as "How deep is the Mariana Trench?" and ask them to brainstorm an experiment that would provide data to answer the question. After the class determines there is no experiment, we introduce the inquiry process, explaining that not every question can be answered through experimentation and these questions must be answered through research and/or observations.

As a first step toward practicing their understanding, we present students with Table 4.1: Questions Already Sorted, which can be used to differentiate between scientific method and inquiry process questions.

Table 4.1   Questions Already Sorted

Scientific method questions	Inquiry process questions
How much does your heart rate increase when you run the 200-m dash?	Why do your muscles hurt after you exercise?
How fast does a toy car have to go to break through a facial tissue?	How have airbags changed throughout the years?
Does food taste differently if you can't smell it?	Is it true that food tastes differently when you get older because your taste buds change?
Which plate boundary causes the most damage to a building made of sugar cubes?	How do scientists measure the strength of earthquakes?

We put students into small groups and assign each one a different question. They must explain why their assigned question is either a scientific method question or an inquiry process question. Students who are assigned a scientific method question must provide the experimental design that would generate data to answer the question. For example, students assigned the first question "How much does your heart rate increase when you run the 200-meter dash?" may describe an experiment involving their classmates running the 200-m dash on a track. Students who are assigned an inquiry process question must provide the type of research and/or observation they would complete that would provide the answer. For example, students assigned the first question "Why do your muscles hurt after you exercise?" may suggest researching the answer online, interviewing the school nurse, or reading books from the school library.

Student groups are given 10 min to create a 2-min whiteboard presentation to share with the rest of the class.

To ensure students understand the difference, we write the following questions on the board. On their own paper, we ask students to individually sort the questions into scientific method questions and inquiry process questions, along with providing evidence for their claims.

- Does toilet water spin in the opposite direction in the Southern Hemisphere? Why or why not?
- What is the chemical difference (i.e., pH) between tap water and bottled water?
- How can we land a rover on the gassy planets?
- Why do eggs have a yolk?
- How does acid rain affect statues made of limestone and granite?

Students are then given time to share their ideas with a partner and make any changes to their answers. We then ask volunteers to share their answers with the class.

SIMILAR RESOURCES FOR THE INQUIRY PROCESS AND THE SCIENTIFIC METHOD

After determining it is necessary to use the inquiry process in a lesson, we leverage the resources available in Chapter 3: Strategies for Teaching the Scientific Method and Its Components, which are referenced in Table 4.2: Resources in Chapter 3 That Can be Used for Teaching the Inquiry Process.

UNIQUE RESOURCES FOR THE INQUIRY PROCESS

The inquiry process can use the same resources from the scientific method for steps 1–3 and 7; however, steps 4–6 require unique resources.

Step 4: Perform More Research and/or Complete Observations

Since there is no experiment in the inquiry process, students aren't required to make a materials list, write step-by-step procedures, or identify controls. Instead they perform additional research or complete observations.

When students ask questions that can be answered with additional research, they may not need to perform observations. For example, during a unit on evolution, a student may ask the question "How did rattlesnake venom evolve?" The student will perform research on evolution and learn that species evolve because environmental changes sometimes cause natural selection to redefine the term "fit." This initial research will be enough to write a hypothesis that would state, "If a snake's prey population evolved to move faster, then natural selection may choose snakes who have evolved an offense mechanism, such as venom, as more 'fit' because when an environment changes, some species evolve." Step four: Perform More Research requires this student to use research to determine if the hypothesis is valid or null. In Chapter 3: Strategies for Teaching the Scientific Method and Its Components, we provide resources that students can use to write hypotheses and perform research.

Table 4.2   Resources in Chapter 3 That Can be Used for Teaching the Inquiry Process

Scientific method/Inquiry process step	Resource name, if applicable
Step 2: Perform research	Figure 3.1: Student Research Organizer
Step 3: Write a hypothesis	Figure 3.2: Identifying independent and Dependent Variables
	Figure 3.3: Identifying Independent and Dependent Variables—Answer Key
	Figure 3.4: How to write a hypothesis
	Figure 3.5: How to write a hypothesis—answer key

In addition to research, or instead of research, other questions may require observations. For example, the question "When will Mount St. Helens erupt next?" requires a student to research the eruption history of Mount St. Helens but can also be answered through various observations, such as interpreting seismograms to identify earthquake patterns near the base of the volcano.

Observations can include viewing a video of a phenomenon, watching a phenomenon first-hand on school grounds or on a field trip, or performing a dissection.

Regardless of the observation type, students should be noticing and recording details. Younger students are often taught to perform observations by using their senses of sight, smell, taste, touch, and sound. As students mature, the expectation is that their observations become more complex; for example, their observations should include quantitative and qualitative data, which we discuss in the next section.

Observations of Phenomena

We teach upper elementary students (and it may be appropriate for older students as well) to include details in their observations by playing an old game Tara's mom conducted at her childhood birthday parties. Tara's mom would place 20–30 unrelated objects on a tray and then cover them with a towel. All of the party attendees would gather around the tray and then the towel was removed. Attendees had one minute to memorize all of the objects on the tray. Then, the tray was put away and each attendee had two minutes to write down all of the objects they could remember. The person with the most remembered items won a prize.

We modify this for our classrooms by making one tray for every group of eight students. The trays have the same 20 items so we include objects that are in high abundance in our supply room or classroom. Examples of objects we've included are a test tube brush, colored pencil, eraser, nickel, beaker, ruler, and textbook. Another option is to use printed images of various objects.

After one minute, the trays are covered and students are instructed to return to their desks and write down all of the objects they can remember. They complete the task individually. Then we pass out a worksheet that asks detailed questions about the objects, such as:

1. What color was the colored pencil?
2. Was the eraser new or had it been used?
3. What year was on the nickel?
4. What were the measurements on the ruler (cm, inches, etc.)?
5. To what page was the textbook open?
6. How many milliliters of water can the beaker hold?
7. What object was under the test tube brush?

We give students about five minutes to answer the questions. Then we uncover the trays again so students can see the objects and instruct them to grade a friend's paper. The student with the most correct answers receives a prize. Afterwards, we ask students to brainstorm why it's important to include details in observations.

To further reinforce the importance of making detailed observations, we provide a mystery for students to solve. In our scenario, a teacher has stolen Ms. White's coffee cup and we want to identify the thief. We ask students to think of details that may help us determine which teacher is the culprit. They brainstorm ideas, such as the last time and location she saw her coffee cup, who else was here at the same time, who has access to Ms. White's classroom, and who else likes coffee (not Mrs. Dale!). After brainstorming about the evidence they've gathered, we ask them again, "Why is it important to include the details in an observation?" We've found this kickstarts a rich conversation.

When we work with middle and high school students, we teach them to perform detailed observations by focusing on quantitative and qualitative data. To teach students the difference between the two types of data, we don't define the terms for them but instead provide materials so they can write their own definitions.

In our experience, when students create their own definitions, they have a deeper understanding of the words. On the other hand, when we simply provide the definitions, many students tend to memorize, instead of learn them. This challenge is explained in the book *Turning Learning Right Side Up*, where the authors argue that memorization doesn't always equal learning (Ackoff & Greenberg, 2008, p. 3). Richard Feynman, a Nobel Prize-winning theoretical physicist, described it eloquently in a 1973 short film, *Take the World from Another Point of View*. He told a story about his father listing the names of a specific bird species in English, Japanese, German, and Chinese. Then his father said to him, "And when you know all the names of that bird in every language, you know nothing, but absolutely nothing about the bird." Mr. Feynman commented after telling the story, "I had learned already that names don't constitute knowledge" (Feynman, 1973).

To ensure our students understand the difference between quantitative and qualitative data, we provide students two lists of data with the titles "Quantitative Data" and "Qualitative Data." See Table 4.3 for an example. We ask students to compare and contrast the data and then write a definition for each of the terms. They work with a partner to complete the task and then we discuss their definitions as a class.

We've found that students notice that quantitative data includes numbers and qualitative does not. However, students often ask questions about the "The jogger at the intersection" example because it also contains a number. We ask them to determine the difference between the numbers in the first column and the phrase "1st Street."

Table 4.3 Example Observational Data That Students Compare/Contrast

Quantitative data	Qualitative data
Four clowns walked down the street.	The clowns had red noses.
There were 23,675 jelly beans in the jar.	The jar sat on top of the counter.
It took the jogger 15 min to run a mile.	The jogger was stopped at the intersection of Main Street and 1st Street.
It was 98°F outside.	It was hot outside.
The light blinked four times.	The light was turned off.

Once students realize that the numbers in the first column all represent a measurement and "1st Street" does not, we instruct them to review their current definitions for *quantitative* and *qualitative* to see if they need to make any changes. Together, we write a class definition for each type of data. For example, quantitative data is defined as data that includes measurements, so it includes numbers. Qualitative data is defined as data that lists characteristics or describes qualities, so it usually doesn't include numbers.

For practice using these concepts, we provide students with Figure 4.1: Quantitative vs. Qualitative Examples, a pair of scissors, and a glue stick. Students are instructed to make a T-chart on their own paper and label one column "Quantitative Data" and the other column "Qualitative Data." Students then cut the examples into individual strips, sort them, and glue them into the appropriate column. The answer key can be found in Figure 4.2: Quantitative vs. Qualitative Examples—Answer Key.

Students then practice making detailed observations, using both quantitative and qualitative data. We provide them with the worksheet in Figure 4.3: Observing with Quantitative and Qualitative Data. Students work with a partner to complete the worksheet while we walk around the classroom monitoring and ensure students who are struggling receive the extra support they need. When students have completed their practice, we go over the answers, which are provided in Figure 4.4: Observing with Quantitative and Qualitative Data—Answer Key.

Observations During Dissections

Dissections are a type of observation, but are becoming more controversial. We suggest teachers check with their administration prior to performing dissections with students. Currently, 18 states and Washington, D.C., have laws that require students be given an alternate assignment if they do not want to participate in a dissection. See the American Anti-Vivisection Society website at https://aavs.org/animals-science/laws/student-choice-laws to see each state's laws.

There are various reasons why students might not feel comfortable performing dissections. For example, dissections are inconsistent with some Native American tribes' cultural beliefs—it is taboo in the Navajo culture to do anything with a dead animal. They believe the dead organism is intended to decompose and replenish the next generation of organisms (Williams & Shipley, 2018).

For students who may not have a cultural or moral objection to dissections but, instead, feel "squeamish" about the activity, we ask them—with no pressure involved—if they are comfortable standing near their group and being an observer. Many students agree to this compromise. For those who are still uncomfortable with the dissection, we offer an alternate electronic assignment. See the Technology Connections section for alternate activities to dissections.

Students can use quantitative and qualitative data to generate questions while performing a dissection. Traditionally, dissections require students to follow step-by-step procedures as they identify body parts and read about their functions. We normally provide these procedures to our students so they know how to dissect a specimen safely and how to isolate the body parts they are supposed to observe.

We require advanced students to write their own step-by-step procedures to increase rigor and give them another opportunity to practice their critical thinking skills. They are provided with three types of resources to write their procedures. Students are instructed to watch a video of the dissection, read another teacher's lesson plan for the dissection, and complete a virtual dissection. As students perform their research they take notes about the following three procedures:

1. Dissection safety
2. Step-by-step procedures to perform the dissection
3. Dissection clean-up

Students work in pairs to write their own procedures and then perform the dissection by following the procedures they wrote. They are encouraged to edit their procedures throughout the lab. We supplement students' procedures with questions that require them to make observations. See Figure 4.5: Owl Pellet Step-by-Step Procedures and Questions as an example of the directions for students to write their own step-by-step procedures.

Our colleague, Colleen Rumer, an anatomy/physiology teacher, engages her students simultaneously in observation and critical thinking by connecting the dissection to students' experiences outside of school. For example, as students dissect a cat, they identify the peritoneum, which is the tissue that lines a mammal's organs in its abdomen. Her dissection worksheet asks students to, "Observe how the peritoneum is connected to the cat's organs. In horror movies, when someone is cut badly through their abdominal cavity their internal organs appear to 'fall out.' Is this possible? Why or why not?" By asking this question, Colleen is requiring her students to observe the peritoneum, hypothesize about its function, and then apply it to a situation beyond her classroom. By connecting the observation to a non-academic situation, Colleen is providing an engaging purpose for the dissection.

After documenting their observations, students engage in reflection, which can include using their quantitative and qualitative notes to generate questions. This assignment can be difficult for younger students, English language learners (ELLs), and students who have learning challenges. To provide support for these students, we give them question stems that have blanks. Students are required to use their critical thinking skills to choose the most appropriate question stems and fill in the blanks. Figure 4.6: Question Stems for Observers is a list of the question stems we use in our classrooms. Older and advanced students are asked to write five questions, each of which must begin with What, Where, When, Why, and How. Figure 4.5: Owl Pellet Step-by-Step Procedures and Questions includes an example. Students then perform research to answer their questions, which deepens their knowledge on the subject.

Once students have obtained all of the necessary information to address the question they initially wrote at the beginning of the assignment, they proceed to steps 5 and 6: Analyze Results and Write a Conclusion.

Steps 5 and 6: Analyze Results and Write a Conclusion

Often, the lack of an experiment means there isn't data that can be represented in a graph. Therefore, when teaching the inquiry process, we choose to combine Step 5: Analyze Results and Step 6: Write a Conclusion. Students still write a Discussion of Results and Conclusion; however, they are combined into one lab report, which is Figure 4.7: Discussion of Results and Conclusion.

DIFFERENTIATION FOR DIVERSE LEARNERS

Students who struggle with organization find Figure 4.8: Using the Inquiry Process helpful. In the younger grades, we give every student a copy and in the older grades we offer it as an optional resource. Students can use this worksheet as a central location for all of their documentation, research, and observational data. On the second page of Figure 4.8, step 5 instructs students to write a lab report, which they can accomplish by completing Figure 4.7: Discussion of Results and Conclusion.

Another differentiation method challenges older and advanced students. When they are writing their own question, we have them ask a question that will require more than a simple Internet search or article to answer it. They must also obtain some of their research through more rigorous approaches, such as reading an academic journal (that could be online) or library book, watching a documentary, visiting a zoo, interviewing a university professor or museum curator via the phone, or attending a lecture or conference. Students are allowed to use the Internet as a tool to view online documentaries, lectures, etc., and read academic journals or online books. Students benefit because they are exposed to additional resources while also developing their listening and interviewing skills.

To help ELL students and those with reading comprehension challenges, we provide dissection videos prior to performing the dissections in class. Students watch the videos, which are sometimes offered in their primary language, at home or in class. This provides them with supportive background knowledge as they read through the step-by-step procedures of the dissection. We've found a myriad of free dissection videos available online.

Generally, the inquiry process is an independent activity; however, sometimes it's appropriate to have students work in pairs. For example, ELL students, those who have learning challenges, and students who struggle behaviorally can pair up with another student who chooses the same research topic.

To assist the pair in working well together, we help them to equally divide the work. We've found more student success when we list each student's responsibilities and add deadlines (see Table 4.4: Inquiry Process Divided for Two Students for an example). Each student is given a copy of the table. We keep a copy as well and then monitor student progress.

By dividing the work, we are chunking a larger project into smaller and more manageable pieces and helping both students be more aware of their responsibilities. Many IEPs (Individualized Education Programs) require teachers to chunk large assignments into smaller pieces, which can also be helpful to all students, and this strategy meets that requirement.

Table 4.4 Inquiry Process Divided for Two Students

Student #1	Student #2	Deadline
Perform research for hypothesis	Help student #1 with research for hypothesis	End of class tomorrow
Identify dependent and independent variables	Write hypothesis, "If. . . .then. . . .because. . ."	End of class tomorrow
Research this topic: _____ by using this resource: _____	Research this topic: _____ by using this resource: _____	End of class Thursday
Write the Discussion of Results portion of the lab report	Write the Conclusion portion of the lab report	End of class Friday
Share the results with _____	Share the results with _____	Beginning of class Monday

Student Handouts and Examples

Figure 4.1: Quantitative vs. Qualitative Examples (Student Handout)

Figure 4.2: Quantitative vs. Qualitative Examples—Answer Key

Figure 4.3: Observing with Quantitative and Qualitative Data (Student Handout)

Figure 4.4: Observing with Quantitative and Qualitative Data—Answer Key

Figure 4.5: Owl Pellet Step-by-Step Procedures and Questions (Student Handout)

Figure 4.6: Question Stems for Observers (Student Handout)

Figure 4.7: Discussion of Results and Conclusion (Student Handout)

Figure 4.8: Using the Inquiry Process (Student Handout)

Figure 4.9: Checklist for Verifying Online Resources (Student Handout)

What Could Go Wrong?

A common problem we encounter during the inquiry process involves students using inaccurate online resources. To address this issue, we help students discern the difference between online fact and fiction.

To teach students how to analyze a website for validity, we challenge them to identify if claims are true or false. To begin teaching this idea, we provide students with the following five claims. They can easily find websites that support all of them, but only one of the claims is true (claim #1).

Claim #1: A new crab species has been found and it's hairy.

Claim #2: A new trout species has been found and it's furry.

Claim #3: You can pop popcorn with your cell phone.

Claim #4: There is an octopus that lives in trees.

Claim #5: Camel spiders eat the legs of their sleeping victims.

We divide our classes into groups of three and randomly assign each one a claim. Students are required to search online to determine if the claim is fact or fiction. We ask them to record their research on mini-whiteboards so they can show and defend their answer. In the younger grades this usually takes about 10 min because we provide the URL links so they can easily find the claims. Teachers at schools with little to no Internet connection can print the sites' information and distribute the hard copies to student groups.

Advanced students and those in the higher grades tend to perform deeper analysis without much instruction (but may need encouragement, nevertheless). Therefore, they may take longer, sometimes as much as 20 min for one website. Regardless of age, we've found that the majority of students tend to believe the claim they were assigned because they search for information that supports the claim instead of information that disproves the claim. This common error creates a prime learning opportunity.

Once groups have completed their research, we distribute Figure 4.9: Checklist of Verifying Online Resources. We model how to use the checklist by displaying a website on the board and showing students how to check for each of the items. For younger students, we shorten the checklist to include only the first four items.

Groups then receive an additional five minutes to compare and contrast their whiteboard notes with the checklist. At this point, many groups realize their first position was wrong and ask if they can change their stance. We encourage them to do so but also ask that they document how they arrived at their new conclusion so they can share it with the rest of the class.

Following the use of Figure 4.9: Checklist of Verifying Online Resources, groups present their conclusions and whiteboards to the class. All students then use the checklist to determine if the group's evidence is strong enough to support their conclusion.

We continue to have students use Figure 4.9: Checklist of Verifying Online Resources throughout the year so they have the support they need to verify online information.

Technology Connections

Many alternate online dissections are available. See Table 4.5 for a list of online resources for the most popular animal dissections in science classrooms.

Classrooms that lack reliable online access have the option of purchasing software programs. Simply search "dissection software" for a list of vendors. These purchases can be good alternatives for schools with a small science budget because unlike preserved specimens, the software can be used repeatedly.

For additional lesson plans that teach students how to identify websites that have inaccurate information, use Larry Ferlazzo's resource. This can be found at "The Best Tools & Lessons for Teaching Information Literacy – Help Me Find More" (http://larryferlazzo.edublogs.org/2015/07/28/the-best-tools-lessons-for-teaching-information-literacy-help-me-find-more).

Attributions

Thank you to Brittany Chase, for drawing the elephant picture we used in Figure 4.3: Observing with Quantitative and Qualitative Data. Her medium was colored pencils.

Thank you, Colleen, for sharing your cat dissection labs with us.

Table 4.5 List of Online Animal Dissections

Animal	Online dissection website
Frog	http://www.mhhe.com/biosci/genbio/virtual_labs/BL_16/BL_16.html
Owl pellet	http://kidwings.com/virtual-pellet
Fetal pig	https://www.whitman.edu/academics/departments-and-programs/biology/virtual-pig
Cat	http://biology.kenyon.edu/heithausp/cat-tutorial/welcome.htm
Cow's eye	https://www.exploratorium.edu/video/cows-eye-dissection
Sheep's brain	https://www.biologycorner.com/anatomy/sheepbrain/sheep_dissection.html
Sheep's heart	http://anatomycorner.com/main/image-gallery/sheep-heart

Figures

Directions: Begin by making a T-chart on your own paper. Title one column "Quantitative Data" and the other column "Qualitative Data."

Below are 15 examples of quantitative and qualitative data. Cut each example into its own strip, sort them, and then glue the strips into the appropriate columns.

1. The cows were large.

2. The doctor's patient had symptoms that included headaches and dizziness.

3. The woman had a fever of 102.3°F.

4. The dog tracked the man through the woods using the scent of an old shirt.

5. The butterflies were a mixture of black and blue.

6. The kittens were too young to separate from their mother.

7. The meteorite was 29% carbon and included crystals that appeared to be blue in color.

8. The sedimentary rock sample was red and brown.

9. The apple tree growing in the sun had 109 more apples than the apple tree growing in the shade.

10. The algae growing in the first tank appeared healthier based on the color of the algae and the water.

11. When we added hydrochloric acid to the rock, it didn't bubble as we had suspected so we concluded it was not limestone.

12. The inside temperature of the black car was 98°F and the inside temperature of the white car was 93°F.

13. The sunflower plant grew three inches in one week.

14. The petri dish had two different species of bacteria.

15. There were 17 worms in the blue bucket.

Figure 4.1 Quantitative vs. Qualitative Examples (Student Handout)

Quantitative Data	Qualitative Data
3. The woman had a fever of 102.3°F.	1. The cows were large.
9. The apple tree growing in the sun had 109 more apples than the apple tree growing in the shade.	2. The doctor's patient had symptoms that included headaches and dizziness.
7. The meteorite was 29% carbon and included crystals that appeared to be blue in color.	4. The dog tracked the man through the woods using the scent of an old shirt.
12. The inside temperature of the black car was 98°F and the inside temperature of the white car was 93°F.	5. The butterflies were a mixture of black and blue.
13. The sunflower plant grew three inches in one week.	6. The kittens were too young to separate from their mother.
14. The petri dish had two different species of bacteria.	8. The sedimentary rock sample was red and brown.
15. There were 17 worms in the blue bucket.	10. The algae growing in the first tank appeared healthier based on the color of the algae and the water.
	11. When we added hydrochloric acid to the rock, it didn't bubble as we had suspected so we concluded it was not limestone.

Figure 4.2   Quantitative vs. Qualitative Examples—Answer Key

Name: _____

Observing with Quantitative and Qualitative Data

Directions: With your partner, use the below elephant picture to practice making detailed observations by using quantitative and qualitative data.

Image by Brittany Chase. Used with permission.

1. Make three detailed observations of the elephant picture using quantitative data.

2. Make three detailed observations of the elephant picture using qualitative data.

Figure 4.3 Observing with Quantitative and Qualitative Data (Student Handout)

Name: _____ *Answer Key*_____

Observing with Quantitative and Qualitative Data

Directions: With your partner, use the below elephant picture to practice making detailed observations by using quantitative and qualitative data.

Image by Brittany Chase. Used with permission.

1. Make three detailed observations of the elephant picture using quantitative data.

   Answers will vary but examples of acceptable answers include
   1. *The mother elephant has two white tusks and the baby has no tusks.*
   2. *The mother elephant appears three times as large as her baby.*
   3. *There are ten trees in the picture.*
   4. *The trees don't appear to have any leaves on them.*

2. Make three detailed observations of the elephant picture using qualitative data.

   Answers will vary but examples of acceptable answers include
   1. *The mother elephant has darker skin than the baby elephant.*
   2. *The two elephants' trunks are touching.*
   3. *The blades of grass in the foreground are shorter than the blades of grass in the background.*
   4. *It's nighttime.*

Figure 4.4 Observing with Quantitative and Qualitative Data—Answer Key

7ᵗʰ Grade Science—Owl Pellet Step-by-Step Procedures

In order to learn about food chains and food webs you will be dissecting an owl pellet. An owl pellet is not owl feces and it is not owl vomit. When an owl eats, it consumes the entire animal, even the bones and the fur. Its digestive system does not break down the bones and fur but instead regurgitates it as a dry, non-odorous owl pellet. Your assignment is to write step-by-step procedures for dissecting your owl pellet.

1. Using the teacher's lesson plan provided to you, take notes about how to practice lab safety and clean up properly.
2. Watch the online video of two girls performing a dissection of an owl pellet. Take notes about the procedure.
3. Go to my website for a link that will allow you to perform a virtual owl dissection. Take notes about the procedure.
4. Now use all of your notes to write step-by-step procedures for dissecting your own owl pellet. Step-by-step procedures are written in step-by-step format so begin with 1, then write 2, then write 3, etc. Do not use complete sentences but be very specific.

After your dissection is complete, observe your bones to answer the following questions:

1. Make three quantitative observations about the bones.
   a.

   b.

   c.

2. Make three qualitative observations about the bones.
   a.

   b.

   c.

Figure 4.5 Owl Pellet Step-by-Step Procedures and Questions (Student Handout)

3. Write five questions about the owl pellet and its contents.
  a. What. . .

  b. When. . .

  c. Where. . .

  d. Why. . .

  e. How. . .

4. The average barn owl produces a pellet every six hours. First, determine how many animals your owl ate in the previous six hours. Then use that data to make a hypothesis about the digestive rate of barn owls.

Figure 4.5   (Continued)

What is the difference between _____ and _____?

How are _____ and _____ similar?

Why did the _____ change?

How can _____ be combined with _____?

What is the meaning of _____?

How can _____ be revised?

How can _____ be summarized?

Why is _____ important?

What is another way to interpret _____?

How can we show that _____ is true?

How can we show that _____ is false?

What is the best way to describe _____?

What is a good way to illustrate that _____?

What is another way to illustrate that _____?

Figure 4.6 Question Stems for Observers (Student Handout)

Name: _____

Discussion of Results and Conclusion

To write your discussion of results and conclusion, complete the sentence starters. The more space there is for you to write, the more writing you'll need to do.

The discussion of results explains what your results mean. It also includes any short-comings you may have experienced. The conclusion is a summary of how your hypothesis and results are connected.

Analysis: Discussion of Results

The question I asked was _____

_____

My hypothesis stated if _____

_____

The most important things I learned through my research and observation were

_____

_____

_____

_____

I performed my observations using these tools and strategies: _____

_____

_____

_____

My research and observations lacked _____

_____

Figure 4.7 Discussion of Results and Conclusion (Student Handout)

Conclusion

My research and observations prove that _____

_____

_____

_____

My hypothesis was _____ *(null or valid)*. This experiment

makes me want to know more about _____

_____

Figure 4.7   (Continued)

Using the Inquiry Process   Name: _____

Directions: You must use the inquiry process instead of the scientific method. This means you'll follow the same steps as the scientific method but instead of performing an experiment, you'll complete research and/or observations.

Ask a Question—Before moving on to step two you must receive your teacher's approval.
Write your question here:

What is your independent variable?_____

What is your dependent variable? _____

Your teacher's approval: _____

1. Research—Perform simple research so that you can create a hypothesis. If you use a reference such as a website or book, write down the author, publication date, etc., as a citation.

    Citation Information:

2. Hypothesis—Use your variables and research. Be sure to write it in "If..... then.....because" format.

Figure 4.8   Using the Inquiry Process (Student Handout)

3. More Research and/or Observation—In addition to searching online, you can also use a survey, interview, observation onsite, movie, book, and/or case study. Be sure to include citation information for your sources.

Citation Information:

4. Data Analysis and Conclusion—Write your lab report.

5. Publish—Explain your project to anyone who is at least 18 years old and have them sign below as proof that you shared your data and conclusion with someone.

Figure 4.8 (Continued)

Checklist for Verifying Online Resources

Directions: To verify if an online resource is a valid resource, ask these questions. Checkmark any question that can be answered with a "yes." If the source has more checkmarks than not, it is probably a valid website.

_____ Does the website end in .org or .edu?

_____ Is the information less than three years old?

_____ If there are hyperlinks, do they link to other valid websites?

_____ Is the author of the website a valid and legitimate person who is considered an expert in their field? What results do you receive when you search for the author's name?

_____ If there is a table or a graph, are the data explained? Does the source indicate where they found the data?

_____ Has the website been updated in the last 12 months?

_____ Does the "About Us" or "Contact Us" link give more information that validates the author?

_____ If there is a table or a graph, can the data be verified using other sources?

_____ Is the author using only facts and omitting emotion? If this is the case, they are less likely to be biased.

_____ Are words spelled correctly and is there proper punctuation?

_____ If Wikipedia is your source, does the Wikipedia page have valid citations to verify the information?

Figure 4.9 Checklist for Verifying Online Resources (Student Handout)

CHAPTER 5

Strategies for Using Project-Based Learning

What Is It?

Project-based learning (PBL) engages students "in solving real-world problems or answering a complex question" (PBLWorks, 2019, in Project Based Learning section, para. 1).

In PBL, students are challenged to solve either personal real-world problems, such as creating a diet for their age and activity level, or larger international problems, like how to rid the ocean of plastic.

What is the difference between doing projects and doing PBL? Projects are generally shorter in nature, don't require the same level of collaboration, and have less rigor. PBL typically requires more classroom time because students are performing research and creating an end product that involves collaboration among their peers (PBLWorks, 2019).

Why We Like It

PBL can engage students because their class work can have real-life relevance. Additionally, they are learning that science requires the use of skills learned in other content areas, such as reading, writing, and math.

We believe the most meaningful benefit of PBL can be the way students perceive themselves after solving the problem or answering the complex question. We've found that many of our students who have a poor perception of their abilities often find they are capable of more than they originally imagined. And some students who easily give up when school becomes difficult can learn how to persevere in the face of challenges.

Supporting Research

PBL may increase both motivation and learning for students because they may relate to the real-world questions being considered in class (Blumenfeld et al., 1991).

Studies have shown that PBL can also increase student communication and teamwork skills, knowledge retention, and the ability to apply learning to other situations, also known as "transfer" (Prince & Felder, 2006, p. 129).

Skills for Intentional Scholars/NGSS Connections

When students participate in PBL, they are using all three Skills for Intentional Scholars. PBLWorks (an organization of educators focused on supporting PBL in K-12 classrooms) states that as a result of participating in PBL, "students develop deep content knowledge as well as critical thinking, creativity, and communication skills" (PBLWorks, 2019, Project Based Learning section, para. 1).

Students can use critical thinking from the beginning of a project to its end. When a problem or complex question is initially presented to students, they first interpret and define the problem. Students creatively problem solve as they brainstorm possible solutions. Once they've designed a solution, they analyze its effectiveness and determine how to communicate their success.

In many ways, PBL is aligned with the Next Generation Science Standards (NGSS), which call for a deeper understanding and application of content (NGSS, 2013a). The NGSS incorporate seven crosscutting concepts, many of which can easily lead to a PBL project. Here are the crosscutting concepts and a brief explanation of each:

1. Patterns—can determine how matter is organized and generates questions about relationships

2. Cause and effect—Mechanism and explanation—cause-and-effect relationships can be used to predict future events

3. Scale, proportion, and quantity—phenomena can behave differently at different scales, proportion, and quantities

4. Systems and system models—models can provide an understanding of systems and can create a testing environment for ideas

5. Energy and matter—Flows, cycles, and conservation—by tracking energy and matter flowing into and out of systems, we can learn system limitations and possibilities

6. Structure and function—an object's shape can determine its properties and functions

7. Stability and change—the description of how a system functions and what causes them to change

See Table 5.1: PBL Projects for the NGSS Disciplines in the Application section for a list of PBL ideas and how they integrate crosscutting concepts.

Application

Some teachers may be hesitant about using PBL in their classrooms for a variety of reasons. One reason may be because they aren't an expert in the field that students are studying. We've found ourselves in the same situation. For example, when Mandi had her students study an environmental issue affecting a human population, she did not know the problems of every country and the budgets necessary for solving them. And, Tara didn't know the carbon footprint of every restaurant when she challenged her students to analyze the footprint of their favorite eating establishment and create three ways the restaurant could be more environmentally friendly.

PBL does not require that the teacher be the expert. Instead, the students become the experts. The teacher's role is to support students by helping them to perform research, document their ideas, and guide their crafting of solutions.

We divide PBL into four steps: planning, working in structured groups, giving authentic presentations, and using scoring guides and rubrics. We also provide examples of PBL ideas for each of the four disciplines of the NGSS (earth and space sciences; physical sciences; life sciences; and technology, engineering, and applications of science) that integrate crosscutting concepts.

PLANNING

Teacher-Initiated Projects

PBL can be initiated by the teacher. For example, after visiting a local fast-food restaurant, Tara was appalled by the amount of waste that was generated—leftover food, wrappers, cups, lids, and straws. She took this problem to her students and challenged them to research the carbon footprints of several restaurants. Students then identified three changes each restaurant could implement in order to reduce their carbon footprints.

In addition to being inspired by events that occur in our lives, such as eating at a restaurant, we also find inspiration within our content standards. We determine what concepts we want our students to learn and the number of class periods we have available to teach these concepts. For example, when we teach a geology unit, our standards require that students learn how rocks and minerals are classified by their observable properties. Our district's curriculum map suggests two weeks to teach this standard.

The next step is to ask, "When would this information be useful for people outside of our classroom?" For example, many of our students spend time on mountain trails (we teach in Arizona), so we determined that they may be able to use the skill of classifying rocks and minerals during their weekend hikes. It is important to us that our students' interests be at the center of their learning because it can increase engagement and enhance retention of newly learned knowledge (Alrashidi, Phan, & Ngu, 2016).

The next step is to create a scenario. Scenario-based projects provide a real-world connection where students can gain a sense of agency and purpose (Mindset Scholars Network, 2015).

Once the scenario has been established, we then construct a problem that doesn't have a right or wrong answer. However, students must be able to justify their conclusion. The book *Overloaded and Underprepared: Strategies for Stronger Schools and Healthy, Successful Kids* explains that PBL is intriguing because "students not only must come to their own conclusions based on their analysis, research, and knowledge, but also explain how they got there" (Pope, Brown, & Miles, 2015, p. 68).

The scenario we created for our geology unit asked students to imagine they were hiking South Mountain, which is just north of our school. The scenario told the story of students who found several rocks with unique physical features and wondered what minerals were in the rocks. Prior to introducing the scenario to our students, the two of us went on a hike and collected several different types of rocks from South Mountain. Students were challenged to create tests that would identify the type of rocks and their minerals. There was no right or wrong answer because they could use traditional tests such as the hardness, streak color, and transparency, which they learned about through research, or they could create their own tests, which required them to use their creative problem-solving skills.

Student-Initiated Projects

An additional type of PBL allows students to identify a problem that personally interests them. We recommend, however, that the class first completes at least one teacher-initiated project so students become familiar with the work involved in successfully completing PBL activities.

There are two methods to manage student-initiated PBL projects. The first one involves placing students into groups and allowing them to choose the problem or complex question they want to address. The second method is allowing individual students to choose a problem or complex question and then forming small groups based on similar interests. To help students brainstorm topics, we use the website "16 Questions to Help Students Brainstorm Project-Based Learning," which can be found at https://teachthought.com/learning-models/4-stages-project-based-learning.

In our experience, giving students all 16 questions can be very overwhelming, especially for younger students. To minimize anxiousness, we ask students only a few of the 16 questions listed on the website. Our favorite questions to begin with are:

1. What interests me? What is important to me?
2. Who in my classroom, school, community, etc., would most benefit from my creativity, passion, and continued effort?
3. What about me is unique and how can I use that to improve something else?
4. What problems exist that I can begin to solve?

There are many times we are not able to simply allow students to have free reign over choosing any project idea they would like. For example, students need to learn specific content based on standards, and classrooms often have time constrictions. In order to allow student choice while also ensuring students are learning our state science standards during the process, we often ask them to answer the above questions within the scope of the content we are aiming to teach. For example, when working in an astronomy unit, we would communicate to students the major concepts we would be learning and tell them to answer the questions within those key ideas.

Regardless of whether a PBL lesson is initiated by the teacher or the students, it begins with an engaging real-life problem or complex question. This is one reason why it's important for teachers to know their students. When a teacher knows their students' interests, the teacher can better plan, engage, and support them. See Chapter 14: Strategies for Cultural Responsiveness for resources that help teachers learn about their students.

WORKING IN STRUCTURED GROUPS

Most PBL activities are completed in small groups of two or three because, in our experience, it is easier to manage the work efforts of individual students in small groups. PBL provides students an opportunity to practice their social emotional skills, such as understanding and managing their emotions, achieving goals, and making good decisions. In Chapter 2: Strategies for Teaching Lab Procedures, we provide several strategies for grouping students and supporting them as they practice their social emotional skills.

Every student should have individual responsibilities with clear deadlines. When we first introduce a problem or complex question in class and students have moved into their learning groups, we ask them to divide the work equally among each team member.

To help students divide tasks equally, we use a worksheet entitled PBL Task Manager. Figure 5.1: Example of PBL Task Manager—Carbon Footprint of a Restaurant shows some of the tasks and deadlines Tara established for a PBL activity focused on reducing the carbon footprint of a restaurant.

Teacher-Initiated Projects

Prior to introducing a teacher-initiated project to the class, we complete the first two columns ("To Do List" and "Task Deadline") in Figure 5.1 and list each task and its corresponding deadline.

We attempt to break up PBL activities into tasks that are similar in difficulty and require the same amount of time to complete. This ensures that regardless of which tasks are assigned to each student, they all have similar levels of rigor. (For an example of how to differentiate, see the section Differentiation for Diverse Learners.) Students work in their groups the first day to complete the third column ("Student Assigned to Task") so that everyone in the group knows who is responsible for each task. It also helps us as teachers because we, too, know which task each individual student is assigned to complete.

The last column ("Teacher Comments") is completed by us. Because many students don't have access to each other outside of class, they receive ample time to complete the entire PBL activity in class (yes, in theory, students could collaborate online, but we are not confident that many could or would). Students are instructed to sit near their group members every day. As they work on their tasks, we meet with each group to provide feedback by filling out the last column. When a student shows us complete and accurate work, we initial the "Teacher Comments" column. But if the work requires improvement, we provide verbal feedback and document the feedback in that column. When a student improves their work, they present it to us again and receive a final grade.

There are many benefits to using this process. In our experience, the quality of student work is higher because we've been providing feedback throughout the project. Additionally, if a student or an entire group gets behind, we know about it before it's too late because we monitor each group several times throughout the activity and proactively communicate with parents.

Student-Initiated Projects

If the project is student-initiated, we distribute Figure 5.2: Blank PBL Task Manager to each student once they have formed their project groups. We guide the class in filling out the first two columns, "To Do List" and "Task Deadline."

We start by having each group break down their project into smaller tasks. Obviously, since all groups have different project topics, their tasks will look different. We instruct them by saying:

You need to break this project into smaller tasks that take the same amount of time. Each group member will be assigned these small tasks so that everyone is working on the project equally. We are going to give you 10 minutes to work with your group members to make a list of tasks that need to be completed in order to answer your project's question. In addition, you need to estimate how long it will take to complete each task. Jot down your ideas on the back of the worksheet so that you can share them with me as I walk around.

We check in with every group as they are working. We want to ensure they are on task and not performing research or solving the problem. Students are often excited to get to work so it may become necessary to slow them down and help them plan their project first.

After 10 min, we stop and remind them about the goal of having an equal amount of work for all group members. We say:

Now check that each task takes the same amount of time. Are there any tasks that can be combined or any that need to be split up to make smaller tasks? You have another five minutes to determine this and finalize your list of tasks. I will be walking around to check and help you, if needed.

To fill out the second column, we provide the students with the number of minutes they will receive each day to work on their project. Groups are responsible for determining each task's due date based on the amount of time they have in class to work.

After the first two columns in Figure 5.2 are complete, we follow the same procedures as teacher-initiated projects:

- Students complete the third column: "Student Assigned to Task."
- Students work on the tasks as we walk around the room, offering guidance.
- When due dates arrive, we check each student's progress and document it in Figure 5.2 and the gradebook.

GIVING AUTHENTIC PRESENTATIONS

Teacher-Initiated Projects

When we initiate a PBL project, we first identify the problem or complex question students will solve, the audience to whom students will present, and the venue for the presentation. Then we determine the final product students will create, which will vary greatly. Here are some examples of products our students have created at the end of a PBL activity:

- Essays and Press Kits: High school ecology students determined how restaurants could reduce their carbon footprint. The students wrote three essays—one for each change they were suggesting to their restaurant. The essays were emailed to the restaurant representative two weeks prior to an in-person meeting on campus. The meeting allowed the representative to ask questions and share concerns. Students also created press kits, which included student-created marketing material that the restaurants could use to advertise themselves as an environment-friendly business. These kits were presented to the representatives when they attended the meeting.

- PowerPoint, Prezi, or Google Slides presentation: Seventh-grade students redesigned a pizza box to make it recyclable. They invited 23 pizza companies to attend a presentation in their classroom. The students dressed up in a professional manner and delivered an oral presentation to the 21 companies who attended.

- Public Service Announcement Video: Students were asked to choose any country with an environmental issue that was negatively affecting the human population. Students then worked to solve the problem and generated a budget to implement their solution. Their video outlined the problem and solution and included a plea for donations to support their endeavor. We posted the videos on a class website.

Student-Initiated Projects

When students initiate a PBL project, we first have them identify the problem or complex question they want to solve, identify the audience to whom they will present, and choose the venue for the presentation. We then ask students to determine their final product. Most often, in our experience, students default to a PowerPoint or Google Slide presentation. They feel most comfortable using this technology, which is why they choose it; however, we also want students to have experience with other presentation types. To help them choose an unfamiliar type of presentation, we offer a list of options, such as:

- videos: action-packed, dramatic, musical, public service announcement
- written: Prezi, poster, essay, press kit
- audio: interview, speech
- visual: skit, Animoto slideshow

We lead the students through a vote so they can decide which product they will create.

See the Technology Connections section for additional ideas for student presentations.

Presenting to an Authentic Audience

After students solve the problem or answer the complex question, the last step is to present their solution to an authentic audience, which is someone who can implement their solution. For example, after Tara's students identified changes for restaurant chains across the country, representatives from each restaurant were invited to the school to meet with her students. Many restaurant owners or their representatives attended the meetings.

Depending on the project, other examples of authentic audience members include engineers, city managers, non-profit administrators, and school district personnel. When the project is student-initiated, we lead the class in a discussion to help them identify to whom they will present. In our experience, students may have personal connections with unique professionals, such as a student's aunt who is a geologist or a parent who works as an engineer.

When we initiate the project or when students don't know someone in an applicable field, we reach out to experts and invite them into our classrooms, either in person or virtually. Some experts visit the school, others participate in a phone call, and yet others use Skype or Google Hangouts to connect with students.

The following advice may seem basic, but we have found it to be critical: To ensure experts are available on the day you need their presence, we suggest connecting with them early. And once the meeting date and time have been established, verify their availability a few days in advance. Some of our experts have had to reschedule a meeting at the last minute so we suggest having an alternate plan, which can be an alternate expert or an alternate date and time. The bottom line is to be flexible.

We've found that many experts are willing to talk to students, so we are not hesitant to ask for a meeting.

To show their appreciation, students write a handwritten thank you letter to the expert who met with them.

When we have difficulty finding an expert, we use the resources in Larry Ferlazzo's blog entitled "The Best Places Where Students Can Write for an Authentic Audience" at http://larryferlazzo.edublogs.org/2009/04/01/the-best-places-where-students-can-write-for-an-authentic-audience. In addition to providing resources that can help students connect with experts, he also includes resources to help students publish online books, make maps, and share their stories.

USING SCORING GUIDES AND RUBRICS

A scoring guide is a list of requirements that are assigned a specific point value. An example of a scoring guide is given in Figure 5.3: Example of PBL Scoring Guide—Restaurant Project. This scoring guide lists every required item with a small description and assigned point value.

A rubric outlines different levels of criteria for different scores. An example of a rubric can be found in Figure 5.4: Example of PBL Rubric—Location of the Next Wind Farm in the U.S.

Teacher-Initiated Projects

Creating a scoring guide or rubric is the last task we do in our planning prior to introducing the activity to students.

Regardless of the final project that students will turn in, they need a scoring guide or rubric beforehand so they know what is expected of them and how they will be graded.

When we make the scoring guide or rubric, we want to ensure that students understand the assignment's expectations. We accomplish this by first providing every student a hard copy when first introducing the PBL activity. Then we ask them to read it silently, underlining the action verbs because these are the words that communicate what students must do. We model this by going through the first item on the scoring guide or rubric. Using the example in Figure 5.3, we read the first item aloud and explain why we would underline the words "provide" and "advertise." Then students are given 3–5 minutes, depending on their age and the length of the scoring guide, to work independently to underline the remaining action verbs. Afterwards they share their answers with a partner. If their answers differ, they work together to decide which words to underline.

To ensure the entire class has the correct answers, we project a copy of the scoring guide or rubric on the board. We randomly choose a student and their learning partner to go to the board and underline the action verbs in the first task. When they are done, another pair is randomly chosen to underline the action verbs in the next task. This continues until all of the tasks have been underlined. At that time, the class is asked if there are any disagreements, at which time we have a class discussion regarding any incorrect answers. To help students feel comfortable, we insist that learning partners go to the board together.

If the final product is an essay or business letter, the final component of the project is always an authentic presentation. If an actual person is not coming in for a presentation, sometimes this written work can be sent to the "audience" for feedback. For example, if business members are not able to come to the school, letters can be mailed to them. However, if community members are available for an oral presentation, students can turn their written work into a presentation format. See the Giving Authentic Presentations section for examples.

Student-Initiated Projects

Once students have chosen their presentation type, we walk older students through a class discussion to create a scoring guide or rubric. We provide them with several examples of each and then work with them to create one common tool that will be used to assess their learning and presentation. See Figure 5.3: Example of PBL Scoring Guide—Restaurant Project for an example of a scoring guide and Figure 5.4: Example of PBL Rubric—Location of the Next Wind Farm in the United States for an example of a rubric. When we work with younger students, we make the scoring guide or rubric for them.

Teacher- and Student-Initiated Projects

If presentations will be shared with the whole class, we ask that students provide each other with feedback. We give each student a copy of Figure 5.5: Peer Presentation Evaluation. As their peers are presenting, students complete the evaluation handout and when the presentation is complete, we collect all of the handouts to give to the presenters.

PROJECT-BASED LEARNING IDEAS

Table 5.1: PBL Projects for the NGSS Disciplines includes a list of example projects for each of the four disciplines in the NGSS. There are also resources in the Technology Connections section that provide additional project ideas.

Table 5.1 PBL Projects for the NGSS Disciplines

NGSS discipline	PBL project idea	Crosscutting concept from the NGSS
Earth and space sciences	Plan and develop a structure where people can live, work, and play on Mars. Students make models using recycled materials.	Systems and system models
Earth and space sciences	Build model rockets to fly the highest, altering one variable, such as the shape or size of the nose cone.	Systems and system models
Physical sciences	Create a process or technology that would prevent the deterioration of outside structures that are degraded by such things as acid rain.	Cause and effect: Mechanisms and explanation
Physical sciences	Design a mechanism to keep the Thanksgiving turkey warm throughout the family gathering.	Energy and matter: Flows, cycles, and conservation
Physical sciences	Create one new game that can be played with various sizes of balls, from beads to bowling balls.	Scale, probability, and quantity
Physical sciences	Analyze the evidence gathered from a car accident to create an improved vehicle design that would minimize the damage to the vehicle, passengers, and/or external structures.	Energy and matter: Flows, cycles, and conservation

Table 5.1   (Continued)

NGSS discipline	PBL project idea	Crosscutting concept from the NGSS
Life sciences (can integrate physical sciences)	Redesign a safety resource currently used in a sport (helmet, pads, shin guards, etc.) that would better protect the body and/or improve its comfort.	Structure and function
Life sciences	Analyze how the current laws regarding animal treatment affect the societal, political, and financial aspects of the pet or food industry.	Cause and effect
Technology, engineering, and applications of science (can integrate life sciences)	Create or improve a technology that is inspired by patterns in nature or improve a current technology based on a natural pattern (biomimicry).	Patterns
Technology, engineering, and applications of science (can integrate life sciences and earth and space sciences)	Develop a technology or process that helps the human body adapt to a warmer Earth.	Structure and function

DIFFERENTIATION FOR DIVERSE LEARNERS

Some students may require accommodations as they work through a PBL activity. In this instance, we help group members divide the work as they complete Figure 5.1: Example of PBL Task Manager—Carbon Footprint of a Restaurant. We strategically give English language learners tasks that can be solved with video research because many online videos have closed captioning available and some are available in languages other than English. We may give some students more time to complete a task. In addition, we may ask another student in the same PBL group to help one of their partners.

Student Handouts and Examples

Figure 5.1: Example of PBL Task Manager—Carbon Footprint of a Restaurant (Student Handout)

Figure 5.2: Blank PBL Task Manager (Student Handout)

Figure 5.3: Example of PBL Scoring Guide—Restaurant Project (Student Handout)

Figure 5.4: Example of PBL Rubric—Location of the Next Wind Farm in the United States (Student Handout)

Figure 5.5: Peer Presentation Evaluation (Student Handout)

What Could Go Wrong?

When students work in groups, the most common struggle is off-task behavior. This often manifests itself in two ways. Either the entire group falls behind or one group member completes the majority of the work. To proactively prevent off-task behavior, we use Figure 5.1: Example of PBL Task Manager—Carbon Footprint of a Restaurant to ensure every student is completing their assigned tasks on time. We've found that a student is more likely to be off-task when they become frustrated that they can't complete a task; therefore, we begin conversations with the student by asking them, "Where are you stuck?" This open-ended question often identifies the problem immediately so that we can provide additional resources or help the student brainstorm solutions. We remain with that student until they are actively working once again and always return to them a few minutes later to ensure they are still productive.

When students are first exposed to PBL, some are uncomfortable that there is no right or wrong answer. They are stifled by this and feel as though they lack direction. We solve this problem by going through the scoring guide or rubric with these students, step-by-step. We point out that the scoring guide or rubric doesn't require them to identify a correct answer but instead requires that they justify why they believe their answer is correct. For example, in Figure 5.2: Example of PBL Scoring Guide—Restaurant Project students are required to explain their answers but also include footnotes as evidence that their explanations are based on facts. And Figure 5.3: Example of PBL Rubric—Location of the Next Wind Farm in the United States requires students to explain their answers, which is how we assess them.

Technology Connections

There are many online resources that provide PBL ideas. PBLWorks (https://www.pblworks.org/get-started) offers onsite training, books, and teaching videos to help teachers of all experience levels.

Samantha Kotey, a technology and learning researcher, offers many unique presentation types in her blog, "20 Best Online Presentation Tools for Students," which can be read at (https://www.codemom.ai/2017/01/15-best-online-presentation-tools-for-students).

Education World has tips and ideas at "Project-Based Learning: Tips and Project Ideas" (https://www.educationworld.com/a_curr/project-based-learning-tips-ideas.shtml).

"Problem and Project-Based Learning Activities" (http://www.mrsoshouse.com/pbl/pblin.html) contains a list of both science and social studies ideas.

There are science and math PBL resources available at "21st Century Educational Technology and Learning" (https://21centuryedtech.wordpress.com/2013/09/15/the-pbl-super-highway-over-45-links-to-great-project-based-learning).

The University of Delaware offers many free PBL resources, including project ideas (http://www1.udel.edu/inst).

Attributions

Thank you to Jeff Sesemann, who gave us the ideas for some of the physical sciences PBL activities. We appreciate the creativity he brings into his classroom and his willingness to share with other teachers

Figures

To Do List	Task Deadline	Student Assigned to Task	Teacher Comments
Choose the restaurant to be researched	Monday	Everyone	
Identify the local chain's address, phone number, manager name, and manager email	Monday		
Identify the supply companies, including their warehouse addresses	Wednesday		
Identify the trucks used by each supply company	Thursday		
Calculate the mileage driven and carbon dioxide emitted by each supply company roundtrip from warehouse to restaurant	Thursday		
Identify current (if any) recycling efforts made by the chain	Wednesday		
Contact the restaurant's corporate headquarters to notify them of your project and ask for their support in helping the environment	Wednesday		

Figure 5.1 Example of Project-Based Learning Task Manager—Carbon Footprint of a Restaurant (Student Handout)

To Do List	Task Deadline	Student Assigned to Task	Teacher Comments

Figure 5.2   Blank Project-Based Learning Task Manager (Student Handout)

Scoring Guide: Reducing Carbon Footprint at Your Restaurant

You've completed three weeks of research and are nearly an expert on your restaurant. You've analyzed and interpreted all of the data to suggest a change the restaurant can make that won't negatively affect their bottom line and will decrease their negative effect on the environment. Now you are writing your persuasive essay, which will be presented to the restaurant manager/owner in May. Your essay must be written well so they know you are a professional.

<u>As you write, remember that your audience is the owner of the restaurant. I am NOT your audience!</u>

Here is your scoring guide. Share your essay with me Friday, when it is due.

Assignment Requirement	Points Possible	Points You Received and Teacher Comments
Provide information about the restaurant's commitment to the environment. What does the restaurant advertise it currently does to help the environment?	4	
Explain the restaurant's current process that hurts the environment	5	
Explain why the restaurant chose to implement their current process that is hurting the environment	10	
Explain why the current process is bad for the environment	10	
Describe your suggestion that will decrease the restaurant's negative effect on the environment	1	
Explain how your suggestion will affect the restaurant's bottom line	10	
Explain how your suggestion will decrease their negative effect on the environment	10	
Present data using a data table or graph and explain why the data is important and applicable to your chosen problem and/or solution	10	
Essay includes all necessary footnotes	10	
Essay has correct grammar, spelling, and punctuation	10	
Total	80	

Figure 5.3 Example of PBL Scoring Guide—Restaurant Project (Student Handout)

#	0 - Missing	1 - You may have tried	2 - You made a concerted effort	3 - You were amazeballs!	Score
Business Letter Format	Did not follow business letter format.	Followed the business letter format a little bit.	Followed the business letter format the majority of the time.	Followed the business letter format for the entire letter. It was perfect!	25%
Benefits of the location you chose	There is no explanation of why this location was chosen.	The explanation was attempted but it was missing crucial parts.	The explanation included all necessary details regarding why this location was chosen.	The explanation went above and beyond, explaining why this location was chosen.	25%
Mitigating drawbacks for your chosen location	There was no mention of how you would mitigate any of the drawbacks.	There was a plan for mitigating the bird migration problem.	There was a plan for mitigating the bird migration problem in addition to one additional problem.	There was a plan for mitigating the bird migration problem in addition to two additional problems.	25%
Compare to the two locations you didn't choose	There is no mention of the other two locations.	The other two locations are mentioned minimally.	The other two locations are mentioned and there is an explanation that addresses why one of them wasn't chosen.	The other two locations are mentioned and there is an explanation that addresses why neither of them were chosen.	25%
					Total Score:

Figure 5.4 Example of PBL Rubric—Location of the Next Wind Farm in the United States (Student Handout)

Presentation Evaluation

Name of Presenter or Presenter Group _____

   Do not write your name on this sheet. Please, however, take it seriously even though you will not be graded on what you write. Help your classmates become better presenters, just as they will do the same for you.

   Write three things you liked about the presentation. You could mention qualities like voice projection, looking at the audience and not just reading from notes, well-organized, original ideas, an attractive PowerPoint, speakers didn't just repeat what was on the PowerPoint slide, told good stories and gave good examples, stood straight, didn't chew gum, all presenters paid attention when one spoke, followed instructions for the presentation, kept to the time limit, smiled, took the assignment seriously, and many more. . .

1.

2.

3.

   Write one, two, or three things the presenters could have done to improve their presentation. Provide constructive criticism—be kind.

1.

2.

3.

Figure 5.5 Peer Presentation Evaluation (Student Handout) *Source:* Adapted and republished with permission from Larry Ferlazzo based on the form he created and featured on his blog, https://larryferlazzo.edublogs.org/2014/11/20/heres-the-form-i-have-students-complete-when-theyre-listening-to-their-classmates-presentations/comment-page-1/

CHAPTER 6

Strategies for Teaching the Engineering Process

What Is It?

The engineering process is a series of steps used by engineers to solve a problem. It generally includes designing an apparatus. Although the steps vary depending on the source, the central idea is the same: solutions must be tested multiple times to ensure a high-quality design.

The Next Generation Science Standards (NGSS) require students to use the engineering design, which consists of these three steps that are formatted as a cycle, with no beginning and no end (NGSS, 2013d):

- Define
- Develop Solutions
- Optimize

The definitions of these three steps vary by grade level, but they have the same basic meaning.

- Define—identify a problem and its criteria.
- Develop Solutions—use research to create solutions or break down big solutions into smaller solutions.
- Optimize—test solutions and then ensure they meet all criteria.

The NGSS emphasize that there is no particular order for these steps (NGSS, 2013d). Most often, the steps are not linear because throughout the process engineers learn new information or think of new ideas. This requires them to return to previous steps to incorporate new learning or ideas into their prototype design.

We've found it helpful to break down these three large steps from the NGSS into nine non-linear smaller steps. In our experience, these nine steps are more concrete, which increases student understanding of what is expected of them. The steps provide a detailed description of how students move through the engineering process. Here are the engineering process steps we teach our students:

1. Ask a question.
2. Perform research.
3. Brainstorm solutions.
4. Choose one solution.
5. Build a prototype.
6. Test the prototype.
7. Reflect on the results and redesign.
8. Communicate results.
9. Begin again with step 1.

This chapter focuses on the engineering process, while Chapter 3 provides strategies for teaching the scientific method, Chapter 4 includes resources for the inquiry process, and Chapter 5 focuses on project-based learning.

All four processes can engage students. In our experience, students most often confuse the scientific method and the engineering process. Based on Table 6.1: Differences Between the Scientific Method and the Engineering Process, the scientific method has a structured beginning and ending; however, the engineering process requires scientists to return to previous steps so that they can incorporate their learning into new designs. The scientific method has only one independent variable because the purpose of an experiment is to determine how that variable affects the experiment's outcomes. However, in the engineering process, there can be many independent variables because scientists can test the efficacy of any aspect of a design.

The engineering process usually includes a diagram of a new design that will be tested, which acts as a substitute for the formal hypothesis that is required by the scientific method. The last difference between the scientific method and the inquiry process is that when an experiment is complete, the scientist determines if the experiment should be repeated with or without alterations. However, in the engineering process, the redesigning never ends because all processes and mechanisms can be improved.

Table 6.1 Differences Between the Scientific Method and Engineering Process

Scientific method	Engineering process
Is a linear process with a clear beginning and ending	Is not linear; does not have a structured beginning and end
Must include only one independent variable	May include multiple independent variables throughout the process
Must include a formal hypothesis	May include a hypothesis
May include retesting	Must include retesting

When we introduce the engineering process to students, we summarize the differences between the scientific method and the engineering process. We explain that when scientists design a new or improved technology, success is almost never accomplished the first time. Engineers create a new design, test it, learn from the testing, apply their learning to another new design, and so on. They don't publish their findings until after they've created a new design that meets the minimum criteria. For this reason, a linear process like the scientific method is disadvantageous.

Why We Like It

When students are using the engineering process, they are also reinforcing the skills they use in the scientific method, inquiry process, and project-based learning. All four of these processes include scientists asking questions, performing research, and communicating their results.

As students work through the engineering process, they are consistently challenged to analyze the effectiveness of their ideas and improve their current designs. Students will often attempt a solution but then realize during or after implementation that their solution isn't as effective as they had originally hypothesized. According to research, making these kinds of mistakes and performing this type of analysis change how a person's brain organizes information (Castro, 2011). Students are certainly learning by using the engineering process, and that is the purpose of science!

Supporting Research

There are benefits to using the scientific method, project-based learning, the inquiry process, and the engineering process in science classrooms. However, the NGSS particularly highlight the engineering process because it clarifies for students, "the relevance of science, technology, engineering, and mathematics (the four STEM fields) to everyday life" (NGSS, 2013g).

The engineering process can also allow for students to use creative thinking, and can help them develop the needed self-confidence to think "outside the box" and solve problems. Becoming skilled in the engineering process promotes critical thinking skills that students can employ as they encounter future problems (Cowan, 2013).

Skills for Intentional Scholars/NGSS Connections

The engineering process incorporates all three Skills for Intentional Scholars. Students use creative problem-solving skills as they brainstorm solutions. They also practice their critical thinking skills as they determine the best possible solution and analyze the effectiveness of their prototype. Finally, students use communication skills to publish their results.

Historically, there's been a division between teaching students science content and science practices. The NGSS attempt to combine the two by requiring the use of engineering practices (National Research Council, 2012, p. 42).

Application

When first presenting the engineering process to students, we introduce Thomas Edison, the inventor of many technological advances, including the phonograph, an incandescent light bulb with a carbon filament, and nickel-iron batteries. We begin by showing students a picture of Thomas Edison and asking them to share with us what they already know about him. After all students have the opportunity to share their knowledge, we tell them the full history of how the light bulb was invented and improved.

Here is the story we tell students:

> The original light bulb was invented in Britain as early as 1802 (Matulka & Wood, 2013). The design was expensive to produce and it had a short lifespan. Beginning in the mid-1800s, Edison worked for several years to improve the design. In October, 1879, he and his team created a light bulb with a carbonized cotton filament that lasted for 14.5 hours. And by January of 1880, they improved their design further by using carbonized bamboo filaments, which remained lit for 1,200 hours and could be produced for a much cheaper price (Engineering and Technology History Wiki, 2015).

We pause at this point in the Edison story to write the following nine engineering process steps on the board:

1. Ask a question.
2. Perform research.

3. Brainstorm solutions.

4. Choose one solution.

5. Build a prototype.

6. Test the prototype.

7. Reflect on the results and redesign.

8. Communicate results.

9. Begin again with step 1.

We explain to students that this is the process engineers use to solve problems, such as improving a current technology like a light bulb. Then we continue the tale...

> The most interesting part of Edison's story involves his tenacity to find a successful design. When he completed Step 7: Reflect on the Results and Redesign, he often realized his proposed design didn't achieve his goals for a cheaper, more efficient light bulb. He chose not to quit but, instead, to return to Step 2: Perform Research or Step 3: Brainstorm Solutions, at which time he identified additional solutions.
>
> The engineering process helped Edison view his failures as learning opportunities—he never gave up! In the 1910 biography, *Edison: His Life and Inventions* (Dyer & Martin, 1910), Edison's friend Walter S. Mallory asked him, "Isn't it a shame that with the tremendous amount of work you have done you haven't been able to get any results?" Mallory reflected on the conversation and recalled that Edison responded quickly, "Results! Why, man, I have gotten a lot of results! I know several thousand things that won't work." (Quote Investigator, n.d.)

After we share the story of Thomas Edison, we ask students to write about an event in their lives when they first failed but chose not to quit. Students share their stories with a partner and then we ask for volunteers to share with the rest of the class. We ask students how they felt when they finally succeeded after trying again and again. Then we ask students how they think Edison must have felt after finally inventing a light bulb that stayed lit for 1,200 hours and was economically feasible. We acknowledge that failing is frustrating; however, we also explain that it's less frustrating when we see mistakes as learning opportunities, like Edison did when his ideas failed. And when people don't quit but instead persevere, they are more likely to meet their goals.

We find this is an excellent opportunity to discuss the concept of a growth mindset with students. We begin by explaining the difference between a fixed mindset (the belief that a person's talents and traits don't change over time) and a growth mindset (the belief that abilities can be developed over time). Then we show the students a quick interview with Carol Dweck, the leading researcher on fixed and growth mindsets. As we do with all videos, we give the students a purpose for watching it by telling them that after the video, they will be responsible for determining which mindset is practiced during the engineering process. The video we show is called "Carol Dweck on the Difference Between a Fixed and Growth Mindset" (2014) and can be found at https://www.youtube.com/watch?v=hXyesVD4EJI. Many others are also available online.

After the video, students have a discussion with a partner about which mindset is practiced during the engineering process. We remind them that the steps of the engineering process are written on the board and encourage them to use the steps as a reference. We walk around, listening to student conversations to ensure students are on task. If students struggle to correctly identify the answer, then we ask them, "Which mindset do you believe Edison had?" This most often leads to students making the growth mindset connection.

As individual groups determine that the answer is a growth mindset, we further challenge their thinking by asking, "Which step of the engineering process provides the most opportunities to practice having a growth mindset and why?" Then we have a classroom discussion by asking for volunteers to share their answers. Students often say, "Step 6 offers the most opportunity because sometimes a prototype won't work as planned." Other students may disagree, which is okay because there is no right or wrong answer. The purpose of the conversation is to have students make a connection between having a growth mindset and using the engineering process.

Once students are aware of the advantages in having a growth mindset, we again point their attention to the board where the nine steps are written. They are directed to discuss with their peers which steps would be the most frustrating to perform but might provide the most learning. Students' answers may include steps 5–7 because Step 5: Build a Prototype requires the actual designing, Step 6: Test a Prototype requires testing the design, and Step 7: Reflect on the Results and Redesign requires analyzing the results. In all three of these steps, engineers may find flaws in their designs.

We pose the question, "What did Edison do when he realized that his design had shortcomings?" Students respond with ideas such as returning to steps 2 and 3 to perform further research and brainstorm more solutions. We agree and then explain this is how engineers use the engineering process. Engineers don't begin with step 1, complete all subsequent steps in order, and neatly end with step 9. Instead, they weave back and forth between researching/brainstorming and building/testing/reflecting. This is a good time to reinforce why engineers can't use the scientific method—it doesn't allow a scientist to return to a previous step.

After students have developed a basic understanding of the engineering process, we launch a lesson that helps them put it into practice.

STEP 1: ASK A QUESTION

The first step of the engineering process is to ask a question, which we address in Chapter 5: Strategies for Using Project-Based Learning. Chapter 5 includes ideas that help both teachers and students generate questions.

To introduce the engineering process to high school students, we challenge them to make a catapult using mousetraps. The question we ask students is, "How can a mousetrap be used to catapult a marshmallow the farthest distance?"

Using mousetraps can be dangerous so, when we work with elementary and middle school students, we instead have them participate in an egg drop challenge or the Pringle potato chip mail challenge. The egg drop challenge requires students to drop an egg from a high distance without it breaking. The question we ask would be "How can an egg be packaged so that it does not break when dropped from the roof?" The Pringle chip challenge requires students to mail a single chip to their house in an envelope and have it arrive in one piece, without any damage. Pringle potato chips are generally the same size and shape, which can be an experimental constant that is unlikely to be found using other potato chip brands. The question for this engineering challenge would be "How can a Pringle potato chip be packaged so it does not become damaged in the shipping process?" Online resources for the egg drop and the Pringle potato chip challenge are available in the Technology Connections section.

We review the following steps specifically discussing the mousetrap catapult example; however, most of these same steps can be applied to any other engineering challenge, including the egg drop or Pringle potato chip challenge. The only exception might be that it would obviously be time-consuming to do multiple tests of the Pringle potato chip challenge.

STEP 2: PERFORM RESEARCH

Before students can define the problem, they must first understand how catapults work.

We begin by showing them two online videos: one of a working trebuchet and another of a catapult (plenty can be found online). Prior to viewing any video with students, we give them a purpose for watching it. We tell students that the purpose of viewing these videos is to learn how trebuchets and catapults launch projectiles into the air. After both videos have been shown, students discuss their observations with a partner. Then we have a class discussion about how catapults use tension while trebuchets use counterweights. We've found that student understanding increases if we show the videos again after the class discussion because now students have a greater ability to comprehend what they are seeing.

After determining how catapults work, students learn about the mechanics of mousetraps. We pass out a mousetrap to each pair of students (after having a serious conversation about safety) and model how to set, hold, and release a mousetrap. Students then practice so they become more comfortable using them.

In the engineering process, students need to research the following two main concepts:

1. Define the Problem: Research any one or all of these questions:
   a. What is the problem?
   b. Why is it a problem?
   c. For whom is it a problem?
2. Identify Current Solutions: Researching any one or both of these questions:
   a. What are the current solutions?
   b. What are the solutions' shortcomings?

In the mousetrap catapult challenge, the question we ask students is, "How can a mousetrap be used to catapult a marshmallow the farthest distance?" In other words, we introduce them to a contest! To provide students with a "starting off point" regarding identifying the problem and its current solutions and shortcomings, we write the following questions on the board or display them on a document camera:

1. What determines the distance a mousetrap can fling a marshmallow?
2. How can those factors be maximized?
3. How can the marshmallow be adhered to the catapult?
4. What additional resources do other people use to make mousetrap catapults?
5. Which designs fling the marshmallow the greatest distance?
6. What are the shortcomings of the solutions other people have used?

We tell students they will need the answers to these six questions in order to design an effective mousetrap catapult. Students work in groups of three or four to complete their research online. See Chapter 3: Strategies for Teaching the Scientific

Method and Its Components for materials to help students perform research. They document their findings in a shared Google document, in their science notebooks, or in their notes.

After groups complete their research, we have a class discussion to define one common problem. Each group is instructed to write their defined problem on a dry erase board, which is 2 × 2 ft. These boards can be purchased and cut for a reasonable cost at any home improvement store. If mini-whiteboards aren't an available resource, a sheet of paper can be an effective substitute.

We instruct students to begin their problem statement with the phrase, "We need to…" They are also instructed to include the dependent variable in their problem statement.

One-by-one, groups share their dry erase boards with the rest of the class. We then facilitate a class discussion to write one problem that will be shared by the whole class. The two most common problems identified by our classes are:

1. We need to use a mousetrap to catapult a marshmallow the farthest distance possible.

2. We need to launch a marshmallow the farthest distance by using a mouse-trap catapult.

We approve the class's problem statement if it includes the main idea of the question and the dependent variable, which in this example is the distance the marshmallow flies.

Then it's time to combine all of the groups' research regarding how other people have attempted to build a mousetrap catapult and the shortcomings of their designs.

We draw a T-chart on the board in the front of the classroom. The first column is titled Current Solution and the second is titled Shortcomings. We ask groups to

Table 6.2 T-chart for Mousetrap Catapult Challenge

Current solution	Shortcomings
Spoon is taped to the mousetrap's metal bar	The spoon can easily be taped on the incorrect side of the bar
Spoon is taped to the mousetrap's metal bar	The spoon can easily be taped facing the opposite direction the bar swings
Spoon is adhered to the mousetrap's metal bar with a rubber band	The rubber bands often break
Mousetrap is taped to the floor	Scotch tape and masking tape aren't strong enough
Mousetrap is triggered with a pencil	Wooden and mechanical (plastic) pencils break

report on their research and we note it on the board. Groups share any current solutions other people have used and the shortcomings of those solutions. This list is kept on the board for the remainder of the challenge so students can use it as a reference.

For the mousetrap catapult challenge, a common T-chart may look like Table 6.2.

STEP 3: BRAINSTORM SOLUTIONS

Now it's time for students to use what they've learned from the research process to brainstorm their own design ideas.

Brainstorming sessions require a structured process that facilitates a creative environment. The goal is that students produce as many possible solutions without parameters or real-life restrictions.

Ideation is the process we use to help students brainstorm ideas. We prefer ideation over all other brainstorming processes because it includes both individual and group think time. It's important to provide the individual think time because research touts that brainstorming sessions include more diverse ideas when people have time to brainstorm individually (Torres, 2016).

Further research finds that when brainstorming sessions begin with the whole group "throwing out" ideas at the same time, only the loudest students are heard. However, when individual brainstorming occurs first and is then followed by a round robin group discussion, student confidence and learning can increase, specifically for English language learners (Asari, Ma'Rifah, & Arifani, 2017).

The ideation process includes two steps.

Step 1: Individual Brainstorm Time

To brainstorm in an organized manner, each student is given a set of sticky notes, index cards, or strips of paper. They are instructed to think quietly and write down every idea that comes to mind. This requires approximately 5–10 min. Students can also draw pictures to represent their ideas, which can be especially helpful for newcomer English language learners.

Students are told to write only one idea on each paper because it helps to keep individual ideas organized during Step 2: Round Robin Discussion.

Step 2: Round Robin Discussion

Students are broken into small groups of three to five. See Chapter 2: Strategies for Teaching Lab Procedures for strategies that can be used to create student groups.

There are several methods for productive round robin discussions. Our favorite is to have each group sit in a circle. One student in the group stands up, shares one idea, and sits down. They place their written idea in the middle of the circle. If another student has the same idea, they immediately pile it onto the previous student's idea. By the end of the round robin discussion, there are multiple piles, each representing a different idea.

We've found some individuals are verbose in their explanations, so using a timer can be helpful. We allow only 30 s of share time for each idea.

In our mousetrap example, students brainstorm designs that would make their marshmallow fly the farthest distance. Some students' ideas focus on the amount of tension, others' ideas are framed around stabilizing the mousetrap when it is released, and yet other students will have ideas that center around how the marshmallow is connected to the mousetrap. The goal of brainstorming is that all of these equally important design ideas are shared so they can be incorporated into the final product that will launch the marshmallow the farthest.

Prior to introducing the ideation process to students, we explain the four rules of ideation. According to Nick Bogaert, there are Four Golden Rules for ideation (Bogaert, n.d.), which we place on the board and teach to the class. The four rules are:

1. There are no bad ideas.
2. Capture everything.
3. Go for hybrid brainstorming.
4. Quantity over quality.

Rule 1: There Are No Bad Ideas

In our experience, this rule is easier for younger students. And conversely, the older the student, the more difficult it can be because they tend to have more social inhibitions and are beginning to see the world through critical eyes. To help older students feel comfortable sharing their ideas, we explain the purpose of this rule.

We explain that the point of the ideation process is not to identify solutions but, instead, to document ideas. No one is allowed to judge anyone's ideas or add restrictions by saying things such as, "yes, but." This is a time for students to be creative and silly. We further explain that sometimes one silly idea will lead to a viable solution so *all* ideas are *good* ideas during an ideation session.

During Step 2: Round Robin Discussion, we walk from group to group and redirect any judgmental comments we hear by saying things like, "Remember that this is a brainstorming session so there are no bad ideas" and "Please don't judge each other's ideas because when we brainstorm there are no bad ideas."

Rule 2: Capture Everything

This rule pertains to both steps of the ideation process. In Step 1: Individual Brainstorm Time, students should document every idea they have; they should not dismiss any of them. During Step 2: Round Robin Discussion, we provide additional sticky notes, index cards, or strips of paper to each student. They are encouraged to write down any additional ideas that come to mind while their peers are sharing. They then share these new ideas, one at a time, when it is their turn.

The ideas students think of during Step 2: Round Robin Discussion may be the best ideas created. When students first begin brainstorming, research states that more and better ideas are generated when individual ideation occurs first and is followed by a group share (Girotra, Terwiesch, & Ulrich, 2010).

Rule 3: Go for Hybrid Brainstorming

This rule encourages students to combine one peer's idea with another during Step 2: Round Robin Discussion. As students are sharing their individual ideas, thoughts might come to group members about how to combine some of them. During this time, they can write their hybrid ideas on a sticky note, index card, or strip of paper and then share them with the group when it is their turn.

Rule 4: Quantity Over Quality

This rule encapsulates the other three rules. The best ideation sessions create the most ideas. We explain to students that they will generate many ideas by being true to the first three rules. We remind them that the goal of brainstorming is to generate multiple ideas in order to synthesize the best possible solution when the brainstorming session is complete.

STEP 4: CHOOSE ONE SOLUTION

After the brainstorming is complete, it is time for students to make a decision about how to proceed with their design. We introduce this step by discussing "universal design principles."

When engineers design a product, they generally design for the average user but should be designing for all types of people (Burgstahler, 2015). Engineers and engineering students can be encouraged to analyze their ideas using the following seven universal design principles:

1. Equitable use—people of all abilities can use the product.
2. Flexibility in use—people of all interests can use the product.

3. Simple and intuitive—people don't need background knowledge to use the product.

4. Perceptible information—people receive easy-to-access information from the product.

5. Tolerance for error—people are safe from harm when using the product.

6. Low physical effort—people don't exert themselves or feel fatigued after using the product.

7. Size and shape for approach and use—people of all shapes and sizes can easily use the product (for example, people who are left-handed).

When we introduce these seven principles, we project them on the board and ask students, "What is the common theme among these seven principles?" After students discuss this with a partner, we facilitate a class discussion. If students are struggling to recognize that each principle revolves around the user, we ask them to identify the common word in all seven principles, which is the word "people." This usually kick-starts a class discussion about how products have no value if people can't use them.

We encourage students to design with the user in mind. For example, when planning their mousetrap, students should design it so that every student in the class—regardless of physical ability—can properly launch the marshmallow with little, if any, instruction.

Research suggests that when engineers use the seven universal design principles, their end products are more user-friendly, especially for people with disabilities (Bigelow, 2012). This is an opportunity for students to practice social emotional awareness because they are designing for people who may be different from themselves.

While in their lab group, we also suggest that students continue brainstorming ideas, especially if they can combine two seemingly different ideas. For example, if one student had the idea to brace the mousetrap by taping it to the floor with duct tape and another student suggested that the marshmallow be placed in a spoon that is taped to the mousetrap, then the chosen solution could incorporate both ideas.

Sometimes, students can't decide between two different design solutions. To help them determine which is the better of the two, we recommend they build the first design and test it multiple times. Then they build and test the second design multiple times. After calculating the average distance for each design, students then choose the design that slung the marshmallow the farthest distance.

STEP 5: BUILD A PROTOTYPE

Once a group decides which ideas to use, we require them to draw a diagram. We teach students that diagrams are pictures with labels indicating the materials used in the design and how the materials will be adhered to one another. We show students Figure 6.1: Student Examples of Mousetrap Catapult Designs, which offers two student examples of well-drawn diagrams. Figure 6.2: Mousetrap Catapult Lab Worksheet is the worksheet we provide to each student so they can record their designs, data, and design changes.

After their diagram is complete, we remind them that they may find that their idea isn't going to be successful, and that is okay. We tell the class that this is a natural part of the engineering process, offer a reminder about having a growth mindset, and encourage them to focus on the fact that they learned something. They simply need to return to their list of ideas and find another. Once this class discussion is complete, the groups gather all necessary materials and begin to build.

STEP 6: TEST THE PROTOTYPE

Once students have a prototype, they test it to gather data that will determine its effectiveness. In the case of the mousetrap catapult, students launch their marshmallows in the classroom, hallway, and/or outside depending on the space available and weather conditions. Students measure the distance the marshmallows fly. They are instructed to document their data in a data table and complete at least two more trials. See Chapter 3: Strategies for Teaching the Scientific Method and Its Components for resources to teach students how to make and use data tables.

To ensure students are launching their marshmallows in a responsible manner, we review lab behavior expectations. See Chapter 1: Strategies for Teaching Lab Safety for resources to teach students proper lab behavior.

STEP 7: REFLECT ON THE RESULTS AND REDESIGN

After students collect at least three trials' worth of data, they analyze the data to determine if their design can be improved. If they determine a change to the design will improve their results, they redraw their diagram, alter the prototype, and test again. Figure 6.1: Student Examples of Mousetrap Catapult Designs includes two student examples of diagrams.

To encourage students to keep designing, testing, and analyzing, we have them compare their data to other groups' data to determine if their design is the most effective or if they should be receiving better results. Students must redesign and retest several times before they find a design that provides optimum results. When a group insists their design cannot be improved, we give them an additional challenge. As an example, in the mousetrap catapult lab, we challenge students to improve their design for accuracy. Using tape, we mark off an X on the wall or floor and challenge the students to hit the X from a specific location.

STEP 8: COMMUNICATE RESULTS

Students can share their results in writing through a lab report, slideshow, an article on a class blog, and/or in many other forms.

In Chapter 3: Strategies for Teaching the Scientific Method and Its Components, we provide resources for students to document their results. In Chapter 5: Strategies for Using Project-Based Learning we've included resources for publishing student results to an authentic audience.

STEP 9: BEGIN AGAIN WITH STEP 1

True engineers never stop designing. To make this point with students, we show them a picture of an original cell phone, informally called a brick phone. We explain that this phone was wireless but could only make phone calls. Students are challenged to list the improvements that cell phones have undergone throughout the years. Students may list such things as access to the Internet and social media, the invention of apps and games, the addition of a calculator or GPS, and texting.

We use the cell phone example as motivation for students to continue improving their design. We ask guiding questions such as, "Can a person in a wheelchair activate your mousetrap?" and "Can a child safely activate your mousetrap?" The goal is that students begin to think about unique users and their needs.

After all students have made revisions and are confident with their designs, they are allowed to complete three official trials to obtain the farthest distance for the contest. The winning group earns a token of our appreciation (extra credit, food, or other incentives).

See Figure 6.3: Mousetrap Catapult Picture for a picture of a mousetrap catapult that was made in our classroom.

GRADING ENGINEERING PROJECTS

There is no right or wrong answer when students use the engineering process. To assess their learning, we grade them based on the documentation they make during the engineering process. When we first introduce an engineering task, we provide each student with a copy of the rubric so they know how they will be graded. We've included an example of our mousetrap catapult rubric in Figure 6.4: Mousetrap Catapult Rubric. Students are provided time to read the rubric and then we ask

Table 6.3 Engineering Project Ideas Based on the Four NGSS Disciplines

NGSS disciplines	Engineering project idea
Physical Sciences: law of conservation of mass	Shrink polystyrene to build a scale model of the classroom, measure the mass of the polystyrene before and after shrinking
Physical Sciences: chemical bonds, activators, polymers	Build the strongest bridge (determined by the mass of pennies held) that is made out of slime; students decide how to make the slime
Physical Sciences: sound waves	Develop a structure that has the most efficient soundproofing
Physical Sciences: air pressure	Build a wind car that can travel a set distance the fastest, powered only by a fan that mimics wind
Physical Sciences: insulators, exothermic, endothermic	Design a cooler that keeps food warm or cold
Earth Sciences: solar energy	Build a solar oven that can cook hot dogs or make s'mores to eat
Earth Sciences: filtration	Create a filtration system that turns polluted water into drinking water
Life Sciences: seed dispersal (can integrate physical science)	Build a device that can disperse a seed the farthest via wind
Life Sciences: osmosis	Develop a membrane that is selectively permeable for some solute but not others
Technology, Engineering, and Applications of Science: erosion (can integrate life sciences or earth sciences)	Design a mechanism that reduces soil erosion to benefit farmers and their crops
Technology, Engineering, and Applications of Science (can integrate physical sciences or earth sciences)	Design a new technology for the International Space Station; it must be composed of materials that are lightweight and its parts must be easily replaceable

them to summarize how their products will be graded. After students identify that it is their documentation that will be graded, we ask them what will *not* be graded. At this point, we help them realize that the effectiveness of their final design isn't part of their grade. We explain that if students desire a grade of an A, they need to document their designs with diagrams and record their experimental results.

ENGINEERING PROJECT IDEAS

Table 6.3 lists engineering projects ideas based on the four NGSS disciplines. See the Technology Connections section for online links to additional resources.

See Chapter 12: Strategies for Incorporating the Arts and Kinesthetic Movement for a specific lesson plan that integrates a historical case study (the story of Filippo Brunelleschi) and the engineering process.

DIFFERENTIATION FOR DIVERSE LEARNERS

When we create groups for engineering tasks, we first take an inventory of the number of supplies we have available. The availability of materials will often be our limiting factor and will dictate the size of the group. If we have ample supplies, then we create groups of two or three because we want every student involved in the task in order to maximize each student's ideas and strengths. See Chapter 2: Strategies for Teaching Lab Procedures for resources to purposefully group students who require extra support.

The most difficult task for students is remembering to document all of their changes throughout the process. Students become very engaged during the testing and redesigning process and often forget about the required documentation. We find this to be especially true for students who don't enjoy writing. To help them, we make an effort to check on every group throughout the process, specifically asking to see their documentation. When we find students who haven't been documenting their results and redrawing their diagrams, we help them backtrack their steps so they can catch up. Once everyone in the group has completed their documentation, we allow the group to continue.

To support English language learners, we provide sentence frames to help them organize their data and design planning. See Figure 6.5: Mousetrap Catapult Sentence Frames for an example of sentence stems that can be used during the engineering process. We provide a copy of the sentence starters to students prior to testing their prototypes. As they document their answers in their lab notebook or on their lab worksheet, they choose the sentence that best supports their writing. They copy their chosen sentence and fill in the blanks with the details. They may use a sentence multiple times and may not use other sentences. They have the choice depending on the documentation they are tracking as they progress through the testing and redesigning steps.

Student Handouts and Examples

Figure 6.1: Student Examples of Mousetrap Catapult Designs
Figure 6.2: Mousetrap Catapult Lab Worksheet (Student Handout)
Figure 6.3: Mousetrap Catapult Picture
Figure 6.4: Mousetrap Catapult Rubric (Student Handout)
Figure 6.5: Mousetrap Catapult Sentence Frames (Student Handout)

What Could Go Wrong?

CLASSROOM MANAGEMENT

There are many moving parts during a lesson plan that uses the engineering process. Students are working in small groups, materials are being added and removed from designs, students are documenting ideas and results, and prototypes are being tested. To mitigate off-task and inappropriate lab behavior, we always review our behavioral expectations, focusing on the rule that horseplay is not permitted. See

Chapter 2: Strategies for Teaching Lab Procedures for resources that help teach students lab rules and expectations.

We also ensure every person in the group has a responsibility. For example, in a group of three, tasks can be divided like this:

- Task 1: Scribe—documents all changes and experimental results (now only one student in the group must document, not every student)
- Task 2: Materials Engineer—manages the provision, use, and clean-up of all lab materials
- Task 3: Lead Engineer—ensures all other group members are on task and facilitates respectful group conversations

Additionally, we walk around the room, guiding students so they are productive and actively participating. If students need to use a different type of location, such as a staircase or field, during Step 6: Test the Prototype, we prefer to have additional adults to help manage student behavior. For example, administrators, office staff, and parents have proven to be helpful assistants. If a classroom consists of a co-teacher, the two teachers can use the co-teaching strategy called Parallel Teaching, which divides a class into two groups and assigns each of the teachers to one of the groups. See Chapter 18: Strategies for Co-Teaching for resources and ideas about how to co-teach with a second adult.

An additional idea is to pair up with another teacher who is also teaching the engineering process. The groups who are still documenting ideas and building their prototypes work in one classroom and the groups that are testing their prototype work in a separate space. Each of the two educational environments can be monitored by one of the cooperating teachers.

MOUSETRAP DANGERS

Regardless of how much practice students are given, it is possible that a student will snap a mousetrap on one of their fingers. We've never seen a mousetrap break the skin but, if it was to happen, we would follow our school's protocol for how to assist an injured student. If students aren't comfortable setting the mousetraps, we always make ourselves available and volunteer to set the mousetraps for them.

Technology Connections

We have a few favorite online resources for egg drop challenges. Northeastern University's Center for STEM Education (https://stem.northeastern.edu/programs/

Table 6.4 Pringle Potato Chip Challenge Rubric

Intactness	Description	Chip score
Perfectly intact	Like it just left the factory	100 Points
Slightly damaged	Cracked, but still in one piece	50 Points
Chipped chip	Broken along the edges, but less than five pieces	20 Points
Split chip	The chip is broken into two fairly equal pieces	10 Points
Significantly damaged	Chipped and/or cracked into less than 20 pieces	5 Points
Pringle dust	Too many pieces to count (more than 20)	1 Point

ayp/fieldtrips/activities/eggdrop), provides differentiation for younger and older students. Buggy and Buddy provide printables, procedures, and extensions for egg drop challenges at "Egg Drop Challenge and Free Planning Printable" (https://buggyandbuddy.com/egg-drop-challenge-and-free-planning-printable-science-invitation-saturday).

The Pringle potato chip mail challenge requires students to create a package that can safely transport a single chip through the US Post Office without cracking or chipping. Students can send the chip to themselves, but for additional fun, two schools from across the country can send their chips to each other. The official challenge rules, which originated from Charles Lindgren, can be found on Brian Bortz's website "Pringles Challenge" (https://sites.google.com/site/newpringle-schallenge/rules). Bortz's site also includes Table 6.4: Pringle Potato Chip Challenge Rubric, which is copied here.

Bortz no longer matches schools so we use social media to find teachers who want to participate in the challenge and are located outside of our state. Larry Ferlazzo includes a list of resources that help teachers match their class with other classes. The resources are available in his blog entitled "The Best Ways to Find Other Classes for Joint Online Projects" (http://larryferlazzo.edublogs.org/2009/05/30/the-best-ways-to-find-other-classes-for-joint-online-projects).

For student examples and additional links to other Pringle potato chip mail challenge resources, see Peggy Reimers's blog at "The Pringles Challenge: A Fun-Filled Stem Activity" (https://blog.tcea.org/pringles-challenge-stem-activity).

For additional ideas of how to incorporate the engineering process into a K-8 classroom, we recommend Engineering Is Elementary (http://www.eie.org). For 4–12 classrooms, we suggest Try Engineering (https://tryengineering.org) and for K-12 resources we like Teach Engineering (https://www.teachengineering.org).

For specific engineering videos, such as the science of football, golf, and the Olympic Games we recommend NBC Learn (https://www.nbclearn.com/portal/site/learn/resources).

Attributions

Thank you to Annika McPeek and Hailey Quick for allowing us to use their examples of mousetrap catapult designs.

Thank you, Brian Bortz, for providing the directions and rubric for the Pringle potato chip mail challenge.

Thank you to Jeff Sesemann who gave us the ideas for some of the physical science engineering activities.

Figures

1. Draw your initial design here. Be sure to label all of the equipment you are using and describe how you are adhering them to one another.

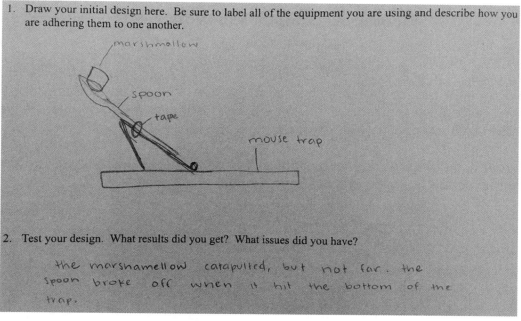

2. Test your design. What results did you get? What issues did you have?

the marshamellow catapulted, but not far. the spoon broke off when it hit the bottom of the trap.

5. Document the changes you will make to improve your results. Redraw your design.

We added cardbord and tape to keep the mouse trap from lifting up when its set off.

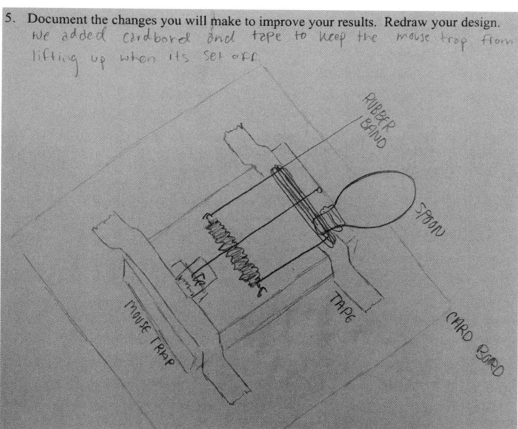

Figure 6.1   Student Examples of Mousetrap Catapult Designs

Name: _____

Mousetrap Catapult Lab Worksheet

Directions: Use this worksheet to record your designs, data, and design changes. You'll notice on the *Rubric for Mousetrap Catapult Designs* that you will not be graded on the distance that your marshmallow flies. The purpose of this lab is to practice the engineering process so you will be graded on how you interpret your data and use it to improve your design.

1. Draw a diagram of your prototype. Label all of the equipment you are using and describe how you are adhering them to one another.

2. Test your prototype. Make a data table to record your data. You need at least three trials.

3. Interpret your data to determine how you can improve your prototype What problems did you encounter? How can you solve those problems? After discussing it with your team, draw a diagram of your new prototype. Again, you need labels of all the tools you are using and how they are adhered to one another.

4. Test your prototype. Make a data table to record your data. You need at least three trials.

Figure 6.2 Mousetrap Catapult Lab Worksheet (Student Handout)

5. Interpret your data to determine how you can improve your prototype. What problems did you encounter? How can you solve those problems? After discussing it with your team, draw a diagram of your new prototype. Again, you need labels of all the tools you are using and how they are adhered to one another.

6. Test your prototype. Make a data table to record your data. You need at least three trials.

7. Continue to redesign and test. There is extra paper on my desk if you need more to draw your diagrams and record your data. Please staple your extra papers to this worksheet.

Figure 6.2 (Continued)

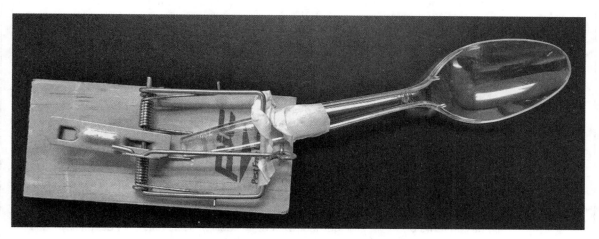

Figure 6.3 Mousetrap Catapult Picture

Rubric for Mousetrap Catapult Designs

Requirement	3	2	1	0
Initial Design	Diagram includes a picture with all materials properly labeled; diagram demonstrates how materials will be adhered to each other	Diagram includes a picture with all materials properly labeled; diagram lacks details about how materials will be adhered to each other	Diagram includes a picture with some materials properly labeled; diagram lacks details about how materials will be adhered to each other	Diagram is missing or diagram is a picture with no labels
Results of Initial Design	Total length documented with units of measurement; includes possible design flaws and changes that will be made in the next design	Total length documented with units of measurement; includes either possible design flaws or changes that will be made in the next design	Total length documented with units of measurement; does not include possible design flaws and missing changes that will be made in the next design	Total length documented without units of measurement; does not include possible design flaws and missing changes that will be made in the next design
Second Design	Diagram includes a picture with all materials properly labeled; diagram demonstrates how materials will be adhered to each other	Diagram includes a picture with all materials properly labeled; diagram lacks details about how materials will be adhered to each other	Diagram includes a picture with some materials properly labeled; diagram lacks details about how materials will be adhered to each other	Diagram is missing or diagram is a picture with no labels
Results of the Second Design	Total length documented with units of measurement; includes possible design flaws and changes that will be made in the next design	Total length documented with units of measurement; includes either possible design flaws or changes that will be made in the next design	Total length documented with units of measurement; does not include possible design flaws and missing changes that will be made in the next design	Total length documented without units of measurement; does not include possible design flaws and missing changes that will be made in the next design
Additional Designs	Diagrams include a picture with all materials properly labeled; diagrams demonstrate how materials will be adhered to each other	Diagrams include a picture with all materials properly labeled; diagrams lack details about how materials will be adhered to each other	Diagrams include a picture with some materials properly labeled; diagrams lack details about how materials will be adhered to each other	Diagrams are missing or diagrams are pictures with no labels
Results of Additional Designs	Total length documented with units of measurement; includes possible design flaws and changes that will be made in the next design	Total length documented with units of measurement; includes either possible design flaws or changes that will be made in the next design	Total length documented with units of measurement; does not include possible design flaws and missing changes that will be made in the next design	Total length documented without units of measurement; does not include possible design flaws and missing changes that will be made in the next design

Figure 6.4 Mousetrap Catapult Rubric (Student Handout)

Mousetrap Catapult Sentence Frames

Directions: Choose the sentence that best matches what you want to say. Rewrite the sentence in your lab packet and fill in the blanks.

1. After launching our marshmallow, it landed an average of _____ centimeters from the catapult.
2. We changed our design. We changed the _____ because _____.
3. We were proud that the _____ launched the marshmallow _____ centimeters.
4. We launched our marshmallow again several times. The average distance was _____ centimeters. We realized that the marshmallow may go further if we _____.
5. We were disappointed that the _____ only launched the marshmallow _____ centimeters.

Figure 6.5 Mousetrap Catapult Sentence Frames (Student Handout)

PART II

Integration of ELA, Mathematics, and the Arts

CHAPTER 7

Strategies for Teaching Vocabulary

What Is It?

Vocabulary is often broken into three tiers based upon research by Isabel Beck, Margaret McKeown, and Linda Kucan (2002). Tier 1 vocabulary is composed of the most basic words that appear in conversations and which children often learn without requiring direct instruction, such as *cat*, *happy*, and *baby*. Tier 2 vocabulary is composed of high-frequency words that appear more often in writing across academic settings and often have multiple meanings. Examples include *obvious*, *analyze*, and *industrious*. Tier 3 vocabulary words are content-specific like *photosynthesis* and *isotope*. Teaching both Tier 2 (academic cross-curricular vocabulary) and Tier 3 (content-specific vocabulary) words should be an important part of every science classroom.

Why We Like It

Teaching vocabulary is vital in all content areas. The more vocabulary words students know, the easier it is for them to understand their reading and to express themselves in their writing.

In our experience, simply memorizing the definitions of these new terms is not going to result in students being able to use them accurately in their reading or writing. To ensure that our students understand word meanings, we explicitly teach the vocabulary while also using strategies that incorporate the new vocabulary words throughout our units. We like that these strategies also present cross-curricular connections to students so they can use their new knowledge in other settings as well.

We like the strategies we write about in this chapter because they provide multiple opportunities to teach and reinforce vocabulary in engaging ways.

Supporting Research

Numerous studies have stressed the importance of using effective strategies to increase student vocabulary. Instructional methods should include connections to other concepts and ideas, repetition, and meaningful use of newly acquired vocabulary (Harmon, Hedrick, & Wood, 2005, p. 266).

Science texts usually contain both Tier 2 and Tier 3 vocabulary words, with many of these words being new to learners. Vocabulary instruction should be more than asking students to look up dictionary definitions. It should enable students to learn and apply words across curricular settings (Rasinski, Padak, & Newton, 2017, p. 41).

Skills for Intentional Scholars/NGSS Standards

Effective instructional strategies for vocabulary focus on more than memorizing new terminology. They also require students to apply the vocabulary in their daily activities. The methods discussed in this chapter require students to think critically and communicate effectively.

Vocabulary skills are also incorporated into the NGSS. From kindergarten through high school, students are required to obtain, evaluate, and communicate information (Achieve, Inc., 2017b). In order to meet these standards, students need to be taught both Tier 2 and Tier 3 vocabulary words.

Application

While there are various ways to teach vocabulary to students, we will focus on four strategies we have found particularly effective: the use of roots, prefixes, and suffixes; interdisciplinary examples; word wall challenges; and "Fast Facts" with clozes. These strategies are not intended to be used for every unit. We alternate the activities to provide our students with varying learning experiences.

ROOTS, PREFIXES, AND SUFFIXES

Teaching roots, prefixes, and suffixes gives students the tools they can use when they come across a new term. This strategy can be effective in building student vocabulary in various academic settings and not only in science classes (Rasinski et al., 2017, p. 42).

At the beginning of a unit, there are multiple ways to introduce new vocabulary. One method we use involves providing students with a list of vocabulary words (see Table 7.1: Basic List of Vocabulary Words—Ecology Unit) they are responsible for learning and using throughout a unit. Students are paired with a partner and challenged to use a list of applicable roots, prefixes, and suffixes to write the words' definitions (see Figure 7.1: The Language of Introductory Ecology for an example). See

Table 7.1 Basic List of Vocabulary Words—Ecology Unit

biotic	abiotic	biology	carnivore	omnivore
ecology	decomposer	ecosystem	biome	invasive species
dispersal	endangered	extinction	renewable	habitat restoration
adaptation	consumer	scavenger	native species	non-native species
trophic level	nonrenewable	producer	habitat	herbivore

the Technology Connections section for our favorite resources that provide lists of prefixes, suffixes, and root words.

We begin the activity by modeling the process of matching the roots, prefixes, and suffixes to the first vocabulary word. We share with the class our thought process of how we would use the word and its parts to write a definition.

For example, with the word "biology," we would say, "Biology can be broken into two parts. As I look at my list, I can see those two parts are 'bio' and 'logy.' According to the list, 'bio' means life or living and 'logy' means the study of. So, when I combine them I can determine biology means the study of life."

Students then work with their partners to complete the same process for the remaining terms. This process should only take about 10–15 min and possibly even quicker as students get better at it.

After students write their definitions, which we refer to as their "hypothesized definitions," we provide the dictionary's definition. Students compare and contrast their definitions with the dictionary's to see if their definitions need to be edited. As usual, we are monitoring throughout the whole process so we can identify students who need more assistance. We emphasize that we want their definitions to be different from the dictionary's, but they do need to communicate the same basic meaning. We tell them that simply copying the definition does not show us they comprehend the meaning.

Once students have written their final definitions, we provide them with Figure 7.2: Vocabulary Definition Worksheet, so they can organize the unit's vocabulary words. When we create this student handout, we pre-fill the first column, titled, "Vocabulary Word," with the vocabulary words that students will learn throughout the unit. Students are instructed to rewrite their final definitions in the second column. Students then complete the last column, where they draw a picture that represents the word. We don't teach all of the unit's words in one class period but, instead, introduce only a few of the words at a time. We will discuss later in this section how we determine the appropriate number of words to teach at one time.

We've found that some students are apprehensive about drawing because they don't identify themselves as artists. We assure these students that we do not evaluate them on their artistic abilities but, instead, on how well they learn the words' definitions.

If the roots, prefixes, or suffixes are going to be used multiple times throughout a unit or across several units, we challenge students to find other words that have the same roots, prefixes, or suffixes. For example, when one of our vocabulary words is *Homo sapiens*, we ask students to find words that have the prefix of *homo* because we know in a future unit we will be teaching the vocabulary terms of homogeneous and heterogeneous. If students are able to come up with words on their own, great! If not, we tell them to use their resources, such as dictionaries, science texts, and the Internet. Of course, saying the prefix "homo" may very well generate giggles and inappropriate comments from students. If this happens, it can create an opportunity to discuss the value and importance of having a classroom and society where everyone is respected.

Research has shown that repeated exposure to new vocabulary words increases retention of those words (Rossiter, Abbott, & Kushnir, 2016, p. 10). In order to provide these repeated exposures, we've found that the optimum number of new vocabulary words for younger students is no more than five each week. At the middle school level, the optimum number increases to eight, and at the high school level we don't exceed 10. We discovered through the years that these maximums meet the requirement of exposing students to new vocabulary words without overwhelming them. If a unit has more than the optimum number of words (more than 10/week), then we either reduce the words in the unit or we extend the unit to provide more instructional time.

USING INTERDISCIPLINARY EXAMPLES

In many science classes, students are given new vocabulary words and asked to look up the definitions on their own or copy them from the teacher or dictionary. In some cases, especially when time is short, this may be a practical method. However, in our experience, students often don't understand the definitions when this is done. We prefer to use a strategy involving context clues.

We give our students three or four sentences containing a vocabulary word and have the students work together to determine the word's meaning. This works best with Tier 2 vocabulary because students are exposed to how the term is used in other content areas apart from science.

One example of using interdisciplinary examples is when teaching the moon phases. Instead of simply giving students a definition of a waning moon, which is a moon that is getting smaller, we give them these four sentences that include the word "waning" outside an astronomy context:

1. Because the king's power is waning, few people listen to him anymore.
2. The man's waning strength was a sign he was dying from the disease.

3. Staring at the waning sun, the lost camper knew it would soon be nighttime.

4. The losing basketball team's confidence was waning in the final moments of the game.

Teachers can create their own sentences or use a resource like "Words in a Sentence" www.wordsinasentence.com to generate them. This website is a helpful tool to save time and to discover how science terms are used in other content areas. The four example sentences with the word "waning" came from this resource.

We provide our students with the four sentences and ask them to use context clues to create a hypothesized definition. We instruct them to work with a partner and write down their definitions.

Once every pair has a definition, we ask for volunteers to share them with the class. Students are allowed to edit their definitions based on the classroom discussion. We monitor to ensure that every student has the correct definition written in their notes.

Now that students know the definition, they can apply it to the content being taught. In this case, it is the phases of the moon. We show the class a picture of how the moon moves from one phase to another, demonstrating all eight phases. We then ask the class to identify the phases where the moon is waning. Students look for instances when the moon's light is decreasing and by doing so, they are practicing their new vocabulary word in context and not just memorizing its definition.

This lesson is another opportunity to use Figure 7.2: Vocabulary Definition Worksheet. Students add their own definitions to the second column and then draw a picture representing each word. ELLs can also write the word in their home language.

WORD WALL CHALLENGE

The Word Wall Challenge was inspired by a student. During our first years of teaching, we started units with a word wall. We would first assign each student a unique vocabulary word. After researching their assigned word, they would create a poster, called a word wall, that included the word's definition, an applicable picture, and an explanation of how it related to our new unit.

After the word walls were graded, we would display them in the back of the classroom, humorously refer to it as the "Word Wall Wall," but never use it again. In the middle of our third year of teaching, we gave our students a survey that asked these four questions:

1. What is one thing you love about class?

2. What is one thing you hate about class?

3. What is one thing we do really well?

4. What is one thing we could do differently that would improve your learning?

One student answered question number 4 by first explaining that the word walls were a lot of work. Then she asked, "Why don't we use them if we put so much effort into making them?"

This got us thinking.

Over the next several months we created the "Word Wall Challenge," which we still use today. At the beginning of a unit, we assign each student a word. We use this opportunity to differentiate instruction. See Table 7.2: Strategies for Assigning Vocabulary Words to Students for the strategy we use to assign words to students based on their individual needs. Of course, this isn't a definitive guide to how we divide up the vocabulary words every time. It is a general thinking strategy that we keep in mind and that may change depending upon the students. For example, an English language learner may be very self-motivated or enjoy challenges, but may not have much background knowledge. In that case, we may give him/her a choice of words from each category.

Once students are assigned their words, we provide them with a piece of construction paper and Figure 7.3: Word Wall Challenge Rubric, which is divided into three sets of requirements aligned with the grades A, B, and C. Students use the criteria to "choose" the grade they want for the assignment. We've found that when assignments require only one class period, students tend to do more work if they can "choose" their grades.

At the minimum, each word wall must include the word, a definition in the student's own words, and an example or picture that shows how it fits with the current concept. Students are permitted to print pictures instead of drawing them. See Figure 7.4: Word Wall Examples for completed student examples.

Table 7.2 Strategies for Assigning Vocabulary Words to Students

Student need	Type of word	Examples
Student is usually self-motivated or engaged, but doesn't always complete assigned work	Something they may find interesting and exciting; sometimes we can ask them ahead of time what word they would prefer	volcano, crystal, fossil, black hole, eclipse, neutron star, predator, prey, tornado, hurricane, sperm, ovary, electromagnetic, nuclear fission
Student has little background knowledge or knows few vocabulary words in this unit	Words that have concrete meanings and can easily be represented with pictures	Galileo Galilei, producer, consumer, herbivore, dispersal, equilibrium, tectonic plate, atom
Student enjoys challenges or is academically advanced	Words that have abstract meanings and cannot be easily explained in one sentence or by pictures	temperature, electromagnetic spectrum, sound, electron, energy pyramid, earthquake, velocity, radiation

As middle school and high school teachers, the biggest struggle we have with this assignment is the interpretation of "a definition in your own words." Some students believe that the definition is "in their own words" when they change just one word in the dictionary's definition. We want students to challenge themselves to research the word, not just look it up in a dictionary.

To help students write the definition in their own words, we add a requirement that to earn an "A" grade, students must write the definition so a 7-year-old can understand it. Students can use complicated words in their definition but then are responsible for defining those words as well.

For example, the term *p wave* is defined by www.dictionary.com as "a longitudinal earthquake wave that travels through the interior of the earth and is usually the first conspicuous wave to be recorded by a seismograph." To receive an A, a student will probably have to perform further research on the term so they can explain it to a 7-year-old. An acceptable definition of a *p wave* is "the fastest energy that travels through the earth after an earthquake." This simple explanation includes vocabulary words that the average 7-year-old understands and requires the student to perform additional research after looking up the term in a dictionary.

We want our grading to be authentic so we used 7-year-old children to initially help us grade. At the time we added this requirement to the rubric, Tara's son was 7-years-old, so he helped us grade. Once he grew too old, her daughter turned 7, so it became her turn to help us. Once she grew up, we used friends' and neighbors' children. We are now experts on the terms that 7-year-olds know and don't know!

If a student does less work than what is required for a C, their word wall is returned and they must redo it. We don't accept any work that has less than the minimum requirements. We provide more one-on-one instruction and feedback to those students so they can improve their work.

Once all word walls are completed and graded, we hang them on the Word Wall Wall for all students to see. This is where the fun part begins. We then use the Word Wall Wall for a game to help students use and understand the vocabulary terms.

In this game, students are challenged to identify when we use a current vocabulary word from the Word Wall Wall during the class period. When we say one of the words, they raise their hand and say, "You said _____." They are required to tell us the word because we want them to practice pronouncing it.

The student who first identifies that we used the word receives a raffle ticket. Then we randomly choose a classmate who must say, in their own words, the vocabulary word's definition. Tara pulls popsicle sticks, Mandi uses index cards, and there are many options for selecting students randomly, which we discuss further in Chapter 10: Strategies for Discussions.

If the chosen student does not know the definition "off the top of their head," they are allowed to access and use any resources they have. For example, students can walk to the Word Wall Wall to read a word wall, ask their partner, leverage a textbook, or use their notes. We provide them with support, resources, and the necessary time to give the definition so that everyone can be successful and receive a raffle ticket as added recognition.

Any students with tickets turn them in at the end of the class period to designated reward cans. These cans are identified by various reinforcers we like to use, such as late homework passes, front of the line passes at lunchtime, one month of music (students can have one earbud in during lab work), and teacher-for-a-day where students are excused from their other classes and teach our class for an entire day. Teacher-for-a-day can take extra preparation for us, as we need to meet with the student and plan a lesson for them to teach and contact the other teachers to get approval for the student to miss class. However, we have found that students really enjoy this reward and so we try to do it a few times throughout the year.

At the end of every unit, we pull one raffle ticket from each reward can. All remaining tickets are thrown away so the reward cans are empty for the next unit. We pull names weekly for items such as bathroom passes and mechanical pencils, but only once in a unit for teacher-for-a-day.

We like to play this game every day of a unit. To ensure the game doesn't take up too much class time, we only allow our students to claim a word once every class period. For example, once we say "centrifugal force" and award the two tickets, the next time we say "centrifugal force" during that same class period, no further tickets are awarded. Additionally, we don't play the game the day before a test because we've found the game then takes the entire period since every word is used during the test review.

Our colleagues who play the game report the same positive test results we've experienced. Test scores increase, especially for ELL students and others who have learning challenges. We believe it's for several reasons. First, the game requires students to pay attention to us when we are talking. Second, students are exposed to the words' definitions every day. And lastly, students must pronounce the words and define the words, which provides them with more practice.

We have had students whose IEPs specifically stated that they could not be called on during class because they had a type of social anxiety called "selective mutism." At the beginning of the year, when we introduced the game to the students, we respectively pulled these students aside and asked if they wanted to participate. They were allowed to provide their answer by writing down "yes" or "no" or shaking their heads. If they indicated that they didn't want to participate, then if we chose their popsicle stick or index card, we would pretend it was another student and call on them instead.

ELL students are accommodated depending on their individual needs. If an ELL student is classified as intermediate or advanced in reading, listening, and speaking, we hold them to the same standards as all other students. ELL students who are classified as beginner or lower intermediate in reading, listening, and/or speaking receive more support when they are called on to provide a definition. For example, we will give them the definition in writing and ask them to read it aloud or we will provide the definition orally and ask them to repeat it. Some of our ELL students have electronic translators or translation apps on their cellphones, which we encourage them to use, especially during the game.

Although this appears to be solely extrinsically motivated, we've found that many students enjoy the game because they have the opportunity to prove they were listening to us during instruction. One specific class period comes to mind. Tara ran out of tickets and promised the last two students she would give them their tickets the next day. Both students responded, "It's okay, Mrs. Dale. We just like pointing out that you said the vocabulary words. It's fun to catch you before others do."

FAST FACTS WITH CLOZES

Fast Facts are exactly what they sound like: a paper with a list of facts that pertain to the current unit. Each Fast Fact is short, only one or two sentences, and contains a bolded vocabulary word. In other words, each one can be completed relatively quickly, which is why it is called a "fast" fact.

Fast Facts use the cloze technique for vocabulary building. Clozes, which are also known as fill-in-the-blanks, are effective tools to help students expand their knowledge of science terms, improve their abilities to use context clues, and enhance their critical thinking skills (Khoii & Poorafshari, 2018, p. 6).

We provide our students with Fast Facts at the beginning of a unit after they make the word walls. The bolded vocabulary words on the Fast Facts are the same words on the word walls.

The Fast Facts are a resource that students can access during the Word Wall Wall game and during other activities in the unit, such as labs.

Figure 7.5: Limiting Factors: Interactive Fast Facts is an example of one of the Fast Facts with clozes we use. It also includes a word bank that has been broken down into smaller sections. Figure 7.6 is the answer key for this cloze.

At the beginning of a lesson, we announce to the class the Fast Fact number we are going to learn first. Students are instructed to read the Fast Fact with a partner and make a guess, using context clues, about what word should go into the blank.

We then randomly choose a pair of students to share their answers. We discuss the word that was chosen by that student and their partner. In other words, we might ask them what context clues they used to make this guess. Sometimes students write a word in the blank that was not the one we had in mind, but it still makes sense. When this happens, it can be an excellent time to ask all of the students if there are other words that could work as well.

We've found that Fast Facts can help students with learning challenges. For example, a student might have an accommodation requiring the teacher to provide him/her with a copy of their notes. The Fast Facts are the notes we use in our classes, so all students receive this accommodation. This is especially helpful to students who have difficulty transferring information from the board or a slideshow to their paper. Note taking can be stressful for them and Fast Facts can make the process less overwhelming.

ELL students and others can be provided with a word bank for the clozes. When we give word banks, we break up the words into smaller groups so students are not overwhelmed with too many choices at once. We have included an example of an optional word bank at the bottom of Figure 7.5: Limiting Factors: Interactive Fast Facts.

During an average one-hour class period, we generally introduce and discuss three to five Fast Facts, teaching the students three to five new vocabulary words. We learned quickly that students will work ahead on their Fast Facts, which can lead to misconceptions and off-task behavior. As soon they complete Fast Fact #1 they sometimes skip ahead to Fast Fact #2 and miss the discussion and instruction pertaining to the first Fast Fact. To avoid this, we don't teach the Fast Facts in order. For example, on day one of a unit we may teach facts 4, 9, and 12 so that students can't predict which words will be taught next. Does this mean students will *never* jump ahead? No. Of course they will, but using this strategy reduces those occurrences.

We keep a running list of the Fast Facts we've learned. This list is maintained on one of our boards so when a student is absent, they can look at the list to identify which Fast Facts were covered during their absence.

DIFFERENTIATION FOR DIVERSE LEARNERS

In addition to the differentiation we explained in the Application section, one tool for differentiating vocabulary instruction is to include pictures with vocabulary words. ELL students can also benefit from seeing the definition in English and from being encouraged to write the definition in their home language.

Student Handouts and Examples

Figure 7.1: The Language of Introductory Ecology (Student Handout)
Figure 7.2: Vocabulary Definition Worksheet (Student Handout)
Figure 7.3: Word Wall Challenge Rubric (Student Handout)
Figure 7.4: Word Wall Examples

Figure 7.5: Limiting Factors: Interactive Fast Facts (Student Handout)

Figure 7.6: Limiting Factors: Interactive Fast Facts—Answer Key

What Could Go Wrong?

There will be times when students come up with inaccurate definitions throughout the various activities. It is obviously important to make corrections without making them feel "dumb." Building positive relationships and rapport with students can help them feel more comfortable making mistakes. It is also important, though, to set this expectation at the beginning of the year. Students need to be told no one will be ridiculed for mistakes because the only wrong answer is, "I don't know."

We encourage our students to have a growth mindset, which means through effort and practice they can get better at something (Dweck, 2006). Therefore, when a student does make a mistake, we may say something like, "That was a great attempt, you're almost there. Take a minute to think about it and try again." Depending on which activity we are using, we can instruct the student to pull out their resources, such as their prefix, suffix, and roots list or their Fast Facts and find the word again. If a student is still having difficulty, we can give him or her time to discuss with a peer before answering again. We have found it is important to give students the opportunity to correct their definitions if possible. This shows students they can do it and helps to build their self-confidence.

Technology Connections

An online dictionary for Greek and Latin roots can be found at "Root Words and Prefixes: Quick Reference" (https://www.learnthat.org/pages/view/roots.html). Another resource is the "English Language Roots Quick Chart" (http://prefixsuffix. com/rootchart.php?navblks=1011000).

A useful resource for creating vocabulary sentences is https://wordsina sentence.com.

There are many tools to help create clozes, which are on Larry Ferlazzo's blog, "The Best Tools for Creating Clozes (Gap-Fills)" (http://larryferlazzo.edublogs. org/2012/04/30/the-best-tools-for-creating-clozes-gap-fills).

Attributions

Thank you to Colby Martin and Ruby Garcia for allowing us to use their word walls for our student examples.

Figures

The Language of Introductory Ecology

Science words can be difficult to understand at times. However, many words can be broken into prefixes, suffixes, and/or roots that are common in science. Use the following prefixes, suffixes, and roots to help you break apart and determine the meanings of new vocabulary words you encounter throughout this ecology unit.

Word part	Meaning
a-	lacking, none
-able	worth, ability
adapt	to fit for a purpose, to adjust
-ate	used to change nouns into verbs
-ation	used to change verbs into nouns
auto-	self
bio-	life, living
calor-	heat
carn-	meat
cell-	storeroom, chamber
circum-	around, about
compose	to create
conserve	to keep safe, to guard
consume	to eat, to purchase
de-	away, from, down, reverse, against
dispersal/disperse	to scatter
diverse	very different
eco-	environment, household
en-	make, put in
ex-	out, out of, away from, lacking, former
extinguish	to wipe out, to obliterate
habitat	a place to live
herba	plant
-ic	quality, relation
in-	into, towards, on, near
invade	to go into, to attack
-ism	a state or condition
-ive	nouns: condition
-logy	study
native	natural, born in
non	not

Figure 7.1 The Language of Introductory Ecology (Student Handout)

Word part	Meaning
omni	all, every
pro-	for, forward
produce	to make, to create
re-	back, again
restore	to build up again, to repair
-trophy	food, nourishment
scavenge	to search for
spir	breath
system	a set of connected things
vor	eat greedily
-y	adjectives: marked by, having

For a more extensive list, see http://prefixsuffix.com/rootchart.php?navblks=1011000.

Figure 7.1 (Continued)

Name: _____

Vocabulary Definition Worksheet

Vocabulary Word	Definition (in your own words)	Picture (represents the word)

Figure 7.2   Vocabulary Definition Worksheet (Student Handout)

Name: _____

Limiting Factors Word Wall Challenge—Rubric

Place your assigned word here: _____ (spell it correctly!).
You get to choose your own grade. Place your desired grade here: _____.
You will turn in this rubric with the word wall but please do not staple them together.
Your word wall is due on _____.
If you want an A:

- the definition must be in your own words
- the definition must be written simple enough for a 7-year-old to understand it
- there can be no spelling or grammar errors
- the word wall must be colorful like a poster, and
- there must be at least three examples or pictures that explain how the word relates to limiting factors or ecology.

   If you want a B:

- the definition must be in your own words
- there can be no more than two spelling or grammar errors
- the word wall must be colorful like a poster, and
- there must be at least two examples or pictures that explain how the word relates to limiting factors or ecology.

   If you want a C:

- the definition must be in your own words
- there can be no more than four spelling or grammar errors
- the word wall must be colorful like a poster, and
- there must be at least one example or picture that explains how the word relates to limiting factors or ecology.

   If you do not earn a C on the word wall, then you will need to redo it until it is at least C work.

Figure 7.3 Word Wall Challenge Rubric (Student Handout)

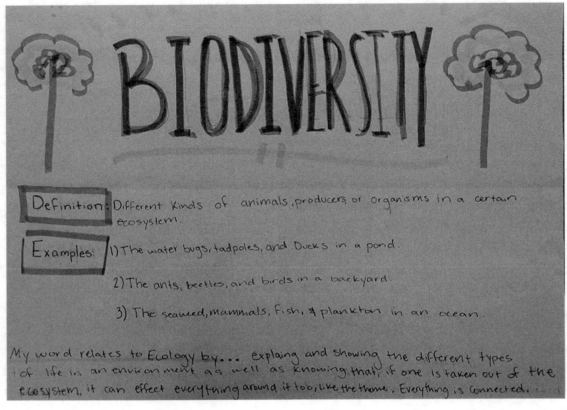

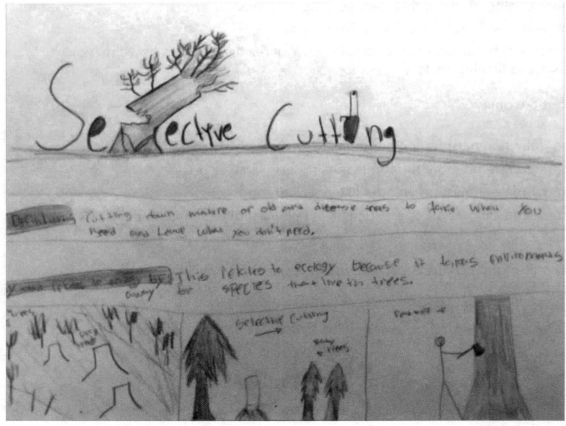

Figure 7.4 Word Wall Examples (Student Examples)

Name: _____

Fast Facts: Limiting Factors

1. A **predator** is the organism that does the _____ in a predation interaction.

2. **Prey** is an organism that is killed and _____ by another organism.

3. A **natural reserve** is a protected area of wildlife (both animals and producers) and _____ factors that support the local communities.

4. **Wildlife strikes** are when an organism (non-human) hits a manmade _____. For example, a deer is crossing the road and is hit by a car.

5. **Competition** is the struggle between organisms to survive as they attempt to use the _____ limited resource.

6. A **limiting factor** is an environmental factor that prevents a population from _____. All organisms have four limiting factors in common: food, water, shelter, and space.

7. **John Muir** (1838–1914) was a _____ who started the movement for wilderness areas to be preserved.

8. **Habitat restoration** is when humans make the effort to restore an _____ that was destroyed.

9. A **suburban** area is one that is just outside of the _____. People who live here usually have to travel into the city (the urban area) for work every day. You often hear people refer to a suburban area as "the burbs."

10. When a company cuts down an entire section of _____, it is called **clear cutting**.

11. **Biodiversity** is the number of different _____ in an area.

12. **Habitat destruction** is the loss of the natural _____.

13. **Conservation biology** is the study of how to _____ biodiversity.

14. **Habitat fragmentation** is when a habitat is divided into sections and the _____ decays.

15. **Urban development** is the process of constructing a larger _____. This means the natural environment is being destroyed as it is turned into roads, homes, schools, businesses, etc.

16. **Selective cutting** is the process of cutting down only some _____ in an area.

17. **Droughts** occur when there isn't enough _____ to sustain the community.

18. **Urban sprawl** is when human populations expand _____ from a central urban area. The best indicator is a population dependent on cars.

19. A **rural** area is one in which the homes and buildings are _____, usually because most of them are farmland. Many people refer to this as living in the country. Human populations are usually very small.

20. An **urban** area is called a city. This is characterized with homes and buildings that are very close together. Human populations are very dense here and there's usually public _____.

21. **Floods** occur when there is too much precipitation, causing excess _____ to accumulate and destroy natural habitats and people's homes.

22. The **Sierra Club** was established in 1892 as an environmental _____ organization.

23. An **urban heat island** is an area that has a considerable higher _____ because of human activity.

24. **Erosion** is caused by water and _____. It slowly wears down rocks, the foundation of buildings, and the sides of a river.

Figure 7.5 Limiting Factors: Interactive Fast Facts (Student Handout)

Word Bank—Choose the word which best fits in the blank for the Fast Facts

Fast Facts 1–4	object	killing	eaten	abiotic
Fast Facts 5–8	same	environment	increasing	conservationist
Fast Facts 9–12	habitat	species	forest	city
Fast Facts 13–16	city	trees	protect	ecosystem
Fast Facts 17–20	spread out	away	transportation	precipitation
Fast Facts 21–24	preservation	water	wind	temperature

Figure 7.5 (Continued)

Name: _____ *Answer Key*_____

Fast Facts: Limiting Factors

1. A **predator** is the organism that does the **killing** in a predation interaction.

2. **Prey** is an organism that is killed and **eaten** by another organism.

3. A **natural reserve** is a protected area of wildlife (both animals and producers) and **abiotic** factors that support the local communities.

4. **Wildlife strikes** are when an organism (non-human) hits a manmade **object**. For example, a deer is crossing the road and is hit by a car.

5. **Competition** is the struggle between organisms to survive as they attempt to use the **same** limited resource.

6. A **limiting factor** is an environmental factor that prevents a population from **increasing**. All organisms have four limiting factors in common: food, water, shelter, and space.

7. **John Muir** (1838 – 1914) was a **conservationist** who started the movement for wilderness areas to be preserved.

8. **Habitat restoration** is when humans make the effort to restore an **environment** that was destroyed.

9. A **suburban** area is one that is just outside of the **city**. People who live here usually have to travel into the city (the urban area) for work every day. You often hear people refer to a suburban area as "the burbs."

10. When a company cuts down an entire section of **forest**, it is called **clear cutting**.

11. **Biodiversity** is the number of different **species** in an area.

12. **Habitat destruction** is the loss of the natural **habitat**.

13. **Conservation biology** is the study of how to **protect** biodiversity.

14. **Habitat fragmentation** is when a habitat is divided into sections and the **ecosystem** decays.

15. **Urban development** is the process of constructing a larger **city**. This means the natural environment is being destroyed as it is turned into roads, homes, schools, businesses, etc.

16. **Selective cutting** is the process of cutting down only some **trees** in an area.

17. **Droughts** occur when there isn't enough **precipitation** to sustain the community.

18. **Urban sprawl** is when human populations expand **away** from a central urban area. The best indicator is a population dependent on cars.

19. A **rural** area is one in which the homes and buildings are **spread out**, usually because most of them are farmland. Many people refer to this as living in the country. Human populations are usually very small.

20. An **urban** area is called a city. This is characterized with homes and buildings that are very close together. Human populations are very dense here and there's usually public **transportation**.

21. **Floods** occur when there is too much precipitation, causing excess **water** to accumulate and destroy natural habitats and people's homes.

22. The **Sierra Club** was established in 1892 as an environmental **preservation** organization.

23. An **urban heat island** is an area that has a considerable higher **temperature** because of human activity.

24. **Erosion** is caused by water and **wind**. It slowly wears down rocks, the foundation of buildings, and the sides of a river.

Figure 7.6 Limiting Factors: Interactive Fast Facts—Answer Key

CHAPTER 8

Strategies for Teaching Reading Comprehension

What Is It?

The strategies in this chapter represent engaging ways to read and work with the many texts found in science classrooms in order to increase reading comprehension.

Why We Like It

Being able to read and comprehend informational text is a skill all students will need in life. Science classrooms provide opportunities to incorporate informational text into lessons. Reading can provide an opportunity for students to build background knowledge around new content. It can also help to extend knowledge after labs and other interactive activities.

The strategies highlighted in this section involve active learning and interaction among students. Additionally, the strategies can give students a purpose for their reading and maintain student engagement. All of the strategies require students to interact with the text multiple times, which can result in an increased understanding, especially of more complex texts.

Supporting Research

Studies have shown that literacy is a key factor in student achievement in science (Education Endowment Foundation, 2017).

Comprehending complex informational text is a challenge for many students. The use of reading strategies during multiple readings of the text can assist with comprehension (Frey & Fisher, 2013, pp. 57–58).

Skills for Intentional Scholars/NGSS Standards

The strategies shared in this chapter use the skills of thinking critically and communicating effectively. Students may think critically when they engage with a text multiple times for a given purpose. We rarely read a text in our classes without discussing it orally or in writing, which also helps students build communication skills.

Reading informational text for details and arguments is also an essential part of the Next Generation Science Standards. This requirement is embedded throughout many of the standards in every grade level (Achieve, Inc., 2017a).

Many of the strategies mentioned in this chapter reinforce the Next Generation Science Standards' crosscutting concepts (National Science Teaching Association [NSTA], n.d.). For example, the crosscutting concept of Systems and System Models requires students to understand how organized groups of objects are related to one another. Students deepen their understanding of systems when they complete various graphic organizers, which we explain in this chapter.

Application

We highlight four strategies for incorporating reading into science classrooms: close reading, graphic organizers, 4 × 4, and jigsaw.

CLOSE READING

Close reading is a strategy we use with complex texts. According to the Common Core Standards, the complexity of a text is determined by three things: (1) qualitative factors, such as levels of meaning, structure, and background knowledge required; (2) quantitative factors, which include grade level, lexile level, and overall measurable readability; and (3) reader and task factors, which consider reader motivation and experience, as well as purpose for reading (Common Core State Standards Initiative, 2019a, 2019b, 2019c). As we expose our students to increasingly complex texts, we need to provide effective strategies they can use to understand them.

Close reading can help students increase their comprehension and application of text because it requires a deeper dive into text to determine purpose, analyze meaning, and make inferences (Dakin, 2013, pp. 56–57). Note that you will not find the term "close reading" in the Common Core Standards; however, it is commonly used to describe the process we discuss in this section.

Our process of close reading starts with choosing a complex text and developing text-dependent questions. Next, we help students gain text annotation skills through multiple readings. Then, students are guided to use textual evidence to support their answers to the text-dependent questions. Finally, we show students how to put it all together through the steps of a "close read."

1. Choosing a Complex Text and Developing Text-Dependent Questions

When we plan for a close reading activity, we first find rich text (one that is complex and will build a deeper understanding) on a science concept. The text does not need to be an entire article. We have found that it works best if it is no longer than a page for younger readers and no more than two pages for older students. It could be an even smaller section of the text containing details we want to emphasize with students.

We next write text-dependent questions. These questions require students to return to the text to find not just the answer, but also evidence to support their response. Text-dependent questions should not ask students for simple facts, but, instead, require them to make inferences (educated guesses based on the text and background experiences) or draw conclusions. See Table 8.1 Examples of Text-Dependent Questions and Non-Text-Dependent Questions for concrete examples. Using text-dependent questions is a key part of meeting the English Language Arts Common Core standards at all levels (Common Core State Standards Initiative, 2010, p. 7).

2. Helping Students Gain Text Annotation Skills Through Multiple Readings

Before we can begin to follow the close reading process, we must first teach students what it means to annotate the text. Annotations are an essential part of close reading because they allow students to focus more deeply on a text (Fisher & Frey, 2013, p. 1). See Figure 8.1: Annotations, for the ones we use in our classrooms. They include noting unfamiliar words or phrases, writing questions, and making connections.

Table 8.1 Examples of Text-Dependent Questions and Non-Text-Dependent Questions

Examples of text-dependent questions	Examples of non-text-dependent questions
Based on what the paleontologist found at the dig site, what can we guess about the people who used to live there?	Was what the paleontologist found at the dig site interesting to you?
Using the article, explain why some people want to go to space.	Do you want to go to space?
The author discusses differences of living on Earth versus in space. What details are used to show this?	Based on the movies you've seen, what is one difference between living on Earth and living in space?

To teach these annotating strategies, we usually go through a text paragraph-by-paragraph with the students. We start by modeling this process through a think aloud, explaining why we are using each annotation. Figure 8.2: Annotations Model Think Aloud Example shows our annotations and the "think aloud" comments we shared with the class (seen in bold). Then, we have students work with a partner to annotate the next paragraph and ask a few to share what they wrote with the entire class. We find that students may favor one annotation and generally only use that one. For example, they may feel comfortable underlining important ideas, but don't use many of the other annotations. To increase their usage of other annotations, we specifically model how to use the "less popular ones."

3. Guiding Students to Use Textual Evidence to Answer Text-Dependent Questions

Once we have practiced the annotations with students, we also take time to model what it looks like to use textual evidence when answering text-dependent questions. We start by explaining why these questions require textual evidence and how the questions are different than others they may see elsewhere. We tell students that these types of questions usually do not ask for their opinions and will require them to understand the text. Text-dependent questions are important because they reinforce the idea of rereading something to ensure comprehension and reveal ideas students may have missed. We further explain that as they grow older, in either the workplace or college, they will need to have a more complete understanding of topics before engaging in important discussions or completing work.

We then model how to answer text-dependent questions by using the following process:

1. Read the question.
2. Re-read the text to find the information (text evidence) that best answers the question.
3. If the parts of the text that answer the question haven't yet been annotated, underline or highlight them.
4. Answer the question by using the quoted textual evidence.

When first writing with textual evidence, it can be helpful to provide students with sentence stems to get them started. Our favorite stems include:

- According to the text. . .
- In the text it states. . .
- The author of the text writes. . .

Once we model the process of answering text-dependent questions, we provide students with examples of questions and appropriate responses. For example, after reading an article about the history of how an intellectual chain reaction (one scientist has an idea that causes other scientists to have additional ideas) discovered fission and how fission itself is another type of chain reaction, we asked our students this text-dependent question: "Which of the two chain reactions in the article is the most important in today's world?" See Figure 8.3: Example of a Text-Dependent Question and Answer for an example of a student's answer. After reading and annotating the text, she made the decision that intellectual chain reactions were more important than fission. Her answer includes a quote regarding Albert Einstein's research that she chose as evidence to support her opinion.

4. Putting It All Together for the Close Reading Process

The close reading process we like to follow is:

1. *First Read*: gather information and annotate text.
   — During this time students are reading the text on their own and marking it with annotations. We are walking around to see if students need help.

2. *First Impressions*: students write down their first thoughts and/or the main idea.
   — Students are expected to write down the main idea of the article and their initial opinion either on the back of the text or a separate sheet of paper. They answer "who, what, where, when, why, and how" to help determine the main idea.

3. *Discussion*: share first impressions with a partner for 2 min.
   — While students are taking turns discussing what they wrote, we walk around to check for main ideas.

4. *Teacher Read*: students listen and make note of what is new to them.
   — We read the text aloud to the students so they can hear it while they are following along. We tell them to make note of new important information they may not have noticed when they read it on their own. We may highlight important parts of the text by either explicitly pointing it out or by emphasizing the words or phrases aloud as we are reading.

5. *Add to first impressions*: students add to their writing from step 2.
   — Students are given a few minutes to add to their initial writing and to adjust any of the "who, what, where, when, why, and how" answers, as well as modify their main ideas, if needed.

6. *Answer text-dependent questions*: students must re-read and support their answers using evidence from the selection either by highlighting or writing it down.

— Students answer the questions using the process explained in step 3.

7. *Optional*: students respond, in writing, to a prompt that is based on the text.

— If teachers would like students to respond to the text with a longer written response, they can present an additional prompt for the students. This prompt should be linked to the text-dependent questions and require students to use textual evidence. For example, a prompt that might relate to the first example in Table 8.1 could be: "Using textual evidence, describe three characteristics that can be inferred about the people who used to live where the paleontologist was digging." The written response could be anywhere from a few sentences to a few paragraphs depending on student writing levels and the overall purpose. See Chapter 9: Strategies for Teaching Writing for more ideas on incorporating writing into science lessons.

GRAPHIC ORGANIZERS

Graphic organizers are tools that help students visually organize information. Research has found that they are effective in helping students identify and recall main ideas from their reading and may increase comprehension (Manoli & Papadopoulou, 2012, p. 351). There are various types of graphic organizers that can be used in all subject areas, but in science class, our favorites are Venn Diagrams, Cause and Effect Organizers, and Concept Maps.

Venn Diagrams are used to compare and contrast two concepts, while Cause and Effect graphic organizers illustrate how causes lead to specific effects. Concept Maps show how concepts are related to each other.

Here are some specific examples of how we use these graphic organizers in our classes:

- Students can be given an article or text, which discusses two types of smog. They fill in the Venn Diagram on their own or with a partner. Figure 8.4: Photochemical and Industrial Smog Venn Diagram is a student example.

- Students can be given several reading selections about the effects humans have on the climate. They then use the information from those texts to fill out a Cause and Effect Graphic Organizer, which is a requirement of the crosscutting concepts published in the Next Generation Science Standards (NSTA, n.d.). Figure 8.5: Cultural Eutrophication Cause and Effect is a teacher's model of how students can complete a Cause and Effect Graphic Organizer.

- Students can be given a text on the water cycle and create a Concept Map during a class discussion. The Concept Map outlines each step of the cycle and how the steps are connected. Figure 8.6: Water Cycle Concept Map is an example of a Concept Map created by one of our students. When students are learning about the biogeochemical cycles, such as the water cycle, they are practicing the crosscutting concept of Systems and System Models (NSTA, n.d.).

- Students can be provided with a text, such as a story about the carbon cycle, found in Figure 8.7: Carbon Cycle Story. We have them read the story individually, underlining any time carbon changes the state of matter or location. Then we take them outside and give each student a piece of sidewalk chalk. Students work in pairs to draw a Concept Map of the carbon cycle. They are instructed to use arrows to depict when and how carbon changes. See Figure 8.8: Example of the Carbon Cycle for an example of what our students created with their chalk. This activity can be accomplished with any of the biogeochemical cycles. This can also be done in the classroom on paper or whiteboards, but going outside and using sidewalk chalk to do it makes it more engaging. It is another opportunity for students to practice the crosscutting concept of Systems and System Models.

- Students can be supplied with hints about a structure and then challenged to draw the structure, which is another example of a Concept Map. As an example, we give our students Figure 8.9: Hints for Drawing the Atmospheric Layers—High School. Students read the hints with a partner and draw the Earth and its five main layers of the atmosphere with details. This particular example was written for high school students so we shuffled the order of the hints in order to increase the rigor. When working with younger students, the hints are written in an order that doesn't require as much reading comprehension, which is provided in Figure 8.10: Drawing the Atmospheric Layers—Elementary and Junior High School. See Figure 8.11: Drawing the Atmospheric Layers—Answer Key for the teacher's answer key. This activity can easily be adapted to teach the layers of the Earth, the organization of a body system, and the structure of a plant or animal cell. When students are learning about structures such as these, they are practicing the crosscutting concept of Structure and Function (NSTA, n.d.), which requires students to understand that the shape of an object often determines its function and properties.

Students can also use Venn Diagrams, Cause and Effect Graphic Organizers, or Concept Maps to capture notes and reference while they are performing research. Students can also refer to their graphic organizers in preparation for assessments and writing projects.

See the Technology Connections section for online resources that offer free "blank" graphic organizers.

4 × 4

The 4 × 4 reading strategy we like requires students to read a text four times for four different purposes.

We start planning a 4 × 4 activity by choosing four topics that could be discussed within an article. For example, after teaching students the drawbacks of nuclear power plants, we have them read an article entitled "The Benefits of Nuclear Power." Four topics from the article that can be discussed are:

1. Cost
2. Land
3. Carbon dioxide (CO_2)
4. Radiation

After we find the article and identify the four topics, we follow these steps during the lesson:

1. Students are divided into groups of four. See later in this section for an explanation of how to divide an uneven class size.

2. Each group is given a large piece of paper or whiteboard and each group member receives a different colored writing utensil so we know the identity of the writer.

3. On the classroom board, we model what we want students to draw on their paper. We begin by drawing a square in the middle, which is where the theme of the article is written. In this case, "The Benefits of Nuclear Power" is written in the middle box. Students are instructed to duplicate this middle square on their paper.

4. Then, on the board, we draw four equal sections (see Figure 8.12: 4 × 4 for an example). Students do the same on their large papers.

5. Once everyone has the basic format written on their paper, we add the four section titles on the board to model how students should label their four sections. In our example, the four sections are titled, "cost," "land," "CO_2," and "radiation." We walk around to ensure students are following directions and correctly constructing their 4 × 4 papers. Note that to save time, these papers can be premade.

6. Each group member receives a copy of the article. They are instructed to read the text searching for any detail that pertains to the section's topic they have in front of them. They receive 2 min to read the text and write down at least one detail.

7. After 2 min, students are instructed to stand up and rotate clockwise so they are sitting in front of a new section. In other words, four students are sitting around one piece of paper and they are rotating around that piece of paper.

8. Students receive 30 s to read what the previous student wrote because they cannot duplicate it.

9. Students then receive 2.5 min (30 s more than the previous time) to read the article a second time, and search for an additional detail that pertains to this new topic.

10. This continues until every student has read the article four times—each time in search of a detail that hasn't yet been written down. And every time students switch seats, they receive an additional 30 s because they'll need this extra time to find the more obscure details their peers didn't find.

For difficult or long texts, students can rotate through the four topics more than one time. Also, the time limits can be flexible.

We provide an example of a completed 4 × 4 board in Figure 8.12: 4 × 4, which is a student-completed example for the Benefits of Nuclear Power.

Students subsequently have a small group discussion answering the following four standard questions, as well as deciding on a spokesperson:

1. What was something that you learned from the article?
2. What was something that surprised you while you read the article?
3. What are questions you have about one of the topics?
4. What was something that confused you during your reading?

In addition, we usually include a fifth question that is specific to the article's content. In this case, it might be "Why do cities choose to use nuclear power?"

They document the answers to these five questions on the backside of their 4×4 paper or article. We then discuss the answers as a class. We begin with the first question and have the spokesperson from each group share out their group's answer. All students have the opportunity to alter their answers based on reports from the other groups.

We love this technique because it allows students to read the text multiple times and work together to expand their understanding.

To extend this particular activity, students could follow the same steps while reading another text about the negative effects of nuclear power. Then, they can take a position and defend it using evidence from the readings either in writing or in an oral debate. This can be done for two sides of any topic using this process. Chapter 10: Strategies for Discussions includes resources for holding a friendly classroom debate.

If class size doesn't permit an even division of four students per group, this activity also works well with three students. Each student still reads the article four times and adds their comments to each of the four sections. And, they still benefit from the five questions they discuss after the activity, just like a group of four would. The only difference is that when the activity is complete, their four sections will have only three details from the article instead of four.

JIGSAW

Jigsaw reading is another strategy we often use in our classes. It requires each student to become an expert in one section of a text. They then teach what they learned to other students who have become experts on different portions of the text. Research has shown that the jigsaw technique can increase engagement and student learning (Tewksbury, n.d.).

To use the jigsaw method, we first divide the text into sections based on concepts or natural breaking points. We attempt to make each section about the same length. However, in order to differentiate for ELL students or students with reading challenges, we often create more accessible sections of text for them (see the "Differentiation for Diverse Learners" section for ideas on how to "engineer" texts to increase their accessibility).

Once we have sectioned the text, the steps are as follows:

1. Inform students which sections they will be reading—if differentiating, we always decide ahead of time so students get the appropriate sections.

2. Students then read their sections to themselves, annotate, and take notes on important ideas—we point out that their goal is to answer the "who, what, where, when, why, and how" for their section.

3. Students meet with other students who read the same section to review notes and add other ideas they may have missed. They may also each create a poster to assist with their teaching.

4. While they are in these groups, students are handed a letter based on the section of the text they read—for example, if there were five sections, the letters A, B, C, D, and E would be used.

5. Students then must get into their letter groups. In other words, each group would have an A, B, C, D, and E representative. Note: if there are not enough group members for each to be represented, the teacher may need to sit in.

6. Students then take turns teaching their section of the text to the other students, while they take notes. The notes can follow the format of answering the "who, what, where, when, why, and how" questions to get the main points of the section. They can use these notes during the following whole-class discussion and refer back to them throughout the unit.

7. We come together as a class and review the key concepts as a whole.

We've often found it helps to have directions up on the board while students are using Jigsaw. Figure 8.13: Jigsaw Instructions is a list of instructions we put on the screen in our rooms and reveal one by one as we are going through the process.

DIFFERENTIATION FOR DIVERSE LEARNERS

In order to "amplify the text" instead of simplifying it, we often take the same text and "engineer it" to increase its accessibility (Billings & Walqui, n.d.). We can "engineer" it by:

- chunking the text into smaller sections
- creating wider margins (i.e., more white space) for annotations
- adding headings
- providing vocabulary definitions
- including focus questions to help guide student reading

For example, if we have an eight-paragraph article, we would break it down into sections of one to two paragraphs with a heading based on the topic of the smaller section. We would also add definitions for any unfamiliar vocabulary words, as well as a focus question for each section. Adding in white space can allow for students to write notes in the text while reading. These steps make longer texts more accessible to students who may have reading challenges.

Some students, however, may require alternative or modified texts. While we want students to feel challenged, we do not want to frustrate them. We will either find a similar text at a lower reading level or only ask them to focus on specific sections. Another tool we have found that is helpful is called Rewordify, https://rewordify.com. This website instructs teachers to place their chosen text into a box and then it will simplify the language. See the Technology Connections section for more online resources.

When using graphic organizers, students who may have difficulty writing can be given premade copies to fill in. We also draw out Concept Maps ahead of time for students who may need the extra help and just have students fill in labels as we go over them.

To help readers facing challenges or ELL students, we often give them the text the day before we read it in class so they can preview it. If available, we can also provide ELL students with the text in their home language (see the Technology Connections section for resources). Another idea for these students is finding videos (in English or in their home language) that are related to the content in the text. The students view the videos prior to the lesson to build necessary background knowledge (see the Technology Connections section for suggested resources).

Student Handouts and Examples

Figure 8.1: Annotations

Figure 8.2: Annotations Model Think Aloud Example (Teacher Model)

Figure 8.3: Example of a Text-dependent Question and Answer (Student Example)

Figure 8.4: Photochemical and Industrial Smog Venn Diagram (Student Example)

Figure 8.5: Cultural Eutrophication Cause and Effect (Teacher Model)

Figure 8.6: Water Cycle Concept Map (Student Example)

Figure 8.7: Carbon Cycle Story (Student Handout)

Figure 8.8: Example of the Carbon Cycle (Student Example)

Figure 8.9: Hints for Drawing the Atmospheric Layers—High School (Student Handout)

Figure 8.10: Drawing the Atmospheric Layers—Elementary and Junior High School

Figure 8.11: Drawing the Atmospheric Layers—Answer Key

Figure 8.12: 4 × 4 (Student Example)

Figure 8.13: Jigsaw Directions

What Could Go Wrong?

While we find close reading to be an excellent strategy for deeper learning, it can take the fun out of reading if used too often. When Mandi first learned of the strategy, she used it several weeks in a row on all texts read in class before realizing the student grumblings were due to her overuse. Reading a text over and over again can begin to get monotonous for students and teachers and is not necessary with all texts. We would suggest that—at most—close reading be used once per month.

Technology Connections

When looking for articles and other science texts, there are many online resources out there. One of our favorites is Newsela: www.newsela.com, which allows you to search by science content, provides multiple written texts, different lexile levels, and contains text-dependent questions. On Newsela, teachers can also set up classes (at a cost) for their students to join and they can access the text and questions online, which is useful practice for online assessments.

Another favorite is CommonLit; www.commonlit.com. While CommonLit is more English-content focused, there are also articles based on science topics. This website allows teachers to create classes and select texts based on lexile levels that come with text-dependent questions.

More options for texts can be found on Larry Ferlazzo's Websites of the Day Blog, "The Best Places to Get the 'Same' Text Written for Different 'Levels'": http://larryferlazzo.edublogs.org/2014/11/16/the-best-places-to-get-the-same-text-written-for-different-levels.

Resources for finding texts and videos in multiple languages can be found at "The Best Multilingual & Bilingual Sites for Math, Social, Studies, & Science": http://larryferlazzo.edublogs.org/2008/10/03/the-best-multilingual-bilingual-sites-for-math-social-studies-science.

For resources to find blank graphic organizers, visit "The Best List of Mindmapping, Flow Chart Tools, & Graphic Organizers": http://larryferlazzo.edublogs.org/2009/02/09/not-the-best-but-a-list-of-mindmapping-flow-chart-tools-graphic-organizers.

Attributions

Thank you to Brianna Miller, who allowed her Venn Diagram to be used.

Thank you to Kaden Neal, Jodi Peterson, Dominic Pedretti, and Conner Anderson for the picture of their 4 × 4 on the benefits of nuclear power.

Thank you to Irelyn Humphries, who allowed us to include her answer to a text-dependent question.

Thank you to Irelyn and her learning partner, Hannah Zicafoose, for their example of the carbon cycle.

Thank you to Emma Wylie, who allowed us to use her water cycle concept map.

Figures

<u>Underline</u> important ideas

○ words or phrases you don't understand

? next to text you are confused about or something you are wondering—write the question

! next to text that surprised you or made you say WOW!

→ next to text when you make a connection to it—write the connection

Figure 8.1 Annotations

Unfortunately, thermal power plants also have potential environmental drawbacks. The environment is harmed because although scrub brushes remove the ash from the coal's smoke, they cannot remove single atoms of pollution. <u>Nitrogen and sulfur are in coal smoke that when released into the air eventually lead to acid rain, changes in soil chemistry, and a loss of forests.</u> (*"I am going to underline this sentence because it is a main idea of an environment drawback of thermal power plants."*) Coal is mined out of the ground, which requires mining companies to ⟨clear-cut forests⟩ (*"I am unsure of the phrase clear-cut forests, so I am circling it to remind myself to go back and look it up."*), which in turn <u>increases the chance of erosion</u> (*"This is another main idea of a drawback so I am underlining it."*). Using coal as an energy source is potentially very negative on the environment.

Thermal power plants can cause health issues in many animal populations, including humans. When coal is burned, it releases pollutants, such as carbon (C) that is so small the scrub brushes miss them. This carbon (C) mixes with oxygen (O_2) to make carbon monoxide (CO2). <u>People who are exposed to too much CO2 experience headaches, vomiting, and eventually death</u> (*"I am going to underline this because it is a main idea, but also am drawing an arrow to show that I made a connection with this statement. It reminds me of a news story I saw on tv one time of a family who was getting sick all of the time and did not realize it was because of elevated levels of carbon monoxide in their home."*). Burning coal also releases carbon dioxide (CO_2). Making electrical energy via the burning of coal causes 25% of all CO_2 that is released into the atmosphere.! (*"I am going to place an exclamation point here because this point makes me think wow!"*). This is bad because CO_2 is one of the major greenhouse gases that accelerates global warming. The average new car weighs about 4,000 pounds. <u>Compare this to the amount of CO_2 that is released by thermal power plants in the United States: 10 billion tons per year, which equates to the weight of 5 million cars.</u>! (*"I am underlining and putting an exclamation point here. It not only shows just how big of a health risk thermal power plants can cause, but also makes me think wow because of how much it is."*). This means that when we breathe, we are breathing CO_2 and that can cause headaches, nausea, a coma, and death. Thermal power plants are a cheap way to make electrical energy but they have serious health and environmental effects.

news story on TV about a family getting sick.

Figure 8.2 Annotations Model Think Aloud Example (Teacher Model)

> **Which of the two chain reactions is the most important in today's world?**
>
> "An intellectual chain reaction is the reaction of one idea being triggered, which triggers more ideas and then even more, etc. In 1943, something known as the Manhattan Project resulted in the formation of the first atomic bomb. This is a perfect example of the intellectual chain reaction. In the article, "What Is Fission," Redd states that, "Einstein noted that such research could be used to create an epic bomb of proportions" (3). To this day, the idea of the atomic bomb is still being recreated and ideas are still being added to make it better."—Irelyn Humphries, 15

Figure 8.3 Example of a Text-Dependent Question and Answer (Student Example)

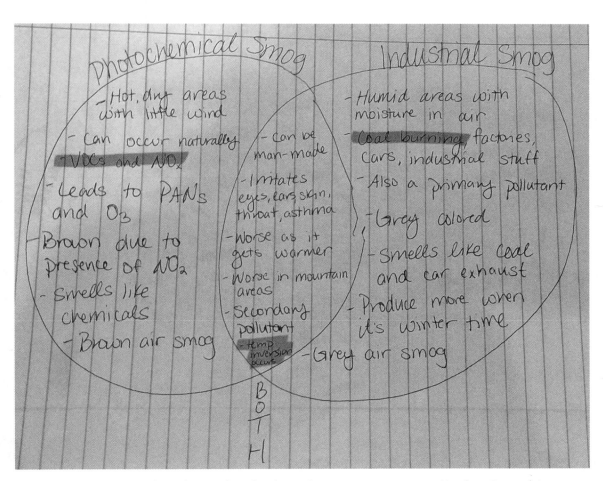

Figure 8.4 Photochemical and Industrial Smog Venn Diagram (Student Example)

Name: _____

Cause and Effect of Cultural Eutrophication

Directions: Below are ten events that need to be put in order from start to finish. Box one is done for you. Can you determine the rest? Hint: As you determine where each event belongs, cross out the event in the word bank, as we've done with box one.

Without oxygen, fish die of hypoxia	Algal blooms occur	Algae eventually die, aerobic bacteria eat it, depleting the lake of dissolved oxygen (these bacteria have high BOD)	Most coliform bacteria are deactivated because they are both aerobic and anaerobic	What little oxygen is left after fish die is used by aerobic bacteria to decompose algae, while anaerobic bacteria increase their productivity
Note: Most often occurs during droughts and hot weather.	Lake's overall productivity begins to lower, reducing fish growth	Anaerobic bacteria produce gas, such as hydrogen sulfide and methane, as they decompose products	~~Anthropogenic sources increase the nutrients (nitrates and phosphates) to an unhealthy level.~~	Algae cover the surface, depleting the sunlight for the lower layers of the lake or river

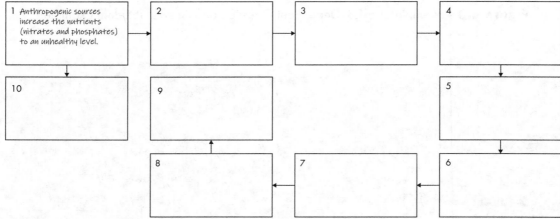

Figure 8.5 Cultural Eutrophication Cause and Effect (Teacher Model)

Figure 8.6   Water Cycle Concept Map (Student Example)

The Carbon Cycle Story

This is a story about how carbon moves through earth systems. There are many steps of the carbon cycle and they do NOT occur in any particular order. In that way, it's very similar to the water cycle.

All living things are made of carbon; we refer to them as organic. Things that are not made of carbon, such as water, gold, and silver, are referred to as inorganic.

Carbon is a part of the ocean, air, and rocks. Because the Earth is a dynamic (ever-changing) place, carbon does not stay still. It is always on the move in a cycle called the carbon cycle!

In the atmosphere, one carbon atom is attached to two oxygen atoms, which makes a gas called carbon dioxide (CO_2). Producers use sunlight and carbon dioxide from the atmosphere to make their food and grow. This is called photosynthesis. The carbon becomes part of the producer.

When producers die, one of two things can happen to them. Some producers are decomposed by bacteria and fungi. During the decomposition process, the bacteria and fungi release the producers' CO_2 into the atmosphere. Some producers do not decompose and are instead buried and turned into fossil fuels. This organic material can eventually be turned into oil or coal. Combustion is when humans burn fossil fuels to make electricity. Combustion releases the carbon that was once in the producers and places it into the atmosphere as carbon dioxide.

Animals obtain their carbon by eating producers or other animals. Animals release carbon into the soil when they excrete waste and release carbon into the air when they fart. Farts aren't CO_2 but are instead made of methane gas, which is CH_4. Animals also exhale carbon back into the atmosphere as CO_2. This is called respiration.

The oceans are large enough to pull carbon dioxide out of the air. But be careful because as the oceans warm, they are less able to do so.

Most people believe that producers only release oxygen into the atmosphere, but producers also release carbon dioxide into the atmosphere, which is called transpiration. And most people believe that humans only release CO_2 into the atmosphere but we also release a little bit of oxygen. When we release these gases, it is called respiration.

Figure 8.7   Carbon Cycle Story (Student Handout)

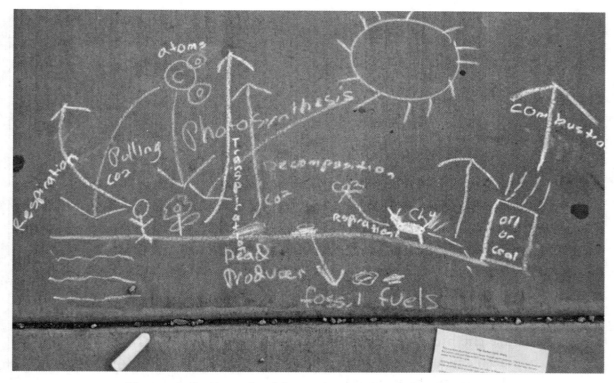

Figure 8.8   Example of the Carbon Cycle (Student Example)

Hints for Drawing the Earth's Atmosphere

Hint #1: The Earth is not a perfect sphere, but is often drawn that way.

Hint #2: The ozone layer is not its own layer but is instead the bottom portion of the stratosphere. It's hot here because O_3, which is called ozone, absorbs the sun's radiation.

Hint #3: The atmosphere has five primary layers.

Hint #4: Organisms breathe the troposphere. This is also where clouds hang out.

Hint #5: The International Space Station revolves around Earth in the thermosphere. The air here is the second to receive the sun's heat so it can be very hot in the thermosphere: positive 815 °C (1,500 °F)!

Hint #6: The troposphere's temperature decreases as altitude increases because the higher air is thinner, so it can't hold on to the sun's heat or the Earth's heat. For example, it's colder at the top of a mountain than it is at the base of the mountain.

Hint #7: Airplanes fly in the stratosphere, so they are above stormy weather.

Hint #8: The mesosphere is where meteorites burn up, which we often refer to as shooting stars. The air here is thick enough to slow down meteorites before they enter the stratosphere and troposphere to bop us on the head.

Hint #9: The exosphere is the outermost layer. It's so hot during the day that it can reach 1,700 °C (3,092 °F) and it's so cold at night that it can reach 0 °C (32 °F).

Hint #10: The stratosphere turns the sun's UV light into heat. It acts as the Earth's sunscreen. Its temperature increases as the altitude increases. It also reflects about 95% of the sun's radiation back into space.

Hint #11: The mesosphere is thinner than the other layers, meaning it doesn't have a lot of air molecules. The higher the altitude, the colder the temperature. This is where the atmosphere is the coldest. Negative 101 °C (-130 °F)!

Figure 8.9   Hints for Drawing the Atmospheric Layers—High School (Student Handout)

Hints for Drawing the Earth's Atmosphere

Hint #1: The Earth is not a perfect sphere, but is often drawn that way.

Hint #2: The atmosphere has five primary layers.

Hint #3: Organisms breathe the troposphere. This is also where clouds hang out.

Hint #4: The troposphere's temperature decreases as altitude increases because the higher air is thinner, so it can't hold on to the sun's heat or the Earth's heat. For example, it's colder at the top of a mountain than it is at the base of the mountain.

Hint #5: Airplanes fly in the stratosphere, so they are above stormy weather.

Hint #6: The ozone layer is not its own layer but is instead the bottom portion of the stratosphere. It's hot here because O_3, which is called ozone, absorbs the sun's radiation.

Hint #7: The stratosphere turns the sun's UV light into heat. It acts as the Earth's sunscreen. Its temperature increases as the altitude increases. It also reflects about 95% of the sun's radiation back into space.

Hint #8: The mesosphere is where meteorites burn up, which we often refer to as shooting stars. The air here is thick enough to slow down meteorites before they enter the stratosphere and troposphere to bop us on the head.

Hint #9: The mesosphere is thinner than the other layers, meaning it doesn't have a lot of air molecules. The higher the altitude, the colder the temperature. This is where the atmosphere is the coldest. Negative 101 °C (-130 °F)!

Hint #10: The International Space Station revolves around Earth in the thermosphere. The thermosphere is the second layer to receive the sun's heat, so it can be very hot here: positive 815 °C (1,500 °F)!

Hint #11: The exosphere is the outermost layer. It's so hot during the day that it can reach 1,700 °C (3,092 °F) and it's so cold at night that it can reach 0 °C (32 °F).

Figure 8.10 Drawing the Atmospheric Layers—Elementary and Junior High School

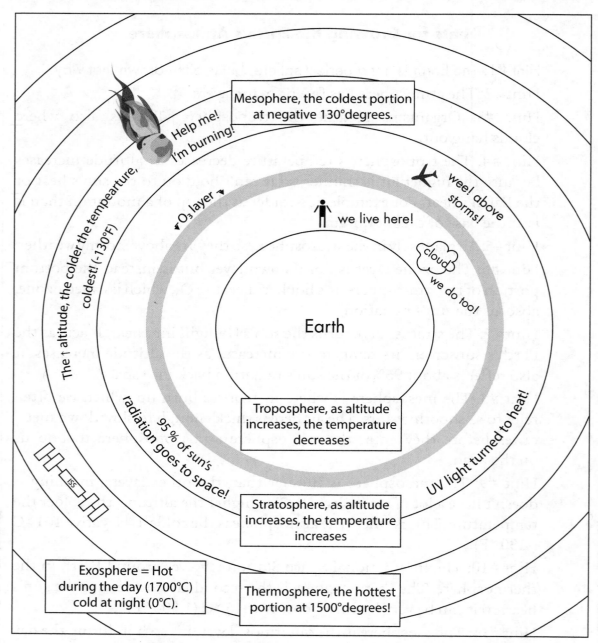

Figure 8.11 Drawing the Atmospheric Layers—Answer Key

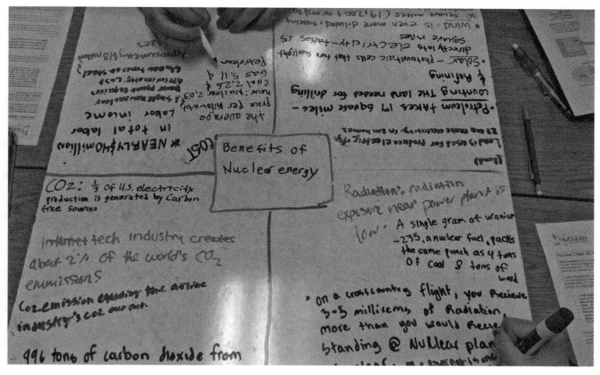

Figure 8.12 4 × 4 (Student Example)

1. Write down and mark off which section of the text you are reading.
2. Read and annotate your section.
3. Write notes about your section:

   - Main ideas
   - Important terms
   - Answer who, what, where, when, why, and how

4. Discuss your notes with the other students who read your section.
5. Add at least two new ideas to your notes.
6. Meet with your letter groups and teach your section to the other students.
7. Take notes as other students are teaching you their sections.

Figure 8.13 Jigsaw Directions

CHAPTER 9

Strategies for Teaching Writing

What Is It?

As with reading, writing is critical to any science classroom. Writing strategies for science can employ active learning and critical thinking as students write about concepts they have been learning in class.

Why We Like It

As science teachers, we are not necessarily teaching the mechanics of writing (however, depending upon the skills of our students, we might be doing some of that, too). The ideas in this chapter are examples of how writing can increase the understanding of science concepts while also helping students become better writers.

When many people think of science writing, they think of lab reports. However, there are other types of writing that occur within a science classroom. Common Core Standards stress the importance of writing in all areas, including science. We create multiple opportunities for expanding students' writing skills through narrative, informative/explanatory, and argument writing (Common Core State Standards, n.d.).

All of the methods we present here require higher-level thinking in order to take science knowledge to a deeper level. Most of them also require research and reading for information before students can begin their writing assignments. Students need to be able to understand a concept in order to write about it effectively. In addition, writing can also be a tool to clarify both understandings and misunderstandings. In our science classes, as the saying goes, "students are learning to write while writing to learn."

Supporting Research

Research has shown that students who write about concepts tend to better under-stand them. Regardless of the length of their writing, students show greater learning when they write about a concept than when they do not write about it (Nevid, Pastva, & McClelland, 2012).

Studies have also found that as students are exposed to more writing opportuni-ties in science class, they improve their abilities to write about science topics and to draw conclusions (Libarkin & Ording, 2012).

Skills for Intentional Scholars/NGSS Connections

Writing can build both critical thinking and effective communication skills for stu-dents. Students must use knowledge they have learned and apply it in written form, which requires them to use higher-level thinking and refine their written communi-cation skills.

Writing is also required in the Next Generation Science Standards. Students are expected to be able to use data and concepts throughout all grades to present argu-ments and communicate information adequately (Next Generation Science Standards, 2017).

Application

We first review three strategies that support all types of student writing: "Following the Writing Process," "Using Rubrics/Checklists," and "Models."

Then, we discuss extended writing activities that fall into the categories of narra-tive, informative/explanatory, and argument. All of these types of writing are included within the Common Core writing standards (Core State Standards Initiative, n.d.).

In addition, our concluding section shares several ways to incorporate writing on a daily basis in science class.

FOLLOWING THE WRITING PROCESS

Students typically learn the writing process through their English Language Arts classes. Research has shown that when students are taught and follow the steps of the writing process, they tend to be more proficient writers (Pritchard & Honeycutt, 2005). Sometimes the writing process steps vary, but most of them include the following five steps:

1. *Prewriting—* students brainstorm their ideas and get them down on paper. It has been found to be one of the most effective steps for students becoming better writers (Kamehameha Schools, 2007).

2. *Drafting*— the stage when students take their ideas from the prewrite to create a draft of their writing assignment.

3. *Revising*— once the first draft is done, students then read back through their writing, receive feedback from others, and make revisions to improve it.

4. *Editing*— students proofread for any spelling or grammar errors.

5. *Publishing*— once students have made all necessary changes, they create their final version. This final version could be "published" by sharing with classmates and turning it into the teacher. It could also be literally published for others to read. See the Technology Connections section for a list of sites.

Most students are familiar with this process from other content areas so, in theory, we don't need to teach it to them. However, it's never good to make assumptions. Reviewing, re-teaching, and supporting these steps in our classes can only result in better writing and learning for our students. The writing process not only allows students to make many changes to improve their writing, but also allows various opportunities for us to check in throughout an assignment to ensure they are on the right track.

Do we and our students follow this precise formula every single time we do an extended writing activity? No! Time, unexpected learning opportunities, teacher illnesses, school vacations, etc., happen. Do we do our best to have students use each of these steps? Yes! Is student writing generally better when they follow all these steps? Yes! Do we beat ourselves up when we have to take shortcuts? No!

USING RUBRICS OR CHECKLISTS

We also give students a rubric or checklist for most writing activities. Providing rubrics tends to increase writing performance because students better understand the requirements (Andrade, 2001). ④

However, we do not simply give them the checklist or rubric and send them off to write. We have found that taking the time to go over the expectations for the assignment leads to better writing. One way we like to introduce a rubric or checklist is by having students highlight key words or phrases and add notes to it while we discuss. For example, the rubric may require students to have three details with text evidence to earn five points. We have students highlight "three details" and "text evidence" so they understand these are required within this assignment. The rubric is a resource that students can reference throughout the writing process to ensure they have all of the required items.

As students develop more writing experience, an alternative to providing them with a rubric is to invite them to help create their own. Research shows that student-created rubrics can lead to a better final product (Ferlazzo, 2019). We discuss this process in the next section. ⑤

MODELS

Using models to demonstrate effective writing is another helpful strategy. Research suggests that using models can be a more effective way to communicate expectations than rubrics (Lemov, 2015a, 2015b). Before we start any type of writing, we show students exemplars of what the writing should look like and walk them through each part. This process does take extra work on our part, though, because we are often the ones who need to write the example or possibly multiple examples, especially if it is the first time we have done this writing type in our classrooms. However, we can also use student examples from previous years.

The models may not be ones responding to the exact prompt students will be using in their assignment. Instead, they may be examples that respond to the same *type* of prompt—narrative, informative/explanatory, or argument. Using those examples reduces the chances of students just copying parts of the model response.

For models to be even more effective, we often go through the rubric or checklist using the model. Having the students use the rubric or checklist to "grade" the example allows them to better understand the expectations on the rubric or checklist. We often go through the example section by section and highlight specific parts that relate to sections of the rubric or checklist. We start by showing the students how to use the first section of the rubric to assess the example, and then have them work together with partners to highlight the other sections according to the rubric. We finish by having a whole class discussion to compare what everyone highlighted and allow them to correct any areas they may have missed.

An alternative to this activity is to have students use the models to assist in *creating* the rubric. This can be done by having students work together to break down each part of the model writing selections. Students can work in pairs or small groups to identify what areas of the writing are strong and essential to include in their work. They can also discuss what aspects of the writing are important in order to effectively respond to the prompt. Once each pair or small group has completed this task, the class can come together and share ideas to decide on which ones they agree should be integrated into the rubric. The teacher can type these expectations into a form to create the rubric during or after the discussion.

We have also found it to be effective to use bad examples, as well. It has been determined that student writing quality benefits from analyzing weak exemplars (To & Carless, 2015, p. 759). This alternative is particularly useful if we see students making similar mistakes in their writing. We can write an example of a section of "bad" writing—for example, it may not provide enough detail. Then, we display this text for the students to see and have them analyze it with partners. We next ask them to identify any areas of improvement. This process allows us to support students as a whole group instead of having to provide the same specific feedback to individual students.

NARRATIVE

Narrative writing is when a story or sequence of events is told through written form. This kind of text can either be fiction, where the events are made up, or nonfiction, when it is based on real-life occurrences (Literary Devices, n.d.).

Narrative writing is often the most creative type of writing we can do in science classrooms. It allows students to have fun while demonstrating their understanding of science concepts. They can often explain a scientific concept or process through the form of a story. An example of a narrative writing activity is to have students write a children's book that explains a scientific concept in "story form." Kristi Simpson, a sixth grade teacher at Mandi's school, has her students write a children's book about a severe weather phenomenon, which is one of the concepts within her curriculum (we share other ideas for the secondary classroom at the end of this section).

She starts by presenting the types of severe weather that students are expected to know, which are hurricane, tornado, thunderstorm, blizzard, flood, and drought. This introduction can be done through playing a short video and/or presentation with pictures of each weather type. The goal is to "hook" students into the project by showing images of severe weather and its impacts before students start the writing assignment.

Once students have been introduced to the weather phenomena, they are asked to choose which one they would like to research and use in their book. Teachers can balance free choice with a need to have a similar number of students reporting on each of the phenomena. They are given the assignment directions, a guide to help them with research, and the scoring guide. Figure 9.1: Severe Weather Book Project Research and Figure 9.2: Severe Weather Book Project Scoring Guide were developed by Kristi to give to students at the start of the project. These two worksheets guide students through the assignment. Figure 9.3: Severe Weather Book Project Research Example is a model of what this worksheet could look like for students.

In Chapter 8: Strategies for Teaching Reading Comprehension, we discussed how graphic organizers are effective in guiding reading and documenting important details. Graphic organizers can also support prewriting. For the Severe Weather Book Project, Figure 9.1 is used to help students take notes during their research and also allows them to better understand the required details of the assignment. Students use this resource to research their chosen weather phenomenon online or with provided texts. See Chapter 3: Strategies for Teaching the Scientific Method and Its Components for more information on performing research.

Narrative writing must have a plot, which is the sequence of events the story follows. Students need to be able to prewrite their story's sequence of events to ensure the proper order. To do this we like to provide students with a plot map outline, which allows them to plan the events so they have all needed parts of a narrative. See Figure 9.4: Plot Map Outline for an example of a blank outline we use often.

Many students are familiar with the elements of a typical story plot (of course, not *all* narratives follow this exact order) from instruction in their English Language Arts classes, but we like to review it with them by going over each part with a quick definition and example.

- *Exposition*— The exposition is the introduction of the story when the characters, setting, and conflict (overall problem) are established.
- *Rising Action*— The series of events that builds within the story and often creates complications within the conflict (often the longest part of the story).
- *Climax*— The turning point of the story and usually intended to create the most excitement and build-up.
- *Falling Action*— The events that occur as the story is wrapping up and complications are being resolved.
- *Resolution*— The conclusion of the story.

Students complete plot maps after we review parts of a story and student research is finished. Figure 9.5: Severe Weather Book Plot Map Example is a model of what a plot map could look like. While students are doing both their research and plot maps, we are monitoring and answering any questions they may have. We tell them that we must check off on both papers before they begin to actually write their books. Teachers checking off on prewriting papers is important so we can conference with students to be sure they are on the right track with their writing ideas before they begin.

Some students may need extra support applying their research to a narrative. This kind of assistance could include:

- Asking students to highlight up to six key words in each box on Figure 9.1 can help them narrow down the research they want to include in their narrative.
- Providing models in real time—as students work on their Plot Maps, the teacher can "borrow" them at various stages of completion to show others or the whole class using a document camera.

The next part of the assignment requires them to create a rough draft of the book. We provide students with blank paper and encourage them to use pencil only so they can erase and do over mistakes. Again, we do not allow them to move on to the final copy of their children's book until we have checked off that they have a completed draft.

After their rough draft is reviewed by the teacher, they begin working on their final copies. In elementary grades, a narrative writing project can take three to five 50–60 min class periods. This time can be adjusted based on the amount of time teachers have allotted for their science classes and based on the levels of students. Secondary students may be able to complete it in less time because their research and writing skills are more advanced than those in lower grades. Teachers should plan for an approximate number of days to ensure ample time if students have difficulty during any part of the process.

To extend the assignment so students learn about all of the severe weather types, teachers can have students present their books to classmates in groups of six in a Jigsaw type activity. See Chapter 8: Strategies for Teaching Reading Comprehension for more details on the Jigsaw process. A class discussion of all the weather types and notes can then take place before any final assessment of their weather phenomenon knowledge. This project can also be done as a final assessment and follow teacher-led instruction on the weather types.

Other narrative writing ideas that could use a similar process (research, prewrite by developing a plot map, create draft, revise, and edit after teacher review, write, and publish final version) and be appropriate for secondary students include:

- a first person narrative of a french fry traveling through the body (digestion)
- a first person narrative of a bumblebee pollinating a flower (pollination)
- a journal entry outlining an astronaut's experiences traveling in the solar system (astronomy)
- a journal entry of a rock changing over millions of years (rock cycle)
- a story about a human who has adapted to a change in the environment, focusing on the adaptation and how it's useful (evolution)

Students can also turn their stories into online presentations. See the Technology Connections section for ideas and resources.

INFORMATIVE/EXPLANATORY

Informative/explanatory writing is an objective form that requires the description of an idea or process. Essentially, the writer is providing information to the reader without adding any opinions (Your Dictionary, n.d.).

Informative writing may not always be the most exciting writing, but it can be an effective tool to determine if students understand specific concepts and ideas. For example, the previous example of the Severe Weather Children's Book from the

Narrative section above can also be used as a form of informative writing. This activity can be done as a step-by-step process in the form of an essay describing how a weather phenomenon occurs, what happens during the phenomenon, and its aftermath. In this case, the writing would be in the third person and, instead of having characters and a story centered on the severe weather, it would reflect an objective explanation of the phenomenon.

When students are writing an informative essay, we like to provide them with additional instruction on transition words for sequencing. Oftentimes students will use *then* and *next* over and over again, which would be fine for basic writing that only requires describing a few steps in a process. However, when completing a longer writing assignment, they will need to utilize other vocabulary. Table 9.1 is an example of transition words that we provide to students. We like to challenge them to only use a particular word once or twice, at most, in their written work. These words are not only effective for informational writing, but can also be used within all three types of writing.

Another example of an informative/explanatory writing assignment is one that our colleagues, Alex Ostrow and Maryann Ramseyer, developed for their sixth grade science classrooms. The curriculum requires them to teach students about various diseases and their effects. Alex and Maryann utilize class notes and videos to teach students about each disease. Students then demonstrate their knowledge by creating a public service announcement (PSA) in the form of a comic strip.

Even though this particular assignment is focused on a comic strip, we use the same steps for every informative/explanatory writing project. They are:

1. Introduce assignment and go over the checklist or rubric.
2. Research topic and prewrite through using a graphic organizer.
3. Create draft of writing project.
4. Teacher/student conference to review draft.
5. Revise and edit project.
6. Write final draft and publish.

Table 9.1 Sequence Transition Words

after	later	last	until	since
then	next	first, second. . .	before	by the time
all of a sudden	now	whenever	eventually	meanwhile
at the same time	as soon as	to begin with	during	prior to
until now	immediately	instantly	suddenly	occasionally
straightaway	in due time	without delay	finally	once

This assignment is introduced by presenting a slideshow containing the following information:

- What a PSA is
  - PSA stands for public service announcement. It is an advertisement shown by mass media (on TV, the Internet, radio, social media, etc.) for no charge to publicize a message in the public's interest. They can come in many forms, including a comic strip.
- Examples of PSA comic strips
  - Alex and Maryann present several examples of comic strip PSAs that students can see to better understand their goal. Examples can be found through an Internet search of comic strip PSAs.
- The requirements/checklist
  - This sheet is also given as a handout to the students. See Figure 9.6: Comic Strip PSA Checklist for an example.
  - It's located at the top of the draft page, which allows students to see the expectations while they are drafting their comic strip.
  - It includes steps that guide students effectively through the process.
- Tips for success
  - Steps to complete, which is also on the handout provided to students. See Figure 9.6: Comic Strip PSA Checklist.

Once the instructions and checklist have been reviewed, Alex and Maryann encourage students to decide on a disease and four important facts about their chosen disease that will be included in their PSA. Once students document these on paper, they can begin planning their story on a provided storyboard. After they plan their story, they can sketch basic illustrations for the draft and have the teacher approve them through a student-teacher writing conference.

Student-teacher writing conferences are one-on-one meetings where students present their writing to the teacher for feedback. If done effectively, student-teacher writing conferences can lead not only to better writing performances, but also to increased student self-efficacy—belief in their competence (Bayraktar, 2013). To be most effective, the teacher can let the student take the lead at the beginning of the conference and provide feedback through open-ended questions (we provide a few examples in the next paragraphs).

For example, when meeting about a rough draft of the Comic Strip PSA, teachers can start off by asking students to read their comic strip to them. Then, the students could be asked to go through the checklist and identify how they have met each requirement. Doing this helps the student realize whether or not they have all of the required pieces and gives an opportunity for the teacher to provide feedback. We always try to give feedback using this sequence:

1. Start by finding positive aspects of a student's writing. This practice can build more rapport between the teacher and the student and increase student confidence. For example, "Your comic strip has a great flow to it and contains four details about the disease."

2. Focus the feedback on the product and not the student. Point out specific parts of the comic strip that may be missing pieces or can be improved. As an example, "Let's look at the number of panels you have in your story board. According to the checklist, do you have enough?"

3. Ask questions to guide the students. We may say, "In looking at your conclusion, there seems to be a missing piece. What could you add to make it more complete?" or "Have you thought about adding more details to this part to better explain the concept?"

By presenting our feedback using this format, we are helping students with their writing skills while building their confidence and challenging them to think about how they can improve their writing product. It's a more effective method than just telling them what to do (Hattie & Timperley, 2007). This process can move students toward becoming more independent and effective writers.

We try to do individual conferences as each student finishes his or her first draft. Other students are still working on their drafts while we are involved in individual meetings. However, if multiple students finish their drafts at one time, we encourage students to take time to prepare for their conference with us. We tell them to use their checklists and highlight what they think they did well so they can share that with us. If they are sure they are ready for their conference, they can work on other enrichment activities, such as a folder activity or online webquest. See Chapter 2: Strategies for Teaching Lab Procedures for more information on possible enrichment tasks.

After our conferences with each student, they revise and edit their comic strips. We provide a final quick check-off at that point. We then give them time to complete their final copies. In total, this type of lesson requires approximately three 55-min class periods. Alex and Maryann suggest students always have access to the Internet for further research. Figures 9.7: Chicken Pox PSA Comic Strip and 9.8: Asthma PSA Comic Strip are student examples of completed projects.

Student projects can be shared with classmates, posted on classroom blogs, or published on a variety of other online sites. See the Technology Connections for ideas.

Some other informative/explanatory writing assignments include:

- a letter to the President pretending to be an alien and explaining several observations of human life forms
- an explanation of what happens during photosynthesis, including all the steps from beginning to end
- the biography of a scientist who contributed to the concepts being taught in class
- a newspaper article outlining the details of an event that students are learning
- an instructional guide that explains how to balance a chemical equation

ARGUMENT

Argument writing requires students to have an opinion and stand behind that opinion with evidence (The Writing Center, 2019). Students must develop an argument based on what they have researched and learned about a topic.

Writing Structures: ICE and CER

Argument writing is probably the most common form of writing used in a science classroom. The key strategy to reinforce during argument writing is supporting claims with evidence. One method we have found to be successful is the acronym ICE. ICE stands for Introduce, Cite, Explain. ICE is a writing structure that assists students in their written work by providing them with prompts to ensure all necessary parts are in their answers. A writing structure is a series of prompts or questions that students respond to as a guide to creating a piece of writing.

ICE is a useful guide for students to add into paragraphs for argument writing. We discuss writing structures further in the Differentiation for Diverse Learners section below. It is important to note that the acronym "ICE" could trigger anxiety for some students familiar with its more well-known public use as an abbreviation for the U.S. Immigration and Customs Enforcement law agency. It is best to acknowledge this similarity and, depending upon the time and local situation, it might be even better to instead use the CER model that is discussed later in this section.

The first step in ICE is to Introduce. As mentioned in Chapter 8: Strategies for Teaching Reading Comprehension, we teach students to always use an introductory phrase before inserting their textual evidence. We give them examples of introduction phrases, such as:

- According to the text. . .
- In the text it states. . .
- The author of the text writes. . .

The next step in the ICE process is to Cite. We tell students whenever they use a quote or direct idea from a text, they must credit the source, which is done at the end of the sentence. The in-text citation will change based on the format of writing being used (Modern Language Association, MLA or the American Psychological Association, APA), but almost always includes the author's or authors' last names and either the year and/or the page number in parentheses after the statement.

The last step in ICE is to Explain the textual evidence. This "writing move" requires students to connect the evidence back to the topic and discuss how the evidence applies to the question and the answer. We often find students will write a quote as their support for the argument but not explain its connection to the prompt. We tell them that after every piece of textual evidence they are required to include an explanation. For example, if supporting an argument suggesting that solar energy is more effective than hydroelectric power, students must first find a quote in the text that supports their opinion. After copying the quote and including the citation, students then need to write another sentence or two that explains how the quote justifies their opinion that solar energy is superior to hydroelectric power. When all three steps are put together, they could look like this:

> According to the text, "Solar energy can be used almost anywhere to power a home, generate electricity or run small appliances like roadside signs or even calculators" (Beach, 2018, Availability and Access section, para. 1). Having the ability to get energy from the sun almost anywhere is an advantage over hydroelectric power since it has to be near larger water sources. More people are able to use solar energy making it a better option for renewable energy.

The ICE method is similar to the CER process that is also commonly used. CER stands for Claim, Evidence, Reasoning. The major difference between the two is the first part. With ICE, the first step is to use an introductory phrase. CER, on the other hand, begins with stating the claim or answering the question. The next two steps are essentially the same. They both require students to provide evidence for their thoughts and then explain how that evidence connects to the answer. An example of CER would look very similar:

> Solar power is superior to hydroelectric power. This is because "solar energy can be used almost anywhere to power a home, generate electricity or run small appliances like roadside signs or even calculators" (Beach, 2018, Availability and Access section, para. 1). Having the ability to get energy from the sun almost anywhere is an advantage over hydroelectric power since it has to be near larger water sources. More people are able to use solar energy making it a better option for renewable energy.

For more information on using CER with students, see the Technology Connections section.

Both methods can be used with students to practice how to incorporate evidence in writing—a key skill needed when producing longer argument essays.

Argument Essay

Tara includes at least one extended argument writing assignment per quarter when teaching seventh grade science. She finds that this is an effective way to assess student learning while also building their writing skills. At the end of each quarter, she presents the students with three or four essential questions that they should be able to answer. Figure 9.9: Ecology Essential Questions Argument Essay shows the four essential questions she uses at the end of an ecology unit.

Mandi often uses a graphic organizer that she developed with a fellow teacher, Lindsay Rij, to help students identify their textual evidence and explanations before they begin writing to the prompt. See Figure 9.10: Argument Essay Organizer for an example. This graphic organizer requires students to identify their main argument or thesis, which includes three supporting reasons. Students then identify quotes from texts to support each reason and copy them into the boxes. Next, they write explanations of the quotations in the boxes next to the boxes containing the quotations. We explain to students that each line of boxes easily becomes a paragraph in their essays. This graphic organizer can be adjusted depending on the amount of support a student requires. Figure 9.11: Ecology Example Argument Essay Organizer is an example of the graphic organizer filled in for one of the above essential questions. Students can use both the graphic organizer and the checklist in Figure 9.9: Ecology Essential Questions Argument Essay to guide them through the steps of what should be in their essays.

By the time students are presented with this writing assignment, they've already been taught the ecology unit so that they have the background knowledge needed to take a stance on one of these questions. Their first step is to decide which one they want to work on. Then, they are told to use their notes, texts, and the Internet to identify reasons that support their argument. During this time, we give them the argument essay graphic organizer to complete while they are researching and planning their essay. They use these notes to begin writing their drafts.

We remind students that writing an essay is more than just copying what they wrote in their graphic organizer. They will need to think about transitions, adding details, and including background for the reader. Providing a model of a finished essay containing these features can be helpful to students in this process.

Peer Editing

Peer editing is a strategy we often utilize for argument writing. Peer editing requires students to exchange their writing with another student in order to get feedback for revisions. In our experience, students need to have a guide to use while they are reviewing the paper in order for peer editing to be effective. Figure 9.12: Argument Essay Peer Editing Checklist is an example of one we often use.

We go over the checklist by displaying it on the board, having students discuss each step in pairs, and then sharing together as a whole class. Once we are sure they know what each element is, we give them the checklist and match them with partners, usually their shoulder buddies or someone near them. If students are not yet done with their rough drafts, we wait and match them after. Then, students sit next to each other while they read their partner's drafts and complete the checklist. If they have questions or need clarification while reading the essay, they can easily ask their partner since that person is sitting next to them. All checklists are turned in for completion grades so we can ensure they completed it. We can also see what types of suggestions students made and if students followed the suggestions.

After peer editing, students are able to write their final copies of their essays. The whole process takes about four to five 60 min class periods if it is the first time using all the steps. Later in the year, it may take fewer periods.

Essay Topics

Some other argument essay prompts include:

- Why is it important to study geology?
- How would Earth be different if there was only one tectonic plate?
- How has space travel changed life on Earth?
- Is there life on other planets?
- How will dark matter (or dark energy) affect the universe in the future?
- What will be the next vestigial feature of human beings?
- If there is an undiscovered state of matter at extreme temperatures, what characteristics would this state of matter have?

DAILY WRITING ACTIVITIES

Below is a list of brief writing activities that can be done daily in class to help increase science achievement.

- *Transfer* – Students can write a short paragraph about how they can apply one thing they learned in a different context—either out-of-school or in another class. Research has shown that this kind of activity can increase learning and engagement (City University of New York, n.d.).

- *Journal/learning log* – Students can write one or two sentences reflecting on what they have learned daily and write any questions they may still have in a notebook. Teachers can then provide feedback.

- *Quickwrites* – Most often in science, we use a quickwrite as an exit ticket at the end of a period. We provide students with a prompt and give students 3–5 min to respond to it in written form. We explain that we want students to document the first answers that come to mind without using any other resources and that we will read them, but they will not be graded. They will instead be used to guide further instruction so they still need to give their best answers. An example quickwrite could be, "Explain the difference between dominant and recessive genes and provide two examples of each."

- *Summaries* — After reading and lab activities, students can write brief three to four sentence summaries of the main ideas or conclusions from the labs. This allows students to synthesize the new knowledge they have learned and put it in their words to increase their learning. Research has shown that summarizing new content can lead to an increase in understanding by as much as 19 percentile points (Marzano, 2010).

DIFFERENTIATION FOR DIVERSE LEARNERS

Some students may become overwhelmed and lost when told to simply go research a topic. Teachers can support these students by providing websites and/or articles to narrow down student research. This kind of scaffolding can also be done with younger students who do not yet have effective research skills.

Teachers can also differentiate by providing students with a certain topic (i.e., specific weather type or disease) instead of allowing them to choose. This allows the teacher to provide students with subjects that are easier to research. On the other hand, teachers can encourage students to choose more difficult topics if they feel students need an extra challenge.

For English language learner (ELL) students and those who may need extra scaffolding with writing, we can provide them with writing frames and writing structures. Writing frames are a series of sentence starters that assist students with a beginning point where they then can insert their ideas. An example of a writing frame would be:

"During the experiment, I observed _____. Based on this observation, I can conclude that my hypothesis was _____ (valid or null) because I stated _____."

Another example of a writing frame can be found in Chapter 6: Strategies for Teaching the Engineering Process.

Writing structures are prompts that students respond to in order to create a longer written response. For example, the ICE and CER strategies that are discussed under the Argument Writing section can be considered writing structures as they prompt students with each part of their answer. These structures are effective at helping guide students through properly setting up written responses, but do not actually provide them with the sentence stems.

See Technology Connections for more resources on writing frames and writing structures.

Students with handwriting challenges can be provided with laptops to type their written assignments. In fact, many students may prefer the benefits of composing and revising on the computer.

Student Handouts and Examples

Figure 9.1: Severe Weather Book Project Research (Student Handout)

Figure 9.2: Severe Weather Book Project Scoring Guide (Student Handout)

Figure 9.3: Severe Weather Book Project Research Example

Figure 9.4: Plot Map Outline (Student Handout)

Figure 9.5: Severe Weather Book Plot Map Example

Figure 9.6: Comic Strip PSA Checklist (Student Handout)

Figure 9.7: Chicken Pox PSA Comic Strip (Student Example)

Figure 9.8: Asthma PSA Comic Strip (Student Example)

Figure 9.9: Ecology Essential Questions Argument Essay (Student Handout)

Figure 9.10: Argument Essay Organizer (Student Handout)

Figure 9.11: Ecology Example Argument Essay Organizer

Figure 9.12: Argument Essay Peer Editing Checklist (Student Handout)

What Could Go Wrong?

We have found one of the biggest challenges with doing writing assignments in science class is managing time. When students enter our classrooms, we may not be sure of their writing abilities and may not plan for the appropriate amount of time. We have found the first writing assignment should be a smaller one so we can determine skill levels and what support and time students may need in order to be successful in writing activities. Time needed will vary for students, so having enrichment activities for students who finish early will be important for teachers to consider before they begin an assignment. See Chapter 2: Strategies for Teaching Lab Procedures for ideas on enrichment activities.

Another problem we have encountered involves the language we use while talking about writing. It is helpful to meet with English Language Arts (ELA) colleagues to learn the terminology they utilize while teaching writing. It is less confusing for students if we use similar language when reinforcing the writing skills they learn in ELA classes. For example, there are many different terms for an introduction section. When Mandi and Tara worked together, ELA teachers used the word *hook*. It was easier for the students to understand since they were hearing the same term in both classes. Also, the process of ICE was one they shared, which helped students make strides in their writing because Tara was reinforcing the process that Mandi taught in her ELA class.

Technology Connections

There are many places students can publish their writings so that other people, in addition to their teachers, can read them. "The Best Places Where Students Can Write for an 'Authentic Audience'" (http://larryferlazzo.edublogs.org/2009/04/01/the-best-places-where-students-can-write-for-an-authentic-audience) offers many potential publication sites.

An online resource that students can use to create stories and comic strips is Storyboard That (www.storyboardthat.com). This site can be beneficial for students who may not be able to write or draw for longer periods of time. Other resources can be found at "The Best Ways to Make Comic Strips Online" (http://larryferlazzo.edublogs.org/2008/06/04/the-best-ways-to-make-comic-strips-online).

Other tools that can be used for creating online stories can be found on Larry Ferlazzo's Best of Blog, "Best Lists of the Week: Web 2.0 Tools" (http://larryferlazzo.edublogs.org/2018/08/30/best-lists-of-the-week-web-2-0-tools).

For more information on using how to teach CER to students, see "The Model Teaching Site" at https://www.modelteaching.com/education-articles/writing-instruction/claim-evidence-reasoning-cer?fbclid=IwAR2PXy6yxewYWfY99RB7-4F-ai5BIo1OuWFlfU3EPgBcHQcmNQt2eTEyfqw or just search "CER" online.

Resources for finding texts and videos in multiple languages to help students while researching for various writing assignments can be found at "The Best Multilingual & Bilingual Sites for Math, Social, Studies, & Science" (http://larryferlazzo.edublogs.org/2008/10/03/the-best-multilingual-bilingual-sites-for-math-social-studies-science).

Visit "The Best List of Mindmapping, Flow Chart Tools, & Graphic Organizers" (http://larryferlazzo.edublogs.org/2009/02/09/not-the-best-but-a-list-of-mindmapping-flow-chart-tools-graphic-organizers) for blank graphic organizers students can utilize while prewriting.

More information and resources for writing stems and writing frames can be found at "The Best Scaffolding Writing Frames for Students" (http://larryferlazzo .edublogs.org/2016/12/01/the-best-scaffolded-writing-frames-for-students).

Attributions

Thank you to Kristi Simpson, Kristen Bren, Alex Ostrow, and Maryann Ramseyer for allowing us to use their writing assignments as examples for the narrative and informational/explanatory sections. We would also like to thank Janica Moirraine and Faith Carrillo for their incredible Comic Strip PSA examples. Another thank you goes to Lindsay Rij for helping Mandi create the argument graphic organizer when they worked in a professional learning community together.

Figures

Name:_____ **Date:**_____ **Period:**_____

Severe Weather Book Project Research

Directions: You will be creating a children's book that will explain a severe type of weather. You may pick from a hurricane, tornado, thunderstorm, blizzard, flood, or drought. Before you begin to create the book, you will first need to do some research on your topic of choice.

What is your topic? Write a definition.	
How is this type of severe weather formed?	
What are common characteristics of your topic?	
Where does your topic occur?	
How does this weather topic impact humans?	
What precautionary measures can humans take to stay safe?	
Interesting facts about your topic. . .	

Figure 9.1   Severe Weather Book Project Research (Student Handout)

Severe Weather Project Scoring Guide

Objective: You will write and illustrate a children's book that informs the reader about a type of severe weather. Use your scientific research from the previous page to help you create your story. Your story must clearly define your severe weather and inform the reader of how your chosen weather is formed, what type of characteristics are associated with your weather, how it impacts humans, and how people prevent injury during this weather.

Use the following checklist to make sure you have all the required elements in your story. Be creative and have fun!

Element	Teacher comments	Teacher score	Self-check
Organization: Book is neat and legible. A cover, title, and author's name are included. 5 points			
Design: Illustrations and dialogue are on every page, illustrations are colorful, it's at least five pages, pages are stapled together in the format of a book. 5 points			
Story: Story flows well with a clear beginning, middle, and end; it's creative; and the chosen weather is clearly stated. 5 points			
Research: Topic is well defined. Author describes how topic is formed and where it is formed. Characteristics associated with topic are included (i.e., heavy rain, wind, lightning, flooding, etc.) 15 points			
Impact: Describe the impact the topic has on humans, communities, animals, the economy, and the environment. Are they long-lasting or short-lived? 10 points			
Precautions: Describe how humans can be prepared for a severe storm. Are there warnings, evacuations, and/or shelters? 10 points			
	Total Score	__/50 Points	

Figure 9.2 Severe Weather Book Project Scoring Guide (Student Handout)

Name:_____ Date:_____ Period:___

Severe Weather Book Project Research

Directions: You will be creating a children's book that will explain a severe type of weather. You may pick from a hurricane, tornado, thunderstorm, blizzard, flood or drought. Before you begin to create the book, you will first need to do some research on your topic of choice.

What is your topic? Write a definition.	tornado—a rapidly spinning column of air that touches both the base of a thunderstorm and the ground
How is this type of severe weather formed? What are common characteristics of you topic?	when there are changes in wind speed and direction, then tipped upward by air moving through the thunderclouds more likely to occur in the spring and summer and during thunderstorms, look like a funnel—grow about 660 ft wide, 10–20 mph speeds up to 70 mph, short-lived
Where does your topic occur?	most occur in the U.S., Texas reports the most—avg. of 120 per year often happen in the late afternoon
How does this weather topic impact humans?	deadly—kill about 70 people per year, destroy structures and homes, about 400 million dollars in damage a year
What precautionary measures can humans take to stay safe?	tornado watches and tornado warnings move to an interior room on a low floor away from windows—a basement if possible
Interesting facts about your topic.....	some people chase them to get more information (like speeds inside the funnel) and take pictures—they use special sensors

Figure 9.3 Severe Weather Book Project Research Example

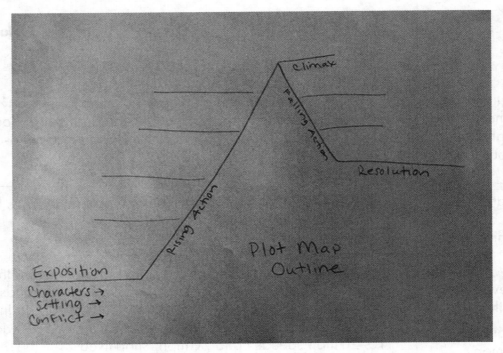

Figure 9.4 Plot Map Outline (Student Handout)

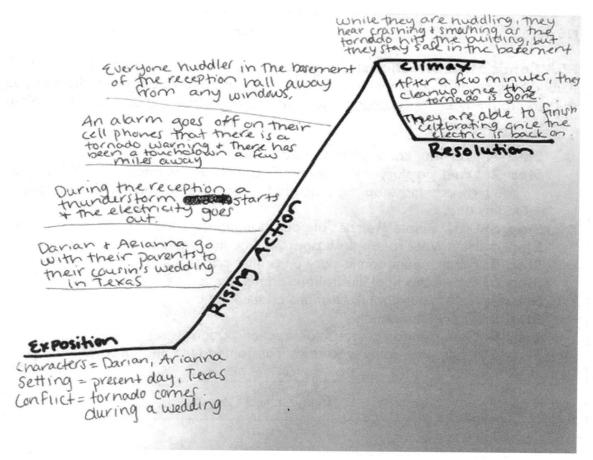

While they are huddling, they hear crashing + smashing as the tornado hits the building, but they stay safe in the basement

Climax

Everyone huddles in the basement of the reception hall away from any windows.

After a few minutes, they cleanup once the tornado is gone.

An alarm goes off on their cell phones that there is a tornado warning + there has been a touchdown a few miles away

They are able to finish celebrating once the electric is back on.

Resolution

During the reception a thunderstorm ~~comes~~ starts + the electricity goes out.

Rising Action

Darian + Arianna go with their parents to their cousin's wedding in Texas

Exposition

Characters = Darian, Arianna
Setting = present day, Texas
Conflict = tornado comes during a wedding

Figure 9.5 Severe Weather Book Plot Map Example

Name_____ Date:_____ Period_____

PSA Comic Strip Directions: Using your video and CDC research, create a PSA (Public Service Announcement) comic strip informing people about the disease you studied. You may either share important information about the disease OR explain how it can be prevented.

Step 1: Plan your comic strip on scrap paper.
Step 2: Write the storyline using the six panels on the backside of this paper. You may add more boxes, if needed. Simply staple another sheet of paper to this one.
Step 3: Draw simple sketches of your planned drawings.
Step 4: Have your rough draft approved by the teacher.
Step 5: Finalize your comic story on printer paper.
Step 6: Draw your final illustrations on the comic.
Step 7: Color your final illustrations on the comic.
Step 8: Cut out the panels.
Step 9: Glue them on colored construction paper.
Step 10: Title your comic and add your name to the final product.

Comic checklist	
Disease identified (5 points)	
At least 4 important facts about the disease included (prevention, treatment, symptoms, etc.) (20 points)	
Illustrations (10 points)	
Dialogue/text is included (20 points)	
Minimum of 6 panels (5 points)	
Comic is neat (5 points)	
Comic is colorful (10 points)	
Comic is presentable (5 points)	
Comic has a title and creator name (5 points)	

Figure 9.6 Comic Strip PSA Checklist (Student Handout)

Figure 9.6 (Continued)

Figure 9.7 Chicken Pox PSA Comic Strip (Student Example)

Figure 9.8 Asthma PSA Comic Strip (Student Example)

Figure 9.8 (Continued)

Name _____

Ecology Essential Questions Argument Essay

Directions: Choose one of the four questions below and write an argument essay. Use the checklist to ensure you have every required element of the essay. You do not have to type your essay but if you want to do so, you can at home.

Answer one of the following four essential questions using an argument essay style:
1. What will be the next big adaptation in human beings?
2. Are humans part of nature?
3. What makes a healthy relationship?
4. Can an organism go extinct without the world noticing?

Requirements	Do I have it?	Points possible	Points awarded
Introduction Paragraph:			
Hook about the subject to reel in the audience			
Background Information (Facts ONLY)			
Thesis Statement with your THREE supporting ideas/claims			
Body Paragraph 1:			
State your first reason			
Introduce the text evidence			
Cite text evidence with proper internal citation			
Explain the reason—at least two sentences!			
Restate your idea and add transition to next paragraph			

Figure 9.9 Ecology Essential Questions Argument Essay (Student Handout)

Requirements	Do I have it?	Points possible	Points awarded
Body Paragraph 2:			
State your second reason			
Introduce the text evidence			
Cite text evidence with proper internal citation			
Explain the reason—at least two sentences!			
Restate your idea and add transition to next paragraph			
Body Paragraph 3:			
State your third reason			
Introduce the text evidence			
Cite text evidence with proper internal citation			
Explain the reason—at least two sentences!			
Restate your idea and add transition to next paragraph			
Conclusion Paragraph:			
Restate your thesis in NEW words from your introduction paragraph			
Give another brief statement or summary different from the introduction (1–2 sentences)			
Clincher to leave the audience wanting more			
Conventions (spelling, grammar, punctuation)			
Total:			

Figure 9.9 (Continued)

NAME:_____   CLASS PERIOD:_____

Argument Essay Pre-Write

THESIS STATEMENT- state your claim and the three reasons you are supporting your claim with:

```
┌──────────────────────────────────────────────────────────────────┐
│                                                                    │
│                                                                    │
│                                                                    │
└──────────────────────────────────────────────────────────────────┘
```

Quote to support reason 1   **Explanation of the quote for reason 1**

```
┌──────────────────────┐          ┌──────────────────────────────┐
│                      │          │                              │
│                      │   ──►    │                              │
│                      │          │                              │
│                      │          │                              │
└──────────────────────┘          └──────────────────────────────┘
```

Quote to support Reason 2   **Explanation of the quote for reason 2**

```
┌──────────────────────┐          ┌──────────────────────────────┐
│                      │          │                              │
│                      │   ──►    │                              │
│                      │          │                              │
│                      │          │                              │
└──────────────────────┘          └──────────────────────────────┘
```

QUOTE that supports the reason 3:   **EXPLANATION** of the quotes that support reason 3:

```
┌──────────────────────┐          ┌──────────────────────────────┐
│                      │          │                              │
│                      │   ──►    │                              │
│                      │          │                              │
│                      │          │                              │
└──────────────────────┘          └──────────────────────────────┘
```

RESTATE THESIS – restate your claim and reasons using new words:

```
┌──────────────────────────────────────────────────────────────────┐
│                                                                    │
│                                                                    │
│                                                                    │
└──────────────────────────────────────────────────────────────────┘
```

Figure 9.10   Argument Essay Organizer (Student Handout)

NAME:_____   CLASS PERIOD:_____

Argument Essay Pre-Write

THESIS STATEMENT- state your claim and the three reasons you are supporting your claim with:

> *A species cannot go extinct without the world noticing because that species' prey. predators. and mutualistic relationships would all be affected*

Quote to support reason 1

> *"Without wolves to keep other animals' number in check, prey populations grew larger" (Bove. 2019)*

Explanation of the quote for reason 1

> *When a species disapperas. their prey species increase in number, which in turn affects other species. In this example, elk numbers went up and they ate more plants causing songbirds to leave the area affecting the whole ecosystem.*

Quote to support Reason 2

> *"The loss of abudant organisms that provide food for a variety of species would also interrupt the food web" (Williams. 2019).*

Explanation of the quote for reason 2

> *if a species is the method of food for a predator than that predatory species suffers. They are than required to relocate to find food or die, which in turn impacts other organisms.*

QUOTE that supports the reason 3:

> *"if bee numbers go down, many flower species are also negatively impacted" (Jones. 2015).*

EXPLANATION of the quotesthat support reason 3:

> Some bee species have a mutualistic relationship with flowers because they pollinate them. allowing them to grow. If bee populations go down, those flowers would decrease as well, which would affect the rest of the ecosystem around them.

RESTATE THESIS – restate your claim and reasons using new words:

> Because every organism has oher organism that depend on its survival like prey predators and mutualistic benefactors a species cannot go extinct without the world noticing.

Figure 9.11   Ecology Example Argument Essay Organizer

Your Name: _____   Partner's Name:_____

Argument Essay Partner Revising and Editing Checklist

Directions: Read your partner's essay. Then go down the checklist, placing a check in the box after you have completed each step. If needed, jot notes in the box for your partner.

Does the writer grab the reader's attention with a strong beginning? Does the introduction state the question being answered clearly? • Underline the hook. Put a check next to the statement of the problem.	
Is there a thesis? • Circle the thesis. Is it at the end of the first paragraph?	
Are there three identifiable reasons to support the argument? • Highlight the reasons in green.	
Do the reasons have supporting details and evidence? • Highlight the supporting details in yellow. • Highlight in another color at least one piece of quoted evidence per paragraph. Is it cited correctly?	
Is there a good conclusion? • Put a star next to the restated thesis.	
Are all sentences complete? • Check for capital letters and punctuation. • Place a cloud around any issues you see.	
Are there any misspelled words? • With a different color pen or highlighter, circle any possible misspelled words.	
Did the writer use transitions? How is the word choice? • Highlight transition words in blue. Add them as needed. Check for and place a box around any repeated or boring words.	

Three revisions/edits I suggest:

1. _____

2. _____

3. _____

Figure 9.12 Argument Essay Peer Editing Checklist (Student Handout)

CHAPTER 10

Strategies for Discussions

What Is It?

Class discussions can be a part of every science classroom. Whether in pairs, small groups, or whole group, students engaging in discourse around scientific concepts is a key component to their learning. However, students often need to learn *how* to appropriately participate in these discussions and need regular practice with these skills.

Why We Like It

Student discussions often reveal valuable insight into student learning. As we listen to our students talk to each other, we can identify their understandings and their struggles. We use discussion as a formative assessment in order to determine if students have adequately learned new material or if we need to provide further instruction.

Student discussions are another opportunity for teachers to incorporate culturally responsive teaching into their classrooms. When students are provided with the opportunity to discuss their ideas and experiences with others, they can be honored as individuals if the teacher has created a culturally responsive environment (see Chapter 14: Strategies for Cultural Responsiveness).

Supporting Research

Research has shown that when students are explicitly taught discussion strategies in the science classroom, they improve both their communication skills and academic achievement (Mercer, Dawes, Wegerif, & Sams, 2004, p. 17).

Another study showed that increasing the amount of discussions in the science classroom helped students develop self-confidence in their speaking abilities and enhanced their understanding of science content (Green, 2012, p. 28).

Skills for Intentional Scholars/NGSS Connections

Teaching and reinforcing discussions within the classroom clearly strengthens effective communication skills. Discussions can also help build both critical thinking and creative problem-solving skills.

Science discourse is also a part of the Next Generation Science Standards (NGSS) at all grade levels (Achieve, Inc., 2017b), as well as the Common Core Standards, where listening and speaking are a part of the English Language Arts Standards (Common Core State Standards Initiative, 2010).

Application

In this section, we will highlight several ways to help students participate in productive discussions.

SET THE GROUND RULES

While every class has its overall behavior expectations, we also set up expectations for student discussions. Since some students may not have experienced productive small and whole group discussions in the past, they can benefit from guidelines that create a safe environment. Some common ground rules we like to use include:

1. Always remain respectful even if you do not agree with what a speaker is saying.
2. Keep an open mind to other perspectives.
3. Listen actively and be sure to let the speaker finish his or her thoughts before speaking—do not interrupt.
4. Give everyone a chance to speak—do not take over the conversation.
5. Ask questions if you do not understand what the speaker is saying.
6. Use evidence to support your statements, when possible.

When these ground rules are first introduced, we take the time to go over each rule one at a time. Students are then placed into groups of three or four to create an example ("Alex sits quiet, looks at Jackie while she is speaking, and waits until she is finished to provide his response to her statement") and a bad example ("Alex listens for only the first part of what Jackie is saying and then interrupts to say why she is wrong") of each of the rules. They are told to write their examples down on one shared sheet of paper. When it is time to share with the class, we invite each group to share either an example or a bad example (we randomly assign one to each group). Their peers then provide feedback by either asking them a question or making a positive statement about their examples.

Another strategy for teaching the rules is to have students write a skit that portrays an example and a bad example. Each group is randomly assigned one of the rules. They write their skits and then perform them in front of the class. An alternate strategy that requires less time is having the teacher lead the skits. For example, when Mandi teaches students how to interact in a small group, she asks three to four students to sit with her in a circle at the front of the class. She asks the group a simple question, such as, "What was the best movie you've seen lately and why?" or "If you could go anywhere in the world, where would you go and why?" As students take turns discussing their answer, Mandi interrupts them, yells over them, and loudly disagrees with their ideas. She then stops the small group to ask the whole class which rules she is *not* following and then asks what she should do instead. If time allows, she asks the participants to express how her behavior made them feel so students can better understand why these rules are important.

Every time students work in groups, we remind them of the behavior expectations by bringing their attention to the rules that are hung in a poster format on one of our classroom walls. Figure 10.1: Discussion Ground Rules is a page that can be displayed on the overhead or made into a poster.

PROVIDE STUDENTS WITH SENTENCE STARTERS

Providing students with sentence starters is an effective way to help them formulate responses during a discussion. Sentence starters can also guide students' critical thinking about the science content as well as what their peers are saying. Additionally, requiring students to use sentence starters can prevent students from blurting out comments during discussions because it forces them to use more time to think out a response.

We discussed debate sentence starters in Chapter 3: Strategies for Teaching the Scientific Method and Its Components. Table 10.1 shows these sentence starters, which can also be used during classroom discussions.

There are other sentence starters that can be used depending on the type of discussion. CommonLit has a list of sentence starters at https://support .commonlit.org/hc/en-us/article_attachments/115001276554/Discussion_ Starters.pdf and others can be found online by searching "classroom discussion sentence starters."

Table 10.1 Debate Sentence Starters

Agreement statements	Disagreement statements
"I agree with you because. . ."	"I like what you were thinking but I was thinking. . ."
"I like what you wrote here. I also wrote. . ."	"Can you explain this answer to me because I wrote something different?"
"I agree that. . ."	"Have you considered. . .?"
"We agree with each other on this question because. . ."	"I notice. . ."
"You made me realize that. . ."	"I wonder. . ."

ENSURE ALL STUDENTS ARE PARTICIPATING

In order for discussions to be effective, all students (or as many as realistically possible) must participate. Teachers can use discussions to build more culturally responsive classrooms by honoring the perspectives of all students (Stembridge, 2017).

To ensure we are tapping into all student perspectives, we use various methods to call on as many students as possible. Tara uses popsicle sticks with student names written on them and Mandi uses index cards with student names. Teachers can randomly pull out a popsicle stick or index card and call the name of the student on the card. There are also online tools, such as www.classdojo.com, that teachers can use to select students at random.

Tara alters her popsicle sticks to help her differentiate. There are some students she wants to "randomly" call on more often, for example, students who are learning English or those who have learning challenges. These students benefit from actively participating in class because they are practicing their thinking, problem solving, and English speaking skills. In order to purposefully pull these students' popsicle sticks, Tara places a dab of hot glue on the tip of their sticks. The glue dries clear so students are unaware of its presence, but Tara can feel for the glue when she reaches into the cup to choose a stick. When a student no longer needs to be called on more often, Tara can easily remove the dab of glue.

If you don't want to deal with popsicle sticks or index cards, but still want to be "strategically" random, note in your mind or on a sticky note the students for whom you want to intentionally include in a conversation. That could mean more than just calling on them, however. It could be important to give quiet students or English language learners (ELLs) a private "heads-up" in advance that you will ask them to share their thoughts with the class.

Regardless of how a teacher randomly chooses students to participate, the simple act of randomly choosing students tends to increase participation. Students are more likely to stay engaged because they do not know when they are going to be required to answer a question or provide an opinion.

It is also important to keep track of student participation when we are not calling on students. We can use tracking data to provide feedback to the students, as well as help inform our decisions for future discussions. For example, if we see a student who is not participating, we may privately encourage them to participate more and/or provide them with additional sentence starters. We can also use the tracking data when we are leading discussions so that we know who we may want to call on more frequently. On the other hand, if we see students monopolizing discussions, we may privately encourage them to look back at the ground rules and remind them of what they can gain by listening.

There are a few easy tricks when it comes to tracking student participation in discussions. We often will use a class roster and record tally marks every time a student shares an answer, opinion, or question. This can also be done with a class seating chart.

When we want to record the quality of a student's participation, we use a check, check minus, and check plus symbol system. A check would be given when a student gives an acceptable statement, such as, "I agree with what _____ said because the experiment showed _____." A check minus would mean the student spoke during the discussion, but it was either inappropriate or a simple statement with no explanation. An example would be, "I don't agree with _____ because she is wrong." The last option would be a check plus for those students who provide responses during the discussion that further the conversation. This would mean a statement, such as, "I agree with _____ because it was determined that _____, but what if we had adjusted the variable by _____?" This statement ends with a question to extend the discussion.

Another way to keep track and assess student participation is through a speaking checklist or rubric. This is effective for grading students on their discussion skills and providing meaningful feedback.

We acknowledge that it is difficult to complete a checklist or rubric for every student during every discussion. We find it is easier to use this method during smaller group discussions where we can focus on one group at a time. Figure 10.2: Group Discussion Ratings Scale is a rating sheet we use during small group discussion activities. Along the side of the scale are the skills we are looking for based on our discussion ground rules and along the top is a space to put student names. As we observe student groups, we take notes and rate students appropriately based on the scale.

Do we document student participation in all class discussions? Of course not! We find that keeping track of this kind of participation is particularly helpful at the beginning of the year to help set expectations. Then, afterwards, we're able to keep track informally, in our own minds, about how students are handling their discussion roles.

DISCUSSION ACTIVITIES

After creating the ground rules and providing students with sentence starters for discussions, it is important to create various opportunities within the classroom for authentic discussions. In addition to the traditional whole class and small group team discussions that often occur naturally during lessons, we have highlighted some additional activities below.

Snowball Strategy

The snowball strategy is a low pressure discussion activity to get students more comfortable with speaking in front of their peers. This is because during the activity they are usually reading what their classmates have written instead of their own words. We typically use it as a brainstorming activity since there is no way of knowing which student wrote each of the ideas. However, it can be a good way to generate ideas for solutions to use with project-based learning and when using the engineering process. More information on brainstorming within these processes can be found in Chapter 5: Strategies for Using Project-Based Learning and Chapter 6: Strategies for Teaching the Engineering Process.

The steps to the snowball activity are as follows:

1. Teachers provide students with a brainstorming prompt. For example, "How can the wheelchair be improved?" or "What will be the next human adaptation?" or "Why do some animals have bones while others have cartilage?"

2. Students write down their ideas on a blank sheet of paper. They should be given no more than 1 min to do this.

3. Students then crumple up their papers and move to the center of the room.

4. Students are instructed to have a "snowball" fight by throwing the paper balls at each other around the room. We typically give students 20–30 s to have fun doing this.

5. Then, once time is up, students pick up any snowball near them and smooth it so they can read what their peer wrote.

6. Students then take turns reading aloud the idea that is written on their "snowball."

As stated above, this is a fun way to help students feel comfortable speaking in front of each other because it removes the fear of having the wrong answer. The snowball strategy has the potential of becoming a bit crazy, so it can't hurt to remind students about behavior expectations prior to any paper-throwing activity.

Think-Pair-Share

Think-Pair-Share is another low pressure discussion activity that can lead to an increase in student participation. We use this strategy often because it also helps ensure full class participation. First developed by Frank Lyman in 1981, Think-Pair-Share requires students to first think independently about a question or problem, then talk with a partner or neighbor, and lastly, share their joint conclusions with the whole class (Lyman, 1981).

We begin a Think-Pair-Share activity by first presenting the students with a question or problem. Students are then given time (1–2 min) to *Think* about the prompt silently and independently. We ask students to write down answers during their think time because, then, as we walk around the class monitoring, we can see if all students have an idea to share with their partners.

We then provide 2–3 min for the *Pairs* to share and another 1–2 min for them to discuss each other's ideas. Lastly, we randomly call on students to *Share* their group's ideas with the class.

Think-Pair-Share can be used with any prompt and at any point in a lesson. Tara finds it useful to review lab safety rules. She asks students, "Now that you've read the directions to the lab, which lab safety rules will you need to follow today?" Mandi uses the strategy as a formative assessment at the end of a lesson. She asks her students any one of these questions after a lesson is complete:

- What was one thing you learned today?
- What was one thing you had difficulty with today?
- What is a question you have regarding today's lesson?
- What is something you want to learn more about now that today's lesson is complete?
- What is one thing you would have done differently today if you had a chance to repeat it?

See Chapter 15: Strategies for the Beginning and Ending of Class for further formative assessment strategies.

When we use this activity as a formative assessment, we also ask students to turn in their written answers. These papers help us identify which students may need additional assistance.

Socratic Seminars

A Socratic seminar is a student-led discussion about a text. Socratic seminars are not intended to be debates. They are often intended to create meaningful discussion about a previously read text and to provide students with an opportunity to practice critical thinking and effective communication.

Before a Socratic seminar, we find a text we want students to read and then write related open-ended questions. See Chapter 8: Strategies for Teaching Reading Comprehension for a list of resources where we find the richest texts and how we write text-dependent questions.

As an example, we have students read an article about how water is recycled on the International Space Station (ISS). Here are the questions we assign to students prior to the Socratic seminar:

- From where does the ISS capture water to be recycled?
- Would you feel comfortable drinking water on the ISS? Why or why not?
- How long will it take to use all of the water on the ISS?
- If you were one of six people on the Station, and a problem occurred with the recycling system so that it only generated enough water for a few of you, what would you do and why?

Note that we begin with text-dependent questions that many students find easy to answer, and then follow with more open-ended, engaging ones.

Students are provided with the text the day before the Socratic seminar. Depending on the complexity and length of the text, we may give students the entire class period prior to the seminar to read and annotate the text alone or with a partner. See Chapter 8: Strategies for Teaching Reading Comprehension for strategies that students can use to annotate texts. Students are also given class time to answer the accompanying text-dependent questions, as well as the more open-ended ones. We remove any element of surprise from the seminar by providing students with time to prepare. This decreases stress for students who may feel anxious about speaking aloud in class.

Students form two concentric circles during a Socratic seminar. The inner circle participates in the discussion, while the students in the outer circle observe, listen, and take notes. Notes can include checklists that track how many times students participate, how many statements they make, and how many questions they ask that further the discussion. These checklists can be used to provide students with feedback so they can reflect on how to improve. Figure 10.3: Socratic Seminar Participation Checklist is an example of a checklist students can fill out during the seminar.

We usually begin a Socratic seminar with a round robin question. We discuss the round robin discussion technique in Chapter 6: Strategies for Teaching the Engineering Process. It would be a similar process here where a question is asked and students take turns answering it one-by-one, going around the inner circle.

Socratic seminars are meant to be student-centered. Teachers are only there as a facilitator, asking new questions, making sure that everyone has had the opportunity to answer, and letting the students know if it is time to wrap up discussions on current questions. This role can lead to more meaningful student discussion because they can't depend on the teacher to further the conversation or their learning; instead, students depend on themselves and each other.

Once we go through the discussion with the inner circle, the students switch spots so that the students who were in the outer circle move in and now have the discussion. We follow the same process with this inner group, starting with a round robin question.

We take time to debrief at the end of a Socratic seminar. Debriefing with students allows them to reflect on the overall seminar, what they have learned, and any changes they will make for future ones. Reflection is a key step because it takes time for students to understand how to effectively participate in Socratic seminars. Questions to be asked during debriefing include:

- How did you feel about the seminar?
- How did you feel about your participation?
- Did you change your mind about anything during the seminar? Why?
- What questions do you still have?
- What was the best part of the seminar? Worst part?
- What would you change for the next seminar?

Here is a list of topics we've discussed in our classes using Socratic seminars:

- Microbes that are growing in the International Space Station
- How biomimicry can help us live a more sustainable lifestyle
- The discovery of the Naica Crystal Cave
- How paleontologists use fossils
- Interpreting the layers of the Grand Canyon
- The differences between bacteria and viruses
- Why the United States does not use the metric system
- How car bumpers protect passengers from bodily harm in an automobile accident
- How the human body uses acids and bases in its daily functions
- The difference between the wavelength, amplitude, and period of a wave and how each affects various attributes of a musical piece

There are huge benefits to Socratic seminars—students develop academic discussion skills, often become more engaged in science topics, and learn to become better listeners. Many things can also go wrong. We discuss those challenges further in the "What Could Go Wrong" section of this chapter.

Debates

Debates are another discussion strategy that can be used in any science classroom. In Chapter 9: Strategies for Teaching Writing, we discuss argument writing and give prompt examples. These same prompts can be used to create debates or friendly arguments within the classroom. In fact, debates can be used as an extension to any writing activity. However, they can also be used independently to generate more discourse.

To facilitate a debate, we follow this process:

1. We first determine an argument prompt. It is important that there be at least two sides to the argument and that there is *credible* scientific evidence that can be used to back up both sides. For example, "Should states use nuclear energy as their primary energy source?" We regularly solicit topic ideas from students.

2. Once we have decided on the prompt, we like to find some resources for the students to use while preparing their arguments. We usually try to find two websites and/or articles for each side of the argument. This provides students with a starting point. If there is no technology available for students to do research, we provide them with additional written resources. We also provide more resources to students who may need extra assistance in finding information. See the Technology Connections section for links to resources.

3. Once our preparation is complete, we present the prompt to the students. In most cases, we allow students to decide their stance on the argument, but still tell them they need to read articles on both sides before deciding. When we are aware that most students are going to desire the defense of the same side, we assign students with the side they will defend. This ensures that we have equal stances on each side. We may also assign a stance to those students who have learning challenges. By doing this, we are ensuring they have the side that has the easiest to find evidence.

4. After the students read the teacher-provided resources and decide on their position, they begin the research process. Information on performing research can be found in Chapter 3: Strategies for Teaching the Scientific Method and Its Components. We tell students to be sure to record their evidence as they are researching. They can use the Argument Essay Prewrite Graphic Organizer

that is in Chapter 9: Strategies for Teaching Writing to help them effectively organize information they find. We encourage them to have three to five reasons in support of their arguments.

5. Once they have completed their research, we have them fill out index cards with each reason and its evidence. This allows them to have more concise notes and helps to reinforce their ideas.

6. The next step is to put students in small groups to have their debate. We prefer to debate in small groups instead of one-on-one because students feel more comfortable when they have an ally or two on their side.

7. Before the actual debates begin, we remind them of the discussion ground rules and how every student needs to be an active participant. Since there are two sides of the debate, students from each side will take turns speaking. Once a speaker from one side has made his or her statement, a student on the other side will speak, and so on. Every student on each side should have the opportunity to speak.

8. To start the debate, we like to flip a coin to determine which side starts. Then, each side takes turns sharing their points and evidence.

9. While the students are debating in their small groups, we walk around to monitor participation. After the debates, students can earn a grade for their graphic organizers and index cards. We can also provide specific students with feedback by using a rating scale, as shown in Figure 10.2: Group Discussion Checklist. Group members can also fill them out for their peers to ensure everyone receives feedback.

Table 10.2: Debate Topics for the Four NGSS Disciplines includes various debate topics for each of the four disciplines in the NGSS, in addition to general science topics that can pertain to all of the disciplines.

Four Corners

Four corners is an activity that incorporates movement into friendly arguments. To set up for four corners, teachers make four signs, one to be hung in each corner of their classroom. The signs say: "Strongly Agree," "Agree," "Disagree," and "Strongly Disagree." These signs should be big enough that they can be seen from across the room and taped onto a wall or cabinet high enough so students can't block them.

We then read a statement to the class that requires an opinion of strongly agree, agree, disagree, or strongly disagree. Students then silently move to the corner of the room that matches their opinion. To prevent students from simply moving with their friends, we first ask students to write their opinions on an index card or sticky

Table 10.2 Debate Topics for the Four NGSS Disciplines

NGSS discipline	Debate idea
Earth and Space Sciences	Should scientists be held liable for natural disasters (i.e., earthquakes and volcanic eruptions) if they fail to accurately predict them?
Earth and Space Sciences	Does life exist beyond Earth?
Physical Sciences	What will it take to define and classify dark matter and dark energy?
Physical Sciences	Can chemistry solve the world's hunger problem?
Life Sciences	Are zoos harmful or helpful to animal populations?
Life Sciences	Should we manage the location and size of beaver dams?
Technology, Engineering, and Applications of Science	Is artificial intelligence dangerous?
Technology, Engineering, and Applications of Science	Should scientists be required to share their research and experimental results with society, free of charge?
General Science	Should governments and private businesses be permitted to own technologies, medicines, etc., for profit?
General Science	Should a country's laws and policies be based on science?

note and list supporting reasons. Then, they are permitted to go to the corner that aligns with their answer. This process also allows students time to think before moving.

Examples of opinion statements are:

- Scientists should be required to publicize all of their data.
- Scientists should not be allowed to profit from their inventions, such as medicine.
- Trophy hunting should be made illegal.
- Mining companies should be required to replant all trees, grasses, and bushes that were clear cut.
- We should clone people.
- Parents should be allowed to choose the gender of their baby.
- Scientists wear white lab coats and spend their day mixing chemicals.
- Salt should no longer be used on icy roads because it rusts our cars.

DIFFERENTIATION FOR DIVERSE LEARNERS

For students who may need more preparation for discussions, such as ELLs and those who may have learning challenges, we find it helpful to provide them with questions ahead of time as often as possible. They can also use translators and/or other resources to develop answers prior to the activity. We use additional materials (summaries, videos, images) to build needed background knowledge. See the Technology Connections section for links to those resources. In addition, students can benefit from extra sentence stems, based on their needs.

Student Handouts and Examples

Figure 10.1: Discussion Ground Rules (Teacher Poster)
Figure 10.2: Group Discussion Ratings Scale
Figure 10.3: Socratic Seminar Participation Checklist (Student Handout)

What Could Go Wrong?

One problem that often occurs during small group and whole group discussions is that some students may not want to participate in the conversations. There are several strategies we use to increase how comfortable students feel when it is their turn to share their opinions.

One is to take advantage of "wait time." Wait time is an idea developed by Mary Budd Rowe referring to the amount of time teachers wait after a question is posed and also how long before a response takes place after a student's statement. Research has found that when wait time is longer than 3 s, the length and quality of student responses, as well as student confidence, increase (Rowe, 1986, p. 44). It can often be challenging because it can feel much longer due to the silence occurring in the classroom. We learned to patiently wait. Once students have properly processed the prompt, they are more willing to share and oftentimes their responses have more depth because of it. During wait time, students can also be encouraged to use their notes and other resources to find answers.

Additionally, we explain to students at the beginning of the year that we have high expectations for each of them and we believe they can achieve these expectations. We want our students to understand why we do not let them off the hook, especially when they respond with "I don't know" and we continue to wait for an answer. During this wait time, we encourage students to use their notes, even directing them to where they can find the information. We may also allow them to ask a friend to point out where they can find the answer. Oftentimes, to minimize the amount of attention focused on an individual student who is looking for an answer, we will tell them we are going to move to the next student, but will return to them after giving them this extra time.

Once students understand they are not going to be excused from answering or participating, they are more likely to be prepared and ready to participate. It's also important to remember that students, like all of us, sometimes have bad days. In those situations when it is clear that a student does not want to participate, we let it go and have a private conversation the following day.

As mentioned above, Socratic seminars can be an excellent tool for discussions in class, but they also have their challenges. Since the seminars are student-led, it can be difficult for students and us, as teachers, to get used to at first. Some issues we have seen arise and ways to overcome them are:

- Students are underprepared for the seminar.
  - Since this can be new for the students, many may not realize how much preparation they need to do in order to sustain a meaningful conversation with peers. To avoid this, we usually spend more time assisting them in preparing for the first seminar.
- Students lack confidence to participate in the seminar.
  - Another common problem for students is that they may not want to participate because they are shy or do not want to talk in front of others. There are a few steps we take to ensure all students are comfortable taking part in the discussion. For example, we always review the ground rules for discussions and refer to the number one rule of being respectful. This is another instance where sentence stems can come in handy for students who may need extra assistance with speaking.
  - We also found that providing "buddy" students is an effective way to help students who may be shy and hesitant during discussions. There are two options for buddies. The first buddy can be someone in the circle participating in the discussion with them. This person can prompt them to speak by inviting them after their comments, such as, "Do you agree or disagree, Susana?" We even include "encourages another student to speak" on Figure 10.3 Socratic Seminar Participation Checklist to prompt students to do it more often. Another buddy the student can have is their partner on the outside of the circle. We try to match the student with someone who they may have a positive relationship with and is able to provide them with feedback in a positive way.
  - The last tip is important for all students. We provide positive reinforcement throughout the seminar. The more positivity we can spread to students and the more encouragement we can offer, the more their confidence will increase for future seminars.
- Too much or too little teacher involvement.
  - We, like our students, need to learn and practice how to work effectively during Socratic seminars. We have to be sure to take a step back and allow the students to carry on a discussion without offering our opinions. This can be a change from many other discussions and activities that occur in

class. However, we also can't completely disappear during the seminar—we need to make sure we help students maintain the flow by encouraging them to move on when we see a break in discussion or when an idea is taking too much time. There is no sure-fire way to master this immediately. One way to reflect on our behavior during the seminar is to invite anonymous student feedback. They often will give honest feedback regarding whether or not we need to be more or less involved and we can use that information to plan for future seminars.

- Student conflict during seminar.

  - The last issue we have discovered during Socratic seminars is the potential of student conflict. One way to avoid this problem is by reminding students that we're having a discussion and there are no winners or losers. We also remind them of the "respect" ground rule.

The biggest tip for Socratic seminars is don't give up; don't stop doing them. The first time may not go as planned, but like with any skill, the more students practice, the better they get.

As with Socratic seminars, there are some challenges that can arise when classroom debates are taking place. Most of these are similar to the ones mentioned above, so the same strategies can be used. For example, to be sure students are prepared for the debate, we give them extra time and check that their graphic organizers and note cards are complete.

Additionally, even though we do the debates in small groups so students have allies and are more comfortable, there will still be students who are shy and hesitant to participate during the activity. To assist these students, we provide them with sentence starters and lots of positive reinforcement. We also request students to encourage other members to participate.

Debates can also lead to conflict among students. We remind students that there is no right or wrong side to the argument and there will be no winners. If we see students taking it too seriously and escalating tension, we pull them to the side to remind them these are friendly debates and everyone will receive the same recognition by participating effectively.

Technology Connections

Additional ideas for sentence stems and other discussion practices can be found at Larry Ferlazzo's blog, "The Best Resources Sharing the Best Practices for Fruitful Classroom Discussions" (http://larryferlazzo.edublogs.org/2014/09/21/the-best-resources-sharing-the-best-practices-for-fruitful-classroom-discussions).

Websites that translate academic language into native languages for ELLs can be found at "The Best Multilingual & Bilingual Sites for Math, Social Studies, & Science"(http://larryferlazzo.edublogs.org/2008/10/03/the-best-multilingual-bilingual-sites-for-math-social-studies-science).

Resources for online debates can be found at "The Best Sites for Students to Create & Participate in Online Debates" (http://larryferlazzo.edublogs.org/2009/10/24/the-best-sites-for-students-to-create-participate-in-online-debates).

Figures

Discussion Ground Rules

1. Always remain respectful even if you do not agree with what a speaker is saying.
2. Keep an open mind to other perspectives.
3. Listen actively and be sure to let the speaker finish his or her thoughts before speaking—do not interrupt.
4. Give everyone a chance to speak—do not take over the conversation.
5. Ask questions if you do not understand what the speaker is saying.
6. Use evidence to support your statements, when possible.

Figure 10.1 Discussion Ground Rules (Teacher Poster)

Group Discussion Ratings

Scores:	3—Mostly	2—Sometimes	1—Rarely	0—Never
	Student Name:	Student Name:	Student Name:	Student Name:
Participates fully				
Remains respectful				
Actively listens				
Takes turns				
Asks appropriate questions				
Provides proof of statements				
Stays on topic				
Total Points:				

Additional Notes:

Figure 10.2 Group Discussion Ratings Scale

Participant's Name: _____ **Observer's Name:** _____

Put an X under the statement every time you observe your partner doing one of the following:

Participates in discussion:

_____

Refers to text to support their statement:

_____

Makes eye contact with other speakers:

_____

Adds to another speaker's statement:

_____

Asks a question to further the discussion:

_____

Encourages another student to speak:

_____

Interrupts a speaker:

_____

Has a side conversation:

_____

Monopolizes the discussion:

_____

What is one thing he or she did well during the seminar?

What is one thing he or she can work on for next time?

Figure 10.3 Socratic Seminar Participation Checklist (Student Handout)

CHAPTER 11

Strategies for Teaching Math

What Is It?

In many ways, science is the application of math. During science lessons, students can use mathematical thinking to solve problems, interpret data, and measure objects and phenomena.

The Next Generation Science Standards (NGSS) authors didn't want science teachers to outpace grade-level math content. Their goal, instead, was to incorporate grade-level math curriculum into science lessons so that science classes were reinforcing the math concepts by applying them to real-life settings (NGSS, 2013e).

To ensure we are complementing our math colleagues, we review the Common Core Math Standards that students have been taught in previous grades and will be taught this current school year. For example, because science lessons require students to measure a myriad of objects and phenomena, we take note of the measurement standards, which include

- measuring length using several different tools (rulers, meter sticks, measuring tape)
- measuring liquid volumes
- measuring masses of objects
- using units of measurement from both the metric and Imperial systems (grams, kilograms, liters, inches, feet, centimeters, and meters)
- adding, subtracting, and dividing liquid volumes, masses, and lengths of the same unit of measurement

Table 11.1 Measurement Standards per Grade Level

Measurement standards	Grade level
Convert units of measurement within the same system (i.e., 3 ft = 1 yard and 100 cm = 1 m)	4
Solve multi-step, real-world word problems by converting units of measurement within the same system	5
Convert units across the measurement systems (metric vs. Imperial) (i.e., 5 in. = 12.7 cm)	6

When we create lessons for elementary students, we consider their math background and the current math skills they are learning, depending on their grade level. Generally, this requires a conversation with the math teacher, who can also provide insight into the struggles students are having in math. We often co-plan with the math teachers so that our lessons are reinforcing their curriculum. For example, Table 11.1: Measurement Standards per Grade Level shares math curriculum expectations that also appear in the Next Generation Science Standards (NGSS, 2013e).

Why We Like It

In our experience, many secondary students have the mistaken perception that because they learn subjects in separate classes, the subjects are independent of each other. For example, when we ask our students to write an essay, some students protest with "but this isn't English class." When students use mathematical concepts in science class, we are strengthening their math skills but also communicating that content areas are often integrated beyond the school environment.

Supporting Research

Math skills are required in many science lessons and everyday applications of science.

Teaching students how to read and make graphs is an essential skill for science learning. Graphs have been found to promote a deeper understanding of science concepts (Kilic, Sezen, & Sari, 2012, p. 2937).

In this chapter, we will provide resources for teaching students how to perform dimensional calculations. Dimensional analysis can help students with calculations in and out of science class because it has been determined that it does not require a high level of mathematical skill (Reichelova & Teleki, 2013).

Chemistry classes are required for most professions in the medical field because chemistry is the basis for how drugs work on the body (Helmenstine, 2019). Chemistry classes usually teach students how to perform dimensional analysis calculations in order to prepare them for future careers. For example, research has found that when nursing students are taught how to determine medication calculations, they tend to make fewer errors when they use dimensional analysis instead of algebraic equations that solve for *x* (Greenfield, Whelan, & Cohn, 2006).

Skills for Intentional Scholars/NGSS Connections

Utilizing math while learning science concepts requires students to practice all three Skills for Intentional Scholars. When students are solving challenging math problems, they can use their critical thinking and effective problem-solving skills. When students use graphs and data tables to record and share their data, they practice their effective communication skills.

In addition to the Skills for Intentional Scholars, the NGSS require students to use math skills in several of the engineering practices. For example, students must use "mathematics and computational thinking" and engage "in argument from evidence" (NGSS, 2013b). This chapter will also provide resources for the engineering practice of analyzing and interpreting data.

The NGSS also require students to use the crosscutting concept of "scale, proportion, and quantity," which has them recognize what is "relevant at different size, time, and energy scales, and to recognize proportional relationships between different quantities as scales change" (National Science Teaching Association, n.d.). This chapter emphasizes using units of measurement in both the metric and Imperial systems because the K-12 Science Education Framework that was used to author the NGSS suggests that students can obtain an understanding of scale by using various units of measurement (Teaching Science as Inquiry, 2019).

Application

We first provide resources for teaching students to make, choose, and interpret graphs. Then we offer strategies to teach students how to complete dimensional analysis problems and how to use the metric and Imperial systems of measurement. This section also provides a specific lesson plan for celebrating March 14, which is known as Pi Day.

See Chapter 3: Strategies for Teaching the Scientific Method and Its Components for resources on another math-related skill: teaching students how to make data tables.

MAKING GRAPHS

Elementary and Middle School

Students can graph data from many experiments that are performed in class. In our experience, elementary and middle school students benefit from proactive lessons that teach them how to make graphs.

The Common Core Math Standards require students in second grade to learn how to make bar graphs (Common Core State Standards Initiative, 2019a, 2019b, 2019c, Math) so we use bar graphs in our examples when we work with fourth grade students. See Figure 11.1: Bar Graph Example for Teaching Graphing to Fourth Grade Students. Note that students need to know the vocabulary words *horizontal* and *vertical* to effectively use Figure 11.1. Line graphs are introduced in the fifth grade Common Core Math Standards (Common Core State Standards Initiative, 2019a, 2019b, 2019c), so this is when we also begin using line graphs and the terms "x- and y-axis." See Figure 11.2: Line Graph Example for Teaching Graphing to Fifth Grade and Beyond.

When we first introduce graphing to students, they each receive a copy of Figure 11.1 or Figure 11.2, depending on their grade level. Using the students' data from a recent experiment, we model, step-by-step, how to turn their data table into a graph. As they work, we walk around the room to ensure they are following the process and to support students as they are creating their graphs.

After their graphs are complete, we provide a widely known science acronym to help them remember the basic parts of every graph. The acronym is DRY MIX. Here is an explanation of what each letter represents:

D = dependent variable
R = responding variable
Y = y-axis (graph information on the vertical axis, also called the y-axis)
M = manipulated variable
I = independent variable
X = x-axis (graph information on the horizontal axis, also called the x-axis)

Another well-known acronym we've found useful is TAILS, which stands for:

T = title (must include all variables)
A = axis labels (DRY MIX)
I = interval marks (ensure they start at zero)
L = label units (units of measurement)
S = scale (ensure the intervals are equal)

To teach these two acronyms, we write the letters on the board. Students then work with a partner to guess what each letter represents. When they guess correctly, they are given a piece of chalk or a dry erase marker to write the answer on the board. Once all correct answers are written on the board, we provide any remaining parts of the acronym they didn't accurately guess. We then have students add the acronyms and their meanings to their notes or to Figure 11.1 and Figure 11.2.

When students make future graphs, we encourage them to use Figures 11.1 and 11.2 and follow the step-by-step procedures to ensure they have all of the requirements for a scientific graph.

See the section "Celebrating Pi Day" for resources students can use to make graphs in Microsoft Excel.

High School

We don't assume high school students know how to create a scientifically accurate graph.

After students perform their first class experiment and collect data, we require them to complete a pretest (see Figure 11.3: Example of Graphing Pretest and Figure 11.4: Example of Graphing Pretest—Answer Key). Our aim is to identify which students know how to make graphs and which students require further instruction.

If half of the class does well on the pretest and the other half proves to need more instruction, we strategically pair students so one student who is already proficient in making graphs is partnered with a student who requires more support. Each student creates their own graph using the data they collected in the class experiment; however, we permit students to work with their assigned partners to complete their graphs.

If a small number of students pass the pretest, then we allow these students to graph their data individually. As they are making their graphs, we model graphing to the remaining students during a class discussion.

If a majority of the students pass the pretest, they make their graphs individually while we meet in a small group with the few students who require more help. Each of these students makes his/her own graph but the graphs are constructed as a group, one step at a time.

Choosing the Type of Graph

In our experience, students of all grade levels often struggle to determine which type of graph is best to use. By the time students reach the secondary level, they may have already been exposed to four types of graphs: bar graphs, single and double line graphs, and pie charts. We use Figure 11.5: Which Type of Graph Should I Use? to give secondary students practice in determining which type of graph they should use with different types of data.

Each student receives their own copy of Figure 11.5. We model how to complete the first problem in front of the whole class. We use a strategy we call "I am thinking. . .," which requires us to think aloud as we work through the problem. By doing this, students witness our thought process live. We start every statement with "I am thinking"; for example, for the first problem we say the following:

1. "I am thinking. . .the data Xee is going to collect is the number of times the flowers are landed on."

2. "I am thinking. . .since that is the data she is collecting during the experiment, it is my dependent variable."

3. "I am thinking. . .that the dependent variable goes on the y-axis."

We draw an x- and y-axis on the board and label the y-axis with "Number of Times the Flowers are Landed on." We continue modeling our thinking.

4. "I am thinking. . .there are three colors: pink, blue, and green. Flower color is the only difference between the flowers so this is my independent variable."

5. "I am thinking. . .that the independent variable goes on the x-axis."

We label the x-axis "Flower Color."

6. "I am thinking. . .that because the x-axis doesn't have numbers, I have to make a bar graph."

We begin making one bar for each flower color to show students what the final product may look like.

Once the first problem is complete, we ask students if they have any questions and address each one for the class.

To differentiate for older and advanced students, we ask them what other type of graph can be used to represent the same data. As shown in Figure 11.6: Which Type of Graph Should I Use?—Answer Key, the first problem on the worksheet has two correct answers. If students struggle to realize that the data can also be graphed using a pie chart, we pose the question, "What if the number of times a flower was landed on was changed to a percentage?" We've found this prompt is enough to guide students toward a pie chart. We ask a volunteer to demonstrate the "I am thinking. . ." process to walk through how they would determine they can use a pie chart.

After modeling the first problem, students are instructed to work with a partner and complete the second one on the worksheet using the "I am thinking. . ." process. This requires them to draw a graph and talk out their thinking as they are drawing. We walk around the classroom and provide assistance to student pairs. We never give the correct answer but, instead, ask guiding questions such as, "What data is the scientist collecting during the experiment?" and "Where does the independent variable go on a graph?"

Once everyone completes the second problem, we ask for a pair of students to demonstrate their "I am thinking. . ." process to the class. Afterwards, we ask students to work with their partners and complete the rest of the worksheet. When everyone is done, student pairs volunteer to use the "I am thinking. . ." strategy to share their thought processes and answers with the class. If anyone has a different answer, it may be because several of the problems have multiple correct answers. We use this opportunity to explain to students that as long as graphs and pie charts are created correctly, there are many times in math and science when there are multiple ways to get to the correct answer.

Analyzing and Interpreting Graphs

In our experience, the best way to teach students how to analyze and interpret graphs is through a lot of practice.

When data and graphs are *analyzed*, statements of fact are documented. For example, when analyzing the data in Figure 11.7: Temperature vs. Number of *Escherichia coli* Colonies, we would write the following analysis statements:

1. The highest temperature where *E. coli* colonies grew was 31 °C. At this temperature, there were 22 colonies.

2. The lowest temperature where *E. coli* colonies grew was 6 °C. At this temperature, there were 68 colonies.

3. As the temperature increased, the number of *E. coli* colonies decreased.

When data and graphs are being *interpreted*, it means that conclusions are drawn regarding the meaning of the data, or the relationship between the variables. For example, using the graph in Figure 11.7 again, these two statements are our assumptions regarding the relationship between temperature and number of *E. coli* colonies:

1. *E. coli* grows more in lower temperatures.
2. Higher temperatures are not the ideal environment for *E. coli* colonies.

In our experience, many students of all grade levels do not know the difference between analyzing and interpreting data. To teach this contrast, we first provide each student a copy of a sample graph while also posting it on the board. Figure 11.8: Year vs. Number of Deer and Wolves is an example of a graph we use.

We explain that when graphs are *analyzed*, scientists write statements of fact and each statement usually includes specific data from the graph, although it's not required. We provide two examples and then ask student pairs to write two additional examples. Here are a few example analysis statements for Figure 11.8:

1. In 2009, there were 11 deer and 1 wolf.
2. Seventeen years later, it was 2026 and there were 10 deer and 6 wolves.
3. In 2015, there were four more wolves than deer.
4. When the deer population is high, the wolf population increases.

While students are writing their two analysis statements, we walk around the room to provide assistance. If students are struggling, we don't give them answers but, instead, ask guiding questions such as, "In your opinion, which year has the most surprising data? How can you analyze it?"

Once all student pairs have two additional analysis statements written on their paper, we ask volunteers to read their statements.

We then explain that when graphs are *interpreted*, we give meaning to the data by making assumptions or drawing conclusions of how the variables are related. We provide two examples and then ask student pairs to write two additional statements. Here are some examples:

1. When the wolf population is at its highest, they are killing the most deer, causing the deer population to decrease.
2. When the deer population is low, the wolves have less food so their population decreases.
3. When the wolf population is decreasing, there are less predators for the prey so the deer population increases.

While students are writing their two interpretation statements, we again walk around the room to help students. To prompt their critical thinking, we don't give answers. Instead, we ask guiding questions such as, "What seems to be the relationship between the wolves and the deer?"

Once all student pairs have two additional analysis statements written on their paper, we ask volunteers to read their statements.

We often use data from local phenomena to create authentic graphs. For example, our school is near a large man-made lake named Tempe Town Lake. When we began an ecology unit, we contacted Phoenix Sky Harbor Airport, which is a 10-minute drive from Tempe Town Lake. The airport officials provided their wildlife strike data (when man-made objects, such as airplanes, hit wildlife), which we turned into a graph that could be used in a lesson. See Figure 11.9: Wildlife Strike Data Analysis and Interpretation for a copy of the worksheet we used to teach students how water attracts animals. It doubled as an opportunity to practice analyzing and interpreting graphs. The answer key is provided in Figure 11.10: Wildlife Strike Data Analysis and Interpretation—Answer Key.

See Table 11.2: Authentic Data Ideas for additional phenomena that can supply authentic data in several different areas of the world. Authentic data that cannot be obtained online most often can be acquired with a phone call. We've found that people are very accommodating when they find out that we are teachers asking for data to use in our class.

DIMENSIONAL ANALYSIS

Dimensional analysis is mathematically changing one unit of measurement into another unit of measurement where both quantities are equal (Garcia, 2019). For example, students perform dimensional analysis when they change inches into miles.

Table 11.2 Authentic Data Ideas

Phenomenon	Authentic data	Possible data resources
Precipitation (snowfall, hail, rain)	Amount in a specific area	Counties
River or lake	Number of times its flooded or how high the water level has been in the past	State Departments of Environmental Quality or the U.S. Geological Survey
Fault line	Number of earthquakes in a specific timeframe or average strength of earthquakes	U.S. Geological Survey
Temperature	High temperatures vs. low temperatures	Counties
Tides	Times or height of high/low tides or spring/neap tides	National Oceanic and Atmospheric Administration
Garbage on a beach	Weight of plastic refuse	State Departments or the U.S. Environmental Protection Agency
Local invasive species	Population dynamics, including the size and average age	State Departments or the U.S. Department of the Interior
Air quality	AQI—Air Quality Index, including amount of ozone, pollen, and particles	State Departments of Environmental Quality
Tornadoes	Number or strength of tornadoes in a specific area or the speed of tornadoes	National Oceanic and Atmospheric Administration
Traffic accidents	Cause of traffic accidents, focusing on speed and impact with inanimate objects	State Department of Public Safety
Bridge inspections	Which bridge designs can withstand high winds, excessive payload, or weathering	U.S. Department of Transportation: Federal Highway Administration

The key to performing dimensional analysis problems correctly is writing the units of measurement for every number. Students attempt to take the easy way out by simply writing numbers, but minor errors can easily be made using this shortcut.

When we introduce dimensional analysis to students, we use examples that involve money or time because these are simple concepts they theoretically learned in the primary grades (Common Core State Standards Initiative, 2019c). See Figure 11.11: Dimensional Analysis Practice for the worksheet we provide to each student.

We have a class discussion and help students to walk step-by-step through the first problem. We model how to complete it on the board. Here is an example of what that discussion might look like:

Us:	When starting a dimensional analysis problem, identify what unit of measurement you need at the end. What is the first problem on your worksheet asking you to find?
STUDENTS:	Dimes.
Us:	Yes, that's correct. So, on the right side of my paper, I'm going to write dimes. Why did I put this on the right side of the paper?
STUDENTS:	Because this will be the answer, which goes at the end of the math problem.
Us:	Good! We are working backwards so what should we draw to the left of 'dimes'?
STUDENTS:	An equal sign.
Us:	That is correct. While I'm writing the answer on the board, you need to copy it onto your paper. I'll walk around in a minute so you can ask me questions. OK, now we are going to go to the beginning of the math problem. We know from the problem that we are starting with $8.00, so I'm going to write 8 dollars. Then I'm going to draw a multiplication sign, which is always the type of math you do in dimensional analysis. To change dollars into dimes, I need to get rid of the dollars. I'm going to make a fraction after my multiplication sign. To cancel out the dollars, should I put dollars in the numerator or the denominator?"
STUDENTS:	The denominator.
Us:	Yes! So let's write 1 dollar in the denominator. Now, how many dimes are in one dollar?
STUDENTS:	Ten.

Us: OK, so then 10 dimes goes into the numerator. Now I'm going to cross out the dollar that's after the 8 and I'm going to cross out the dollar in the denominator. They cancel each other. The last step is to multiply across so that you multiply 8 by 10. Do this now while I walk around the room, checking to see if you need help. You may work with your partner.

As we walk around, we help struggling students by guiding them through the math problem. If they get stuck and don't know what to do, we go back to the questions we asked during the class discussion; for example, we ask, "Which unit do you need to cancel out?"

After students correctly complete the first problem, we ask them a conceptual question, such as, "The answer is 80 dimes. What does the number '80' represent?" Students are provided time to discuss the answer with their partner and then we randomly call on a student to explain that the number 80 represents the number of dimes in $8. Research shows that by asking conceptual questions after students complete a math equation, they tend to understand the purpose of the equation and answer, which can lead to enhanced problem-solving skills (Thompson, Philipp, Thompson, & Boyd, 1994).

Students then complete the remaining math problems on the worksheet. The third problem requires students to switch the data in the numerator and denominator. Some students may have the math skills needed to figure this out while other students may struggle at this point. This is another time when walking around the room is imperative because we may need to guide students. If several student groups can't figure out that they need to switch the denominator and numerator, we obtain the attention of the whole class and model how to work the problem.

Once all students are done with the money problems, we move to multi-step dimensional analysis problems using time as the unit of measurement. This is the second half of Figure 11.11: Dimensional Analysis Practice.

We first model problem number five on the worksheet and ask students to copy down everything we write on the board. After setting up the answer to the problem by placing "seconds" on the right side of the paper, we ask students questions, such as, "How many seconds are in one minute?" We continue to guide them through the math problem by asking other leading questions so they recognize that their goal is to use new units to cancel existing units.

As students complete this problem correctly, they are instructed to work with their learning partner to complete the worksheet and to ask if they have any questions. We continue walking around the room, stopping to check on every student group so that all students receive support and immediate feedback. The answer key for Figure 11.11 is Figure 11.12: Dimensional Analysis Practice—Answer Key.

Table 11.3 Measurement Examples for Content-Related Dimensional Analysis Problems

Content area	Variable examples to be measured and changed
Chemistry	Density, mass, moles, molar mass, volume, temperature, time
Physics	Velocity, speed, momentum, force, acceleration, temperature, time, wavelength, frequency, work, kinetic energy, electrical potential
Biology	Mass, area, growth rate, carrying capacity, population density, time, birth rate, death rate, pulse, pressure, volume
Earth Science	Velocity, speed, mass, area, distance, volume, density, miles per gallon, time
Engineering	Mass, area, temperature, speed, velocity, distance, time, fluid mechanics (i.e., chimney flow, surface waves, and ship waves), elasticity, critical load, density

After students complete this practice worksheet, we assign dimensional analysis problems that pertain to the unit we are teaching. Table 11.3: Measurement Examples for Content-Related Dimensional Analysis Problems provides specific ideas of variables that can be measured and changed using dimensional analysis.

There are many dimensional analysis worksheets available online for every content area. Many of these online worksheets also include the answer key. When we use other teachers' worksheets that we have obtained from the Internet, we require that all student work be completed in class to prevent students from searching for the answers.

METRIC AND IMPERIAL SYSTEMS

Grade-Level Math Skills and Standards

Most science lessons require students of all ages to measure objects and phenomena, including how they change over time. For example, science labs collect data that measure distance, temperature, mass, weight, energy, force, and volume.

Which measurement system should we teach in our classes: the metric or Imperial system? The NGSS and Common Core Math Standards require that students know both the metric and Imperial systems (NGSS, 2013e). Students need to know the two systems for real-life applications. For example, NASA uses both the metric and Imperial systems (NASA, 2014).

At which grade should each of the measurement systems be introduced to students? The NGSS require that students use both measurement systems to measure objects prior to the third grade (NGSS, 2013e). Between fourth and sixth grade, the NGSS require students to learn how to convert within and between the two measurement systems.

Nevertheless, many students still do not have—or do not remember—this knowledge by the time they enter high school. We regularly teach it to our secondary classes.

Teaching the History of the Measurement Systems

To help students understand why it's important to use the same measurement system as other societies and governments, we introduce the history of the two systems. We ask students if they know the history of the Imperial system (also known as the standard system) or if they know the history of the metric system. We provide time for students to share any of their knowledge. In our experience, students who have lived in other countries are most likely to volunteer their personal stories with the class. This sharing is an excellent opportunity for us to develop a culturally responsive classroom. See Chapter 14: Strategies for Cultural Responsiveness for additional strategies to make your classroom culturally responsive.

Sometimes students provide misinformation or are missing information, so we share the history based on an Encyclopedia Britannica article (Zupko & Chisholm, 2019). Here is how we tell it:

> For centuries, many countries were using their own measuring techniques. But as the world's population increased and technology advanced, people from different countries began trading with each other. But they found it difficult to trade because they weren't measuring the same object with the same unit of measurement. Think about it: *How would you know if you were getting a deal or getting ripped off when someone from another country offered you 3 yayas of candy for your 2 pounds of sugar?* Without knowing what a "yaya" is, you can't determine if you are making a good trade.

At this point, we stop the story and have students share out their feelings. Then we ask them how all of these different countries should solve their trading problem. Students share any ideas they come up with and then we continue with the story.

> About 800 years ago, many countries decided they needed to use the same units of measurement. This is called a standardized system. For example, maybe one yaya is equal to 2 pounds and this is true everywhere you go and with everyone you trade.

> After we won the American Revolution, the U.S. Constitution went into effect, which states that it's the job of Congress to determine a standard measurement system. Several famous people debated the issue, including the current president, George Washington, and the future president, John Quincy Adams. They decided they wanted to

continue trading with the British people so they adopted the Imperial system to maintain a standard between the two countries.

During this time, the metric system was being established in France, but Britain had yet to adopt it. So although using the metric system was discussed, the Founding Fathers decided on the Imperial system. The metric system was finalized in France in June, 1799, just 16 years after the end of the American Revolution.

The metric system spread through Europe as France conquered other lands. When France took over a new city or country, they would require the people living there to use the metric system. And sometimes France required other countries to use the metric system in treaties. By the mid-1800s much of Europe, Latin America, Russia, Japan, and China had adopted the metric system.

I have a thinking question for you: *If the rest of the world is beginning to use the metric system and the United States is using the Imperial system, what problems do you think they may have experienced?* (If students struggle to realize that trade and the economy would be negatively affected, we remind them of why a standard unit of measurement was created 800 years ago.)

Many industries in both Britain and the United States knew they were going to have a problem selling their goods if they didn't also begin using the metric system. Throughout the 1900s, many industries in both countries began adopting the metric system. For example, in the United States the chemical, automobile, electronic, and power industries adopted the metric system.

Here's a second thinking question: *Why is it important for you to learn both the Imperial and metric systems?* We give students time to talk with their learning partners first and then call on volunteers. Correct answers may include "Some of the industries in the U.S. use the metric system while other industries use the Imperial system" and "Although we live in the U.S. where the Imperial system is the official measuring system, we may work for a company whose customer base is located outside of the U.S."

After discussing their answers, we continue our story. "In 1965, Britain officially adopted the metric system but the United States never did. Here's another thinking question for you: *What objects in the U.S. would have to be changed if the U.S. Congress officially adopted the metric system?* Talk to your learning partner first and then I'll call on volunteers." Students often list items such as road signs, cookbooks, and rulers. Then we ask, *"Knowing that all of these objects in the entire United States would have to be replaced, why do you think the U.S. hasn't adopted the metric system?"* We then have a discussion about who would have to pay for all of the changes. We honor every student's answer because there is no correct or incorrect answer to this question.

Now that students know the history of both systems of measurement and why they need to learn both of them, we begin teaching about measurement.

Converting in the Imperial System

We recognize that conversions within the Imperial system and metric system (and between the two systems) can be accomplished using online calculators. However, the NGSS, Common Core State Standards, and National Council of Teachers of Mathematics (NCTM) state that students need to develop an understanding of measuring units and their relationships, in addition to the ability to apply both systems to real-world situations (NCTM, 2015). In other words, the purpose of teaching measurement is to teach students how units are related to each other so they have a conceptual understanding of a measurement. This knowledge will help them to problem solve when they are required to perform measurements as adults, such as altering a recipe, designing the landscape in their backyard, or building a birdhouse.

To teach students how to convert within the Imperial system, we have them complete Figure 11.13: Practice Measuring Your Friends and Their Things. Each student receives a copy of the worksheet and various measuring tools such as a ruler, measuring tape, yardstick, electric scale, triple-beam balance, measuring spoons, and measuring cups. Students work in pairs to measure their partner's height and belongings. In the case that a partner doesn't own one of the items on the list, we provide our belongings.

The first measuring problem is done for them so we discuss this problem as an example of what they should do to convert measurements. As students are working in their pairs, we walk around to ensure they are using the measuring tools correctly, including rounding to the nearest tenth as the instructions require, and are completing the math conversions accurately.

Students often struggle to know when to multiply and when to divide. We simplify this process by telling students that they will always multiply. They do have to determine if they are going to put the conversion in the numerator or the denominator. To help them, we provide the hint that if they are converting to a larger unit

(1 mile is longer than 1 yard), they need to put the conversion in the denominator. Here is an example:

$$5.6 \text{ yards} \times \frac{1 \text{ mile}}{1,760 \text{ yards}} =$$

And vice versa: if they are converting to a smaller unit (1 pound is less than 1 ton), they need to put the conversion in the numerator. Here is an example:

$$1.2 \text{ tons} \times \frac{2,000 \text{ pounds}}{1 \text{ ton}} =$$

We explain that by doing it this way, the beginning units of measurement cancel out (yards and tons based on the above examples), leaving only the new units (miles and pounds).

Once the class completes the activity, we review the answers together. The answer key is provided in Figure 11.14. Students volunteer with their partner to come to the board and write out how they found their answer. Then we challenge students to create three conversion math problems: volume, mass, and distance. They must create an answer key, too. The NGSS require students to learn about volume, mass, and distance prior to fourth grade (NGSS, 2013e). However, if students don't recall this background knowledge (or didn't attend schools that implemented the NGSS), we remind them that volume is how much space a substance occupies, mass is an object's weight on Earth (or how much matter an object contains), and distance is the measurement between two objects.

Each group is then randomly paired with another group. They switch math problems and grade each other's work. Next, groups are randomly matched again. We continue having them practice until the majority of the class can work the problems on their own without much help from us or their partners.

Converting in the Metric System

When we introduce the metric system to students, we begin by showing them how it uses a base of 10. We teach students the prefixes of kilo- through milli- because these are the most commonly used. However, there are larger and smaller prefixes, such as mega- and giga- that are larger than the kilo- prefix, and micro- and nano- that are smaller than the milli- prefix. Students naturally learn these larger and smaller prefixes as they advance through math and science classes, which can be easily learned when they have the background knowledge of the kilo- through milli- prefixes.

We begin by telling students there is only one base unit for distance (meter), one base unit for volume (liter), and one base unit for mass (gram). Then we explain how these bases can get bigger or smaller by adding a prefix. We write the prefix and the base *meter* on the board in the shape of a ladder so that the smallest prefix is at the bottom of the ladder and the largest prefix is at the top. Figure 11.15: Metric System Ladder is an example.

In our experience, many students use the mnemonic, "King Henry Died By Drinking Chocolate Milk" to remember the order of the prefixes. However, we've had two negative experiences with this phrase. First, students sometimes believe that it's a historical fact that chocolate milk killed King Henry! Second, students can't use this phrase to differentiate between deka- and deci- because they both begin with the letter *D*.

When we introduce the prefixes, we teach "King Henry Died By Drinking Chocolate Milk," but then explain that it's not historically accurate. We also tell students that the first D word should begin with the letters *da* because that will help them remember that deka is first and is abbreviated *da*. We challenge each student to rewrite the mnemonic, giving them the responsibility of correcting the two problems that exist with the original mnemonic. We've found that students are more likely to remember the prefixes and their order when they develop their own mnemonic. An example of a student-created mnemonic is "Kangaroos Hop Daringly Because Dingos Chase Mammals."

After everyone has written their mnemonic, we explain that you multiply by 10 for every step down the ladder. For example, if you want to convert 9 kilometers to hectometers, that requires one step down so you multiply by 10 one time, which results in 90 hectometers. And when you begin with 9 km and want to convert to dekameters, that is two steps down the ladder so you multiply by 10 two times, resulting in 900 dekameters.

Students practice these conversions by completing Part 1 of Figure 11.16: Converting Within the Metric System. Each student receives a copy of the worksheet and is assigned a learning partner. They begin by drawing their ladder at the top of the worksheet.

We instruct them to add the abbreviation for each unit of measurement and the prefixes so that their ladders look like Figure 11.17: Metric System Ladder and Abbreviations.

In our experience, students make two common errors. We draw their attention to these errors so they can avoid making them. Here are the two errors:

1. Capitalization: many students don't follow the capitalization rules when they write their unit of measurement abbreviations. We point out that all of the abbreviations need to be lower case except the abbreviation for liter, which is the capital *L*. Scientists use the capital *L* to avoid confusion with the number 1 (one). That being said, yes, in the field of science, we usually abbreviate 'liters' with a lower case L when there is a prefix, such as milli- or deci-.

2. Confusion with the abbreviations of lower case *m*: the abbreviation for meter is lower case *m* and the abbreviation for the prefix milli- is also lower case *m*. Many students confuse these two because they are identical. We point out that the abbreviation for milli- is never going to be by itself. It will always be paired with one of the three bases and will always appear first (mg, ml, and mm). The abbreviation for meter may be by itself, but if it is paired, it will always be the last letter (km, hm, dam, dm, cm, and mm). We also explain to students that when the two *m*'s are combined (mm), it stands for millimeter.

In Part 1 of Figure 11.16, the first problem is already completed for them. We walk the class through the steps for completing the problem. Then, learning partners work together to solve the remaining problems in Part 1. We walk around the room, helping students who are struggling. Once everyone is done with Part 1, students change learning partners to compare answers. If any of their answers are different, they both rework the problem to determine the correct answer. We then provide the correct answers for all of the problems and ask if students have any questions.

Part 2 of Figure 11.16 requires students to move up the ladder. We ask students what the opposite of multiplication is. When they answer "division," we explain that we are going the opposite direction on the ladder (up), so we must do the opposite of multiplication (division). This means we must divide by 10. We return to Figure 11.16 and do the first problem as a class. We then repeat the process that we performed with Part 1.

As students work these types of conversion problems, some may find mathematical shortcuts. Before moving on to Part 3, we stop the class and ask if anyone is doing the math differently. We ask these students to share their shortcuts with the class. One popular variation is to multiply (or divide) all of the steps first and then do the conversion. Here is an example:

> Converting 3 km to m requires three steps down the ladder. Students first multiply $10 \times 10 \times 10$ to get 1,000 and then multiply 3 and 1,000, which equals 3,000 m.

Another mathematical shortcut is to move the decimal point instead of multiplying and dividing. We explain that when we move down the ladder, we move the decimal point to the right every time we take a step down, and when we move up the ladder, we move the decimal point to the left every time we take a step up. Here is an example:

> Converting 85 km to hm requires one step down the ladder. We remind students that when there is no decimal point in a number, it's

at the end of the number, like a period goes at the end of a sentence. We draw the decimal point so that it looks like this: "85." Then we move the decimal point one time to the right and fill in the empty place with a 0 (zero) so that the answer is 850 hm.

Here is another example:

Converting 620 ml to dal requires four steps up the ladder. We remind students that when there is no decimal point in a number, it's at the end of the number. We draw the decimal point so that it looks like this: "620." Then we move the decimal point four times to the left and fill in the empty place with a 0 (zero) so that the answer is 0.0620 dal. We like this example because it shows students how to add decimals to the front of a number but also gives us an opportunity to explain that 0.0620 dal and .0620 (without the preceding zero) and 0.062 (without the last zero) are the same number. We instruct them to always include the preceding number because this is how professional mathematicians and scientists write numbers.

As we work through Part 3 of Figure 11.16, which includes a mixture of conversions that move up and down the ladder, we announce to students that they should use the mathematical method they find the easiest to use. Students are again paired with a learning partner, we walk around to help struggling students, and when everyone is done, students work with a new partner to compare and discuss their answers. Afterwards, we provide the answers and ask if students have any questions or if we should do any of the problems on the board. The answer key can be found in Figure 11.18: Converting Within the Metric System—Answer Key.

As a closing activity, students complete three stations in the classroom. We give each student a copy of Figure 11.19: Metric System Measuring Challenge and instruct them to draw their ladder on the top of the paper. We remind them to add their abbreviations.

The first station is located at their desk and is completed with a learning partner. Station 1 requires students to answer four thinking questions. Students first discuss with their learning partner how to solve the problems. As students are working, we walk around the room. If students are struggling, we do not give them the answer but instead we ask guiding questions, such as, "How can you use the metric system ladder to solve these problems?" Once they think of a solution, they complete the work to find the answers and then move to Station 2.

Station 2 requires some prep work on our part. Prior to the activity, we measure the length of 10 items and randomly line them up on the edge of a table. Items we've measured include a chocolate Easter bunny, candy dispenser, pencil, pencil sharpener, and toy cell phone. See Figure 11.20: Example of 10 Items to Be Measured for a picture of the items on the edge of a table as an example of how to set up Station 2.

When students arrive at Station 2, the directions tell them they may not touch or measure the items but they must determine each item's length. There is only one solution to the challenge and students must figure out what it is. The solution at Station 2 requires students to first convert the 10 measurements into the same unit. It doesn't make a difference which unit they choose; for example, they can convert them all into kilometers, meters, or decimeters. Then, finding the smallest item on the table, they assign it the smallest length. The second smallest item on the table is assigned the second smallest length, and so on until all 10 items have been assigned a specific length.

When they complete Station 2, they move to Station 3, which is where the teacher is located. To ensure we are monitoring the class for on-task behavior, we place ourselves in the room so that we have full view of Stations 1 and 2. When students approach us, we ask them to explain how they solved the problems in both stations. Then we check their answers. We circle incorrect answers and instruct students to rework those problems and to return to us when they are done, at which time we check their answers again. This continues until everyone has the correct answers. The answer key can be found in Figure 11.21: Metric System Measuring Challenge—Answer Key.

Converting Between the Metric and Imperial Systems

We begin by telling infamous stories about conversions between the metric and Imperial systems that went very badly. For example, in 1983, an Air Canada plane was developed using the metric system, the first of its kind. The refueling process hadn't yet been converted to the metric system, causing too little fuel for the plane. Approximately half-way through its flight, the airplane ran out of gas. Luckily, the pilots were able to land the plane safely and avoided all fatalities (Witkin, 1983).

Another story occurred in 1999 when NASA lost an orbiter in space because a contracted engineering team used the Imperial measurement system while NASA used the metric system. The orbiter was supposed to land on Mars but instead is probably orbiting the sun (Lloyd, 1999).

Once students understand why it's necessary to learn how to convert correctly between the two measurement systems, we ask them to share with us an item from their backpack that can be measured. A common example is a bottle of water, which has an Imperial measurement of 16.9 fluid ounces and a metric measurement of 500 ml. As students share, we ask, "Which is greater—16.9 fluid ounces or 500 ml?" Students answer that they are the same.

We explain that the purpose of today's lesson is to learn how to convert a measurement in one system to an equivalent measurement in the other system. Each student receives a copy of Figure 11.22: Metric and Imperial System Internet Search Lab, which requires students to read online articles that include one of the two systems, for example, the length and mass of the longest snakes on Earth. When technology is limited, we print the articles and provide hard copies to the students.

We work on the first problem as a class. We model how to complete the problem using the conversion table at the top of the worksheet. As students work through the Internet lab, we walk around to help those who are struggling. We check the correctness of their answers as they work. If they have an incorrect answer, we bring it to their attention and ask them to work the problem again. We watch them work the problem so if they make an error, we can easily identify where they are struggling and help them to correct it.

Students most often become confused when they are trying to determine if they will multiply or divide by the conversion. We simplify this by telling students that they will always multiply. They are responsible for determining if they are going to put the conversion in the numerator or the denominator. To help them, we provide the hint that the unit of measurement they began with goes in the denominator and the unit of measurement they want to end up with goes in the numerator. This "cancels out" the old unit and leaves only the new unit.

The answer key is available in Figure 11.23: Metric and Imperial System Internet Search Lab—Answer Key.

Table 11.4: Topics That Can Integrate Measurement into the Four NGSS Disciplines lists lesson plan ideas of how measurement can be purposefully integrated into the four NGSS disciplines.

Table 11.4 Topics That Can Integrate Measurement into the Four NGSS Disciplines

NGSS discipline	Measurement lesson plan
Earth Sciences	Measure the rate of erosion as the incline changes
Earth Sciences	Measure porosity and permeability of different soil profiles
Physical Sciences	Measure the change of volume of a gas as its temperature increases and decreases
Physical Sciences	Measure the force exerted on objects of different masses using spring scales
Life Sciences	Measure the change in the mass of an object that underwent osmosis
Life Sciences	Measure rate of reaction with and without catalysts
Engineering, Technology, and Applications of Science	Calculate the pounds per square inch as the number of standard atmospheres and pascals
Engineering, Technology, and Applications of Science	Calculate the dimensionless quantity of the drag force of a turbine placed in the ocean to create tidal energy

CELEBRATING PI DAY

The world celebrates Pi Day on March 14. Sometimes Pi Day lands on a weekend or while a school is on break. When this occurs, we celebrate Pi Day the school day prior to March 14.

We allow our students to bring in circle-shaped snacks to share with the class, such as pizza, donuts, cookies, and blueberries. We caution teachers to check with their administration prior to allowing food into the classroom because some districts have policies regarding what food is allowed, if any.

When teaching elementary students, we use lessons offered at www.piday.org, which is the official Pi Day website and offers K-12 lesson plans, focusing on algebra 1 & 2, geometry, and pre-calculus at the high school level. See the Technology Connections section for additional resources to celebrate Pi Day, including lesson plans for K-12 grade students.

However, when we work with seventh to twelfth grade students, we use our own lesson plan. The Common Core Math Standards require that beginning in the seventh grade, students learn how to calculate the circumference and area of a circle, which is why we use this lesson with students who are no younger than seventh grade.

We were inspired years ago when we realized how little students know about spreadsheet software applications, such as Microsoft Excel. The following lesson can be accomplished using Microsoft Excel, Apple Numbers, or Google Sheets; however, we use Microsoft Excel because it's considered by many to be the most flexible, and hence the most preferred, of the three software options (Hattersley, 2016). We provide links for online tutorials that teach how to use Apple Numbers and Google Sheets in the Technology Connections section for those teachers who don't have access to Microsoft Excel.

While students are sharing and eating their snacks for their Pi Day celebration, we use pi to determine the surface area and volume of several celestial objects. Students use Microsoft Excel as a calculator. We've been able to adapt the lesson plan when we work in schools that don't offer the Excel software. We allow students to use scientific or graphing calculators because the numbers they are going to calculate are too large for a regular calculator. However, scientific and graphing calculators only have the display capabilities for 10 digits, and the largest number in this lesson has 26 digits. Therefore, students need to know how to convert numbers into scientific notation in order to use calculators instead of spreadsheet software.

Setting Up Excel

Before beginning the lesson (which assumes that each pair of students has access to a computer or laptop), students must first format the cells on their spreadsheet. We instruct them to open Excel and follow along as we also set up our computers, which are projected on a screen that all students can view. Here are the instructions we read as we format our cells and instruct students to format theirs:

1. Go to the top left corner of the Excel spreadsheet and click on the little gray triangle as shown in Figure 11.24. This will highlight and select all of the cells in the spreadsheet. See Figure 11.24 for a screenshot that shows where the little gray triangle can be found.

2. Right-click anywhere on the spreadsheet so that a pop-up box appears.

3. Choose the Format Cells option.

4. Under Category, choose the option Number and set the decimal places to a value of 2, as shown in Figure 11.25.

5. Click OK.

Teaching Excel Vocabulary

Students must also know some vocabulary before we can begin. We explain the difference between a row (the cells that are going from left to right) and a column (cells that are going up and down). Rows are titled with numbers and columns are titled with letters. A visual is provided in Figure 11.26.

When we talk about a cell, we call it by its name, which is the column first, followed by the row. As an example, the first cell in Figure 11.26 is called A1. The cell below A1 is A2 and the cell to its right is B1.

To ensure students understand how cell nomenclature works, we randomly highlight a cell on our screen that is projected for all of them to see. We ask students for the cell's name. We do this for three or four cells to provide practice because the cell names will be used when they use Excel as a calculator.

Modeling How to Use Excel as a Calculator

Students are paired with a learning partner. Each group of two receives a copy of Figure 11.27: Celebrating Pi Day in the Sky. One of the students in the pair is the scribe and is responsible for documenting the answers onto the worksheet. The other student is the computer programmer who works with Excel. To ensure learning partners have an equal experience, we instruct students to switch roles when they are halfway through the activity.

We model how to set up the spreadsheet so that students can keep track of each cell's meaning. In cell A1, we type "Celestial Object." Then we type "sun," "earth," and "moon" into cells A2, A3, and A4, respectively.

In cell B1 we type "Diameter," C1 "Divided by 2," and D "Equals Radius." See Figure 11.28 for a picture.

Then we model how to use the cells as a calculator. We type the diameter of the sun into cell B2. Note that the diameter is provided to students in Figure 11.27. Then we type "2" into cell C2. We want the math answer of the sun's radius to appear in D2. To do so, we tell students to first type an equal sign (=) and then the math equation they want Excel to complete (B2/2) so that D2 has "=B2/2" typed into it. Students then hit the enter key and Excel automatically completes the math problem, placing the answer into D2. The final product will look like Figure 11.28.

Students now follow the same logic to calculate the Earth's and moon's radii. We walk around the room, helping students. There are a few common errors students may make at this point.

1. Students will forget to include an equal sign (=) first.

2. Students will use B2 and C2 in their formula instead of B3 and C2 for Earth's radius.

3. If a student's answer is given in scientific format, such as 6.2E+07, this indicates that their cells are not formatted correctly. When this happens, we help them one-on-one to execute the steps that are outlined in the section Setting Up Excel. This corrects the problem immediately.

4. Students will often hit the enter key and their answer will result in a collection of hashtags (#). Excel does this when the information inside the cell is too long to display. To correct this, the cell needs to be widened. The easiest way to accomplish this is to go to the top of the spreadsheet and place the cursor on the line that separates two columns. Left-click on that line and drag it to the right to make the column wider. Figure 11.29 includes two screenshots depicting before the fix and afterwards.

To easily see what a student has typed into a cell, click on the cell and look just above the C column for the formula bar. Figure 11.30 is a screenshot for when we click on cell D2, whose equation is in the formula bar. Equations can be altered in the individual cells or in the formula bar, whichever the user prefers. We find it easier to use the formula bar when we are troubleshooting student work. Figure 11.30 includes a screenshot of the formula bar.

Once the students are done calculating the radii, we model how to calculate the sun's surface area. We first set up the spreadsheet so that all data is labeled. We walk students step-by-step to create a second section that, when complete, looks like the screenshot in Figure 11.31.

Here is the step-by-step process:

1. Type the title "Celestial Object Surface Area" into cell G1.

2. Type the titles "sun," "earth," and "moon" into cells G2, G3, and G4, respectively.

3. Type "4" into cells H1 (this is the title of the column) and H2 (this is the 4 from the surface area calculation that is provided to students in Figure 11.27).

4. Type the titles "Multiplied by Radius Squared" into cell I1, "Pi" into cell J1, and "Equals Surface Area" into cell K1.

5. Type the equation "=H2*D2*D2" into cell I2. The cell D2 has the sun's radius. By multiplying it by itself, its square has been calculated, and by multiplying the product by H3, it's been quadrupled as the formula requires.

6. Type the value of pi (3.14) into cell J2.

7. Type the formula "=I2*J2" to multiply the product in cell I2 with Pi.

Students begin working with their partners to calculate the surface area for the Earth and moon. As students are working, we walk around the room to answer questions, check their answers for accuracy, and help them troubleshoot problems. The answer key is provided in Figure 11.32: Celebrating Pi Day in the Sky—Answer Key.

Students most commonly become frustrated because they don't know the keyboard symbols for multiplication (*) or division (/). We usually have to teach that the (*) means to multiply, and we type it by holding down the "shift" key while at the same time hitting the "8" key. And to type the division slash we use the key that has the question mark on it (no "shift" key is necessary).

The common non-technological error students make is writing the incorrect unit. We've noticed they write km (kilometers) as the unit for every answer on their paper. These students haven't yet made the connection that because the radius was squared to calculate the surface area, the unit of measurement should also be squared (km^2). And they struggle to make the connection that the volume required the radius to be cubed so the units of measurement should be cubed too (km^3). We point this out to students as we walk around, verifying their answers.

Making Graphs in Excel

Students who finish early are provided with Figure 11.33: Making Graphs in Excel. They use the step-by-step procedures to make a bar graph in Excel depicting the relative volumes of each celestial object. They draw the graph onto their copy of Figure 11.27: Celebrating Pi Day in the Sky. Figure 11.34 is an example of what a final graph should look like.

Students usually display a feeling of dismay when they don't see data for the Earth or moon. When they ask what they've done incorrectly, we explain that their graph's data is correct and ask them to brainstorm an explanation for the lack of data for the Earth and moon. They write their answer next to the graph on their worksheet. If they struggle to figure out that the Earth's and moon's volumes are too small to be seen at this scale, we ask them the guiding question, "How many moons and Earths fit inside the sun?"

DIFFERENTIATION FOR DIVERSE LEARNERS

In addition to the individual differentiation we offer with each resource, we also find there are a few general strategies that can help students with learning challenges. One way to help these students with both graphing and dimensional analysis is by providing them with a multiplication chart. This can help students identify intervals as they are making graphs and allow them to quickly multiply numbers if calculators are not available. Another strategy for these students is to ensure they are paired with a peer "buddy." Peer buddies who work well with these students assist them in a way that is less obtrusive and can be more comfortable for the student.

ELLs may need support when analyzing and interpreting graphs. To assist them, we provide sentence frames. For example, when students are analyzing Figure 11.8: Year vs. Number of Deer and Wolves, we provide them with the following stems:

1. When the number of deer was 12, the number of wolves was _____.
2. In the year _____, the number of deer was 14 and the number of wolves was 6.
3. From 2011 to 2015, the deer population _____ (increased/decreased).

Student Handouts and Examples

What Could Go Wrong?

We've found that when many elementary students use math in science class, they can transition easily from math to science. However, when middle and high school students are required to leverage their math knowledge in our science classes, we find that many struggle to bridge what they've learned in math to solve problems in science. We remind them at the beginning of a math activity that the math we will be using was previously taught in their math classes and reassure them that although we are science teachers, we are indeed good mathematicians so they can ask us for help.

In our experience, some students feel very comfortable declaring that they aren't good at math. When we hear a student say they aren't good at math, we address it immediately. First, we remind them that there is value in having a growth mindset (see Chapter 6: Strategies for Teaching the Engineering Process for resources that help students to develop a growth mindset). We also reassure them that they have a lot of support in our class, such as their learning partners and us. And, then, we follow through by checking in with these students first and often. When they accomplish a mathematical task, we provide positive feedback, such as a high five or verbal praise.

When students measure objects, we've noted that regardless of grade level, most students will round to the nearest whole number if not instructed otherwise. We instruct them in written and oral directions what decimal they need to measure to, such as the nearest 10th or 100th.

Technology Connections

Purchasing graph paper can be an expensive investment. To provide all students with graph paper but without spending a lot of funds, we print free graph paper from the Internet. Our favorite resources are Free Online Graph Paper (http://print-graph-paper.com) and Math-Aids.Com (http://www.math-aids.com/Graph_Paper).

There are 31 Pi Day lesson plans at the We Are Teachers website, which can be found here: WeAreTeachers (https://www.weareteachers.com/pi-day-activities). These are intended mostly for elementary and middle school students. High school Pi Day lesson plans can be found at (http://web.archive.org/web/20080118155630/http://www.nvnet.org/nvhs/dept/math/pi/trig.html) for Trigonometry classes and at (http://web.archive.org/web/20080118155620/http://www.nvnet.org/nvhs/dept/math/pi/algebraii.html) for Algebra II classes. The School District of Philadelphia offers lesson plans for K-12 students at "Pi Day Activities" (http://web.archive.org/web/20070317225901/http://www.phila.k12.pa.us/offices/curriculum/supports/CIGuides/PiDayActivities2006Final(2).pdf).

There are many online tutorials for using Apple Numbers as a calculator, such as Nabtech's "Formulas and Functions in Apple Numbers 2017" (https://www.youtube.com/watch?v=qwojJ0VJyv0) and MacMost's "9 Mac Calculator Tricks" (https://macmost.com/9-mac-calculator-tricks.html). There are also plenty of tutorials for using Google Sheets as a calculator, such as GCF Global's "Google Sheets - Creating Simple Formulas" (https://edu.gcfglobal.org/en/googlespreadsheets/creating-simple-formulas/1) and Flipped Classroom Tutorials' "15 Functions in Google Sheets You NEED to Know" (https://www.youtube.com/watch?v=mRHlvRRERgs).

Figures

Name: _____

How to Make a Bar Graph

1. Place the independent variable on the horizontal line. Your independent variable is _____.

2. Place the dependent variable on the vertical line. Your dependent variable is _____.

3. Label the horizontal line with all of the values for the independent variable. Each value needs to be separated by two boxes on the graph paper.

4. To label the vertical line, begin by placing the value of 0 (zero) where it crosses the horizontal line.

5. To add more values to the vertical line, first identify the highest number that you will graph. Use the following guidelines to determine the graph's scale:

  — If the highest data point is 10 or less, then each box on the vertical line will represent a change of 1

  — If the highest data point is 11–20, then each box will represent a change of 2

  — If the highest data point is 21–50, then each box will represent a change of 5

  — If the highest data point is 51–100, then each box will represent a change of 10

6. Title the horizontal line with the independent variable, including the units of measurement, if necessary.

7. Title the vertical line with the dependent variable, including the units of measurement, such as centimeters, °C, or age.

8. Look at the first value in your data table. Use it to determine where the bar in the bar graph will end above the horizontal line. Fill in all of the boxes from the horizontal line to that point.

Figure 11.1 Bar Graph Example for Teaching Graphing to Fourth Grade Students (Student Handout)

9. Title your graph, which needs to include the independent and dependent variables.

Here is an example of a bar graph that includes all of the requirements:

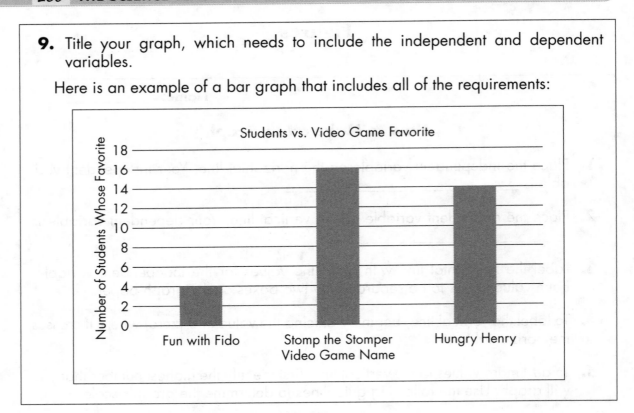

Figure 11.1 (Continued)

Name: _____

How to Make a Line Graph Using a Data Table

1. Determine which data will be placed on each axis.

  — x-axis (horizontal) = independent variable
  — y-axis (vertical) = dependent variable

2. Place a 0 (zero) where the x- and y-axis meet.

3. Start your x- and y-axes at 0 (zero). Create equal intervals along the x-axis using the following guidelines:

  — Identify your highest data point for the independent variable
  — If the highest data point is 10 or less, then each box on the vertical line will represent a change of 1
  — If the highest data point is 11–20, then each box will represent a change of 2
  — If the highest data point is 21–50, then each box will represent a change of 5
  — If the highest data point is 51–100, then each box will represent a change of 10
  — Repeat this step for the dependent variable

4. Title each axis with the correct variable, including the units of measurement, such as centimeters, °C, or year.

5. Plot the points on the graph.

6. Connect the points to create a line. Begin with the first data point in your data table.

7. Give your graph a title, which needs to include the independent and dependent variables.

Figure 11.2 Line Graph Example for Teaching Graphing to Fifth Grade and Beyond (Student Handout)

8. Provide a key, if necessary.

Here is an example of a line graph that includes all of the requirements:

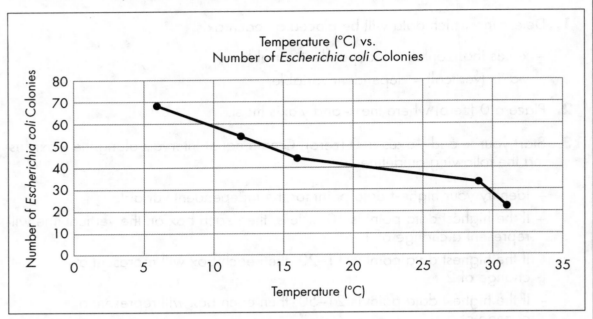

Figure 11.2 (Continued)

Name: _____

Graphing Pretest

Directions: Graph the below data so I can learn what you already know about graphing.

Temperature vs. *Escherichia coli* Colonies After 20 Days

Temperature (°C)	Number of *Escherichia coli* Colonies
22	31
33	29
44	16
54	12
68	6

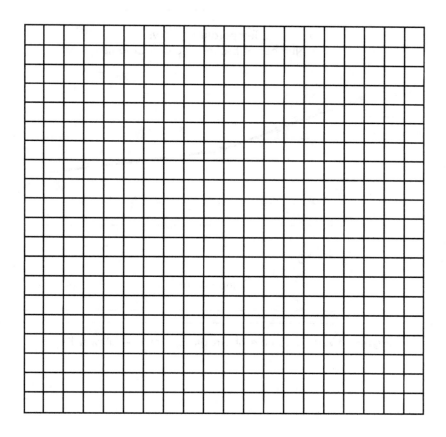

Figure 11.3 Example of Graphing Pretest (Student Handout)

Name: _____ *Answer Key*_____

Graphing Pretest

Directions: Graph the below data so I can learn what you already know about graphing.

Temperature vs. *Escherichia coli* Colonies After 20 Days

Temperature (°C)	Number of *Escherichia coli* Colonies
22	31
33	29
44	16
54	12
68	6

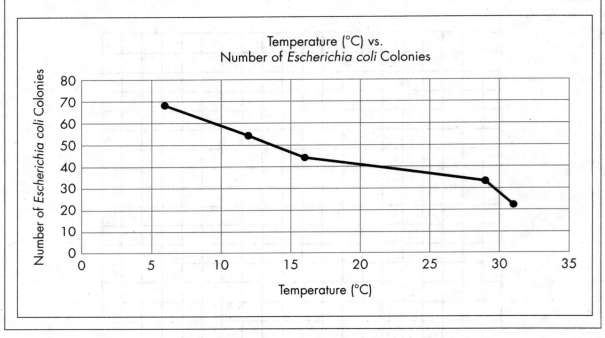

Figure 11.4 Example of Graphing Pretest—Answer Key

Name: _____

Which Type of Graph Should I Use?

Directions: Using the information for each experiment, determine the type of graph that should be used. Then write down why you chose that type of graph. We will do the first one as a class.

1. Xee wanted to know if flower color determines which flower a butterfly lands on. She used the same brand of spray paint to paint white roses the following colors: pink, blue, and green. She left the roses in a butterfly garden at her local zoo and focused a camera on the flowers. When she reviewed the film, she counted how many times a butterfly landed on each colored rose.

    a. What type of graph will Xee use to graph her data? Draw an example here:

    b. What information helped you to answer question a?

2. Juan performed an experiment to determine what fruit to bring to the next class party. His mom said he could bring one of the following: apples, oranges, bananas, or grapes. He performed a survey, asking each classmate which fruit they would prefer for the class party.

    a. What type of graph will Juan use to graph his data? Draw an example here:

    b. What information helped you to answer question a?

3. Tom was curious to find out if hiking with his two dogs altered the pace of his hike. He chose the same trail to hike and began each hike on the same day of the week at the same time of day. He completed the hike every day for 30 days, alternating between taking his dogs and not taking his dogs.

    a. What type of graph will Tom use to graph his data? Draw an example here:

Figure 11.5 Which Type of Graph Should I Use? (Student Handout)

b. What information helped you to answer question a?

4. Jazmin wanted to know if the amount of rain increased or decreased during her birthday month of November. Beginning on November 1, she recorded the amount of rain captured in a bucket. She continued to do so every day through November 30.

   a. What type of graph will Jazmin use to graph her data? Draw an example here:

   b. What information helped you to answer question a?

Figure 11.5 (Continued)

Name: _____ *Answer Key*_____

Which Type of Graph Should I Use?

Directions: Using the information for each experiment, determine the type of graph that should be used. Then write down why you chose that type of graph. We will do the first one as a class.

1. Xee wanted to know if flower color determines which flower a butterfly lands on. She used the same brand of spray paint to paint white roses the following colors: pink, blue, and green. She left the roses in a butterfly garden at her local zoo and focused a camera on the flowers. When she reviewed the film, she counted how many times a butterfly landed on each colored rose.

   a. What type of graph will Xee use to graph her data?

   Xee could create a bar graph or a pie chart.

   b. What information helped you to answer question a?

Figure 11.6 Which Type of Graph Should I Use?—Answer Key

Xee has only one set of data that will be represented quantitatively (with numbers), which is the number of times the butterflies land on each flower. The second set of data is qualitative (with no numbers), which is the color of the roses. This is an indicator that the scientist could use a bar graph.

Xee can also choose to create a pie chart because the data can be represented using percentages. Xee can calculate the percentage of times each colored flower was landed on.

2. Juan performed an experiment to determine what fruit to bring to the next class party. His mom said he could bring one of the following: apples, oranges, bananas, or grapes. He performed a survey, asking each classmate which fruit they would prefer for the class party.

   a. What type of graph will Juan use to graph his data?

   Juan could use a pie chart or a bar graph.

   b. What information helped you to answer question a?

   A bar graph would be acceptable because there is only one set of quantitative data (the number of students).

   A pie chart would be acceptable because the data can be represented in percentages. Juan could graph the percent of his classmates that chose each of the fruit options.

3. Tom was curious to find out if hiking with his two dogs altered the pace of his hike. He chose the same trail to hike and began each hike on the same day of the week at the same time of day. He completed the hike every day for 30 days, alternating between taking his dogs and not taking his dogs.

   a. What type of graph will Tom use to graph his data?

   Tom could make a bar graph or a double line graph.

   b. What information helped you to answer question a?

   Tom could make a bar graph because there is one set of qualitative data (the time it takes to complete the hike) if he chooses to average his times. The x-axis would indicate whether the dogs were with him and the y-axis would indicate the time it takes to complete the hike.

   Tom could also make a double line graph if he doesn't average his data. Both of his variables are quantitative. The independent variable (each day of the month)

Figure 11.6 (Continued)

will go on the x-axis and the dependent variable (the time it took to complete the hike) will be on the y-axis. Tom will then have two lines of data, which means he will need a key. One line will represent when the dogs were with him and the other line will represent when the dogs weren't with him.

Teacher's Note: This is an excellent opportunity to discuss variables and averages. Tom has two independent variables (the presence of the dogs and the day of the month), which is not recommended in science but is sometimes unavoidable because it's nearly impossible to control every factor. The preferred approach for communicating Tom's data is to average the hike times because the average better represents the month as a whole.

4. Jazmin wanted to know if the amount of rain increased or decreased during her birthday month of November. Beginning on November 1, she recorded the amount of rain captured in a bucket. She continued to do so every day through November 30.

a. What type of graph will Jazmin use to graph her data?

Jazmin should make a line graph.

b. What information helped you to answer question a?

Jazmin has two sets of quantitative data. She can plot the independent variable (each day in November) on the x-axis and the dependent variable (the amount of rain collected) on the y-axis. She will not need a key.

Figure 11.6 (Continued)

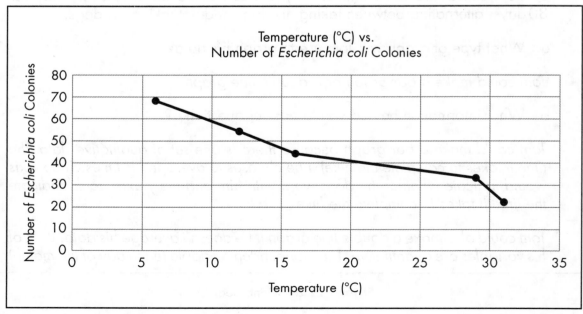

Figure 11.7 Temperature vs. Number of *Escherichia coli* Colonies

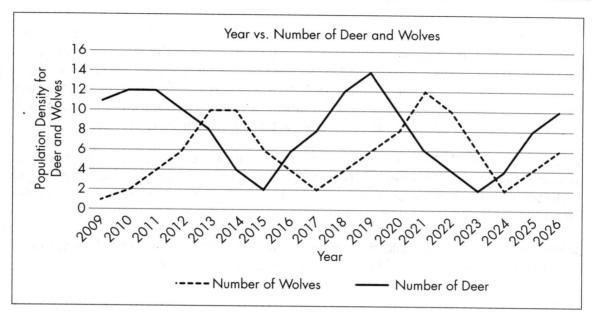

Figure 11.8 Year vs. Number of Deer and Wolves

Name: _____

Wildlife Strike Data Analysis and Interpretation

What is a wildlife strike? It is a collision that occurs between a wild animal and a man-made object. One example is when a bug comes into contact with your parents' windshield while you are driving down the street.

Ha! That reminds me of a great joke.

Q: What is the last thing that goes through a bug's mind when it hits your car?

A: Its butt! (I love this joke!)

With your learning partner, think of three other examples of wildlife strikes. These can be events you've experienced, read about, or saw on TV/online.

1.

2.

3.

Figure 11.9 Wildlife Strike Data Analysis and Interpretation (Student Handout)

Another example of a wildlife strike is when a wild animal, such as a bird, collides with an airplane. In freshwater coastal states, such as Florida, the more common wild-life strike at the airport is with alligators, who sit on the runaway trying to warm themselves. As a plane is speeding up to take off or is coming in for a landing, it sometimes runs over an alligator. In highly forested states, such as Oregon, it is more common for airplanes to collide with deer who are running across the airport's runway.

When airplanes collide into wildlife, it costs a lot of money. Every year, the U.S. aviation industry incurs over $1 billion in damages because of wildlife strikes! In addition to costing a lot of money, more than 100 people die every year in the United States because of a wildlife strike with an airplane.

Below are the historical data from Phoenix Sky Harbor Airport regarding the number of bird strikes per year. Use this data to answer the questions below.

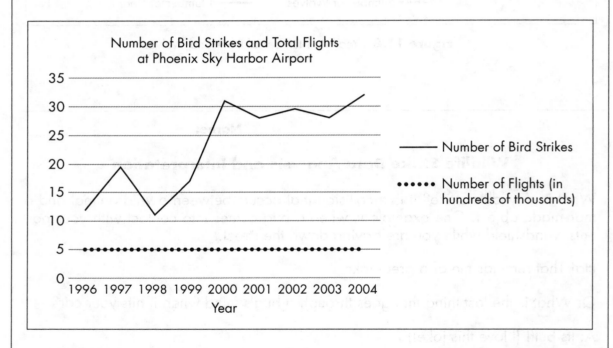

1. Analyze the data in the graph: Between what two years did the number of wildlife strikes increase dramatically?

2. Analyze the data in the graph. During that same year, how much did the flights at Phoenix Sky Harbor increase?

Figure 11.9 (Continued)

3. Interpret the data in the graph: In the summer of 1999, the Tempe Town Lake was filled with water, attracting birds. Using the data you observed in the graph, write a hypothesis that explains when you increase the amount of water in an environment (the independent variable), you cause an increase in the number of wildlife strikes (the dependent variable). NOTE: Use the proper "If. . .then. . .because. . ." format.

Figure 11.9 (Continued)

Name: _____ *Answer Key*_____

Wildlife Strike Data Analysis and Interpretation

What is a wildlife strike? It is a collision that occurs between a wild animal and a man-made object. One example is when a bug comes into contact with your parents' windshield while you are driving down the street.

Ha! That reminds me of a great joke.

Q: What is the last thing that goes through a bug's mind when it hits your car?

A: Its butt! (I love this joke!)

With your learning partner, think of three other examples of wildlife strikes. These can be events you've experienced, read about, or saw on TV/online.

1. *Answers will vary but acceptable ones include hitting a squirrel while driving.*

2. *When a bird flies into a clean window.*

3. *When a bird flies into a wind turbine.*

Another example of a wildlife strike is when a wild animal, such as a bird, collides with an airplane. In freshwater coastal states, such as Florida, the more common wildlife strike at the airport is with alligators, who sit on the runaway trying to warm themselves. As a plane is speeding up to take off or is coming in for a landing, it sometimes runs over an alligator. In highly forested states, such as Oregon, it is more common for airplanes to collide with deer who are running across the airport's runway.

When airplanes collide into wildlife, it costs a lot of money. Every year, the U.S. aviation industry incurs over $1 billion in damages because of wildlife strikes! In addition to costing a lot of money, more than 100 people die every year in the United States because of a wildlife strike with an airplane.

Figure 11.10 Wildlife Strike Data Analysis and Interpretation—Answer Key

Below are the historical data from Phoenix Sky Harbor Airport regarding the number of bird strikes per year. Use these data to answer the questions below.

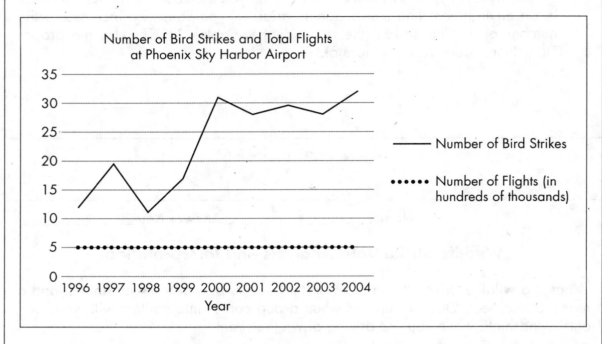

1. Analyze the data in the graph: Between what 2 years did the number of wildlife strikes increase dramatically?

   Between 1999 and 2000.

2. Analyze the data in the graph. During that same year, how much did the flights at Phoenix Sky Harbor increase?

   There was no increase.

3. Interpret the data in the graph: In the summer of 1999, the Tempe Town Lake was filled with water, attracting birds. Using the data you observed in the graph, write a hypothesis that explains when you increase the amount of water in an environment (the independent variable), you cause an increase in the number of wildlife strikes (the dependent variable). NOTE: Use the proper "If. . .then. . .because. . ." format.

   Answers will vary but this is an example of an acceptable answer: If the amount of water is increased in an environment, then the number of wildlife strikes increase because wildlife is attracted to water.

Figure 11.10 (Continued)

Name: _____

Dimensional Analysis: Practice

Directions: Dimensional analysis is a fancy term that simply means you are changing a number from one unit of measurement (such as meters, degrees Fahrenheit, and hours) into a different unit of measurement (such as centimeters, degrees Celsius, and seconds).

To ensure you successfully change the unit of measurement, you must write down the unit of measurement for every number!

We'll practice using money first.

Quarter = 25¢ = 4 in one dollar
Dime = 10¢ = 10 in one dollar
Nickel = 5¢ = 20 in one dollar
Penny = 1¢ = 100 in one dollar

1. How many dimes are in $8.00?

2. How many nickels are in $7.65?

3. How many dollars do you have if you have 56 quarters?

4. How much money do you have if you have 31 nickels?

Now we're going to practice with units of measurement that pertain to time. These are multi-step dimensional analysis problems.

60 s = 1 min
60 min = 1 hr
24 hr = 1 day
7 days = 1 week
365 days = 1 year

Figure 11.11 Dimensional Analysis Practice (Student Handout)

5. How many seconds are in 4.5 hours?

6. How many minutes are in 2 days?

7. Convert 4 years into seconds.

8. Convert 3 weeks into hours.

Figure 11.11 (Continued)

Name: _____ *Answer Key*_____

Dimensional Analysis: Practice

Directions: Dimensional analysis is a fancy term that simply means you are changing a number from one unit of measurement (such as meters, degrees Fahrenheit, and hours) into a different unit of measurement (such as centimeters, degrees Celsius, and seconds).

To ensure you successfully change the unit of measurement, you must write down the unit of measurement for every number!

We'll practice using money first.

Quarter = 25¢ = 4 in one dollar
Dime = 10¢ = 10 in one dollar
Nickel = 5¢ = 20 in one dollar
Penny = 1¢ = 100 in one dollar

1. How many dimes are in $8.00?

$$8 \text{ dollars} \times \frac{10 \text{ dimes}}{1 \text{ dollar}} = 80 \text{ dimes}$$

2. How many nickels are in $7.65?

$$\$7.65 \times \frac{20 \text{ nickels}}{1 \text{ dollar}} = 153 \text{ nickels}$$

3. How many dollars do you have if you have 56 quarters?

$$56 \text{ quarters} \times \frac{1 \text{ dollar}}{4 \text{ quarters}} = \$14.00$$

4. How much money do you have if you have 31 nickels?

$$31 \text{ nickels} \times \frac{1 \text{ dollar}}{20 \text{ nickels}} = \$1.55$$

Figure 11.12 Dimensional Analysis Practice—Answer Key

Now we're going to practice with units of measurement that pertain to time. These are multi-step dimensional analysis problems.

60 s = 1 min
60 min = 1 hour
24 hr = 1 day
7 days = 1 week
365 days = 1 year

5. How many seconds are in 4.5 hours?

$$4.5\,hr \times \frac{60\,min}{1\,hr} \times \frac{60\,s}{1\,min} = 16{,}200 \text{ seconds}$$

6. How many minutes are in 2 days?

$$2\,days \times \frac{24\,hr}{1\,day} \times \frac{60\,min}{1\,hr} = 2{,}880 \text{ min}$$

7. Convert 4 years into seconds.

$$4\,years \times \frac{365\,days}{1\,yr} \times \frac{24\,hr}{1\,day} \times \frac{60\,min}{1\,hour} \times \frac{60\,s}{1\,min} = 126{,}144{,}000 \text{ seconds}$$

8. Convert 504 hours into weeks.

$$504\,hr \times \frac{1\,day}{24\,hr} \times \frac{1\,week}{7\,days} = 3 \text{ weeks}$$

Figure 11.12 (Continued)

Name: _____

Practice Measuring Your Friends and Their Things

Directions: Today you are going to practice measuring and converting measurements in the Imperial system. Using any of the measuring tools available to you, measure the below items using the unit of measurement that is indicated. Then use the conversion table to convert your units of measurement into your new unit of measurement. The first one is done for you.

Conversion Table Using the Imperial System: Distance

3 ft = 1 yard	12 in. = 1 ft
1 mile = 1,760 yards	1 mile = 5,280

NOTE: your measurements must be rounded to the nearest 0.1, or tenth.

1. Measure your teacher's height: _____67_____ inches = _____ 5.6 _____ feet

$$67 \text{ in.} \times \frac{1 \text{ ft}}{24 \text{ in.}} \times \frac{1 \text{ ft}}{7 \text{ in.}} = 5.6 \text{ ft}$$

2. Measure your friend's height: _____ inches = _____ feet

3. Measure your friend's pencil: _____ inches = _____ feet

4. Measure the distance from your friend's desk to the door: _____ feet = _____ inches

5. If your friend lives 2.3 miles from school, how many yards do they live from school?

6. If your friend lives 9,504 ft from school, how many miles do they live from school?

Figure 11.13 Practice Measuring Your Friends and Their Things (Student Handout)

Conversion Table Using the Imperial System: Mass

16 oz = 1 pound	2,000 pounds = 1 ton

7. Measure the mass of your friend's calculator: _____ ounces = _____ pounds

8. Measure the mass of your friend's full backpack: _____ pounds = _____ ounces

9. If your friend's parent drives a car that weighs 3,341 pounds, how many tons does the car weigh?

10. If your friend owned an elephant that weighed 3.7 tons, how many pounds would your friend's pet weigh?

Conversion Table Using the Imperial System: Volume

16 cups = 1 gal	16 tablespoons = 1 cup
1 cup = 48 teaspoons	4 quarts = 1 gal

11. Measure your friend's water in their water bottle: _____ cups = _____ teaspoons

12. If your friend had 16 tablespoons of apple sauce at lunch, how many cups of apple sauce did your friend eat?

13. If your friend drank 2.3 gal of water in 3 days, how many quarts did your friend drink?

14. Your friend was making chocolate chip cookies and the recipe called for 3.5 cups of flour. Your friend couldn't find a measuring cup, but there was an easy-to-reach tablespoon. How many tablespoons of flour would your friend need to measure for the recipe?

Figure 11.13 (Continued)

Thinking Questions

15. You and your friend are at the store but you are the only one who remembered to bring money. Your friend offers you a deal: If you buy 42 oz of candy for your friend right now, your friend will give you 3 pounds of candy when you two get home. Is this a good deal? Show your work and then explain your answer using at least one sentence.

16. Why can't we convert pounds to meters or meters to gallons?

Figure 11.13 (Continued)

Name: _____ *Answer Key*_____

Practice Measuring Your Friends and Their Things

Directions: Today you are going to practice measuring and converting measurements in the Imperial system. Using any of the measuring tools available to you, measure the below items using the unit of measurement that is indicated. Then use the conversion table to convert your units of measurement into your new unit of measurement. The first one is done for you.

Conversion Table Using the Imperial System: Distance

3 ft = 1 yard	12 in. = 1 ft
1 mile = 1,760 yards	1 mile = 5,280

NOTE: your measurements must be rounded to the nearest 0.1, or tenth.

1. Measure your teacher's height: _____67_____ inches = _____ 5.6_____ feet

$$67 \text{ in.} \times \frac{1 \text{ ft}}{12 \text{ in.}} = 5.6 \text{ ft}$$

2. Measure your friend's height: _____ inches = _____ feet

3. Measure your friend's pencil: _____ inches = _____ feet

4. Measure the distance from your friend's desk to the door: _____ feet = _____ inches

Figure 11.14 Practice Measuring Your Friends and Their Things—Answer Key

5. If your friend lives 2.3 miles from school, how many yards do they live from school?

$$2.3 \text{ miles} \times \frac{5,280 \text{ ft}}{1 \text{ mile}} \times \frac{1 \text{ yard}}{3 \text{ ft}} = 4,048 \text{ yards}$$

6. If your friend lives 9,504 ft from school, how many miles do they live from school?

$$9,504 \text{ ft} \times \frac{1 \text{ mile}}{5,280 \text{ ft}} = 1.8 \text{ miles}$$

Conversion Table Using the Imperial System: Mass

16 oz = 1 pound	2,000 pounds = 1 ton

7. Measure the mass of your friend's calculator: _____ ounces = _____ pounds

8. Measure the mass of your friend's full backpack: _____ pounds = _____ ounces

9. If your friend's parent drives a car that weighs 3,341 pounds, how many tons does the car weigh?

$$3,341 \text{ pounds} \times \frac{1 \text{ ton}}{2,000 \text{ pounds}} = 1.7 \text{ tons}$$

10. If your friend owned an elephant that weighed 3.7 tons, how many pounds would your friend's pet weigh?

$$3.7 \text{ tons} \times \frac{2,000 \text{ pounds}}{1 \text{ ton}} = 7,400 \text{ pounds}$$

Conversion Table Using the Imperial System: Volume

16 cups = 1 gal	16 tablespoons = 1 cup
1 cup = 48 teaspoons	4 quarts = 1 gal

11. Measure your friend's water in their water bottle: _____ cups = _____ teaspoons

12. If your friend had 16 tablespoons of apple sauce at lunch, how many cups of apple sauce did your friend eat?

$$16 \text{ tablespoons} \times \frac{1 \text{ cup}}{16 \text{ tablespoons}} = 1 \text{ cup}$$

Figure 11.14 (Continued)

13. If your friend drank 2.3 gal of water in 3 days, how many quarts did your friend drink?

$$2.3 \text{ gal} \times \frac{4 \text{ quarts}}{1 \text{ gal}} = 9.2 \text{ quarts}$$

14. Your friend was making chocolate chip cookies and the recipe called for 3.5 cups of flour. Your friend couldn't find a measuring cup, but there was an easy-to-reach tablespoon. How many tablespoons of flour would your friend need to measure for the recipe?

$$3.5 \text{ cups} \times \frac{16 \text{ tablespoons}}{1 \text{ cup}} = 56 \text{ tablespoons}$$

Thinking Questions

15. You and your friend are at the store but you are the only one who remembered to bring money. Your friend offers you a deal: If you buy 42 oz of candy for your friend right now, your friend will give you 3 pounds of candy when you two get home. Is this a good deal? Show your work and then explain your answer using at least one sentence.

$$42 \text{ oz of candy} \times \frac{1 \text{ pound}}{16 \text{ oz}} = 2.6 \text{ pounds}$$

Yes, this is a great deal. I am purchasing 2.6 pounds of candy but when we return home, I'm going to receive 0.4 pounds more.

16. Why can't we convert pounds to meters or meters to gallons?

We can't determine how tall something is based on its mass. And we can't determine an object's volume by its mass.

Figure 11.14 (Continued)

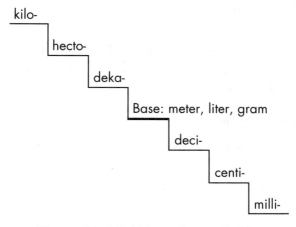

Figure 11.15 Metric System Ladder

Name: _____

Converting Within the Metric System

Draw your ladder here:

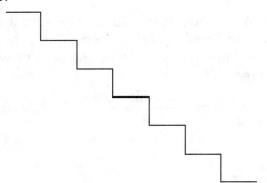

Part 1 Directions: Use your ladder to convert from one unit of measurement to another. Every time you take a step, multiply by 10 because you are going down the ladder. The first one is done for you.

1. Convert 72 kl into hl.

72 kl X 10 (1 step) = 720 hl

2. Convert 87 L into cl.

3. Convert 902 dam into mm.

4. Convert 3 dm into cm.

5. Convert 1.8 kg into mg.

6. Convert 0.34 cg into mg.

Part 2 Directions: Use your ladder to convert from one unit of measurement to another. Every time you take a step, divide by 10 because you are going up the ladder. The first one is done for you.

7. Convert 2,000 mm to meters.

2,000 mm / 10 (1 step) = 200 cm / 10 (1 step) = 20 dm / 10 (1 step) = 2 m

8. Convert 189 dal to kl.

Figure 11.16 Converting Within the Metric System (Student Handout)

9. Convert 5 g to hg.

10. Convert 0.8 cl to dl.

11. Convert 0.03 m to km.

12. Convert 4,900,000 mg to kg.

Part 3 Directions: Use your ladder to convert from one unit of measurement to another. Be careful because now you may move up or down the ladder. You have to determine the direction and then complete the conversion.

13. Convert 76 km to m.

14. Convert 20.45 L to dal.

15. Convert 18.890 hg to mg.

16. Convert 0.000567 ml to kl.

17. Convert 8.07 meters to dekameters.

18. Convert 23.801 decigrams to centigrams.

Figure 11.16 (Continued)

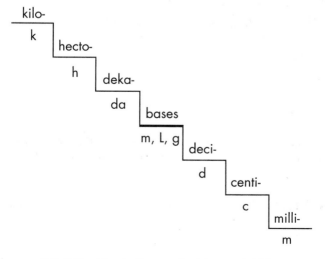

Figure 11.17 Metric System Ladder and Abbreviations

Name: _____ *Answer Key*_____

Converting Within the Metric System

Draw your ladder here:

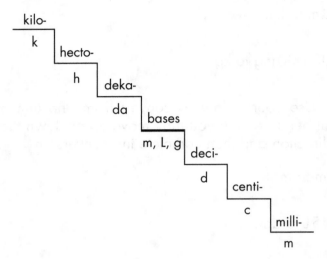

Part 1 Directions: Use your ladder to convert from one unit of measurement to another. Every time you take a step, multiply by 10 because you are going down the ladder. The first one is done for you.

1. Convert 72 kl into hl.

   72 kl × 10 (1 step) = 720 hl

2. Convert 87 L into cl.

   87 L × 10 (1 step) = 870 dl × 10 (1 step) = 8,700 cl

3. Convert 902 dam into mm.

   902 dam × 10 (1 step) = 9,020 m × 10 (1 step) = 90,200 dm × 10 (1 step) = 902,000 cm × 10 (1 step) = 9,020,000 mm

4. Convert 3 dm into cm.

   3 dm × 10 (1 step) = 30 cm

5. Convert 1.8 kg into mg.

   1.8 kg × 10 (1 step) = 18 hg × 10 (1 step) = 180 dag × 10 (1 step) = 1,800 g × 10 (1 step) = 18,000 dg × 10 (1 step) = 180,000 cg × 10 (1 step) = 1,800,000 mg

Figure 11.18 Converting Within the Metric System—Answer Key

6. Convert 0.34 cg into mg.

0.34 cg × 10 (1 step) = 3.4 mg

Part 2 Directions: Use your ladder to convert from one unit of measurement to another. Every time you take a step, divide by 10 because you are going up the ladder. The first one is done for you.

7. Convert 2,000 mm to meters.

2,000 mm/10 (1 step) = 200 cm/10 (1 step) = 20 dm/10 (1 step) = 2 m

8. Convert 189 dal to kl.

189 dal/10 (1 step) = 18.9 hl/10 (1 step) = 1.89 kl

9. Convert 5 g to hg.

5 g/10 (1 step) = 0.5 dag/10 (1 step) = 0.05 hg

10. Convert 0.8 cl to dl.

0.8 cl/10 (1 step) = 0.08 dl

11. Convert 0.03 m to km.

0.03 m/10 (1 step) = 0.003 dam/10 (1 step) = 0.0003 hm/10 (1 step) = 0.00003 km

12. Convert 4,900,000 mg to kg.

4,900,000 mg/10 (1 step) = 490,000 cg/10 (1 step) = 49,000 dg/10 (1 step) = 4,900 g/10 (1 step) = 490 dag/10 (1 step) = 49 hg/10 (1 step) = 4.9 kg

Part 3 Directions: Use your ladder to convert from one unit of measurement to another. Be careful because now you may move up or down the ladder. You have to determine the direction and then complete the conversion.

13. Convert 76 km to m.

76 km × 10 (1 step) = 760 hm × 10 (1 step) = 7,600 dam × 10 (1 step) = 76,000 m

14. Convert 20.45 L to dal.

20.45 L/10 (1 step) = 2.045 dal

15. Convert 18.890 hg to mg.

18.890 hg × 10 (1 step) = 188.9 dag × 10 (1 step) = 1,889 g × 10 (1 step) = 18,890 dg × 10 (1 step) = 188,900 cg × 10 (1 step) = 1,889,000 mg

Figure 11.18 (Continued)

16. Convert 0.000567 kl to ml.

0.000567 kl × 10 (1 step) = 0.00567 hl × 10 (1 step) = 0.0567 dal × 10 (1 step) = 0.567 L × 10 (1 step) = 5.67 dl × 10 (1 step) = 56.7 cl × 10 (1 step) = 567 ml

17. Convert 8.07 m to dekameters.

8.07 m/10 (1 step) = 0.807 dam

18. Convert 23.801 decigrams to centigrams.

23.801 dg × 10 (1 step) = 238.01 cg

Figure 11.18 (Continued)

Name: _____

Metric System Measuring Challenge

Draw your ladder here:

Station 1: Thinking Questions—Use your critical thinking skills to figure out how to answer these questions.

1. Which distance is longer: 53 km or 530,000 m?

2. Which item weighs more: a 4.5 dag bag of oats or a 4,500 cg bag of oats?

3. Which has more volume: 623 ml or 0.623 dl?

4. Which item is longer: a fish that is 0.00823 hm or a fish that is 823 mm?

Station 2: Go to the back of the room where you'll find 10 items on the edge of a table. Without measuring these items, determine their length. You may not touch the items!

1. Which item is 5.5 cm long?

2. Which item is 80 mm long?

3. Which item is 1.05 dm long?

4. Which item is 0.175 m long?

Figure 11.19 Metric System Measuring Challenge (Student Handout)

5. Which item is 0.00025 hm long?

6. Which item is 0.000095 km long?

7. Which item is 0.0085 dam long?

8. Which item is 0.22 m long?

9. Which item is 0.00016 km long?

10. Which item is 13.8 cm long?

Station 3: Find your teacher.

Figure 11.19 (Continued)

Figure 11.20 Example of 10 Items to be Measured

Name: _____*Answer Key*_____

Metric System Measuring Challenge

Draw your ladder here:

Station 1: Thinking Questions—Use your critical thinking skills to figure out how to answer these questions.

1. Which distance is longer: 53 km or 530,000 m?

— *53 km = 53,000 m so 530,000 m is larger than 53 km*

2. Which item weighs more: a 4.5 dag bag of oats or a 450 cg bag of oats?

— *4.5 dag = 4,500 cg so 4.5 dag is larger than 450 cg*

3. Which has more volume: 623 ml or 0.623 dl?

— *623 ml = 6.23 dl so 623 ml is larger than 0.623 dl*

4. Which item is longer: a fish that is 0.00823 hm or a fish that is 823 mm?

— *0.00823 hm = 823 mm so the two fish are the same length*

Station 2: Go to the back of the room where you'll find 10 items on the edge of a table. Without measuring these items, determine their length. You may not touch the items!

1. Which item is 5.5 cm long?

— *Rubik's cube*

2. Which item is 80 mm long?

— *cotton swab*

3. Which item is 1.05 dm long?

— *candy dispenser*

4. Which item is 0.175 m long?

— *chocolate Easter bunny box*

5. Which item is 0.00025 hm long?

— *pencil sharpener*

Figure 11.21   Metric System Measuring Challenge—Answer Key

6. Which item is 0.000095 km long?

— *toy cell phone*

7. Which item is 0.0085 dam long?

— *pink timer*

8. Which item is 0.22 m long?

— *water sock (shoe)*

9. Which item is 0.00016 km long?

— *3D glasses*

10. Which item is 13.8 cm long?

— *clip*

Station 3: Find your teacher.

Figure 11.21 (Continued)

Name _____

Metric and Imperial System Internet Search Lab

Directions: Practice converting measurements from the Imperial system to the metric system and vice versa. For each answer, you must include measurements! You can use your own calculator, borrow a calculator from me, or use the calculator on your computer. You are NOT permitted to use your phone's calculator. Show all of your work and round your answers to the nearest tenth.

Use this table for your conversions:

1 m = 3.3 ft	1 kg = 2.2 lbs
(°C × 9/5) + 32 = °F	(°F – 32) × 5/9 = °C
1 gal = 3.8 L	3,280 ft = 1 km
1 km = 0.6 miles	1 m = 1.1 yard

The World's Biggest Snakes

1. Go to https://www.livescience.com/34444-biggest-snake-largest-snake-longest-snake.html.

2. Read the article about the longest and most massive snakes to have slithered the Earth.

3. What is the longest anaconda's length (use feet)?

4. How many meters does this equal?

5. What is the estimated mass for the prehistoric *Titanoboa cerrejonensis* in pounds?

6. How many kilograms does this equal?

7. Based on your answers and the conversion information in the table, which is larger? Underline one:

1 ft	1 m

8. Based on your answers and the conversion information in the table, which is larger? Underline one:

1 pound	1 kg

Figure 11.22 Metric and Imperial System Internet Search Lab (Student Handout)

The World's Deepest Fish

1. Go to http://www.extremescience.com/deepest-fish-video.htm and read the article.

2. What is the depth, in feet, at which the snailfish is found?

3. How many kilometers under the ocean can snailfish be found?

4. How many miles does this equal?

5. Based on your answers and the conversion information in the table, which is larger? Underline one:

1 mile	1 km

Microorganisms in Extreme Temperatures

1. Go to http://archive.bio.ed.ac.uk/jdeacon/microbes/thermo.htm and read the article.

2. Thermophiles are microorganisms that prosper in extremely hot temperatures, such as near volcanoes. What is the maximum temperature, in Celsius, that these microscopic creatures can live in?

3. How hot is that in Fahrenheit?

4. Polar bears maintain a body temperature of about 98.6 °F but live in environments that are as cold as negative 92 °F (-92 °F). What is the difference, in °C, between a polar bear's internal body temperature and its external environmental temperature? Hint: convert the temperatures to Celsius first and then subtract to find the difference.

5. Based on your answers and the conversion information in the table, which is hotter? Underline one:

1 °C	1 °F

Figure 11.22 (Continued)

Olympic Pools

1. Before you go to the next website, estimate how many liters of water are in an Olympic-size pool. If it helps, think of a 2 L bottle, which, coincidently, holds 2 L.

2. Convert your guess into gallons.

3. Go to https://www.livestrong.com/article/350103-measurements-for-an-olympic-size-swimming-pool and read the article.

4. How many gallons are in a regulation, Olympic-size pool?

5. How many liters does that equal?

6. Calculate for both liters and gallons, how close your estimates were.

7. Based on your answers and the conversion information in the table, which is larger? Underline one:

1 gal of water	1 L of water

Figure 11.22 (Continued)

Name: _____ *Answer Key*_____

Metric and Imperial System Internet Search Lab

Directions: Practice converting measurements from the Imperial system to the metric system and vice versa. For each answer, you must include measurements! You can use your own calculator, borrow a calculator from me, or use the calculator on your computer. You are NOT permitted to use your phone's calculator. Show all of your work and round your answers to the nearest tenth.

Use this table for your conversions:

1 m = 3.3 ft	1 kg = 2.2 lbs
(°C × 9/5) + 32 = °F	(°F − 32) × 5/9 = °C
1 gal = 3.8 L	3,280 ft = 1 km
1 km = 0.6 miles	1 m = 1.1 yard

The World's Biggest Snakes

1. Go to https://www.livescience.com/34444-biggest-snake-largest-snake-longest-snake.html.

2. Read the article about the longest and most massive snakes to have slithered the Earth.

3. What is the longest anaconda's length (use feet)?
   30 ft

4. How many meters does this equal?
   30 ft × 1 m/3.3 ft = 9.1 m

5. What is the estimated mass for the prehistoric *Titanoboa cerrejonensis* in pounds?
   2,500 pounds

6. How many kilograms does this equal?
   2,500 pounds × 1 kg/2.2 pounds = 1,136.4 kg

7. Based on your answers and the conversion information in the table, which is larger? Underline one:

1 ft	<u>1 m</u>

Figure 11.23 Metric and Imperial System Internet Search Lab—Answer Key

8. Based on your answers and the conversion information in the table, which is larger? Underline one:

1 pound	<u>1 kg</u>

The World's Deepest Fish

1. Go to http://www.extremescience.com/deepest-fish-video.htm and read the article.

2. What is the depth, in feet, at which the snailfish is found?

25,000 ft

3. How many kilometers under the ocean can snailfish be found?

25,000 ft × 1 km/3,280 ft = 7.6 km

4. How many miles does this equal?

7.6 km × 0.6 miles/1 km = 4.56 miles

5. Based on your answers and the conversion information in the table, which is larger? Underline one:

<u>1 mile</u>	1 km

Microorganisms in Extreme Temperatures

1. Go to http://archive.bio.ed.ac.uk/jdeacon/microbes/thermo.htm and read the article.

2. Thermophiles are microorganisms that prosper in extremely hot temperatures, such as near volcanoes. What is the maximum temperature, in Celsius, that these microscopic creatures can live in?

70 °C

3. How hot is that in Fahrenheit?

(70 °C × 9/5) + 32 = 158 °F

4. Polar bears maintain a body temperature of about 98.6 °F but live in environments that are as cold as negative 92 °F (−92 °F). What is the difference, in °C, between a polar bear's internal body temperature and its external environmental temperature? Hint: convert the temperatures to Celsius first and then subtract to find the difference.

Figure 11.23 (Continued)

(98.6 – 32) × 5/9 = 37 °C

(–92 – 32) × 5/9 = –68.9 °C

37 – (–68.9) = 105.9 °C is the difference between the polar bear's body and its environment's temperature

5. Based on your answers and the conversion information in the table, which is hotter? Underline one:

<u>1 °C</u>	1 °F

Olympic Pools

1. Before you go to the next website, estimate how many liters of water are in an Olympic-size pool. If it helps, think of a 2 L bottle, which, coincidently, holds 2 L.

Answers will vary.

2. Convert your guess into gallons.

Answers will vary.

3. Go to https://www.livestrong.com/article/350103-measurements-for-an-olympic-size-swimming-pool and read the article.

4. How many gallons are in a regulation, Olympic-size pool?

660,253.1 gal

5. How many liters does that equal?

660,253.1 gal × 3.8 L/1 gal = 2,508,961.8 L

6. Calculate for both liters and gallons, how close your estimates were.

Answers will vary.

7. Based on your answers and the conversion information in the table, which is larger? Underline one:

<u>1 gal of water</u>	1 L of water

Figure 11.23   (Continued)

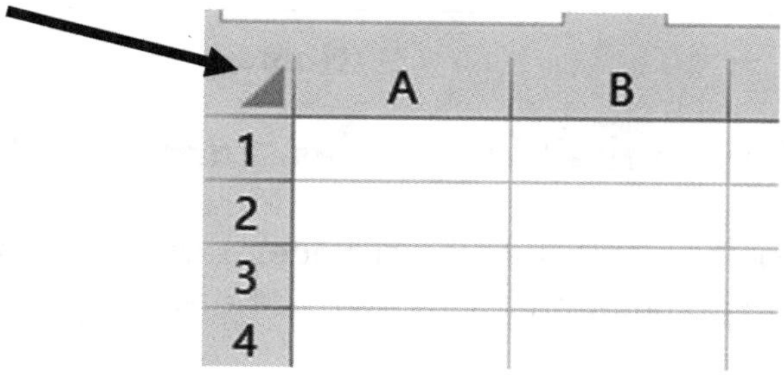

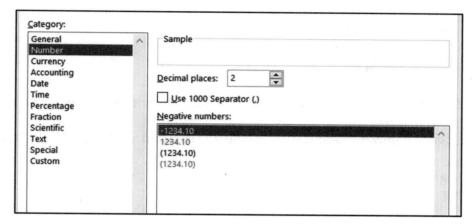

Figure 11.24   Excel—Selecting All Cells in a Spreadsheet

Figure 11.25   Excel—Pop-up Box

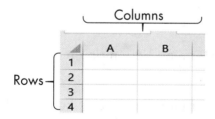

Figure 11.26   Excel—Rows vs. Columns

Name: _____

Celebrating Pi Day in the Sky: Sun vs. Earth vs. Moon vs. Antares

Using the diameters below, calculate the surface area and volume of the sun, earth, and moon. Here is the calculation for the surface area of a sphere:

$$4r^2\pi$$

Here is the calculation for the volume of a sphere:

$$(4/3)r^3\pi$$

Sun diameter: 1,392,700 km
Earth diameter: 12,756.32 km
Moon diameter: 3,474 km

NOTE#1: these are diameters, not radii. How do you turn a diameter into a radius?
NOTE#2: Pi = 3.14
NOTE#3: Every number needs a unit—some will be squared and some will be cubed.

Sun Surface Area: _____
Sun Volume: _____

Earth Surface Area: _____
Earth Volume: _____

Moon Surface Area: _____
Moon Volume: _____

Now using the volumes, determine how many moons fit inside Earth:

Now using the volumes, determine how many Earths fit inside the sun:

Antares is one of the largest stars in the Milky Way. Its radius is 400 times larger than the sun's radius. Calculate Antares's volume:

Now using the volumes, determine how many suns fit inside Antares:

Figure 11.27   Celebrating Pi Day in the Sky (Student Handout)

◢	A	B	C	D
1	Celestial Object	Diameter	Divided by 2	Equals Radius
2	sun	1392700	2	696350
3	earth			
4	moon			

Figure 11.28   Excel—Calculating Radius

Before

◢	A	E
1	######	
2	######	
3		
4		
5		
6		

After

◢	A	B
1	16806.00	
2	61918484.00	
3		
4		
5		
6		
7		

Figure 11.29   Excel—Screenshots of Before and After Cell Fix

D2's equation

D2	▾	⋮	✕	✓	f_x	=B2/C2

◢	A	B	C	D	E
1	Celestial Object	Diameter	Divided by 2	Equals Radius	
2	sun	1392700	2	696350	
3	earth				
4	moon				
5					

Figure 11.30   Excel—Screenshot of the Formula Bar

G	H	I	J	K
Celestial Object Surface Area	4	Multiplied by Radius Squared	Pi	Equals Surface Area
sun	4	1939613290000	3.14	6090385730600
earth				
moon				

Figure 11.31   Excel—The Sun's Surface Area

Name: _____ *Answer Key*_____

Celebrating Pi Day in the Sky: Sun vs. Earth vs. Moon vs. Antares

Using the diameters below, calculate the surface area and volume of the sun, earth, and moon. Here is the calculation for the surface area of a sphere:

$$4r^2\pi$$

Here is the calculation for the volume of a sphere:

$$(4/3)r^3\pi$$

Sun diameter: 1,392,700 km
Earth diameter: 12,756.32 km
Moon diameter: 3,474 km

NOTE#1: these are diameters, not radii. How do you turn a diameter into a radius?
NOTE#2: Pi = 3.14
NOTE#3: Every number needs a unit—some will be squared and some will be cubed.

Sun Surface Area: *6,090,385,730,600 km²*
Sun Volume: *1,413,680,034,501,100,000 km³*

Earth Surface Area: *510,952,417.82 km²*
Earth Volume: *1,086,312,091,079.10 km³*

Moon Surface Area: *37,895,642.64 km²*
Moon Volume: *21,941,577,088.56 km³*

Now using the volumes, determine how many moons fit inside Earth: *49.51 moons*

Now using the volumes, determine how many Earths fit inside the sun: *1,300,000 Earths*

Antares is one of the largest stars (by volume) in the Milky Way. Its radius is 400 times larger than the sun's radius. Calculate Antares's volume:

90,475,522,208,070,600,000,000,000 km³

Now using the volumes, determine how many suns fit inside Antares: *64,000,000 suns*

Figure 11.32 Celebrating Pi Day in the Sky—Answer Key

Making Graphs in Excel

Follow these step-by-step procedures to turn your Pi Day measurements into a bar graph using Excel.

1. Highlight and copy the four cells that list the Celestial Objects title and names.

Celestial Object Volume	
	sun
	earth
	moon

2. Paste these four cells to four new cells.

3. Highlight and copy the four cells that list the title and volumes of these celestial objects.

Equals Volume
14136800345011100000
1086312091079
21941577089

4. Place the cursor in the cell next to the cell that reads "Celestial Object Volume" that was created in step 2 above.

5. Right click the mouse. Choose Paste Special and then Values. Click OK. The final product should look like this:

Celestial Object Volume	Equals Volume
Sun	14136800345011100000.00
Earth	1086312091079.10
Moon	21941577088.56

6. Highlight all eight cells.

7. Click Insert at the top of the Spreadsheet. Then in the Charts section, click on the picture of a bar graph as shown here:

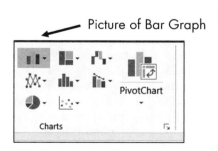

Figure 11.33 Making Graphs in Excel (Student Handout)

8. The bar graph will appear but it isn't finished. It's missing many of the items a scientific graph requires. Click on the title and change it so that it includes both the independent and dependent variables.

9. Click on the graph so that these three symbols appear on the right side:

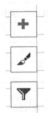

10. Click on the addition symbol, which opens a pop-up box. Click on the option "Axis Titles."

11. Return to the graph, click on the titles for the x- and y-axis to change the titles so they read as independent and dependent variables. Be sure to include units of measurement. To make the cube a superscript so that it rides above the line, type "km3" and then highlight the 3. Right-click on the 3, which opens a pop-up box. Choose "Font" and then "Superscript." Click OK.

Figure 11.33   (Continued)

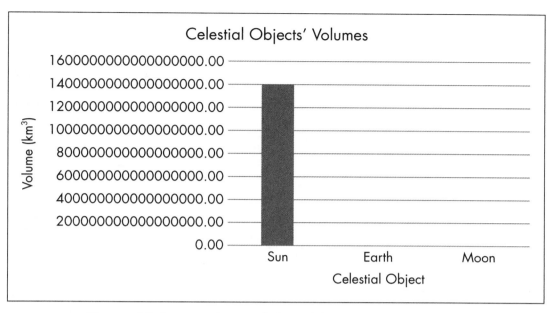

Figure 11.34   Excel—Graph for Celebrating Pi Day in the Sky

CHAPTER 12

Strategies for Incorporating the Arts and Kinesthetic Movement

What Is It?

On February 2, 2016, John Maeda, the former president of the Rhode Island School of Design, gave a speech at the fifth annual Governor Victor Atiyeh Leadership for Education Awards. The speech told his story of leading the national movement to integrate the arts into STEM (science, technology, engineering, and math) so it would read STEAM (Concordia University, 2016).

Maeda's message is that the arts teach students to design creatively, which leads to innovation (Gunn, 2017). Incorporating the arts into science means there is purposeful integration of "humanities, language arts, dance, drama, music, visual arts, design and new media" (Wade-Leeuwen, Vovers, & Silk, 2018). Kinesthetic movement is not simply students moving but is "the use of creative movement in the classroom to teach across the curriculum" (Griss, 2013).

Why We Like It

Art and kinesthetic strategies can be an effective way to engage students who have a passion for dance, music, drawing, and sports. In our experience, students have a deeper understanding of new content why we incorporate the arts and kinesthetic activities into our teaching.

Supporting Research

Research has found that arts-integration strategies can lead to increases in science achievement along with the other content areas (Ludwig, Boyle, & Lindsay, 2017,

p. 43). Incorporating the arts in content instruction can also have positive impacts on student attitudes, critical thinking, and social-emotional learning (Ludwig et al., 2017, p. 43).

Studies show that using arts-integrated lessons to aid in teaching science can increase student long-term retention of content, especially for students who are at basic reading levels (Hardiman, JohnBull, Carran, & Shelton, 2019, p. 30).

There are also numerous studies showing how kinesthetic learning increases motivation and retention for students (Lai, Luong, & Young, 2015, p. 49; Novak, 2017, p.125).

Skills for Intentional Scholars/NGSS Connections

All of the Skills for Intentional Scholars are being practiced when using arts-integration and kinesthetic strategies. Students can think critically and use problem-solving skills when transferring knowledge into an art form or utilizing movement while learning content. They also can improve communication skills by using arts and movement to express new knowledge.

The Next Generation Science Standards (NGSS) incorporate eight Science and Engineering Practices, one of which is Developing and Using Models. They define models as, "diagrams, drawings, physical replicas, mathematical representations, analogies, and computer simulations" (National Science Teaching Association [NSTA], 2014). Many of the lesson plan ideas we share in this chapter incorporate diagrams, drawings, and/or physical replicas.

Application

We've shared ideas throughout this book that incorporate the arts and kinesthetic movement. See Table 12.1: Where to Find STEAM and Kinesthetic Lesson Ideas in Other Chapters for a quick reference of where to find these lessons.

This chapter will provide additional specific lesson plan examples that incorporate the arts as they are defined by Wade-Leeuwen, et al. (2018): humanities, language arts, dance/music, drama, visual arts, design, and new media. We will also include lesson plans that purposefully get students moving out of their seats. The lesson plans target middle school classrooms; however, we provide ideas for modifying each plan for elementary and high school students. See the Technology Connections section for specific STEAM resources, such as how to become a STEAM certified teacher.

Table 12.1   Where to Find STEAM and Kinesthetic Lesson Ideas in Other Chapters

Chapter	Lesson ideas
Chapter 1: Strategies for Teaching Lab Safety	Visual Arts: Draw a cartoon and create a poster
	Digital and New Media: Produce a video
	Drama: Write and act a skit
Chapter 3: Strategies for Teaching the Scientific Method and its Components	Digital and New Media: Publish a blog, Prezi, Google Slides, or PowerPoint presentation
Chapter 5: Strategies for Using Project-Based Learning	Digital and New Media: Create a press kit, Animoto slideshow, PowerPoint, Prezi, or Google Slides Presentation
	Drama: Create and share a public service announcement video or a skit
Chapter 6: Strategies for Teaching the Engineering Process	Humanities: Share historical stories of inspiring scientists
	Kinesthetic Movement: Make a mousetrap catapult, drop an egg from a significant height, and mail a potato chip without it breaking
Chapter 7: Strategies for Teaching Vocabulary	Linguistics: Teach prefixes and suffixes
Chapter 8: Strategies for Teaching Reading Comprehension	Visual arts: Create cause-and-effect graphic organizers, concept maps, and chalk drawings
	Kinesthetic Movement: 4×4 reading strategy
Chapter 9: Strategies for Teaching Writing	Visual arts: Create a comic strip public service announcement
Chapter 10: Strategies for Discussions	Humanities: Debate scientific topics
	Kinesthetic Movement: Four corners activity
Chapter 11: Strategies for Teaching Math	Kinesthetic Movement: Measure objects
Chapter 16: Strategies for Reviewing Content	Kinesthetic Movement: Play Quizlet or the Box Game
Chapter 17: Strategies for Assessing Student Learning	Visual arts: Create models
Chapter 18: Strategies for Co-teaching	Kinesthetic Movement: Create the tallest structure and use Station Teaching

HUMANITIES

Here we share a lesson plan that integrates history with the engineering process, which is discussed in Chapter 6: Strategies for Teaching the Engineering Process.

We first teach the engineering process and have students complete a simple engineering challenge. Then, they complete the lesson in Figure 12.1: Engineering Process: A Case Study in Inventions.

We provide each student with a copy of Figure 12.1 because students work on their case studies individually; however, we do allow students who require extra support to pair up with a peer.

We introduce the lesson by reading the directions aloud: "The engineering process became a systemic approach to design in the 1970s." We then stop reading and tell the story of Filippo Brunelleschi, the designer of a cathedral in Florence, Italy, around the year 1420. The story we tell comes from an article entitled, "An Extremely Abbreviated History of Engineering Design" (Salustri, 2003). We also show an easily available online image of him.

Our story begins,

> It was around the year 1420 and one notable architect in Italy was Filippo Brunelleschi. He had been hired to design and build a dome for the Florence Cathedral. Prior to this time, architects would begin building without a lot of planning. If their design started to fail and they couldn't fix the flaws, they would destroy what they had built and then begin building all over again. Architects weren't known for being creative and rarely tried anything new to avoid this waste of time, materials, and money.

> Brunelleschi wasn't all that worried about the waste of time, materials, and money, but he was worried about something else. Can anyone guess what he would be nervous about?

We allow students to share their guesses and then we continue.

> He was worried that other architects would steal his ideas, so he put a lot of effort into brainstorming different ideas. He kept a journal that contained sketches and mathematical calculations. He kept the journal very well guarded.

> As he sketched and planned, he realized that some of his ideas wouldn't be successful so he brainstormed more designs. Once he decided on what he thought was the best design, Brunelleschi encountered a problem. If he gave his design to a construction crew, they would know all of his design secrets. So what did he do to solve this problem? What do you think?

We allow students to share their guesses and then we continue.

> He drew sketches that included only parts of the dome and sent each of the sketches to a different construction crew. These crews built the individual parts without knowing they were constructing a dome.

When all of the parts arrived in Florence, Brunelleschi hired a small crew of men who promised to keep his design a secret. They worked to put all of the dome's individual parts together to construct one full dome. They did encounter a few minor design issues that Brunelleschi had to solve, but ultimately the dome was complete and, 600 years later, is still standing in Florence, Italy.

At this point, we show a picture of the Florence Cathedral. The photo can be found online using these search words: "filippo brunelleschi florence cathedral image."

We explain that Filippo Brunelleschi had unknowingly been the first person (that history remembers—there may very well have been others) to plan and document the construction of a building, which would eventually become the foundation for the engineering process. We then put the steps of today's engineering process on the board and ask students to identify which steps he used. Here are the steps for the current engineering process:

1. Ask a question.
2. Perform research.
3. Brainstorm solutions.
4. Choose one solution.
5. Build a prototype.
6. Test the prototype.
7. Reflect on the results and redesign.
8. Communicate results.
9. Begin again with step 1.

If students struggle to identify all of the steps that Brunelleschi used, we go through each step individually and ask guiding questions. For example, we point to Step 1 and ask students, "What question did Brunelleschi ask?" We allow students time to think and answer that his question was "How do I design a new dome for the Florence Cathedral?" By the end of this exercise, students will have identified that Brunelleschi used all of the steps to build the dome except for Step 9: Begin Again with Step 1. However, when he designed future projects, he certainly incorporated his learning from the dome project, meaning that he ultimately used Step 9: Begin Again with Step 1. Here is how he used those first eight steps:

1. Ask a question—"How do I design a new dome for the Florence Cathedral?"
2. Perform research—Brunelleschi knew of previously designed domes.
3. Brainstorm solutions—in his journal, he kept sketches of possible designs.

4. Choose one solution—he eliminated some of his ideas and ultimately chose one.

5. Build a prototype—this was the dome.

6. Test the prototype—while putting together the individual pieces, the dome had issues and failed the test.

7. Reflect on the results and redesign—Brunelleschi had to solve the issues that were identified in Step 6.

8. Communicate results—we can assume the Church celebrated that they finally had a roof.

We continue reading the directions in Figure 12.1: "In order to apply your new knowledge of the engineering process, you will choose an invention that was created after 1870." We explain that we prefer inventions post-1870 because there is sufficient documentation available for them to research. Additionally, we want them to choose an invention that was created prior to 1970 because this is when the engineering process was introduced to most engineering degree programs and became a standard in engineering practices (Mathes, 2017). Therefore, these earlier inventions are more likely to have been designed using only parts of the engineering process, which makes for a richer learning experience. In other words, it is more likely that they might find that a step was missed along the way.

We continue to read the directions and review the checklist with students. They then perform research using library books, the Internet, or phone interviews. See Chapter 3: Strategies for Teaching the Scientific Method and Its Components for resources that help students to research effectively.

We allow students to choose the media they will use to present their research. Their options are included in Figure 12.1. One option includes building a website. See the Technology Connections section for several website-making tools for students.

Here are options for modifying this assignment for elementary school students:

1. Provide a list of vetted inventions that have plenty of information online or in the school library. Students choose from the list. We've found these are the easiest to research:
   a. Airplane
   b. Microwave
   c. Gas-powered car
   d. Telephone
   e. Wireless phone
   f. Radio
   g. Handheld camera

2. Allow students to work in pairs (see Chapter 2: Strategies for Teaching Lab Procedures for ideas of how to effectively pair students).

3. Remove the requirement of how the invention's improvement followed the engineering process.

Here are options for modifying this assignment for high school students:

1. Require text evidence and a bibliography.

2. Require the history of the patent including the patent number, year, and a copy of the submitted diagram.

3. Require that students propose an improvement to the current design and that they include a diagram of what the new design would look like and how it would be different.

Additional science lesson ideas that incorporate the humanities include:

- Studying human evolution by learning about fossils and archeology. Many archeological lesson plans are available online, including from the Archaeological Institute of America (Archaeological Institute of America, n.d.).

- Reading excerpts from well-known novels such as *Silent Spring* (Carson, 1962), *On the Origin of Species* (Darwin, 1859), or *A Brief History of Time* (Hawking, 1988) and then discussing their impact on society today.

- Researching the work of James Hannam, who has a PhD in the history and philosophy of science. His work focuses on the collaboration of scientists and religious leaders to achieve a common goal: to explain the unknown.

LANGUAGE ARTS—POETRY

We enjoy adding poetry to our lesson plans. Our favorite poet is Shel Silverstein, who authored *Where the Sidewalk End*s (1974) and *A Light in the Attic* (1981). Prior to Silverstein's death in 1999, he recorded himself reading his poems in *Where the Sidewalk Ends*, which is available online and on CD.

The following activity uses Silverstein's poem entitled, "Sarah Cynthia Sylvia Stout Would Not Take the Garbage Out" (Silverstein, 1974). Although we don't describe the entire lesson plan here, this portion can be used to launch several different types of activities—depending on the grade level.

In elementary and middle school, we use the poem to introduce a lesson that teaches the NGSS's disciplinary core idea of ESS3.C (Earth and Space Science): Human Impacts on Earth Systems. The focus in elementary school is on what happens to garbage after it leaves our houses, and in middle school we use this to introduce the difference between decomposition, incineration, composting, and recycling. In high school, this activity is used as a hook to introduce the laws of conservation of matter and mass at the macro level so students can more easily understand what occurs at the atomic level, which is the NGSS of HS-PS1: Matter and its Interactions.

We put the poem under the document camera so students can follow along as we play the CD twice (of course, teachers could read it themselves, instead). As students listen to Silverstein dramatically read his humorous poem, they are instructed to write down the items in Sarah Cynthia Sylvia Stout's garbage can. Students then share their lists with their learning partners who write down any of the items they were missing.

Students are next instructed to brainstorm with their learning partner the answer to this question: "If Sarah Cynthia Sylvia Stout had indeed taken the garbage out, where would it have gone and what would have happened to it when it reached its destination?" Students document their answer by drawing a sketch, which may include any of the following ideas, depending on the students' background knowledge about garbage:

- dumped in a landfill
- sent to a recycling plant
- incinerated
- dumped in the ocean
- deposited in a composting pile

When teaching elementary students, we then launch into a lesson about the purpose of landfills and how they negatively affect the environment when they release gas and leach into the soil and groundwater. We next teach a lesson about composting to make garden fertilizer as an alternative to landfills. After that lesson is complete (usually a day or two later, depending on the specific plan), we ask students to pull out the list of items that were in Sarah Cynthia Sylvia Stout's garbage can and circle all of the compostable items. For example, they would circle the bananas, peas, and potato peelings, but they would not circle the cottage cheese because it's a dairy product, which attracts pests that will eat the fertilized garden.

When teaching middle school students, we use their sketches as a pre-test to determine what students know and don't know about decomposition, incineration, composting, and recycling. We use this information to plan our Human Impacts on Earth Systems unit because it teaches students the positive and negative effects of garbage decomposing in landfills, burning in incinerators, composting for fertilizer, and recycling.

High school students who are about to learn the law of conservation of mass or the law of conservation of matter are asked to use their sketches to indicate what happens to the garbage after it reaches its final destination. Here are some options for their answers:

- At a recycling plant—the garbage is broken down and reused.
- In a landfill—the garbage decomposes, releasing leachate and methane.
- At a composting plant—made into fertilizer for agriculture.
- Is incinerated—becomes ash and gases such as carbon dioxide, sulfur dioxide, and nitrous oxides.

If students struggle to determine what happens to the garbage, we pair them up with another group who sketched the same destination so they can work through the problem together. We aren't too concerned that they know exactly what happens to the garbage, but we do want them to realize it's being changed into something else: Garbage doesn't stay garbage forever.

We then ask the class, "Clearly garbage doesn't simply disappear just because it leaves your house. Will it stay garbage forever? Why or why not?" We provide students the opportunity to brainstorm with their learning partners and then ask some to share with the class. As students explain that garbage is stored or changed, we introduce the laws of conservation of mass or matter, depending on what we are teaching. We explain that garbage being recycled, composted, burned, or decomposed are macro examples of the law. This law is also obeyed at the atomic level.

At some point in the unit, we can return to the poem and ask students to pull out their list of items that were in Sarah Cynthia Sylvia Stout's garbage can. We explain to them that carbon is included in all food and ask the class to circle any items they listed in Sarah's garbage can that contained carbon. Then we ask, "If that food was eaten, where would the carbon have gone?" Students should be able to explain that it was used by the body and/or excreted as waste: The carbon doesn't just disappear. The amount of carbon in the food that was eaten equals the amount of carbon that was received by the body after digestion because of the law of conservation of mass. The law states that the products must equal the reactants.

Additional science lesson ideas that incorporate poetry include:

- Reading and discussing poems about specific content, such as J. Patrick Lewis's *Chromosome Poem*, *Said the Little Stone*, and *The Loneliest Creature* (Robb & Lewis, 2007).
- Writing haiku or tanka poems about the specific content students are studying.
- Analyzing the accuracy of historical poems, such as *An Anatomy of the World*, written in 1611 by John Donne, *Sonnet—To Science* by Edgar Allan Poe in 1829, and *The Horrid Voice of Science* by Vachel Lindsay in 1919.

DANCE/MUSIC

This lesson plan can incorporate dance, music, and design and new media. The basic idea is that students first learn a new concept and then "show off" their learning by writing a song about the concept.

In our example, we first teach about the life cycles of stars, how scientists measure distances in space, and the layers of the sun. Students are then divided into groups of three. See Chapter 2: Strategies for Teaching Lab Procedures for ideas on creating student groups.

Each group is provided with a copy of Figure 12.2: Rewriting a Song, which instructs them to rewrite the song *Twinkle Twinkle Little Star*. We focus specifically on this song for two reasons. First, the chorus has many incorrect statements. After teaching about stars, we ask students to identify the errors in the song, which are:

- Stars don't twinkle.
- Stars aren't diamonds.
- Stars aren't little.
- We don't "wonder" about them as much as we did when the song was written because we've learned a lot about stars since 1806, the year the song was probably composed.
- Stars aren't located solely above our location on Earth.

The second reason we focus on *Twinkle Twinkle Little Star* is because it is a universally known tune, so there is a very high chance that every student will have some familiarity with it. The same melody is used to sing a version of *Twinkle Twinkle Little Star* in China, the Philippines, most English-speaking countries, and in some nations where Arabic is the primary language. Germany and the Netherlands also use the melody in a popular Christmas carol (Doggart, 2011). Several years ago, we had a student from Japan who didn't speak English. As we were singing *Twinkle Twinkle Little Star* to the class, without prompting, she stood and sang the song with us in Japanese. It was the first time she spoke in class voluntarily and the students erupted in applause when she was done. That moment offered a special connection among her, the other students, and us.

Each member of the group is responsible for writing his/her own stanza, but they work on them together so that all the lines complement each other as a full song when the assignment is complete. We provide the groups with a list of concepts that must be covered in each stanza. As an example, in the *Twinkle Twinkle Little Star* lesson, we put students in groups of three and instruct them to write about these three concepts in their stanzas (one person in each group chooses a different concept):

1. Layers of the sun
2. Life cycle of the sun
3. Light years and astronomical units

As students are working on their stanzas, we walk around the room to keep students on task and help anyone who hits a roadblock. Many students want their lines to rhyme but we remind them that this is not a requirement of the assignment.

We also give groups the choice of how they will perform their new songs. In Figure 12.2: Rewriting a Song, we list the options given to students for the *Twinkle Twinkle Little Star* lesson. They can create:

- a music video
- a live presentation with vocals and/or instruments
- a pre-recorded presentation with vocals and/or instruments
- an interpretative dance that is performed while someone dramatically reads the song lyrics

See the Technology Connections section for applications students can use to make music videos or record a performance at home.

Figure 12.2: Rewriting a Song also includes the scoring guide we use to grade the groups' performances. See Figure 12.3: Example of the First Rewritten Stanza for *Twinkle Twinkle Little Star* for an example of what the first stanza may look like.

With modifications, this lesson can be applied to many other songs. An online search of "science songs" can provide a good start for other ones to use.

Additional science lesson ideas that incorporate music include:

- students creating parodies. For example, they can choose their favorite song and rewrite the lyrics to reflect a science concept and perform their creation.
- watching parodies others have created that are available online, such as AsapScience's parodies. Our favorites are their parody of *Star Wars* entitled, "Science Wars"; Dua Lipa's "New Rules" titled, "Lab Rules"; and Taylor Swift's "Style" titled, "Science STYLE Cover."
- changing a common children's song, such as Humpty Dumpty, into a parody and then creating a dance that accompanies the new lyrics.

DRAMA

This lesson plan incorporates drama into the science classroom.

We love to tell students stories and students enjoy hearing them. But sometimes the story is so long or complicated that students would become bored if we told it. To simplify a story and make it more engaging, we break it into parts. Each part is then assigned to a small group. In this lesson, we have eight "parts," so there are eight groups with four or five students in each one.

The purpose of this lesson is to teach students the story of how scientists' discoveries over several centuries contributed to the cell theory and germ theory. We begin by listing all of the scientists who will be the focus of student learning. Here are the scientists we chose, including each person's contribution:

- Hippocrates—believed incorrectly that bad air made people sick.
- Athanasius Kircher—blamed the bubonic plague on microorganisms he saw in a microscope.
- Robert Hooke—credited with inventing the microscope and coining the term *cell*, after seeing cells in a piece of cork.
- Francesco Redi—disproved the belief of spontaneous generation.
- Anton van Leeuwenhoek—improved the microscope and was the first to document microbes.
- Marcus Antonius Plenciz—theorized without proof that specific "seeds in the air" (today these "seeds" are known as microbes) cause specific illnesses.
- Matthias Schleiden—concluded that all plants are made up of cells.
- Theodor Schwann—concluded that all animals are made up of cells.
- Karl von Siebold—concluded that all microbes are made up of one cell.
- Ignaz Philipp Semmelweis—a doctor who, when he washed his hands, had a lower death rate.
- Rudolf Carl Virchow—discovered that cells come from other cells.
- Louis Pasteur—identified microbes as the cause of milk spoiling and that these microbes could be killed if the milk was heated to a minimum temperature.
- Florence Nightingale—improved sanitary conditions in military hospitals.
- Joseph Lister—used chemicals to kill microbes.
- Robert Koch—proved that specific microbes cause specific illnesses.
- William Stewart Halsted—a doctor who used rubber gloves.

We group the scientists into pairs, which creates eight groups. They are paired together based on the year of their contributions; the two earliest years are paired together, then the next two years are paired together, and so on.

Each pair of scientists is then assigned to a group of students. We've found that younger students usually need help dividing the work among them, so we visit each group individually to model how a division of labor can be accomplished. Older students are more likely to have the social skills to divide the labor among themselves as long as we provide whole class instruction for a suggested process. With student groups of four, we suggest that two students work together to research one scientist. If there are five students in a group, then two students can research one scientist and the remaining three students can research the other scientist. By pairing students in this fashion, they are receiving support from a peer "buddy," which is especially useful for students who have learning challenges or who are English language learners.

For this lesson plan, the groups research the following questions for their assigned scientists:

1. What time period was it? When did your scientist make their contribution? What important dates pertain to your scientist?

2. What important discovery did your scientist make?

3. What process did your scientist go through to make his/her contribution? How did they make their discovery? What proof (if any) did they provide to prove their contribution was valid?

4. How accurate was your scientist? What was the response from the rest of the scientific field (did people believe him/her or not)?

5. How did your scientist's contribution advance the cell and/or germ theory?

See Chapter 3: Strategies for Teaching the Scientific Method and Its Components for resources to help students effectively perform research.

After students complete their research, they are instructed to create a skit they will perform in front of the class to teach their peers about their scientists. We provide a copy of Figure 12.4: Rubric for Cell and Germ Theories Skit to each group so they know grading expectations for the assignment. We have many of the props students may need for their skit, such as flasks and petri dishes, so the day before their performance, we ask each group to write their desired props on an index card and turn it in. This assignment gives us ample time to collect the props from our supply room, other teachers' supply rooms, the drama teacher, the cafeteria, and from anyone else on campus who may be able to donate.

On the day of the performances, each student receives a copy of Figure 12.5: Timeline Graphic Organizer for the Cell and Germ Theories. As students are watching the other groups' performances, they complete the timeline. At the end of the lesson, we display the answer key on the board, which we've provided in Figure 12.6: Timeline Graphic Organizer for the Cell and Germ Theories–Answer Key. In addition to ensuring that students have captured the correct information on their timelines, this also provides an opportunity for students to practice their critical thinking skills. They analyze their timelines to discern differences between their versions and ours. They then update their timelines for accuracy. This activity can easily be differentiated for students with learning challenges. We provide these students with a hard copy of the answer key. Some students' challenges make it difficult for them to copy from the board so they use the hard copy to analyze and improve their timelines and we collect the answer key from them when they are done. Other students benefit from keeping the answer key as an attachment to their timeline.

See Table 12.2: Ideas for Telling Stories Through Skits for specific stories that can be told in each of the NGSS disciplines. Each story will take some research and preparation by teachers, but after the initial preparation, it can be used for many years with minor adjustments. The steps to create and execute these lessons are:

1. Determine which scientists could be included in the story and identify each of their contributions. Create a list like the one above that shows those involved with Cell and Germ Theories.

2. Determine the number of student groups you want. Then we typically group scientists into pairs based on the dates of their scientific contributions. For example, above we wanted 8 student groups, so we paired the 16 scientists.

3. Group students and assign each group the scientists they will be researching.

4. Provide student groups with these questions to guide their research:

   a. What time period was it? When did your scientists make their contributions? What important dates pertain to your scientists?

   b. What important discoveries did your scientists make?

   c. What process did your scientists go through to make their contributions? How did they make their discoveries? What proof (if any) did they provide to prove their contributions were valid?

   d. How accurate were your scientists? What was the response from the rest of the scientific community (did people believe them or not)?

   e. How did your scientists' contributions advance . . . (insert the specific idea they are learning about here)?

5. Use Figure 12.4: Rubric for Cell and Germ Theories Skit to assist students in planning their skits. This rubric is general and can be used for any concept by just changing the title of it. Go over the rubric with the student groups and give them two to three 50-min class periods to prepare their skits. Have them list any props they require on an index card and collect them from storage rooms, the theater room, cafeteria, and anyone else who is willing to donate.

6. On performance day, provide students with copies of a timeline graphic organizer. See Figure 12.5: Timeline Graphic Organizer for the Cell and Germ Theories for an example. Students should fill in their graphic organizers while groups are performing.

7. Once all groups have performed, display a timeline answer key for the class to be sure all students have them filled out correctly.

In addition to the ideas in Table 12.2, the NGSS suggest the teaching of specific scientists. While teaching these historically significant scientists, we intentionally identify a female scientist or scientist of color that can also be incorporated into the lesson. This strategy is an example of culturally responsive teaching, which is discussed further in Chapter 14: Strategies for Cultural Responsiveness. Table 12.3 couples the NGSS's suggested scientists with women scientists and scientists of color who made important contributions in the same areas and can be easily integrated into lessons.

This lesson is naturally differentiated for elementary and high school students by its content.

Table 12.2 Ideas for Telling Stories Through Skits

NGSS discipline	Story to be told through skits
Earth Sciences	History and current effects of climate change
Earth Sciences	Chicxulub lands on Earth, alters the Earth's surface and climate, which ultimately kills the dinosaurs
Physical Sciences	Evidence of plate tectonics, beginning with Alfred Wegener and ending with satellite images from the late twentieth century
Physical Sciences	Discoveries of fission and fusion and how they lead to the invention of the atomic and nuclear bombs
Life Sciences	How cadavers have been used throughout the history of the United States
Life Sciences	Evidence of evolution and survival of the fittest, including Darwin, fossil record, embryology, and DNA
Technology, Engineering, and Applications of Science	Causes of the Chernobyl explosion, focusing on the differences between the designs of the Chernobyl Nuclear Power Plant and other nuclear power plants around the world
Technology, Engineering, and Applications of Science	How fishing technology has evolved, causing overfishing in today's lakes and oceans

Table 12.3 NGSS Scientists Paired with Women Scientists and Scientists of Color

NGSS scientist and contribution	Women scientists and scientists of color
Nicolaus Copernicus—proved heliocentrism and studied planetary movement	A list of women in planetary science, including Natalie Batalha, can be found at https://womeninplanetary science.wordpress.com/profiles
	Maria Cunitz, who furthered Kepler's work to determine a planet's location as a function of time
Isaac Newton—established Newtonian Mechanics	A list of Black physicists, including John McNeile Hunter, can be found at http://www.math.buffalo.edu/mad/physics/physics-peeps.html
Charles Lyell—developed the Doctrine of Uniformity	Adriana Ocampo, NASA's leading geologist, studies new impact craters on Earth and other celestial bodies
	Carol Gardipe, a geologist who maps and studies geography and natural resources
John Dalton and Antoine Lavoisier—proposed that all matter is made up of atoms	Maria Goeppert Mayer, a physicist who identified the structure of the atomic nucleus
Charles Darwin—used evidence to establish the theory of evolution	Nancy A. Moran, an evolutionary biologist who studies the mutualistic relationships between insects and bacterial species
Louis Pasteur—discovered that heating milk kills its microbes	Florence Nightingale, a nurse who established sanitary procedures and increased the survival rates of soldiers
James Watson and Francis Crick—discovered that DNA is a double helix	Rosalind Franklin, whose X-ray data inspired Watson and Crick's discovery

VISUAL ARTS

A popular lesson plan in physics classrooms instructs students to use their learning of simple machines to build a Rube Goldberg machine. The six simple machines included in a Rube Goldberg machine are:

1. lever
2. pulley
3. inclined plane
4. screw
5. wheel and axle
6. wedge

The purpose of a Rube Goldberg machine is to use a chain reaction of the six simple machines to accomplish a simple physical task, such as opening window blinds, popping a balloon, starting the microwave, or closing a door.

We share our Rube Goldberg lesson plan here and provide additional online resources in the Technology Connections section.

Rube Goldberg machines are notorious for being silly and fun. To emphasize this, we encourage students to choose a personal interest, such as their favorite song, sport, or hobby, as a theme for their machine. Elementary and middle school students incorporate the visual arts into their machine by drawing a cartoon that depicts how their machine works.

The NGSS of 5-PS2–1 for fifth grade includes the requirement that students know that "gravitational interactions are attractive and depend on the masses of interacting objects" (NGSS, 2013h, MS-PS2). When we use this lesson plan for elementary students, we emphasize the simple machines that depend on gravity: level, pulley, and inclined plane. In middle and high school, all six simple machines must be included. The Rube Goldberg machine lesson is done after we have taught students about the simple machines.

We begin the lesson by showing them a video of a Rube Goldberg machine in motion. See the Technology Connections section for video resources. Prior to viewing the video, we tell students that after the video is complete we will ask them, "What was the purpose of building the machine?" After the video, we discuss how much work went into creating a machine to perform such a simple task. We then show them a second video and tell them that after the video is complete we will ask, "Which of the six simple machines were included in the machine?" After the video, students share which simple machines they did (or did not) see.

Students are then paired with a learning partner. Each pair receives a copy of Figure 12.7: Directions and Scoring Guide for Rube Goldberg Cartoon. We read the directions as a class and answer student questions.

Students work with their partners to draw the six simple machines. We walk around to check for understanding. Then, students complete the Brainstorming section of Figure 12.7.

When students are done with the Brainstorming section, each pair is given a blank sheet of paper. We show the class one example of a cartoon, which can easily be found through an Internet search using the terms "Rube Goldberg cartoon images." We only show one cartoon because we want students to develop their own ideas. Student pairs are instructed to work together: (1) to sketch the Rube Goldberg machine, labeling each of the simple machines; and (2) to write an explanation of what is happening from one machine to the next.

The NGSS of HS-PS3–3 for high school requires students to "Design, build, and refine a device that works within given constraints to convert one form of energy into another form of energy." The "clarification statement" for this standard specifically mentions Rube Goldberg machines as an example (NGSS, 2013i). Taking this point into account, we require high school students to include how energy is changing form when they write their explanation of what is occurring at each simple machine on their diagram. For example, they would explain that mechanical energy is changed to sound energy when a ball hits a wall and produces the sound of "thud," and how electrical energy is changed into heat energy when a lightbulb is lit.

We challenge our high school students (and some in middle school) to build their machines. After drawing their sketches and writing their explanations, they use recycled materials to build them. To obtain all of the necessary materials students need, we ask our administration to send an email to the community asking for donations of recycled materials, nails, screws, plywood, toilet paper/paper towel rolls, cardboard, aluminum foil, etc. We then ask our friends and family to borrow their hammers and screwdrivers. Marbles can be expensive. Instead, we've used golf balls donated from local courses. For an example of an eighth grade student's constructed Rube Goldberg machine, see Figure 12.8: Picture of a Student's Constructed Rube Goldberg Machine, which was made using only recycled materials.

Additional science lesson ideas that incorporate visual arts have students identify the many connections between science and art. There are many examples of how science influences art and how art influences science. When students recognize these connections, we've found that their perception of science can change. Instead of generalizing a scientist as a person who works in a lab, wearing a white coat and lab safety goggles, students can realize that science influences many fields.

To help students make this connection between science and the arts, we assign them one of the following challenges:

- Analyze art pieces like Edvard Munch's *The Scream*, Luke Jerram's glass models of microbes and viruses, and Fabian Oefner's photographs of natural phenomena, such as fire and centripetal forces, to determine how science has influenced artists.

- Analyze historical art pieces like Maria Sibylla Merian's sketch of a tarantula eating a hummingbird and Anna Atkins' photographs of algae, to learn how science influences the field of art.

- Describe how art and science can intersect by studying people who have been both artists and scientists, such as Samuel Morse (the inventor of Morse code), Leonardo da Vinci (studied human anatomy), and Maria Sibylla Merian (documented the interactions between animals and plants).

- Identify careers that integrate science and art, such as those that contribute to NASA's Art Program, graphic design, architecture, video game design, and art restoration.

Students complete research to identify the interdependence between art and science and then either write a paragraph explaining the connection or, as an enrichment assignment, they can create their own art piece and write a description that explains how their artwork was inspired by science.

DESIGN AND NEW MEDIA

In our experience, students enjoy building their own websites, and technology has made it simple to create them. A website can be built to effectively communicate any concept, but is especially useful when highlighting concepts that have a visual element, such as diagrams, pictures, and videos. Websites can also provide students with an authentic audience. See the Technology Connections section for resources that help students identify authentic audiences with whom they can share their websites.

The focus of this lesson is examining the benefits and drawbacks of dams. We require students to create a website because we've found that students' understanding is deeper when they have access to pictures and videos that depict the effects of dams. Additionally, many of the solutions that engineers and farmers have created to make dams less destructive are more appreciated if students can see them through pictures or videos. For example, we've found that students are more amazed by the effectiveness of fish ladders, which allow fish to swim upstream and over a dam, when they see a video of one in action.

We begin this lesson by dividing students into pairs. With our colleague, Melissa Posey, we developed Figure 12.9: Dams! Are They Constructive or Destructive? We provide each student with a copy of Figure 12.9 and explain they will ultimately be designing a website that states, with evidence, whether dams are constructive or destructive.

As a class, we read the directions and checklist in Figure 12.9. We define the terms *constructive* and *destructive*. We ask students, "What does it mean to construct something?" Students often answer "to build" or "to create." We affirm their answer and then explain that when dams are built, they construct lakes so in that sense they can be considered constructive. Then we ask students "What does it mean to destroy something?" Students typically respond "to demolish" or "to hurt/injure." Again, we affirm their answer and then explain that the rivers below the dams are destroyed so in that sense dams can be considered destructive. Their task is to perform research about dams around the world and determine if they are constructive or destructive. Then, they must support their position with evidence.

We answer student questions regarding the directions and checklist in Figure 12.9 and then provide time for them to perform their research. See Chapter 3: Strategies for Teaching the Scientific Method and Its Components for resources to differentiate for students while they are researching, along with other resources that can be applied to this activity.

We walk around the room as students are researching on their devices and provide support. We encourage them to research several of the dams listed in Figure 12.9 because no one resource is going to provide all of the information they need to complete this task.

Table 12.4 Topics for Website Projects for the Four NGSS Disciplines

NGSS discipline	Website lesson plan idea
Earth Sciences	How buildings are designed to withstand earthquakes
Earth Sciences	Differences between a lunar and solar eclipse
Physical Sciences	Structure of electron shells and how they determine chemical bonds
Physical Sciences	Use vectors to solve real-life problems, such as throwing a football to another player or landing an airplane
Life Sciences	Benefits and drawbacks of natural disasters, such as forest fires and floods
Life Sciences	How life survives in the depths of the ocean, especially in the absence of sunlight
Technology, Engineering, and Applications of Science	A chronicle of how a specific technology has changed from its inception to today
Technology, Engineering, and Applications of Science	Design a city layout that minimizes vehicular traffic jams and maximizes foot and bicycle traffic

We offer many resources when students are ready to begin building their websites. Google Sites is one option but there are also many other tools. See the Technology Connections section for resources that students can use to make their own websites and for videos they can watch to learn how to use Google Sites.

Table 12.4: Topics for Website Projects for the Four NGSS Disciplines lists lesson plan ideas that have students create their own website. As we previously mentioned, the topics that are most appropriate for websites are content areas that are better understood with a visual tool. For example, the first earth science lesson plan idea is to have students make a website explaining how buildings are designed to withstand earthquakes. On their website, students can include two opposing videos: one video of a building with base isolators swaying during an earthquake and another video that shows a building without base isolators swaying during an earthquake. The comparison of these two videos greatly enhances a student's understanding of how engineering is improving structures during natural disasters. The topics are broken down by the NGSSs' four disciplines.

This lesson plan is naturally differentiated for elementary and high school students by its content.

KINESTHETIC MOVEMENT

The term *kinesthetic* relates to a person's awareness of their body movements.

Researchers have concluded that when students are moving, their learning can be deeper and longer lasting (Bauernfeind, 2016, pp. 42–55).

We use kinesthetic movement in two types of "mix-and-match" activities.

Posted Answers

This type of lesson plan requires some planning on our part. Prior to meeting with students, we create a worksheet that includes questions or incomplete sentences. An example of a worksheet we use is shown in Figure 12.10: Meiosis vs. Mitosis Review. The questions we ask on the student worksheet can be new or previously taught material. When we are teaching new material, we only use 10–12 answers. However, we use as many as 30 answers when we are reviewing material that's already been taught.

We print each question's answer on one sheet of paper and hang the answers around the perimeter of the room in a random order. Students receive copies of Figure 12.10: Meiosis vs. Mitosis Review and are instructed to work in pairs. We tell them they will be walking around doing a "mix-and-match" review activity. They are told to begin at any one of the posted answers. They read the answer, match it to the related question on their worksheet, and then copy the answer below the question on their worksheet copy.

During this activity, we periodically monitor student learning using kinesthetic movement. Every time we "check-in" with a group, we instruct students to act out a mitosis or meiosis stage. For example, we look at the phases they've already addressed in the activity and then ask them to act out one of those stages, such as the anaphase stage of mitosis. Students are provided a few minutes to prepare their kinesthetic movement. By the end of an hour-long class period, every group will have acted out approximately three stages.

Table 12.5: Purposeful Kinesthetic Movement in the Four NGSS Disciplines includes ideas of content that can be taught or reinforced through purposeful body movements.

Table 12.5 Purposeful Kinesthetic Movement in the Four NGSS Disciplines

NGSS discipline	Content to be taught or reviewed with purposeful body movements
Earth Sciences	Plate boundaries: using two flat hands students demonstrate subduction, divergence, and convergence
Earth Sciences	Water and/or wind currents: students demonstrate the Coriolis Effect in the Northern Hemisphere by moving counter-clockwise around the classroom
Physical Sciences	Types of chemical reactions: students move chemical equations to opposing sides of the room that represent exothermic and endothermic reactions
Physical Sciences	Electrical circuits and their components: on the floor, students use tape to draw the path of an electron in a circuit and then walk the path, describing each part of the circuit; they can also compare/contrast series and parallel circuits
Life Sciences	Photosynthesis and respiration: students represent sunlight, water, glucose, oxygen, and carbon dioxide, acting out both equations
Life Sciences	Functions of cell parts: each student represents an organelle and uses their body movements to depict the organelle's function
Technology, Engineering, and Applications of Science	Students randomly choose two technologies out of a hat and act out how they are connected; the class must guess the two technologies
Technology, Engineering, and Applications of Science	Complete an engineering challenge, such as building the tallest structure, but constraints are added to the challenge every 10 min

QR Codes

A fun and different way to present answers is to use QR codes. A QR code is a black and white array of cubes that can be read by a device, usually a smartphone. There are many free apps available on both Android phones and iPhones, in addition to tablets, Chromebooks, and laptops. The only requirement is a connection to the Internet for the apps' download and a camera so the device can scan the QR code.

When the QR code is scanned by a device's camera, it translates the code into a message, which can be any number of items such as a URL, sentence, song, or video. Here is an example of what a QR code looks like. If you can scan it, the translation will state, "This is an example of a QR code."

We use a free QR creation website such as QR Code Generator (https://www.qr-code-generator.com) or QRCode Monkey (https://www.qrcode-monkey.com) to make an individual QR code for each of the worksheet's answers. For example, the first question on Figure 12.10: Meiosis vs. Mitosis Review stated, "There are some very large differences between somatic cells and gamete cells. In fact, there are _____ differences we will be reviewing today." The associated QR code, once scanned and translated, says "five."

As each QR code is generated, we copy it onto a document, which will be printed after all of the QR codes are made. Each QR code receives a random number. In our meiosis/mitosis example, we use the numbers 1 through 28 because that's how many questions are on our review worksheet. We then populate the randomly assigned number into the answer key so we know which QR code contains the answer. As an example, question one on our worksheet is assigned QR code 26.

After all of the QR codes are made, we print the document, cut out each QR code, and randomly tape them around the classroom. Students walk around the room, scanning each QR code with their device, determining which QR code completes which review question, and then writing down the answer. And, of course, we still monitor students and ask groups to act out a stage of mitosis or meiosis.

We have found that we must tell students that the QR code numbers were randomly assigned. Some believe the numbers are associated with the worksheet's questions and attempt to use them as a shortcut. We are proactive with this disclosure by announcing it at the beginning of the activity because it's not a good use of their time to find out the real purpose of those numbers, which is our answer key.

These types of kinesthetic lesson plans are naturally differentiated for elementary and high school students by their content. The most difficult challenge with using QR codes is a lack of smart devices. In some circumstances, we've had so few devices that we had to put students into groups of three.

DIFFERENTIATION FOR DIVERSE LEARNERS

Each lesson includes differentiation strategies.

Student Handouts and Examples

Figure 12.1: Engineering Process: A Case Study in Inventions (Student Handout)

Figure 12.2: Rewriting a Song (Student Handout)

Figure 12.3: Example of the First Rewritten Stanza for *Twinkle Twinkle Little Star*

Figure 12.4: Rubric for Cell and Germ Theories Skit (Student Handout)

Figure 12.5: Timeline Graphic Organizer for the Cell and Germ Theories (Student Handout)

Figure 12.6: Timeline Graphic Organizer for the Cell and Germ Theories— Answer Key

Figure 12.7: Directions and Scoring Guide for Rube Goldberg Cartoon (Student Handout)

Figure 12.8: Picture of a Student's Constructed Rube Goldberg Machine

Figure 12.9: Dams! Are They Constructive or Destructive? (Student Handout)

Figure 12.10: Meiosis vs. Mitosis Review (Student Handout)

What Could Go Wrong?

Many of these lesson plans require students to perform online research. In our experience, students often enter search words into a search engine and read the summaries of the websites that are listed on the first results page. If the answers they are looking for aren't in those summaries and aren't on the first page, we often hear them say, "I can't find it" or "It's not on the Internet." We help them broaden their search by instructing them to click on one of the websites listed on the results page. Then we teach them to hold the "CTRL" key and the "F" key at the same time to open the *Find and Replace* dialog box. In this box they can type in one or two key words, which will be highlighted when they hit the "ENTER" key. This shortcut helps them to quickly identify if this specific website has the information they are researching. By using this procedure, students often find useful information on a website that was not included in its summary on the results page.

Storytelling is an art. If teachers are going to tell a story, it's important to practice it beforehand. Nothing can kill engagement more than forgetting the details of a story and having to look them up.

When students are free to move around a space, they are more likely to stay on task if we set behavioral expectations prior to the activity. We preface every kinesthetic activity with a reminder that students are expected to remain on task, keep their hands to themselves, and be respectful of their peers. When a classroom is too small to accommodate a large group of students, we attempt to use other sites on campus, such as a hallway, the gym, or a sports field.

Technology Connections

Teachers who want to become STEAM certified can access all necessary resources for certification through All Education Schools, which is available online at "Resources for Current & Future STEAM Educators" (https://www.alleducationschools.com/resources/steam-education).

See "The Best Ways for Students or Teachers to Create a Website" (https://larryferlazzo.edublogs.org/2008/12/12/the-best-ways-for-students-or-teachers-to-create-a-website) for easy website-creation tools.

Music videos can be made on multiple applications, such as the five that Matthew Lynch lists in his article "5 Movie Making Apps for Student Projects" (https://www.thetechedvocate.org/5-movie-making-apps-student-projects). In Larry Ferlazzo's blog post, "Making Instagram Videos with English Language Learners" (http://larryferlazzo.edublogs.org/2013/10/22/making-instagram-videos-with-english-language-learners), he offers suggestions and tips for using Instagram.

The official site for everything Rube Goldberg is https://www.rubegoldberg.com and includes many lesson plan resources and videos online of Rube Goldberg machines that can be used as examples to show students. TeachEngineering (https://www.teachengineering.org/activities/view/cub_simp_machines_lesson05_activity1) also offers a two-part lesson plan and a video for Rube Goldberg machines.

When we have difficulty finding an expert, we use the resources in Larry Ferlazzo's blog entitled "The Best Places Where Students Can Write for an Authentic Audience" (http://larryferlazzo.edublogs.org/2009/04/01/the-best-places-where-students-can-write-for-an-authentic-audience). He includes links to online resources where students can publish online books, make maps, share stories, and contact experts.

Students can watch online videos to help them build a website using the Google Sites tool (https://www.youtube.com/watch?v=tnr-_0UC50Y). Google also provides step-by-step directions (https://support.google.com/sites/answer/6372878?hl=en).

Erin Macpherson, an author for WeAreTeachers, offers sample STEAM lesson plans that are broken down by grade level. Her lesson plans can be found at "15 Ways Art Can Increase Innovation in Your Science Class" (https://www.weareteachers .com/15-ways-art-can-increase-innovation-in-your-science-class-2).

Jenn Horton, an editor at WeAreTeachers, offers "50 Tips, Tricks, and Ideas for Teaching STEAM" (https://www.weareteachers.com/teaching-steam).

Attributions

Thank you, Melissa Posey, for helping us to develop the lesson plan entitled, "Dams! Are They Constructive or Destructive?"

Our sincerest gratitude to Taryn Mazanec, who allowed us to include a picture of her 8th grade Rube Goldberg machine.

Figures

Name: _____

Engineering Process: A Case Study in Inventions

The engineering process became a systemic approach to design in the 1970s. In order to apply your new knowledge of the engineering process, you will

- choose an invention that was created between 1870 and 1970. It must be a tool or technological invention. If you are unsure, check with your teacher.
- answer the following questions:
  1. Who invented it? Describe this person, such as the country the person was from and the person's education.
  2. Which steps of the engineering process did the inventor use to create their invention? Use specific examples of each step the inventor followed.
  3. How has the invention changed since it was originally designed? Be sure you incorporate the steps of the engineering process in your answer.
- include at least two pieces of text evidence and a bibliography.

You may present your case study using any of the following formats:

- PowerPoint, Prezi, or Google Slides
- a website
- a poster
- an essay
- a trifold brochure

Here is how you will be graded for this assignment:

Required item	Points possible	Points earned
Description of inventor	5	
Identify and explain which steps of the engineering process the inventor followed	10	
Description of how the invention has improved since its original design	5	
Explanation of how the engineering process was or was not used while the invention was being improved	10	
Spelling, punctuation, and neatness	5	
Total Points Possible:	35	

Figure 12.1   Engineering Process: A Case Study in Inventions (Student Handout)

Name of Person #1: _____
Name of Person #2: _____
Name of Person #3: _____

Rewriting the Song: *Twinkle Twinkle Little Star*

The song, *Twinkle Twinkle Little Star*, was written probably around 1806. At the same time, astronomers were learning about the life cycle of stars. If you notice, the song even states that the composer doesn't know anything about stars: "How I wonder what you are." Here is the first stanza of the song:

> Twinkle Twinkle Little Star
> How I wonder what you are
> Up above the world so high
> Like a diamond in the sky

Directions: Now that you know about stars, your lab is to rewrite the song with accurate information. You will work in groups of three. Your song must be at least three stanzas long, each written by a different member of your group. Here is what must go in each stanza:

Stanza One: Layers of the sun
Stanza Two: Life cycle of the sun
Stanza Three: Light years and astronomical units

Your group is responsible for turning in the lyrics to your new song in addition to one of the following musical presentations:

• a music video

• a live presentation with vocals and/or instruments

• a pre-recorded presentation with vocals and/or instruments

• an interpretative dance that is performed while someone dramatically reads your song

Here is the scoring guide I will use to grade you:

Presence/language Skills   5   4   3   2   1   0

    body language & eye contact

    spoken/sung loud enough to hear easily

    understandable

    physical organization

    appropriate vocabulary and grammar

Figure 12.2   Rewriting a Song (Student Handout)

Mastery of the subject	5	4	3	2	1	0
thorough information						
accurate information						
correct use of new vocabulary words						
Visual/auditory aids	5	4	3	2	1	0
instruments, if applicable						
costumes						
high audio and/or video quality						
Overall impression	5	4	3	2	1	0
entertaining						
all group members participated						
well organized/easy to understand						

Total score _____ / 20

Figure 12.2 (Continued)

Core is hot, convection moves,
you can see the photosphere.
Chromo is red, fusion in
radi, Corona is last.

Figure 12.3 Example of the First Rewritten Stanza for *Twinkle Twinkle Little Star*

Rubric for Cell and Germ Theories Skit

	Poor— 1 point	Needs improvement— 2 points	Good— 3 points	Excellent— 4 points
Mastery of the Subject: Thorough information	Missing the answer to more than two of the required questions	Missing the answer to two of the required questions	Missing the answer to one of the required questions	All required items included; teacher learned something!
Mastery of the Subject: Accurate Information	More than 3 incorrect pieces of information	3 incorrect pieces of information	1 or 2 incorrect pieces of information	All information is correct
Visual Aids/ Props/Costumes	No use of props, costumes, and/or other visual aids that helps the audience learn	Includes props, costumes, and/or other visual aids but they don't help the audience learn	Includes the basic props, costumes, and/or other visual aids that helps the audience learn	Creative use of props, costumes, and/or other visual aids that helps the audience learn
Presence/Language Skills	One person participates or lacks planning and no one knows what to do, difficult to hear and understand, ineffective tone and volume	Not every member participates, usually difficult to hear and understand, boring, and ineffective tone and volume	Every member participates, often is easy to hear and understand, somewhat entertaining and somewhat effective tone and volume	Every member participates, easy to hear and understand, entertaining, effective tone and volume

Figure 12.4   Rubric for Cell and Germ Theories Skit (Student Handout)

Timeline for Cell and Germ Theories

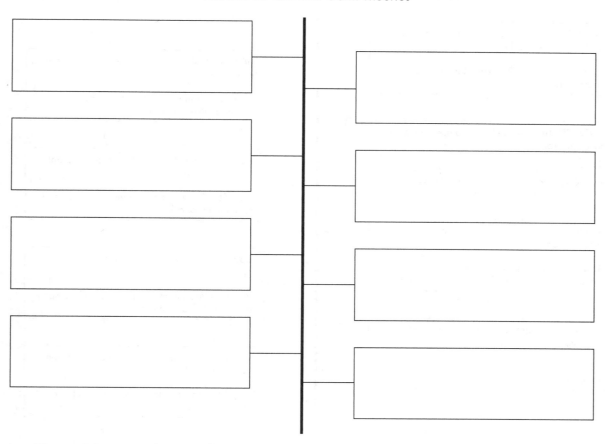

Figure 12.5   Timeline Graphic Organizer for the Cell and Germ Theories (Student Handout)

Timeline for Cell and Germ Theories - Answer Key

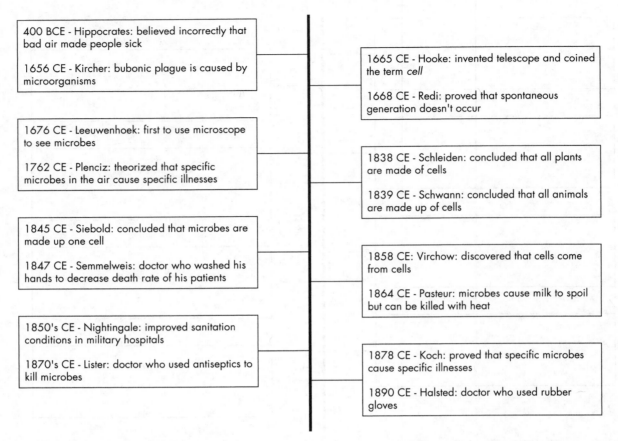

400 BCE - Hippocrates: believed incorrectly that bad air made people sick

1656 CE - Kircher: bubonic plague is caused by microorganisms

1665 CE - Hooke: invented telescope and coined the term *cell*

1668 CE - Redi: proved that spontaneous generation doesn't occur

1676 CE - Leeuwenhoek: first to use microscope to see microbes

1762 CE - Plenciz: theorized that specific microbes in the air cause specific illnesses

1838 CE - Schleiden: concluded that all plants are made of cells

1839 CE - Schwann: concluded that all animals are made up of cells

1845 CE - Siebold: concluded that microbes are made up one cell

1847 CE - Semmelweis: doctor who washed his hands to decrease death rate of his patients

1858 CE: Virchow: discovered that cells come from cells

1864 CE - Pasteur: microbes cause milk to spoil but can be killed with heat

1850's CE - Nightingale: improved sanitation conditions in military hospitals

1870's CE - Lister: doctor who used antiseptics to kill microbes

1878 CE - Koch: proved that specific microbes cause specific illnesses

1890 CE - Halsted: doctor who used rubber gloves

Figure 12.6 Timeline Graphic Organizer for the Cell and Germ Theories—Answer Key

Name Partner #1: _____ **Name Partner #2:** _____

Directions and Scoring Guide for Rube Goldberg Cartoon

Directions: You are going to use your knowledge of simple machines to develop a Rube Goldberg machine, which is a chain reaction of events that, when complete, accomplishes a simple goal.

Here is how your Rube Goldberg machine will be graded:

Requirement	Points possible	Earned points and teacher comments
All six simple machines must be actively included at least once	6	
The written explanation provides, in detail, how each simple machine moves	6	
The final task accomplished by the Rube Goldberg machine is simple	2	
The idea is silly and fun while creatively incorporating the theme	2	

Let's first do a quick review. Draw a picture of each of the simple machines.

Lever: Pulley:

Inclined plane: Screw:

Wheel and axle: Wedge:

Figure 12.7 Directions and Scoring Guide for Rube Goldberg Cartoon (Student Handout)

With your partner, identify a favorite hobby, movie, game, sport, or book that will be the theme of your Rube Goldberg machine. Document your theme here, including the goal/task that your Rube Goldberg machine will accomplish:

Brainstorming: You and your partner will use this section to brainstorm how the simple machines will be used together to accomplish a goal. We suggest you work backwards so the following questions will begin at the end and work toward the beginning of your Rube Goldberg machine.

1. Which of the simple machines will be used to accomplish the last step of your goal (the popping of the balloon, the feeding of your pet fish, the banging of the piano)?

2. What can be attached to the simple machine in #1 to make it move?

3. What can be attached to the simple machine in #2 to make it move?

4. What can be attached to the simple machine in #3 to make it move?

5. What can be attached to the simple machine in #4 to make it move?

6. What can be attached to the simple machine in #5 to make it move?

7. What will begin the movement so that the simple machine in #6 moves? (for example, you will push a book off the table to trigger a pulley system)

8. Below, create a draft of a cartoon showing all of the machines working together to accomplish your goal/task. Be sure to include images and written explanations. After reviewing your draft cartoon, create a final version on another sheet of paper or on a poster.

Figure 12.7 (Continued)

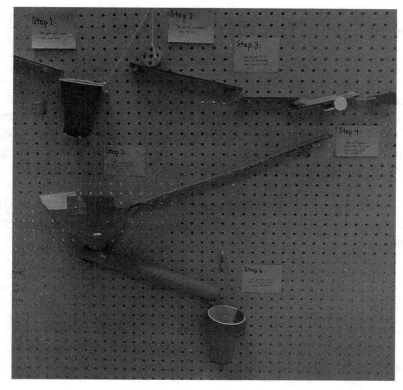

Figure 12.8   Picture of a Student's Constructed Rube Goldberg Machine

Name Partner #1: _____ **Name Partner #2:** _____

Dams! Are They Constructive or Destructive?

Directions: You and your learning partner must determine if dams are constructive (they build new landforms) or destructive (they destroy existing landforms). YOU MUST CHOOSE ONE OR THE OTHER! You will not be graded on the answer to the question but instead on the thoroughness of your research and examples. A checklist is available below so you can see how you will be graded.

There are many dams in the world. You can focus your research on any dam you choose. If you aren't familiar with dams, we suggest researching one of these because there is a lot of information available:

- Aswan Dam, located in Egypt
- Three Gorges Dam, located in China
- Hoover Dam, located in Arizona, United States
- Hirakud Dam, located in India
- Belo Monte Dam, located in Brazil

Using your research, you will come to your own conclusion and publish your findings on a website. Here is a checklist so you know what is required and how you will be graded.

Are Dams Constructive or Destructive? Checklist

Description	Teacher comments	Points
• Explanation of why dams are constructive or destructive must be stated clearly • Opinion must be supported by three descriptive examples from your research that are cited and included in a bibliography		__/15 pts
• Include two "counter-arguments" to support your opinion. This should include statements that support your reasoning and counter the arguments of the opposing position. • Both should be cited and included in a bibliography		__/10 pts

Figure 12.9 Dams! Are They Constructive or Destructive? (Student Handout)

• Include at least two quotes as text evidence • Properly cite your text evidence and include the resources in your bibliography		__/10 pts
• Includes three videos and/or pictures that represent how the dam is constructive or destructive		__/10 pts
Neatness and spelling		__/5 pts
Sizzle! If you are able to create a product that teaches me something new or is out of this world, you have the chance to receive these extra credit points!		__/5 pts extra credit
Total		__/50 pts

Figure 12.9 (Continued)

Name: _____

Meiosis vs. Mitosis Review

Directions: Posted around the room are the answers to all of the questions on this worksheet. When you approach a posted answer, read it, and then match it to a question. Document the answer exactly as it's written.

1. There are some very large differences between somatic cells and gamete cells. In fact, there are _____ differences we will be reviewing today.

Difference #1—The Number of Chromosomes

2. In humans, how many chromosomes are found in somatic cells and what special name do they have?

3. What is the opposite of a gamete cell and how many chromosomes does it have if it is a human cell?

4. Gamete cells are not diploid because they have half the number of chromosomes. What is their special name?

5. The two sets of 23 chromosomes are referred to as what kind of chromosomes?

Difference #2—Meiosis, not Mitosis

6. Gamete cells don't undergo mitosis but instead meiosis. Meiosis begins with what kind of cell?

7. The first phase of Meiosis 1 is called Interphase 1, but what happens in Interphase 1?

8. The second phase of Meiosis 1 is called Prophase 1, but what happens in Prophase 1?

9. Prophase 1 creates a special type of chromosome. What is it called?

Figure 12.10 Meiosis vs. Mitosis Review (Student Handout)

10. What happens between Prophase 1 and Metaphase 1?

11. The third phase of Meiosis 1 is called Metaphase 1, but what happens in Metaphase 1?

12. The fourth phase of Meiosis 1 is called Anaphase 1, but what happens in Anaphase 1?

13. The fifth phase of the Meiosis 1 is called Telophase 1, but what happens in Telophase 1?

14. The final phase of Meiosis 1 is called Cytokinesis, which is the same as cytokinesis in mitosis; the cell rips into two cells. But the result is different. Crossing over causes one difference between these two daughter cells and the resulting daughter cells of mitosis. What is the difference?

15. Mitosis and Meiosis 1 both begin with diploid cells; however, the daughter cells in mitosis are different from the daughter cells in meiosis. How are they different?

16. At the end of Meiosis 1, what is the definition of a chromosome?

Difference #3—Meiosis Happens Twice But Mitosis Only Occurs Once

17. After Meiosis 1, there is another round of meiosis called Meiosis 2. In Meiosis 2, what phase doesn't exist?

18. In Meiosis 2, the first step is Prophase 2. What happens in Prophase 2?

19. In Meiosis 2, the second step is Metaphase 2. What happens in Metaphase 2?

20. In Meiosis 2, the third step is Anaphase 2. What happens in Anaphase 2?

21. In Meiosis 2, the fourth step is Telophase 2. What happens in Telophase 2?

Figure 12.10 (Continued)

22. The final phase of Meiosis 2 is called Cytokinesis, which is when the two daughter cells split into a total of four cells. What is special about these four daughter cells?

23. After this cytokinesis phase, what is the definition of a chromosome?

Difference #4—The Results Are Very Different!

24. At the end of mitosis, how many daughter cells are there and what is special about them?

25. At the end of Meiosis 1 and 2, how many daughter cells are there and what is special about them?

Difference #5—The Purpose of Mitosis Is Very Different Than the Purpose of Meiosis

26. Mitosis has one job—to make new cells. What are two reasons a body would need to make more cells?

27. Meiosis has one job—to make gametes (sperm and egg). Knowing that men make sperm from the time they begin puberty to the time they die, when do men experience meiosis?

28. Meiosis has one job—to make gametes (sperm and egg). Knowing that women make all of their eggs before they were born, when do women experience meiosis?

Figure 12.10   (Continued)

PART 3

Additional Resources

CHAPTER 13

Strategies for Activating Prior Knowledge

What Is It?

Activating prior knowledge entails "eliciting from students what they already know and building initial knowledge that they need in order to access upcoming content" (Ferlazzo & Hull Sypnieski, 2018).

Before we can activate prior knowledge, we must learn what students currently know. And once we have determined what they understand, we can take the additional time to build on that knowledge to ensure they have the foundations to learn new content.

Why We Like It

Ensuring that students have the necessary prior knowledge before beginning new learning is essential to their understanding of science concepts. We cannot make any assumptions about student knowledge. We must allow them to share what they currently know, tap into that knowledge, and continue to build on it. This process creates a more successful learning environment.

Supporting Research

Research supports that it is easier to learn new knowledge when there are familiar pieces within it. Students achieve higher rates of learning when they are familiar with and have a working memory of previous concepts (EurekAlert, 2015).

Education researcher Robert Marzano found through various studies that what students already know about a concept is one of the most important factors in how well they will learn new content (Marzano, 2004, p. 1).

Skills for Intentional Scholars/NGSS Connections

When students can leverage their background knowledge, they are practicing their critical thinking skills because they are connecting prior knowledge to new learning. Many of the strategies also allow for building effective communication skills as students share their background knowledge and begin to make connections.

Application

The activities highlighted below help to identify background knowledge students currently have, as well as develop additional knowledge needed before they begin learning new concepts. The strategies we find most effective include KWL charts, anticipation guides, Blind Kahoot!s, videos, and identifying misconceptions.

KWL CHARTS

KWL charts are graphic organizers used to gauge what students know before beginning a new concept. They are composed of three columns.

Students complete the first two columns before instruction begins. The first one is the "K" column, which stands for what students already *know* about a concept (or, in reality, what they *think they know* since it may not be accurate). "W" is the second column and is where students write down questions about what they *want* to know about the concept.

Students complete the last column during and/or after instruction. This is the "L" column, which indicates what students have *learned.*

We like to use KWL charts not only to determine background knowledge but also as a way to help students organize notes throughout a lesson or unit. It is a helpful tool for students to use when they need to refer back to concepts, such as when they are completing a lab or studying for a test.

Figure 13.1: KWL Chart Example—States of Matter shows an example of a completed KWL chart. KWL charts can be used at any time during a unit; however, we tend to introduce a KWL chart when we begin a new concept. We announce that the class is going to learn about a specific topic, for example, the states of matter. They each get out a sheet of paper and make three columns. If this is the first time we've used KWL charts, we have students title the columns: "What I Know About States of Matter," "What I Want to Know About States of Matter," and "What I Learned About States of Matter." We then have them circle the words "know," "want," and "learned." In subsequent KWL charts, we instruct students to use the letters (KWL) when they title their columns. Teachers can also save class time by distributing a pre-made blank KWL chart.

We instruct students to complete the first and second columns individually. We give them an example and ask, "Do you know how many states of matter there are? If you do, you can put that statement in your *K* column and, if you do not, you can add it to your *W* column." When we use KWL charts, students often ask how many items they need to write in each column. We explain that there are no minimum requirements; however, if they have less written in the *K* column then they should have more written in the *W* column and vice versa.

As students work, we walk around the room to assist those who are struggling to complete the first two columns. In our experience, this usually occurs because they don't have enough background knowledge to fill out the *K* column or to ask questions in the *W* column. To help these students, we ask them questions, such as, "What are the states of matter?" and "Why is it important to learn about the states of matter?" If they can answer the question, they place the answer in the *K* column, and if they don't know the answer, they write the question in the *W* column.

If students are struggling to create questions for the *W* column, we suggest they create a different question for each of the five W's and the H (who, what, when, where, why, and how). We've found this to be an effective trick to get students started. Another option is to have a list of "question starters" on the wall that students can use as a reference source. Teachers can search "question starters" online for examples.

Once students complete the first two columns, which usually requires about 5 min, we provide time for students to share their *W* column with their learning partners and to work together to add new questions.

We rarely instruct students to share what they *know* because sometimes a student's entry in their *K* column is incorrect and we want to prevent them from teaching inaccurate information to their learning partner. However, this "knowledge" is important information because it helps us to identify students' misconceptions. Additional resources for identifying misconceptions and how to address them can be found in that section later in this chapter. If we're confident that most students have a substantial amount of accurate prior knowledge on the concept, we may have students share what they "know" with their partners and with the entire class. We might even have students contribute to a class chart in those cases.

We collect the students' KWL charts so we can read each one to determine the extent of students' background knowledge. Our lesson is then differentiated based on this information. When we read our students' KWL charts about the states of matter, we discovered that every student knew solid, liquid, and gas, but only two of them knew there were other states. Our district requires us to teach solid, liquid, gas, and plasma, so we knew the emphasis of our lesson would have to be plasma.

We then teach our lesson about the states of matter. Afterwards, students are provided time to record their learning in the *L* column.

Once the students have completed the third column, we ask if there are any questions from the *W* column that weren't answered. There are two different types of questions that go unanswered and we treat each type differently.

KWL—Unanswered Questions "Parking Lot"

Student questions from the *W* column may be unanswered because the questions are off-topic or require a deeper teaching and learning experience than what we had planned. For example, when we taught the states of matter, a student asked, "Who invented plasma TVs?" We didn't know the answer, but it is an interesting question.

Students who have these types of questions are instructed to write each one on a single Post-it note and stick them to the door, which acts as a "parking lot" for questions. As students leave the classroom, they can choose to grab one of the Post-it notes (it could be one of their own questions), complete the research, and share the answer with the class the following day. We offer these students a small reward, such as extra credit points.

KWL—Unanswered Questions But the Content Was Taught

Another reason students' questions may not be answered is because they did not learn the content as it was being taught. In this case, their unanswered questions are an effective formative assessment tool. If the majority of students missed the same information during the lesson, we know the lesson needs to be altered and the content needs to be retaught. If only a few individual students didn't learn the content, then we address and answer these questions as a class. Students are instructed to discuss the topic with their learning partner and then we ask for volunteers to explain the answer to the class.

An extended variation of KWL charts is KWL-S charts where the *S* stands for "What I *still* want to know." In this fourth column, students list any remaining questions they might have after we have completed teaching our content. We often use this column for additional lesson ideas because student engagement is likely to be high. For example, after learning about the states of matter, several students wrote down that they still wanted to know the state of matter of milkshakes, fire, and slime. We used these ideas to develop an assignment where students could choose one ambiguous object, such as a milkshake, to determine its state of matter.

ANTICIPATION GUIDES

Anticipation guides are tools used to activate prior knowledge and peak interest in new concepts. They are most often used prior to reading texts but can also be utilized before introducing new science concepts. The guide presents a series of opinion statements to which students indicate the extent to which they agree or disagree. Students then write a quick sentence explaining their reasons. Figure 13.2: Astronomy Anticipation Guide is an example of one we use when introducing an astronomy unit.

We begin by providing a copy of the anticipation guide to every student. We want students to feel comfortable sharing their candid thoughts, so we explain that these are opinion statements and there are no right or wrong answers. We also clarify that it is common for students to change their minds as they learn new material and they will have the opportunity to revise their answers. After students have completed their anticipation guides, we collect them for later use.

At the end of the unit, we return students' anticipation guides. Students now have the opportunity to document new opinions and change their answers. We then take time for students to share why they changed their minds. This process can also be used as a formative assessment because student comments can indicate their level of understanding.

Another way of using anticipation guides is incorporating the four corners strategy that is discussed in Chapter 10: Strategies for Discussions. The four corners of the classroom are titled "Strongly Disagree," "Disagree," "Agree," and "Strongly Agree." After completing the anticipation guide individually or with a partner, we read the first statement to the class. Students move to the corner that represents their opinion. We invite specific students to share their reasoning with the rest of the class. This format can provide physical movement and increase engagement. There are ideas for incorporating kinesthetic movement into lesson plans in Chapter 12: Strategies for Incorporating the Arts and Kinesthetic Movement.

BLIND KAHOOT!

In this section, we provide resources for creating and using a specific online game called a Blind Kahoot!, in addition to variations that do not require technology. A Blind Kahoot! is used to introduce new material to students and provides them with an opportunity to use prior knowledge they bring into the classroom. In addition, the game itself helps students learn the prior knowledge they need to learn new concepts. In Chapter 16: Strategies for Reviewing Content, we discuss additional online games that can be used to review content.

A Blind Kahoot! is an online game played with a class of students. To play, the teacher must be able to project their teacher Kahoot! account on a screen or board that all students can see in order to access the game questions. Ideally, every student uses their own technology (laptop, computer, smartphone, tablet, or Chromebook). However, students can be grouped into pairs if there is a shortage of devices.

Every question is multiple choice and has two to four answer options. Students compete against one another for the highest score. Points are awarded for correct answers and the sooner an answer is chosen, the more points a student earns.

If students have played a Kahoot! game before, it's important to first explain that the Blind Kahoot! they are about to play covers content that has not yet been taught. We tell our students, "We are going to play a Blind Kahoot!. It's 'blind' because the game is going to ask you questions about topics we haven't yet taught you. It's your job to do your best at guessing and learning. Each question will provide you with information that will help you answer the next one, so it will be important to be attentive."

To create a Blind Kahoot!, we begin with the end in mind. We first decide what concept(s) we want students to have learned by the end of the Blind Kahoot!. As an example, we wanted students to learn the difference between the central and peripheral nervous systems. We use the following step-by-step process to create the Blind Kahoot!. To provide an example for each step, we used the Blind Kahoot! that we created for the nervous system.

1. What is the first thing students need to know? What background knowledge is important for them to have? Write a multiple-choice question. This is called a "blind question."

   — Students should learn the basic body parts that are part of the nervous system: brain, spinal cord, and nerves.

   Q: Which of the following body parts is NOT part of the nervous system?

   A. Brain

   B. **Blood**

   C. Nerves

   D. Spinal cord

2. Identify what students learned in the previous question and ask a similar question to test that they learned the content. This is called a "reinforcement question."

   — Students should have learned that the brain, nerves, and spinal cord are body parts that are in the nervous system.

Q: Which body system includes the brain, nerves, and spinal cord?

    A. Immune system

    B. Muscular system

    C. Endocrine system

    D. **Nervous system**

3. Decide what students should learn next. Write a blind question in multiple-choice format.

    — Students should know the function of the nervous system: detect information, execute responses, and process information.

    Q: Which of the following is NOT a function of the nervous system?

        A. Detect information

        B. Execute responses

        C. **Circulate fluids**

        D. Process information

4. Combine the learning in the previous three questions to ensure students are learning and making connections. Ask a reinforcement question.

    Q: What is the nervous system?

        A. **Brain, spine, and nerves that receive and process information**

        B. Brain, spine, and blood that receive and process information

        C. Brain, spine, and nerves that receive and process waste

        D. Brain, spine, and nerves that handle information

5. Decide what students should learn next. Write a blind question in multiple-choice format.

    — Students should understand there are two major divisions of the nervous system: central and peripheral.

    Q: What are the two major divisions of the nervous system?

        A. Peripheral and medial

        B. Medial and peripheri

        C. Peripheri and central

        D. **Peripheral and central**

6. Identify what students learned in the previous question and ask a reinforcement question to test that they learned the content. It's effective to add learning from previous questions to this reinforcement question because it reinforces student learning.

   — Students learned there are two divisions to the nervous systems called the peripheral and central nervous systems.

   Q: What is the function of the peripheral and central nervous systems?
   - A. To detect information and respond
   - B. To process information and respond
   - C. **To detect and process information and respond**
   - D. To respond to new information

7. Decide what students should learn next. Write another blind question in multiple-choice format.

   — Students should know one of the differences between the central and peripheral nervous systems: the central is in the bone and the peripheral is not

   Q: What is the difference between the peripheral and central nervous systems?
   - A. P = all of the system that is in the bone; C = not in the bone
   - B. P = all of the system that is in the bone: C = in the tissue
   - C. **P = all of the system that isn't in the bone: C = in the bone**
   - D. P = all of the system that is in the blood: C = in the bone

8. Identify what students learned in the previous question and ask a reinforcement question to test that they learned this content.

   — Students learned that the peripheral system isn't in the bone and the central nervous system is.

   Q: Which body parts are part of the central nervous system?
   - A. Spinal cord and nerves
   - B. Brain and nerves
   - C. Nerves and tissue
   - D. **Brain and spinal cord**

This questioning pattern (first a "blind question" followed by a "reinforcement question") continues until the original learning goal is complete.

Blind Kahoot!s are teacher-paced so that the whole class answers the same question at the same time. This process prevents students from working ahead and provides time between questions. We use this time to answer student questions, ask them questions, or expand on content. Students can also use the time to take notes in their science notebooks. English language learners or students with learning challenges can use a graphic organizer, such as Figure 13.3: Blind Kahoot! Nervous System Notes, to help them take notes. The answers remain on the screen after each question, giving students time to write notes or complete their graphic organizer.

As we play the game, we ask some students who answer "blind questions" correctly, "How did you know the answer?" Students may have gotten lucky and guessed correctly, while others may have had background knowledge they leveraged to answer the question. We allow them time to share this knowledge with the class so that everyone can benefit from this student's experience.

While the game is in play, we stand in the back of the room if they are on computers or walk around if they are on smartphones. We want to see the students' screens because we can use the color of their screen to identify students who may need support. Green screens indicate students who answered the questions correctly and red screens indicate students who answered the questions incorrectly. We want to provide extra learning opportunities to the students who answer a "reinforcement question" incorrectly. We may have a one-on-one conversation at their desk to clarify information, but in the case that the majority of the class missed a "reinforcement question," we have a whole class discussion.

We create an answer key and a script to help us guide students through the Blind Kahoot!. Figure 13.4: Blind Kahoot! Teacher Notes—Nervous System is an example of the notes we use while students complete the nervous system's Blind Kahoot!. The notes include a summary of the questions and answers, in addition to a suggested script of how to introduce some of the questions. As we facilitate the Blind Kahoot! and walk around the room, we carry the notes with us so they're easily available.

See the Technology Connections section for the many resources available for making Blind Kahoot!s. When a teacher logs into their Kahoot! account, there is a search feature that allows teachers to find and use Blind Kahoot!s that have already been created. To search for these Kahoot!s, enter "#blindkahoot" or "blind kahoot" in the search bar. To narrow the search, other words can be added such as, "#blindkahoot rock cycle." After finding another teacher's Kahoot!, we make a copy and modify it to meet the needs of our students.

When devices aren't available, Blind Kahoot!s can be played with individual mini-whiteboards. The only required adjustment is for keeping score. We allow each student to track his or her own score. They earn one point for every question they answer correctly.

As in all of our instruction, we do not assume that everything that comes up in a Blind Kahoot! is automatically retained by students the first time they hear it. Games are just one additional way to introduce and/or reinforce academic content.

VIDEOS

Videos that are 3–6 min in length are an effective tool for science teachers to activate and build knowledge before introducing a new concept. Videos can also increase interest and engagement.

We always give students a purpose for watching videos because we want to focus their attention on a specific concept. For example, we used a 4-min video to introduce wind turbines.

Prior to teaching about wind turbines, we surveyed our students to determine their background knowledge. We teach in Arizona, so we asked students, "By a show of hands, how many of you have driven to California and seen the wind turbine farm in San Gorgonio Pass?" Students shared their experiences and vacation stories. We then asked, "Has anyone seen any other wind farms?" Again, students shared their stories with the class. When we asked students the two survey questions, *we* were activating their background knowledge.

We next introduced the 4-min video, which highlights a female wind turbine technician who climbs and repairs 300-ft turbines. Prior to starting the video, we advised our students, "After the video, we are going to ask you how wind turbines become damaged and why it's important to fix them quickly." While students were watching the video, they were building the background knowledge they would need to complete the lesson.

English language learners can be encouraged to watch the same video the night prior to learning the information in class or a similar one in their home language (ideally, time can be made for them to do this previewing activity in class). Then, when we watch the video in class, we play it at a slower speed, in English, and add closed captioning. These modifications help everybody! The Technology Connections section provides links to multilingual videos and other video-related resources.

IDENTIFYING MISCONCEPTIONS

Students often enter their science classrooms with misconceptions from previous learning and/or life experiences. These misconceptions can prevent students from learning new concepts. We need to determine what misconceptions our students have and address them before moving on with new content.

According to the National Research Council, there are five types of science misconceptions (National Research Council, 1997, p. 28):

1. *Preconceived notions*—those based on previous experiences or observations that may not be correct. For example, some people may believe that statistics are unbiased and error-free.

2. *Non-scientific beliefs*—misconceptions based on non-scientific references, such as religious beliefs. An example is the belief that Earth is significantly younger than 4.6 billion years old.

When we know we will come across non-scientific beliefs, such as those embedded in religion, mythology, or astrology, we address them proactively. For example, before teaching evolution, we tell the class, "Today we will begin learning about evolution. There are many ideas that explain how humans were created and we are not dismissing any of them. However, because this is a science class, we will be focusing on the scientific theory of evolution." We suggest that teachers acknowledge opposing ideas when necessary but follow their state's science standards when teaching a concept that may not be aligned with a community's belief system. Of course, there may be rare situations where "opposing ideas" need to be immediately challenged beyond an "acknowledgment," such as if a student suggests intelligence is based on ethnicity.

3. *Conceptual misunderstandings*—occur when students do not understand a basic science principle, which then creates faulty ideas of science concepts. For example, the difference between a hypothesis, theory, and law can cause conceptual misunderstandings. People may think that because something is "only" a theory, it's not been proven by science.

4. *Vernacular misconceptions*—occur when words are being used differently in science than in everyday use. The word "work" has a different meaning in everyday life than it does in physics.

5. *Factual misconceptions*—are formed in early years due to various sources such as adults, movies, etc., that remain unaddressed throughout the years. Examples include the belief that going outside with wet hair in the cold will make you sick and lightning never strikes twice in the same place.

There are various ways to identify student misconceptions. KWL charts and anticipation guides are both tools that can be used because they allow students to share their knowledge or opinions on science concepts before learning begins in class.

Dr. Annette Taylor, an experimental psychologist and university professor, provides six steps for addressing student misconceptions (Taylor, 2017):

1. *Pretest students*—ask questions that help to identify if students have misconceptions that are common in the content area. See the Technology Connections section for online resources that list students' most common misconceptions.

2. *Teach the facts*—engage students in activities that explore fact-based content.

3. *Describe the misconception*—acknowledge the misconception but avoid the "familiarity backfire effect," which is when students' misconceptions are strengthened because they hear what is said first (the misconception) and then stop listening so they miss the refute. Taylor suggests that to avoid the "familiarity backfire effect," teachers shouldn't put a lot of emphasis or focus on the misconception.

4. *Refute the misconception*—provide the explanation and proof that the misconception is false.

5. *Fill the gap*—there was a gap of knowledge created when the misconception was refuted so reteach the facts that were taught in Step 2: Teach the Facts.

6. *Inoculate*—prepare students for the next time they encounter the misconception. Teach them how others will convince them that the misconception is the truth and how to respond when this occurs.

We provide two examples of how we use this process. The first example is how we use Dr. Taylor's six steps to teach altitude and the second example pertains to climate change.

Step 1: *Pretest Students:* When we write pretests for the purpose of uncovering misconceptions, we ask only short-answer questions so that we can identify students' background knowledge and see how well they use reason. See Figure 13.5: Altitude Pretest for Misconceptions for an example of a pretest that tests specifically for misconceptions.

When we teach altitude, our pretest usually uncovers the misconception that as altitude increases, the temperature increases. Students may answer question #2, "Does the temperature increase or decrease as the altitude increases and why?" with, "The temperature increases because you are getting closer to the sun." This is an example of a conceptual misunderstanding because students don't know or understand that air is thinner as altitude increases.

Step 2: *Teach the Facts:* We create a lesson that teaches students that temperatures decrease as altitude increases. Students analyze and interpret data from graphs to determine this negative relationship. See Chapter 11: Strategies for Teaching Math for resources to teach students how to analyze and interpret graphs.

Step 3: Describe the Misconception: Once students interpret the graph and realize that as altitude increases, the temperature decreases, we mention the misconception. We tell the class, "Some people believe that as the altitude increases, the temperature increases because they are closer to the sun but this is not correct."

Step 4: Refute the Misconception: We then provide students with a reading assignment that includes a graph displaying altitude versus atmospheric pressure. Students read the article and analyze and interpret the graph. They work in groups to write a paragraph that refutes the misconception.

Step 5: Fill the Gap: We pair up with another class, preferably one that is not learning about altitude. The students are challenged to explain to a person in the other class why the temperature decreases as the altitude increases.

Step 6: Inoculate: We return to the classroom and ask students, "What will you say to someone who believes that as the altitude increases, the temperature increases?" Students work with a partner to create a response and then student volunteers share their answers with the class.

This next example pertains to teaching climate change.

Step 1: Pretest Students: See Figure 13.6: Climate Change Pretest for Misconceptions for our climate change pretest.

When we teach climate change, our pretest often uncovers many misconceptions. The first one we focus on is the difference between weather and climate. We've found that most students are unaware there is a difference and they use the two terms interchangeably.

Step 2: Teach the Facts: We create a lesson that teaches students that weather is the daily (and sometimes hourly) status of temperature, precipitation, humidity, wind speed and direction, cloud cover, and air pressure, but climate is the average temperature and precipitation from the last 30 years (World Meteorological Association, n.d.). Students analyze and interpret weather reports and graphs to determine the differences. See Chapter 11: Strategies for Teaching Math for resources to teach students how to analyze and interpret graphs.

Step 3: Describe the Misconception: Once students interpret the data and realize that weather is daily but climate is an average of 30 years of data, we tell the class, "Some people believe there is no difference between the two terms, but they are incorrect."

Step 4: Refute the Misconception: We then challenge students to compare today's weather report in various land biomes around the world (desert, rainforest, grasslands, savannah, chaparral, deciduous forest, taiga, and boreal forest) with the climate for these same biomes. Students work in groups to calculate the difference between today's temperature and precipitation with the climate's temperature and precipitation.

Step 5: Fill the Gap: We provide a meme that confuses the terms weather and climate. Students rewrite the meme so it's correct.

Step 6: Inoculate: We ask students, "What will you say to someone who confuses weather and climate as the same thing?" Students work with a partner to create a response and then student volunteers share their answers with the class.

DIFFERENTIATION FOR DIVERSE LEARNERS

One method of differentiation for English language learners is to present them with background material in their home language. We mentioned doing this with videos, but we can provide them with articles in their home language as well. See the Technology Connections section for a list of these resources.

To build necessary background knowledge, students with learning challenges can also benefit from previewing videos. Student learning can be easier when articles are "engineered," which means white space is added between paragraphs, headings are added to paragraphs, and new vocabulary terms are defined. See Chapter 8: Strategies for Teaching Reading Comprehension for additional information.

Student Handouts and Examples

Figure 13.1: KWL Chart Example—States of Matter

Figure 13.2: Astronomy Anticipation Guide (Student Handout)

Figure 13.3: Blind Kahoot! Nervous System Notes (Student Handout)

Figure 13.4: Blind Kahoot! Teacher Notes—Nervous System

Figure 13.5: Altitude Pretest for Misconceptions (Student Handout)

Figure 13.6: Climate Change Pretest for Misconceptions (Student Handout)

What Could Go Wrong?

Sometimes it is assumed that students do not have the background knowledge about a topic because it is different from our own. We need to remember that students from different cultures often bring varied experiences and different prior knowledge into the classroom. It is important to draw on their experiences to benefit *all* of our students. For example, students from Central America may be able to talk about the impact climate change has had on refugees fleeing that area (Sample, 2019).

Technology Connections

Stephanie Castle is the spokesperson for Blind Kahoot!s. Her blog, "The Art of Blind Kahoot!ing," is available at https://kahoot.com/blog/2015/10/28/art-blind-kahooting. It includes an instructional video for how to make Blind Kahoot!s.

There is a Blind Kahoot! template available at the Kahoot! Website (https://create.kahoot.it/share/blind-kahoot-template/fca0f1d5-29bf-4693-8a4e-87be19362617). And K!Academy offers a detailed instructional manual for Kahoot!, including Blind Kahoot!s. It can be accessed at https://files.getkahoot.com/academy/Kahoot_Academy_Guide_1st_Ed_-_March_2016_-_WOA.pdf.

In addition to a Blind Kahoot!, there are many other online games available for classroom use. Larry Ferlazzo provides a list in his blog post, "The Best Websites for Creating Online Games" (http://larryferlazzo.edublogs.org/2008/04/21/the-best-websites-for-creating-online-learning-games).

The New York Science Teacher offers a list of the most common misconceptions in astronomy, biology, chemistry, geology, meteorology, and physics (https://newyorkscienceteacher.com/sci/pages/miscon/subject-index.php). The National Science Teaching Association published a list of misconceptions that are common in the elementary grades (http://static.nsta.org/connections/elementaryschool/201209AppropriateTopics-ElementaryStudentScienceMisconceptions.pdf).

Larry Ferlazzo compiled a list of resources that are available in multiple languages. This list is available in his blog post, "The Best Multilingual and Bilingual Sites for Math, Social Studies, & Science" (http://larryferlazzo.edublogs.org/2008/10/03/the-best-multilingual-bilingual-sites-for-math-social-studies-science). It is frequently updated. "A Potpourri of the Best & Most Useful Video Sites" (http://larryferlazzo.edublogs.org/2012/11/06/a-potpourri-of-the-best-most-useful-video-sites) offers additional resources.

Attributions

Thank you, Caroline Woody, for helping us to develop the Blind Kahoot! graphic organizer students can use to take notes.

Figures

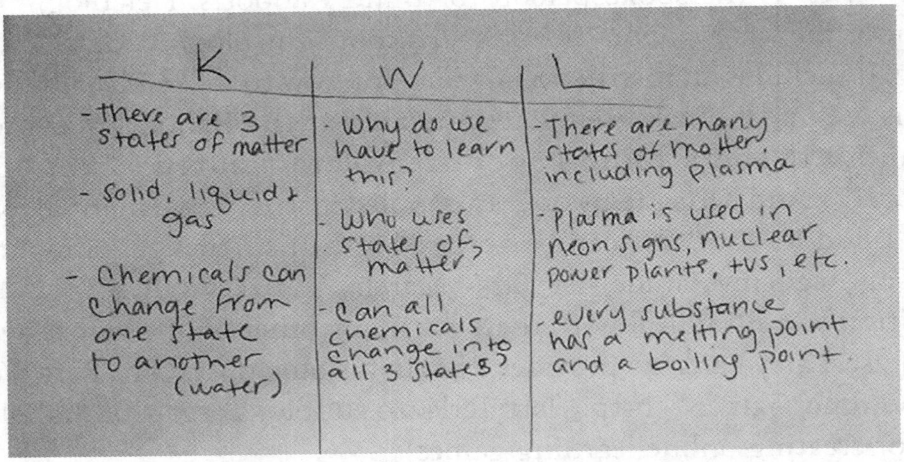

Figure 13.1 KWL Chart Example—States of Matter

Name: _____

Directions: Read the series of statements below and circle your opinion of strongly disagree, disagree, agree, or strongly agree. Then write 1–2 sentences explaining why.

1. There are other forms of life in the universe than those that reside on Earth.

Circle one:	Strongly disagree	Disagree	Agree	Strongly agree
Explain your opinion here:				

2. The Earth will be sucked into the sun when it moves into its red giant phase.

Circle one:	Strongly disagree	Disagree	Agree	Strongly agree
Explain your opinion here:				

3. The universe began with the big bang.

Circle one:	Strongly disagree	Disagree	Agree	Strongly agree
Explain your opinion here:				

4. Dark matter and dark energy will be defined in my lifetime.

Circle one:	Strongly disagree	Disagree	Agree	Strongly agree
Explain your opinion here:				

5. The moon was a passing meteoroid that was captured by Earth's gravitational pull.

Circle one:	Strongly disagree	Disagree	Agree	Strongly agree
Explain your opinion here:				

6. Pluto should be considered a planet again.

Circle one:	Strongly disagree	Disagree	Agree	Strongly agree
Explain your opinion here:				

7. We will eventually colonize Mars.

Circle one:	Strongly disagree	Disagree	Agree	Strongly agree
Explain your opinion here:				

Figure 13.2 Astronomy Anticipation Guide (Student Handout)

Name: _____

Blind Kahoot! Nervous System Notes

1. Which of the following body parts is NOT part of the nervous system?	
2. Which body system includes the brain, nerves, and spinal cord?	
3. Which of the following is not a function of the nervous system?	
4. What is the nervous system?	
5. What are the two major divisions of the nervous system?	
6. What is the function of the peripheral and central nervous systems?	
7. What is the difference between the peripheral and central nervous systems?	
8. Which body parts are part of the central nervous system?	

Figure 13.3 Blind Kahoot! Nervous System Notes (Student Handout) *Source:* Reproduced with permission of Caroline Woody.

Nervous System Notes and Script for the Blind Kahoot!

1. Not part of the nervous system?   =   blood (nerves, brain, spinal cord)

Say: "Blood is part of the circulatory system."

2. Which body system?   =   nervous system
3. Not function of nervous system?   =   circulate fluids (detect, process, execute)

Ask: "Which system circulates blood?" (circulatory system)

Say: "In this next question, you'll put it all together."

4. What is the nervous system?   =   brain, spine, nerves that receive and process

    Say: "You probably don't know the answer to this question because we haven't taught it to you. But do your best to guess."

5. Two divisions of the nervous system? =   peripheral and central
6. Function of the PNS & CNS   =   detect, process, and respond
7. Difference between PNS & CNS   =   P isn't in the bone and C is in the bone
8. Body parts in the CNS?   =   spinal cord and brain

Ask: "Why do you think we say the brain pertains to bone when the brain doesn't have any bone in it?" (Because the skull is a bone and holds the brain.)

Say: "Now you have to determine the function of each one, knowing that the brain and spinal cord are the central nervous system and the nerves are the peripheral nervous system."

9. Which moves muscles?   =   PNS
10. Heart faster: good-looking people   =   PNS
11. Notice the sun is warm?   =   PNS
12. Causes sweat?   =   PNS

Say: "Using the four examples of the PNS' functions, what do you think the function of the PNS is?"

13. Function of PNS?   =   complete automatic tasks
14. Causes you to wake up with alarm   =   CNS
15. Causes you to feel pain/touch   =   CNS
16. Realizes you are careless   =   CNS

Figure 13.4   Blind Kahoot! Teacher Notes—Nervous System

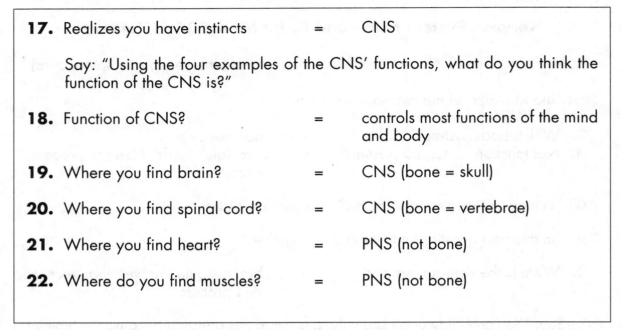

17. Realizes you have instincts   =   CNS

Say: "Using the four examples of the CNS' functions, what do you think the function of the CNS is?"

18. Function of CNS?   =   controls most functions of the mind and body

19. Where you find brain?   =   CNS (bone = skull)

20. Where you find spinal cord?   =   CNS (bone = vertebrae)

21. Where you find heart?   =   PNS (not bone)

22. Where do you find muscles?   =   PNS (not bone)

Figure 13.4 (Continued)

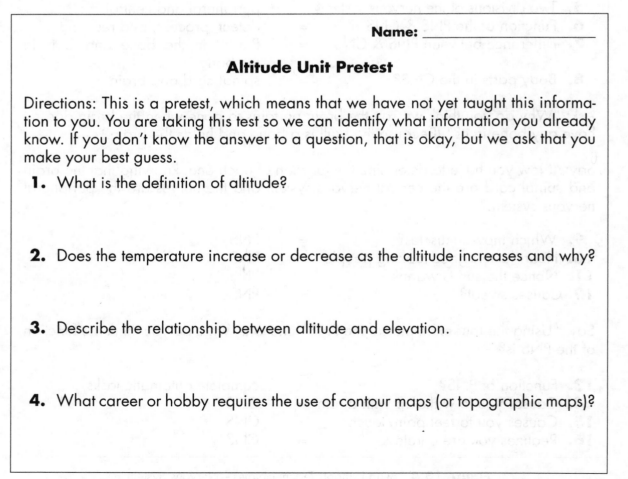

Name: _____

Altitude Unit Pretest

Directions: This is a pretest, which means that we have not yet taught this information to you. You are taking this test so we can identify what information you already know. If you don't know the answer to a question, that is okay, but we ask that you make your best guess.

1. What is the definition of altitude?

2. Does the temperature increase or decrease as the altitude increases and why?

3. Describe the relationship between altitude and elevation.

4. What career or hobby requires the use of contour maps (or topographic maps)?

Figure 13.5 Altitude Pretest for Misconceptions (Student Handout)

Name: _____

Climate Change Unit Pretest

Directions: This is a pretest, which means that we have not yet taught this information to you. You are taking this test so we can identify what information you already know. If you don't know the answer to a question, that is okay, but we ask that you make your best guess.

1. What is the difference between climate and weather?

2. What are two methods used to measure climate?

3. What does the theory of climate change state?

4. How do we know that humans are causing climate change?

Figure 13.6 Climate Change Pretest for Misconceptions (Student Handout)

- Personal goal: Learn 2 new things.

CHAPTER 14

Strategies for Cultural Responsiveness

What Is It?

By 2027, it is estimated that students of color will represent 55.3% of total public school enrollment in the United States (National Center for Education Statistics (NCES), 2019) while White teachers account for 80% of the teaching profession (National Center for Education Statistics (NCES), 2018). This chapter will focus on two perspectives for guiding teachers in culturally relevant pedagogy.

The first philosophy is called culturally relevant teaching (CRT), which is not a set of strategies but, instead, is more of a mindset stating that every student has the ability to learn and contribute to the learning experience of their peers. We will provide specific examples of how teachers can embrace CRT and incorporate it into their lessons and interactions with all students.

Culturally sustaining pedagogy (CSP) is the second philosophy, which was proposed by social science and educational justice researchers Django Paris and H. Samy Alim. It is defined as pedagogy that sustains "linguistic, literate, and cultural pluralism as part of schooling for positive social transformation" (Callaway, 2017, p. 1). CSP involves pedagogical strategies to respond to a classroom's diversity while simultaneously sustaining diversity as the focus for teachers as they plan their lessons and classroom procedures.

Both philosophies acknowledge that it is important to include students' cultural experiences in all aspects of the classroom, as emphasized in *The Dreamkeepers* (1994) by Gloria Ladson-Billings. Ladson-Billings helped pioneer culturally relevant pedagogy with her research in critical race theory. Cultural responsiveness is a pedagogy that creates a classroom where all student cultures are represented, accepted, and nurtured.

use student's assets to your advantage!!

Why We Like It

Culturally responsive and sustaining teaching can create a more meaningful education for all students. It is student-centered and focuses on high achievement for *all* learners. Culturally responsive classrooms can increase student engagement, a student's sense of belonging, and academic achievement (Ferlazzo, 2016).

The classroom is enriched for everyone when students are looked at through the lens of assets and not deficits. For example, when students are raised in rural agricultural communities, they likely have a deep knowledge of the natural world and its many interactions (Coley, Vitkin, Seaton, & Yopchick, 2005). These students are assets in the classroom because they may provide a unique perspective that can be leveraged as they and their peers are learning about agriculture, ecology, earth science, and biology.

An additional example of student diversity enriching our classroom occurred during a lesson about invasive species (introduced species that cause harm to the environment and/or human populations). Knowing that two of our students were from Uganda, we chose to teach about the harm of the Nile perch in Lake Victoria. Prior to the lesson, we met with both students and their parents to learn why the British government decided to introduce Nile perch to the lake. The history of this case study differs greatly depending on who tells the story. The ecologists and biologists explain that it was an ineffective solution because they knew that Nile perch would overpopulate and destroy the lake's ecological balance. The government officials justify their decision by explaining that the lake had been overfished and the only way to avoid an economic depression was to populate the lake with a large, fast-reproducing fish species that would support the fishermen and their families.

Neither of the families made their living through fishing, but both had family members or friends who fished commercially. Through these discussions, we were able to document both sides of history, which were then presented to our students. After listening to the audio tapes (while also reading the manuscripts), students participated in a debate. Half of the class posed as scientists and the other half as government officials who were responsible for their country's economy. See Chapter 10: Strategies for Discussions for resources that support classroom debates.

By knowing about our students and honoring their unique experiences and cultural differences, all of our students benefit. Student uniqueness is an asset and never a deficit.

Supporting Research

Research has shown that culturally relevant teaching strategies can lead to an increase in student perceptions at school. Student surveys show higher interest in school and a greater sense of belonging when culturally relevant teaching is used in the classroom (Byrd, 2016, p. 6).

Cultural understanding and responsiveness can lead to better relationships among students and teachers and improve the quality of teaching in the classroom (Callaway, 2017, p. 19).

Skills for Intentional Scholars/NGSS Connections

In a culturally responsive and sustaining classroom, the Skills for Intentional Scholars can be practiced because all students have the opportunity to use their unique skills. Culturally responsive strategies can increase a lesson's effectiveness and support students while they achieve at higher rates. They can enable students to build their critical thinking, creative problem solving, and effective communication skills.

The authors of the Next Generation Science Standards (NGSS) make it very clear that teachers should do everything possible to make science content accessible to *all* students. The NGSS Diversity and Equity Team (DET) documented seven case studies, most of which highlighted specific examples of culturally responsive teaching (NGSS, 2013a).

Four of the seven studies focused on student groups who have been traditionally underserved by the education system. For example, one of the case studies was an eighth grade life science class that consisted mostly of students from different race and ethnic backgrounds. The teacher in this class demonstrated the effectiveness of building on student backgrounds and connections through multiple modes of representations (NGSS, 2013a).

Another of the case studies involved a high school where 66% of the student population qualified for free or reduced lunch. The chemistry teacher used her students' "funds of knowledge" to teach states of matter. "Funds of knowledge" presumes that every person is capable and knowledgeable because they have gained knowledge through life experiences (González, Moll, & Amanti, 2005). The case study demonstrated that when students have the opportunity to use and share their previous knowledge, they are more likely to learn new concepts (NGSS, 2013f). See the Technology Connections section for information about accessing these case studies.

Application

Culturally responsive teaching isn't a specific set of strategies to be used within classrooms. So, then, how is it achieved? Culturally responsive teaching is a shift in mindset that motivates how we plan for every aspect of learning and overall classroom experiences. Zaretta Hammond, author of *Culturally Responsive Teaching and the Brain* (2015), created the Ready for Rigor Framework, which highlights four main areas for culturally responsive teaching. Those areas are Awareness, Learning Partnerships,

Information Processing, and Community of Learners and Learning Environment (Hammond, 2018). Below we will discuss strategies we use within this framework for culturally responsive teaching.

AWARENESS

The area of awareness centers around educators understanding their own cultural lenses and biases they bring into the classroom. We have to actively and constantly reflect on our own biases.

Many years ago, we attended an equity class hosted by our school district. We were told to bring two things with us: scores from a recent test and an open mind. As the class began, we were instructed to analyze our students' test scores to identify patterns or surprises. Some patterns that emerged among class participants included poor performance of students with learning challenges and English language learners (ELLs).

After analyzing our test results, Tara wrote, "I'm surprised our two Asian American students only earned Cs." We were then challenged to use our patterns and observations to identify our biases and link them to our teaching practices. During the exercise, Tara realized she had a bias that Asian American students don't require extra support and because of her bias, she didn't always monitor their learning. This mistake in judgment explained her surprise but also may have contributed to these two students earning a C when the class average was 81 percent.

The equity class was led by Dr. Adama Sallu, a diversity leader at Arizona State University. Dr. Sallu asked, "Who is biased?" We learned that everyone has biases. Research has found that in addition to having biases, most people are unaware of their own biases even though they may be able to identify them in others (Rea, 2015).

Dr. Sallu also asked us, "Where do our biases come from?" She explained that biases are developed automatically in middle childhood and can unconsciously drive behavior towards others (Chadiha, 2019).

We further learned that biases are not permanent; in fact, they are so malleable they may change without a person making an effort to do so (Dasgupta, 2013). But we chose to make an effort. We collaborated with Dr. Sallu and Dr. Daniel D. Liou, an equity and inclusivity researcher at Arizona State University, to develop the Equity Institute, which is a one-day professional development class offered to teachers.

Dr. Liou begins the class by explaining the results of his research showing specific actions teachers take when they have high (and low) expectations of students (Liou, 2011). For example, when teachers have high expectations, they tend to offer students more positive encouragement and feedback. However, when they have low expectations, students may receive more negative criticism and reviews. We then facilitate an activity where teachers reflect on Dr. Liou's research so they can identify the frequency of their actions that align with teachers who have high and low expectations for students.

Dr. Liou and Dr. Sallu then present other studies regarding how teacher expectations can affect student performance. For example, in 1965, Robert Rosenthal and Lenore Jacobson performed an experiment in elementary classrooms that concluded if teachers have high academic expectations for their students, their test scores tended to be higher than the students who had teachers with low academic expectations (Rosenthal & Jacobson, 1968).

We then introduce the author of *Rigor is NOT a Four-Letter Word*, Barbara Blackburn, who defines rigor as, creating an environment in which:

- each student is expected to learn at high levels;
- each student is supported so he or she can learn at high levels;
- each student demonstrates learning at high levels (Blackburn, 2008).

Then we lead the teachers through an activity that helps them to reflect on the current level of rigor in their classrooms.

The class continues in this pattern: Dr. Liou and Dr. Sallu present research and data and then we facilitate activities that help teachers identify areas of improvement in their classroom and how to make needed adjustments.

The week prior to the Equity Institute, we ask teachers to document how often they find themselves thinking things like this:

- If only Johnny did his homework, he would perform better.
- If only Johnny's parents made him study, he would pass tests.
- Johnny is always late or absent so, of course, he is failing.
- Johnny's from *that* part of the city.
- Johnny has an IEP (or 504 or is an ELL). He shouldn't be in my class.

They use this data during the Equity Institute because statements such as these reveal a bias toward students based on their family structure, socioeconomic status, intellectual ability, and culture. These biases can result in teachers having lower expectations for particular students.

Another bias that occurs often in schools is racial bias. Many teachers would say they are not biased when it comes to race; however, research shows these biases do occur when it comes to both academics and behavior even without teachers being aware of them. For example, many studies have confirmed that students of color are more likely to be issued disciplinary punishments (Gregory et al., 2016).

Two studies conducted at Stanford University demonstrate how racial bias affects school discipline. The first study involved presenting teachers with discipline files for a student who had two minor infractions for classroom disturbance and defiance. However, some teachers were given files with what the authors described as "stereotypically black" names, such as Dashawn or Darnell, and others were given files with what the authors described as "stereotypically white" names, like Greg or Jake. The study found that while the teachers' opinions of the student remained the same after reading the details of the first behavioral infraction, teachers who received files labeled with "stereotypically black" names revealed more feelings of the student being a troublemaker after the second infraction. The second study was an extension of the first. The teachers were asked to predict if the student would be suspended in the future. The results revealed that the teachers predicted a higher possibility of suspension when the student was assigned a "stereotypically black" name (Okonofua & Eberhardt, 2015).

The first step in eliminating our biases is to identify them. One way is through self-reflection. When confronting our own biases, it is important to be humble, honest, and open-minded. We cannot be defensive about them, but rather understand they are a natural occurrence based on our experiences that we can correct. Studies have shown that our brains can be reprogrammed with repetition (Staats, 2015–2016).

While it is important to identify and understand our biases, we also need to confront them in the classroom. One step that is suggested by the American Federation of Teachers is taking time to process the situation before taking action. While it's not always easy because we are often dealing with a classroom full of students and time constraints, we have to take the time to consider if our biases are preventing us from acting equitably (Staats, 2015–2016). For example, before reacting to a student who is "acting out," we should take a moment to evaluate the situation to be sure our response is appropriate and is the one that we would make for other students who are demonstrating the same behavior.

There are online resources that can help people identify their implicit biases. Implicit biases are subconscious prejudices and attitudes that affect the way people act without intention (Brownstein, 2019). See the Technology Connections section for an online test that reveals people's hidden biases.

LEARNING PARTNERSHIPS

In addition to awareness, Dr. Hammond stresses the importance of the teacher-student relationship functioning as a partnership within her framework (Hammond, 2018). In order for this to happen, teachers must take the time to get to know their students, build rapport, and provide continuous support for them to be successful.

Many researchers and practitioners suggest teachers begin building culturally responsive classrooms by getting to know their students (Kozleski, 2010; Deady, 2017). Getting to know students is multifaceted. It means learning about them as students (how they learn, what engages them, their academic strengths, and where they struggle), as individuals (their hobbies, interests, social-emotional gifts and challenges), and as members of family units and broader communities (family traditions, socio-economic challenges). By understanding our students and their backgrounds, we can create ways for them to use their assets in class.

There are three strategies we use throughout the school year to get to know our students as individuals: share time, surveys, and greeting students daily. easy !!! :)

Share Time

One strategy that is popular in the elementary grades is called share time or rug time, which is a dedicated amount of class time for students to talk about themselves. A structured variation of share time is Show and Tell, where students bring an item from home and describe its importance to their peers.

A specific version of share time for older students is called restorative circles. This is when the class comes together to form a circle and engage in dialogue about topics, such as building relationships, resolving conflict, and making decisions (International Institute for Restorative Practices, n.d.). The teacher starts the circle with an opener, such as a poem, quote, or song, and students are encouraged to discuss their thoughts and experiences based around it. This share time allows for students to spend time getting to know each other and build upon their relationships. It also assists in increasing cultural competencies in students as they understand the perspective and backgrounds of diverse peers. To facilitate respectful discussion that gives every student the opportunity to participate and not be interrupted, some teachers use a talking stick, which can be any object, such as a ruler or rubber ball. The student who is holding the talking stick is the only person who is permitted to talk. When the student is done sharing, they pass it on to the next person in the circle.

Another version is called "All About Me!," which highlights a different student every week. The chosen student completes a form (Figure 14.1: All About Me!) and presents it to the class. The student can present the form "as is" or transfer the information onto poster board. A variation incorporates Show and Tell so students the option of bringing meaningful items to share during their presentation.

Rebecca Hammer, a colleague of ours, teaches middle and high school. She altered share time to meet her secondary students' interests. Each of Mrs. Hammer's students make an online Kahoot! that completes the sentence stems in Figure 14.1: All About Me! Form. When students share their Kahoot! with the class, all of their peers play the Kahoot! game. The student-creator of the Kahoot! game facilitates it, expanding on their personal information as their peers ask them questions. We provide instructions and tips for making Kahoot!s in Chapter 13: Strategies for Activating Prior Knowledge.

Surveys

At the middle and high school level, we ask students to complete a survey so we can learn about them. The survey is available in Figure 14.2: First Day of School Student Survey. This survey collects basic information about students, such as their hobbies and interests, but also school-specific information; for example, we ask how they best learn. We use the survey information to connect lessons to students' interests.

On a broader level, this information influences topics we teach. For example, if students like basketball, we can incorporate basketballs into a lesson on kinetic and potential energy and have the students participate with the demonstration of dropping and bouncing basketballs along with smaller and larger sports balls.

On a much smaller scale, we use this information in writing questions for students to answer throughout the year. This strategy is very easy to do and we've found it can have a surprisingly positive effect on student engagement. For example, when we teach selective breeding, we use a dog breeding lesson that incorporates a student who owns a dog. If a student named Rosa has a dog named Rocky, we write the directions as, "Rosa decided to begin a dog breeding business. Her dog, Rocky, had specific qualities that other dog owners would be interested in having. Rosa's challenge is to determine which dog Rocky should breed with so the puppies have these desired qualities."

To gather student information from parents, we use a welcome letter or syllabus that is sent home the first week of school. We ask parents for the usual information (their email address, phone number, and signature) and, "What information would you like us to know about your child?" When parents choose to respond to this question, we reach out to them so they know that we have read their note and appreciate the information. For example, one parent wrote, "My daughter is the sweetest child. She is quiet and shy at school but she talks endlessly at home. She loves science but struggles in math." We called this student's mother to thank her for the note and to ask if her daughter is comfortable answering questions in class. This spurred a conversation that allowed us to learn more about the student and it began a positive relationship with her mother.

Both Figure 14.1: All About Me! Form and Figure 14.2: First Day of School Student Survey inquire about how students best learn. We are always impressed with how well they know themselves and how honest they are about their strengths and struggles. Students have answered, "I learn best when I can listen to music" and "It's hard for me to pay attention when I'm just sitting because I have a lot of energy." Their answers help discover ways we can best provide instruction and support.

We give a second survey to high school students, which is in Figure 14.3: High School Student Survey. We find this survey especially helpful at the high school level because students may be solidifying their future plans. We want to support their post-high school plans, and one of the best ways to start is to ask them about their goals.

We use the bottom section that instructs students to rate their interest in various topics, such as math and engineering, reading and writing, and the arts and music. After collecting the surveys from all students, we first look for trends. Do the majority of our students have interests in the arts and music? If that's the case, we know our lesson plans should incorporate activities, such as sketches, cartoons, songs, and dance. See Table 14.1: Chapters for Teaching Specific Student Interests to discover the chapter that offers resources in the interests listed on the survey.

We also use the survey to identify our influence as science teachers. The top section instructs students to rank the four core content areas from most important to least important and most interesting to least interesting. Near the end of the school year, we ask students to complete this section a second time. We compare their ratings from the beginning to the end of the school year because we want to identify if students' science interests have increased, decreased, or remained the same. We use this information to assist us in lesson planning for the next school year. For example, if student interest in science decreases, then we know we need to make changes so content is more engaging and relevant. To determine what changes need to be made next, we ask students the following follow-up questions:

1. What was something you loved about science class this year? Please explain why.

2. What was something you would have changed about science class this year? Please explain why.

3. How could we have made science more engaging for you? Please explain why.

4. What was something that you learned that was relevant to you and your interests? Please explain why.

5. What was something that you learned that you didn't find meaningful or relevant? Please explain why.

Table 14.1 Chapters for Teaching Specific Student Interests

Student interests from survey	Chapter in this book
Math	11: Strategies for Teaching Math
Engineering	6: Strategies for Teaching the Engineering Process
Writing	9: Strategies for Teaching Writing and 7: Strategies for Teaching Vocabulary
Reading	8: Strategies for Teaching Reading Comprehension and 7: Strategies for Teaching Vocabulary
The Arts/Music	12: Strategies for Incorporating the Arts and Kinesthetic Movement
Nonfiction Stories	5: Strategies for Using Project-Based Learning and 8: Strategies for Teaching Reading Comprehension
Technology and Gaming	5: Strategies for Using Project-Based Learning

The most common thing we learn from asking these five questions is that students have difficulty making real-life connections with some of our content. For example, we learned that students don't know why they must learn about mitosis and meiosis or how electricity is made. To increase the relevancy of our content, we altered our lessons so concepts are being taught with current trends, such as the possibilities of curing diseases with stem cells, which divide rapidly for long periods of time. And how electromagnetic fields can be used to transmit energy wirelessly, which has recently led to the invention of wireless cell phone chargers.

Greeting Students Daily

When we greet students as they enter the classroom, we say "hello" or "good morning" and in the elementary and middle school settings, this is usually enough to spark a conversation. However, with high school students, we've noticed they are often less responsive to this kind of greeting.

Harry and Rosemary Wong, the authors of *The Classroom Management Book*, share a strategy they witnessed in other schools where students enter a classroom and have the option to give their teacher a hug, handshake, or high five. (Wong, Wong, & Jondahl, 2014, pp. 53–56). We use this strategy and refer to it as the "Say Hi with an H" strategy.

Tara implements the "Say Hi with an H" strategy with her high school students after the first month of school has passed. She often notices during that first month, as she stands by the door greeting each student individually, many pass right by her, ignoring her "hello" or "how are you?," especially if they are using earbuds. She gives students the first four weeks to warm-up to her and each other and then explains what the expectations will be going forward. Once she introduces the strategy to students, they slow down as they enter her classroom, often stop their music to return a "hello," and give her a few moments of their time.

At first, students seem shy to participate but after a few days, they become more comfortable. Students easily determine what they want to use as their greeting because they all know their own comfort level. As she gets to know her students more, she focuses on asking specific questions about them, such as, "Did you work last night? How was your shift?" and "How's your mom doing after the surgery?" She is able to better connect with them during the 5-min passing period as she learns more about them as individuals.

But that isn't all! Many students themselves will begin greeting each other with a hug, handshake, or high five. By implementing the "Say Hi with an H" strategy, she alters the culture of their classroom. There is a connection that doesn't exist until after the "Say Hi with an H" strategy has been implemented. Tara also finds that students' on-task behavior increases, which has been identified as a positive consequence for teachers who greet their students at the door (Allday, Bush, Ticknor, & Walker, 2011).

After we greet students, they are expected to walk in and get started on the warm-up, which is displayed on the board or overhead projector. This procedure is taught in the beginning of the year when we introduce students to the classroom procedures. Once the passing period is over and the bell rings, we enter class to ensure all students are on task and beginning their work. See Chapter 15: Strategies for the Beginning and Ending of Class for more information on how to structure warm-ups.

There are a few alterations to the "Say Hi with an H" strategy. We added the option of students giving us an elbow bump, which some are more likely to choose when they are sick and we appreciate that! Another option is the verbal acknowledgment of, "Hello Mrs. Dale" or "Hello Ms. White." We've found students who are uncomfortable with physical touch most often choose this verbal greeting.

Differentiated greetings are a specific way to be respectful of all cultures. For example, not all cultures are comfortable with hand shaking or hugging. When students are given options for how to greet their teachers, they are in control of their bodies and can interact in a comfortable fashion.

Regardless of the strategies used to get to know our students as individuals, we are always looking for opportunities to highlight their cultures and to model curiosity about them and respect for them. We might have a Muslim student in our class who is fasting for Ramadan and, after checking in with them to see if it would be okay, we invite him/her to share with the entire class about what it means and what it entails. We could do the same during the Lunar New Year. And if we have a student who we know is a cricket fan, we might ask him or her to explain the game when the Cricket World Cup is played.

We acknowledge that share time, surveys, and greeting students can seem like we are taking away from instructional time; however, it is vital that this time is invested because it can help to build rapport with students.

Positive teacher-student relationships and trusting student-student relationships are the building blocks of a culturally responsive teaching environment. We teachers have to do more to solidify those relationships than just learn about the lives and interests of our students. We need to extend the information we learn into culturally relevant learning and lessons in order to continue building a classroom of respect and acceptance. In the next two sections, we will demonstrate ways we use our student partnerships in the classroom to expand learning and growth for all students.

INFORMATION PROCESSING

The next section within Dr. Hammond's Culturally Responsive Teaching Framework is Information Processing. Information processing encompasses how students are learning within the classroom and includes providing appropriate challenge to increase growth of all students, using strategies rooted in oral traditions to assist in learning new information, and making authentic, real-world connections (Hammond, 2018).

High Expectations for All Students

While we worked with Dr. Daniel Liou in creating the Equity Institute, he shared his research on expectations in the classroom. His research connects the expectations teachers have toward their students with their overall achievement. He found that students experienced higher academic achievement when their teachers had high expectations for their learning and vice-versa (Liou, 2011).

Dr. Liou performed many hours of classroom observations in an attempt to identify concrete examples of teaching strategies that aligned with teachers who have high expectations and those who have low expectations. His results are documented in Table 14.2: Teacher Expectancy Practices.

The practice from Table 14.2 that jumped out at us was "Let students get by without challenging work." Liou discovered that when teachers don't believe students can learn, regardless of the reason (their culture, efforts, abilities, or family support), teachers tend to lower their expectations and make classwork easier (Liou, 2011).

An example of teachers lowering their expectations might relate to students who have an identified learning challenge and are on an IEP (individualized education program). Sometimes, teachers decrease the required learning for these students. The purpose, however, of the accommodations listed in an IEP is to maintain high learning expectations and provide extra support systems so these students have the ability to learn alongside their peers. Note that the modifications on an IEP are different than the accommodations. Modifications change what a student is taught or expected to learn (The Understood Team, 2019).

Table 14.2 Teacher Expectancy Practices

High expectation practices	Low expectation practices
Attentive to student needs and feelings	Inattentive or impatient with student needs and feelings
Effective communication style	Ineffective communication style
Positive feedback on coursework	More negative criticisms than feedback
Receptive to student responses to teacher questions	Student response to teacher's questions is ignored
Use of ideas from student	Hostility and discouragement
Offer praises and encouragement	Skeptical and dismissive
Friendly and warm	Pessimistic, detached or indifferent,
Trusting, optimistic, caring, demanding	Lets students get by without challenging work
Comfortable in teacher-student interaction	Nervousness and spends less time in teacher-student interaction

Source: Reprinted with permission from Dr. Daniel Dinn-You Liou.

Throughout this book we've emphasized that when students are working, we walk around the room to check in with *every* group. We make this concerted effort because we want to support every student as they rise to our high expectations.

We've also mentioned in Chapter 10: Strategies for Discussions that when we ask students questions and they do not know the answer, we allow them to look up the answer in their notes or to ask a partner. This is another strategy for having a culturally responsive classroom as we are maintaining the high expectations that all of our students are capable of learning the material. At the beginning of the school year, we establish this norm. We explain to students that, "in the past, you may have been asked a question and not known the answer. The teacher may have then called on a second student to help you with the answer. This will not happen in our classroom. If we ask you a question and you don't know the answer, it's your opportunity to learn the information you don't know. You will receive time to find the answer because we believe in each of you and will not lower our expectations for you." While the student is looking up the answer, the rest of the class looks up the answer in their notes as well, even if they feel they already know it.

The effectiveness of this strategy is apparent by the second month of school. During the first month, when students don't know the answer to a question, we respond with, "we'll wait for you to find the answer because you are worth our time." Students sometimes sluggishly attempt to find their class notes or ask a partner. But after the first 4 weeks of school, students realize we do believe in each of them and they find the answer with a higher sense of urgency.

In addition to having high academic expectations, teachers should also have high and consistent behavioral expectations. In addition to teaching, Tara is an instructional coach. Mandi is an academic and behavior specialist. In these roles, we often support teachers who are struggling with effective classroom management. For example, we helped a math teacher who only addressed off-task student behavior about 12% of the time. He would redirect one group of students who were not engaged in the activity but then ignore the same off-task behavior from other groups.

During a post-observation meeting, we asked him how this inconsistency might be interpreted by the students who were redirected. He answered, "They may think I'm picking on them." He quickly explained that this was not the message he wanted to send to those students. Then we asked him, "How might the other students, who are participating in the same off-task behavior but not being redirected, perceive your inconsistency?" After some discussion, he realized that, "Those students may think that I don't believe in them. They may think that I don't want them to succeed or that I don't believe they can succeed."

There are many reasons we make a conscious effort to reinforce rules consistently. We, of course, want students to perceive the classroom as fair. We also want every student to know that we believe in their ability to be successful. By enforcing classroom procedures and rules equitably, we can also begin to eliminate the biases that appear in student behavioral data across the United States.

These kinds of practices do not preclude applying effective differentiation strategies—as the saying goes, treating people "fairly" does not always mean treating them "equally" (Wormeli, 2007). This is why each chapter in this book includes a section "Differentiation for Diverse Learners."

⚓ Utilize Oral Tradition Strategies ⚓

In addition to maintaining high expectations for all students, another culturally responsive lesson strategy is to use repetition and rhythm and/or music to assist in students learning new information. Many of our students come from cultures that have strong traditions of passing on information through these methods, and using them in the classroom can assist in the learning of all students. In Chapter 12: Strategies for Incorporating the Arts and Kinesthetic Movement, we discuss ways to use songs and poetry in the classroom.

Another example of this in the classroom is the work of Dr. Christopher Emdin. Dr. Emdin uses hip hop music to teach science to students. Not only can this kind of repetition and rhythm increase learning, but hip hop makes it more engaging and culturally relevant for his students. Dr. Emdin also founded Science Genius (https://genius.com/artists/Science-genius), which encourages students to create raps that teach scientific concepts.

Make Learning Authentic Through Real-World Connections

Students learn better when they can make connections to the material. One of our responsibilities is to ensure that we teach lessons that allow our students to make cultural connections to the science content.

Incorporating Diverse Role Models

When we first came upon research suggesting that we purposefully incorporate role models of color, we immediately thought of Black History Month. We use Dr. Hammond's article entitled, "Five Things Not to Do During Black History Month" (2013) to guide our celebration of African Americans' contributions to science. Here is a summary of Dr. Hammond's five suggestions and how we incorporate them in our classrooms:

1. Instead of the superficial practice of simply changing names or situations in an existing lesson plan, teachers should incorporate local culture in their daily instruction. Dr. Hammond suggests that teachers include local people of color who are making changes daily. To identify local people, we completed

an Internet search with the words "Arizona people of color diversity" and found resources such as Local First Arizona, One Arizona, and the Arizona Memory Project. Each one of these resources included local people of color who were contributing to Arizona. An example of how we included them into a lesson plan is when our students wanted to create a public campaign making plastic bags illegal in the state. We connected with the leaders at One Arizona who guided our students through the process of contacting their legislators and proposing a bill.

2. The focus of Black History Month should not be only on the first African American to succeed at something or popular celebrities of color. See the Technology Connections section for resources that list scientists of color who can be incorporated into multiple lessons.

3. Dr. Hammond's third suggestion is to include people of color in stories we tell. For example, during an ecology unit when we learn about agriculture, we teach students about George Washington Carver's life. He taught local farmers how to alternate crops using peanuts and sweet potatoes so soil would be naturally replenished with nutrients. In addition to teaching students about individuals, we also incorporate stories about groups of people, such as when we teach a chemistry unit about polymers. We tell students how the Olmec, a civilization who inhabited today's Mexican Gulf lowlands, were the first to harvest the rubber tree to produce rubber balls.

4. The purpose of Black History Month is not to "sprinkle" African American themes "atop the existing curriculum" (Hammond, 2013). Dr. Hammond offers the suggestion that teachers choose a focus and dive deeply into it. A biology example is while teaching about blood, we teach the history of blood banks, which were first established by Dr. Charles Drew. Students first study how blood was donated and stored and the limitations of doing so prior to Dr. Drew's established methods. Then they document how his methods affected the field of medicine, focusing on Worls War II soldiers who received blood transfusions from donors thousands of miles away.

5. The last statement Dr. Hammond (2013) makes is, "Don't think you can't talk about black history because you are a white educator." She explains that white teachers can and must teach about black history. At the same time, they must be willing to learn about the topic, including being open to exploring their own privilege, and building alliances with teachers of color.

After reading Dr. Hammond's article, we realized there was no reason to wait for February to begin using her suggestions and that we needed to be able to apply these lessons for other cultures, as well. LGBTQ Pride Month (June), Women's

History Month (March), Asian Pacific American Heritage Month (May), and National Hispanic Heritage Month (mid-September to mid-October) are just some of the national celebrations of diversity. Of course, teachers should also incorporate these connections year round. These national celebrations, however, do provide opportunities and reasons to highlight the value of diversity even more. One way we incorporate these ideas is by always including people from diverse backgrounds who connect to our units of study. Table 14.3: Diverse Contributors for Each Branch of Science includes examples.

Chapter 12: Strategies for Incorporating the Arts and Kinesthetic Movement contains a table (Table 12.3: NGSS Scientists Paired with Women Scientists and Scientists of Color) that presents examples of women scientists and scientists of color whom we can incorporate throughout our curriculum, as well.

See the Technology Connections section for resources that we use to identify people from diverse backgrounds who have contributed to or are currently contributing to science.

Once we choose whom to highlight in a specific unit, we provide each student with a copy of Figure 14.4: Contributors to Science in addition to an article, video, or podcast that provides the person's biography. As students learn about the chosen contributor, they complete Figure 14.4. They need to make connections with the contributor in order to complete that last box, "I have the following in common with this person. . ." To ensure every student will find something in common with

active learning can be CRT

Table 14.3 Diverse Contributors for Each Branch of Science

Branch of science	Contributor's name and contribution
Earth and Space Sciences	Adriana Ocampo—a planetary geologist who first identified a ring of cenotes around the Chicxulub crater
Earth and Space Sciences	Gladys West—developed models of the Earth that were eventually used to create the Global Positioning System (GPS)
Earth and Space Sciences	Madam C.J. Walker—created a hair care product using the Earth's natural minerals
Physical Science	Percy Lavon Julian—duplicated natural chemicals in the lab for mass production
Physical Science	J.V. Martinez—a physicist who worked with the Atomic Energy Commission
Physical Science	Leland D. Melvin—an engineer and astronaut responsible for using optical fiber sensors to measure temperature
Life Science	Henrietta Lacks—her cancer cells were harvested to create an immortalized human cell line (we always discuss how racism contributed toward how she and her family were treated by the medical establishment)
Life Science	Lisa Stevens "the Panda Lady"—the assistant curator for pandas and primates at the Smithsonian National Zoo
Life Science	Patricia Bath—ophthalmologist who pioneered cataract surgery
Life Science	Cherish Ardinger—a neuroscientist that studies addiction

the contributor, we use biographies that include the contributor's childhood, family structure, and hobbies. After everyone has completed Figure 14.4, we have a class discussion so students can share their connection to the contributor.

Including Culture in Lessons

Many advocates of culturally responsive teaching suggest intertwining students' cultures into lessons (Lynch, 2015; Deady, 2017; Tarasawa, 2018). For example, in Chapter 11: Strategies for Teaching Math, we provide examples of how to use local authentic data when teaching students how to make, analyze, and interpret graphs.

Another example occurs during a health unit in biology. We teach about the lead contamination in Flint, Michigan, which is not simply a case study of how lead affects children but also a study of how society and science are connected. We begin by providing students with a glance at the cultural and economic makeup of Flint. Forty percent of the population is living below the poverty line and 57% of the citizens are African American (Martinez, 2016).

Then we define "environmental racism," which is a term that was coined in the 1970s that refers to environmental injustices that harm people of color (Green Action for Health and Environmental Justice, n.d.).

To help students understand the connection between society and science and to provide an example of how "environmental racism" exists, we provide them with two articles: one written by a local Flint citizen and another written by a Flint politician.

Although the two authors tell a story about the same event, they have two very different perspectives regarding the safety of the water today. Local citizens insist their water is still not lead-free but the politicians resolve that the contamination has been corrected and the water is safe to drink.

When presenting a story to students, it's important that they don't receive the subtle message that both sides are equal (Collins, 2019). To avoid this perception of equality, we lead a class discussion about who has the power in this case study: the politicians or the citizens? Then we discuss the impacts of the pollution, asking how the citizens were affected and how the politicians were affected.

Students then debate if the citizens should trust the politicians' message that the water can be safely consumed. For ideas and tips for using debate in the classroom, see Chapter 10: Strategies for Discussions.

Women and Science

According to The Society of Women Engineers (2016), only 12% of American engineers are female, which is unexpected considering that 49% of eighth grade females report science being their favorite subject (The Society of Women Engineers, 2019).

The aim of the American Association of University Women (AAUW) is to use research and education to promote equity and education for women and girls. They have been advocating for gender equality since 1881, when they were originally founded (AAUW, n.d.). Dr. Catherine Hill, a former Vice President of Research for the AAUW, explains that females are not equally represented in STEM fields because of implicit bias (which we discussed earlier in the Application section) and stereotype threat (Hill, 2010).

Stereotype threat is when a person is at risk of confirming a negative stereotype about their social group (Stroessner & Good, n.d.). The stereotype threat may be one way to explain why females are not equally represented in science fields. Girls may have self-doubt about their ability to be successful in science because of subtle cultural messages that tell them boys are scientists, not girls (Berwick, 2019). We know students harbor the stereotype that science is for males. In the 1960s and 1970s, students were asked to draw a scientist. Fewer than 1% of the 5,000 pictures depicted a female as a scientist (Terada, 2019). The experiment has been repeated over the past 50 years and the results are promising. Based on a meta-analysis of 78 experiments, students now draw female scientists 27% of the time (Miller, Nolla, Eagly, & Uttal, 2018). In addition, the meta-analysis discovered that female students are the ones increasingly drawing female scientists, not male students. In the original 1966 study, only 1.2% of the girls drew a female scientist but in a 2016 study, girls drew female scientists 58% of the time. Male students still draw male scientists 9 out of 10 times (Terada, 2019).

To continue breaking the stereotype that science is solely for males, we incorporate female role models into lesson plans, classroom decor, and reading materials. A study from 2010 demonstrated that female students who were exposed to textbooks with female scientists tended to perform better than those female students whose textbooks didn't include females (Good, Woodzicka, & Wingfield, 2010). See the Technology Connections Section for free posters that highlight female contributors in science.

Another barrier that females face in STEM fields is discrimination during the hiring process. Females are less likely to be hired and are likely to receive less pay than their male counterparts (Flaherty, 2019). For those women who work in predominantly male STEM fields, such as engineering, the proportion of them who report discrimination is 78% and 50% report harassment (Jordan, 2018).

We make sure our students are aware of these challenges, not as a form of discouragement but, instead, to help equip them with the tools they can use to effectively respond to these issues. In addition to explicitly teaching about laws regarding workplace discrimination, we support other recommendations made by advocates and researchers in the field, including joining women in science organizations and encouraging our students to seek out mentors once they enter the field (Settles, 2014; Mitchell, 2018).

Additional Strategies to Reach All Students Through Connections

In addition to strategies that specifically address student culture, CRT also includes additional student-centered strategies that increase student achievement. Brown University offers a general list (The Education Alliance, Brown University, n.d.):

- Ensure student engagement by providing students with choices.
- Develop a student-centered classroom by using cooperative learning strategies.
- Involve the community.
- Encourage students to learn by forming literature discussions where students are talking with their peers about what they are reading in class.

Throughout this book we've provided specific examples of each of these four strategies. See Table 14.4: Examples of Brown University CRT Strategies for other chapters that offer resources for accomplishing the CRT strategies listed by Brown University.

As a quick reminder to ourselves of how to ensure a culturally responsive classroom, we post near our desk a copy of Figure 14.5: 13 Culturally Responsive Teaching Ideas, created by Valentina Gonzalez (Gonzalez, 2017), a previous language arts teacher who currently works as a Professional Development Specialist, focusing on English language learners. Gonzalez's list includes 13 specific things teachers can do to ensure all students feel safe, honored, and included in any classroom.

Table 14.4   Examples of Brown University CRT Strategies

Brown university CRT strategy	Resources available in this book
Ensure student engagement by providing students with choices	Chapter 4: Strategies for Teaching the Inquiry Process
	Chapter 5: Strategies for Using Project-Based Learning
	Chapter 6: Strategies for Teaching the Engineering Process
	Chapter 12: Strategies for Incorporating the Arts and Kinesthetic Movement
	Chapter 17: Strategies for Assessing Student Learning
Develop a student-centered classroom by using cooperative learning strategies	Every chapter in Parts I and II includes lesson plan ideas that include cooperative learning
Involve the community	Chapter 5: Strategies for Using Project-Based Learning
Encourage students to learn by forming literature discussions	Chapter 8: Strategies for Teaching Reading Comprehension
	Chapter 9: Strategies for Teaching Writing
	Chapter 10: Strategies for Discussions
	Chapter 13: Strategies for Activating Prior Knowledge

COMMUNITY OF LEARNERS AND LEARNING ENVIRONMENT

The fourth area represented in Dr. Hammond's framework is focused around creating an environment where all students feel supported and safe to learn and grow. This requires allowing for student voice and having procedures in place to support continuous learning (Hammond, 2018).

Throughout the book and in the previous sections we have outlined ways to invite student voice in the classroom. Students are encouraged to participate in discourse every day in the science classroom in a variety of ways, such as discussing their personal experiences and backgrounds, planning and executing scientific experiments and outcomes, debating hot topics within a field of science, and many more. Through these activities, diverse opinions emerge, which allow for students to increase their understanding of each other and different backgrounds.

Another way to build this community of learners is through cooperative learning, which is present in many lesson ideas throughout the book. Cooperative learning lends itself to what is known as the contact hypothesis. The contact hypothesis centers around the idea that prejudices are naturally reduced when diverse groups of people are required to work together (Pious, n.d.). Thus, by creating diverse groups of students within our classroom, students are being exposed to other cultures and learning from each other. This can break down the prejudices that occur in order to solidify a classroom of respect and acceptance so that all learners feel supported and safe. Refer to Chapter 2: Strategies for Teaching Lab Procedures for further information on grouping strategies.

Another way to build a community of respect is one we referred to in Chapter 4: Strategies for Teaching the Inquiry Process. In that chapter, we discuss dissections and how in some Native American cultures they are not permitted to be present to perform a dissection. In order to create an environment that is accepting and respectful of this belief, we find a safe space for them to go and work during this time. We also invite them to teach other students about the history and basis of their traditions. We can make these kinds of modifications in advance because we make an effort to know our students and their backgrounds.

Lastly, an aspect of creating a community of learners and learning environment is using restorative practices. We talk earlier in this chapter about the role of restorative circles in encouraging this kind of culture.

DIFFERENTIATION FOR DIVERSE LEARNERS

Although this chapter's focus is differentiating for specific groups of students, there is a simple change that science teachers can make that benefits all students. One study found that if science teachers change their vernacular from "be scientists" to "do science," students were more likely to demonstrate greater persistence in future science activities (EurekAlert!, 2019). For example, instead of saying, "Today you are going to be a scientist and perform an experiment," we now say, "Today you will do science as you perform your experiment."

The study also found that both male and female students and students of color reported less interest and confidence in "being a scientist" but maintained their interest and confidence when "doing science" (EurekAlert!, 2019).

Student Handouts and Examples

Figure 14.1: All About Me! Form (Student Handout)

Figure 14.2: First Day of School Student Survey (Student Handout)

Figure 14.3: High School Student Survey (Student Handout)

Figure 14.4: Contributors to Science (Student Handout)

Figure 14.5: 13 Culturally Responsive Teaching Ideas

What Could Go Wrong?

Sometimes, as we introduce the videos celebrating Black History Month, a student asks why we celebrate Black History Month or why we don't celebrate a White History Month. In reply to the student, we explain, it is important to recognize that not all races have been treated equitably in the United States. In addition to honoring Black History Month, we also celebrate Hispanic Heritage Month, Native American Heritage Month, and Asian Pacific Heritage Month in order to recognize races that have been marginalized throughout our history. We further explain that much of what is taught in schools, and what we see and experience every day outside of school, is, in fact, predominantly "white culture." In other words, whites have been the dominant voice and power in our country for many years and have had a disproportionate role in shaping our society.

Technology Connections

To read Appendix D of the Next Generation Science Standards (NGSS), "All Standards, All Students, see NGSS (2013a).

The seven case studies that were documented by the NGSS Diversity and Equity Team are available online (https://www.nextgenscience.org/appendix-d-case-studies). The Team specifically states that the case studies are not, "intended to prescribe science instruction but to illustrate an example or prototype for implementation of effective classroom strategies with diverse student groups" (NGSS, 2013a).

To identify hidden biases, complete the test offered by Harvard University's "Project Implicit" (https://implicit.harvard.edu/implicit).

We use the following resources to identify diverse scientists:

- Famous Women Inventors (http://www.women-inventors.com)
- Famous Black Inventors (http://www.black-inventor.com)
- Stories in Science (https://storiesinscience.org)
- Queer Scientists of Historical Note (https://www.noglstp.org/publications-documents/queer-scientists-of-historical-note)
- 500 Queer Scientists (https://www.500queerscientists.com)
- SACNAS Biography Project: Advancing Chicanos/Hispanics & Native Americans in Science (https://www.sacnas.org/biography-project), which also includes Native Hawaiian and Indigenous Pacific Islander peoples
- Hispanic Heritage Month: Latino Doctors, Scientists, and Educators (https://www.umhs-sk.org/blog/hispanic-heritage-month-latino-doctors-scientists-educators)
- Latinos in Math and Science (https://www.loc.gov/rr/scitech/SciRefGuides/latinos.html)
- Famous Asian American Scientists (https://www.infoplease.com/people/asian-american-scientists)
- Famous Asian Women Scientists (https://www.asianscientist.com/2018/03/features/female-scientists-slay-as100)
- Famous Scientists: The Art of Genius (http://www.famousscientists.org) with an emphasis on Muslim scientists (https://www.famousscientists.org/famous-muslim-arab-persian-scientists-and-their-inventions)
- Jewish Scientists, Inventors, and Philosophers (https://www.juliantrubin.com/schooldirectory/jewishscientists.html)
- Arts and Culture (https://artsandculture.google.com)

The Best (Free) Posters of STEM Women suggests three resources for free posters of female scientists, some of which are offered in multiple languages (https://www.edutopia.org/article/best-free-posters-stem-women).

To engage colleagues in learning more about culturally responsive literacy, check out this module produced by The National Center for Culturally Responsive Educational Systems (NCCRESt) on culturally responsive literacy (http://www.niusileadscape.org/docs/FINAL_PRODUCTS/NCCRESt/practitioner_briefs/%95%20TEMPLATE/DRAFTS/AUTHOR%20revisions/annablis%20pracbrief%20templates/Literacy_Brief_highres.pdf). We've found this resource especially useful to initiate and guide discussions during our professional learning community

(PLC) meetings. The resource includes a list of authors who write children's literature that incorporates the African American, Native American, Asian American, and Latino American cultures.

To learn more about current issues in education that relate to culturally responsive education, subscribe to Arizona State University's "Equity Matters" blog (http://www.equityallianceatasu.org/ea/equity-matters-newsletter).

Dr. Zaretta Hammond offers workshops and is a guest speaker but also has a blog that helps teachers to implement the philosophy of culturally relevant teaching (https://crtandthebrain.com/about).

Larry Ferlazzo offers a list of online resources, including podcasts, articles, interviews, and research regarding culturally responsive teaching. His blog, "The Best Resources About Culturally Responsive Teaching and Culturally Responsive Pedagogy—Please Share More!" is available at http://larryferlazzo.edublogs.org/2016/06/10/the-best-resources-about-culturally-responsive-teaching-culturally-sustaining-pedagogy-please-share-more.

Attributions

Thank you to our colleague, Rebecca Hammer, for allowing us to share her strategy for getting to know secondary students using Kahoot!.

Thank you to Dr. Daniel D. Liou and Dr. Adama Sallu, for sharing their research, strategies, and passion for equity in every classroom for every student.

We appreciate the generosity of Valentina Gonzalez, who allowed us to reprint her poster with 13 culturally responsive teaching ideas.

Figures

All About Me!

My name is _____. I am _____ years old.

My family consists of...

My hobbies include...

My favorite foods are...

I learn best when...

My favorite thing about school is...

Figure 14.1   All About Me! Form (Student Handout)

Student Survey for _____
(enter name here)

1. What is your favorite class and why?

2. Do you have any pets? If so, describe them. If you don't have pets now, what pets would you like to have in the future, if any?

3. Do you have any siblings (brothers/sisters)? What are their ages?

4. How do you learn the best?

5. What is your favorite food?

6. What do you do for fun?

7. Have you ever been out of the United States?

8. What is your favorite animal?

9. Do you like to read for fun?

10. What is your favorite movie?

11. What kind of career do you want to pursue? If you're not sure, what are some careers you would like to learn more about?

12. What do you need to do in order to accomplish the career you listed in question #11 (for example: go to a post-secondary school, get good grades, attend school regularly)?

Figure 14.2 First Day of School Student Survey (Student Handout)

Student Interest Survey   Your name: _____

Directions: Please rank each subject based on how important it is to you, your life, and your future. 1 is the most important and 4 is the least important.

_____ language arts
_____ math
_____ science
_____ social studies

Directions: Please rank each subject based on how interesting it is to you. 1 is the most interesting and 4 is the least interesting.

_____ language arts
_____ math
_____ science
_____ social studies

Directions: Answer each question as fully as you can.

1. What careers (jobs) interest you?

2. What would you change about school if you were the principal?

3. What do you love about school?

Directions: Using a scale of 1 to 10, how you would you rank your interest in the below items where 1 is "not interesting at all" and 10 is "extremely interesting"?

Math/Engineering	1	2	3	4	5	6	7	8	9	10
Writing	1	2	3	4	5	6	7	8	9	10
Reading	1	2	3	4	5	6	7	8	9	10
The Arts/Music	1	2	3	4	5	6	7	8	9	10
Nonfiction Stories	1	2	3	4	5	6	7	8	9	10
Technology/Gaming	1	2	3	4	5	6	7	8	9	10
Learning/Knowing	1	2	3	4	5	6	7	8	9	10

Figure 14.3 High School Student Survey (Student Handout)

Name: _____

Contributor to Science

The person I'm studying is named...

This person's education includes...

This person contributed to science by...

I have the following in common with this person:

Figure 14.4 Contributors to Science (Student Handout)

Figure 14.5 13 Culturally Responsive Teaching Ideas *Source:* Used with permission from Valentina Gonzalez (https://elementaryenglishlanguagelearners.weebly.com/blog/are-you-practicing-culturally-responsive-teaching)

CHAPTER 15

Strategies for the Beginning and Ending of Class

What Is it?

What happens at the beginning and ending of class is just as important as the learning during class.

Nearly every lesson plan template includes an activity at the beginning of science class to review, preview, or build anticipation for content. The 5E Instructional Model calls it "Engage" (BSCS Science Learning, n.d.), and Madeline Hunter refers to it as an "anticipatory set" (Hunter, 2004).

Although there are many terms describing the short activity students do for the first few minutes of science class, we refer to it as a "warm-up." Reviewing, previewing, and building anticipation for new content can all take place during warm-ups.

The last few minutes of class are when "cool down" activities can occur, which may offer time for students to reflect, make new connections, or complete a formative assessment.

Why We Like It

In secondary schools, the practice of using warm-ups and cool downs is referred to as "bell-to-bell instruction." Bell-to-bell instruction consists of students working on any variety of activities from the moment class begins until the bell rings (Ginsburg, 2014). The purpose of bell-to-bell instruction is to maximize the amount of time students are engaged and learning.

Warm-ups are effective tools to begin bell-to-bell instruction. While students are completing their warm-up, it provides us with the opportunity to take attendance, check homework, and address individual student needs, including "catching up" students who were absent the previous day.

We use cool downs at the end of the class for formative assessments or to engage students in reflection activities. Cool downs can provide data and drive instruction because they can let us know when students are struggling or if they are ready to move to the next concept. Wrapping up learning at the end of the lesson can also help students make new connections with their learning (The Teacher Toolkit, n.d.).

Supporting Research

Research shows that warm-ups used as a daily review of previously learned material can help students recall previous information and make new connections (Rosenshine, 2012, p. 13).

An action-research project found that using exit tickets to review vocabulary words with English language learners increased their usage and comprehension of the words (Larson, Dixon, & Townsend, 2013, p. 18,). Another study in science classes found that exit slips improved student engagement and quiz scores (Mastromonaco, 2015).

Skills for Intentional Scholars/NGSS Connections

All three Skills for Intentional Scholars are incorporated with beginning and ending of class strategies. Whether it is a quick review, activation of prior knowledge, learning goal self-reflection, or a quick formative assessment, students are using their critical thinking skills, creative problem solving, and effective communication skills.

Warm-ups and cool downs can be used to informally assess students' depth of knowledge of the Next Generation Science Standards' three dimensions: Science and Engineering Practices, Crosscutting Concepts, and Disciplinary Core Ideas.

Application

At the beginning of the school year, we teach students the classroom procedure for beginning science class. We practice for the first one or two weeks so students can become familiar with the classroom routine. We ask them to sit in their seats, take out required materials, and begin the warm-up, which is written on the board or projected onto the screen.

Prior to the beginning of class, we also list all of the lesson's necessary materials on the board. These may include pencils, lab notebooks, and highlighters. As part of the classroom procedure, students know to get these materials out prior to beginning their warm-up and to put everything else away. (We, of course, provide the lab supplies, such as beakers, chemicals, and test tubes.) We have students obtain the materials first because it helps them to transition smoothly into the lab after completing the warm-up.

We also practice cool down procedures during the first two weeks. After the main lesson is complete, students return to their desks and begin the cool down, which is available on the board or screen.

In this chapter, we discuss how warm-ups and cool downs can be used in classroom management, as formative assessments, and we address the frequency of their use. We will first briefly review those three areas, and then discuss more specific activities teachers can use—first for warm-ups, then for cool downs.

CLASSROOM MANAGEMENT

While students are working on their warm-ups and cool downs, we can address some "housekeeping" needs, such as taking attendance. However, once those tasks are complete, we walk around the room and try to check in with every student. Another classroom procedure we teach students during the first two weeks of school is how to complete their warm-ups and cool downs quickly. We begin by telling students that we will not move on to the next part of the lesson until everyone is done. This action reinforces the message that every student is important. We walk around and provide one-on-one support to anyone who may have questions. We also encourage partners to work together, because, as we remind them, "Two heads are better than one." Once every student is done with their warm-up or cool down, we say something like "Now that everyone is done, let's talk about your answers."

Once this kind of routine is established, it becomes a vital part of daily classroom management. Students know what to expect when they enter the room. Knowing that a cool down related to that day's lesson will often be their "ticket" out the door may help maintain student engagement during the period.

WARM-UPS AND COOL DOWNS AS FORMATIVE ASSESSMENTS

Sometimes warm-ups and cool downs can be used as formative assessments. The purpose of formative assessments is to provide students with practice so they can receive meaningful feedback, and continue their learning prior to the graded summative assessment (Miller, 2011; Dyer, 2013). In addition, formative assessments can provide valuable information to the teacher so that instruction can be aligned to student needs. We discuss formative and summative assessments in Chapter 17: Strategies for Assessing Student Learning.

FREQUENCY OF USE

Generally speaking, we use warm-ups and cool downs at the beginning and end of every lesson. If a lesson only requires one day, then the warm-up and cool down will occur on the same day. However, if a lesson is three days long, then the warm-up may occur on day one and the cool down occurs on day three. There are times when a lesson teaches many concepts, in which case we may use a cool down at the end of each day so we know how students are progressing. The bottom line is that teachers should decide what frequency makes sense for their situation. For example, some particularly "active" classes might benefit from knowing that there will be a warm-up and/or a cool down every day.

SPECIFIC IDEAS FOR WARM-UPS

Warm-ups can be written in any number of formats, including as a set of questions, brain teasers, jokes, memes, political cartoons, demonstrations, or videos.

Regardless of the format in which the warm-up is written, we use them for four different purposes, which include:

1. previewing new material to build anticipation
2. teaching or reviewing background knowledge
3. reviewing previous material
4. formative assessment

We discuss how to use warm-ups as formative assessments in Chapter 17: Strategies for Assessing Student Learning. The next three sections discuss the remaining purposes for using warm-ups.

Warm-Ups: Previewing New Material to Build Anticipation

Warm-ups can be used to preview new material in order to build anticipation for an upcoming lesson. When we say we are building student anticipation, we mean that we are trying to spark their curiosity.

Curiosity activates specific areas of the brain. Research shows that when people are curious, their prefrontal cortices are activated because their brains are getting ready to learn something (Kang et al., 2009). It's important to stimulate the prefrontal cortices because some of those functions include decision-making, self-control, and problem solving, which are skills that students can actively use to learn new content (UCD Neuropsychology Lab, 2018).

There are multiple ways to build anticipation. One activity could be demonstrating a phenomenon, such as lighting a match and dropping it into a 5-gal water bottle that secretly holds a teaspoon of rubbing alcohol. The match ignites the alcohol and a small explosion occurs. Then light a second match and drop it into the water bottle but nothing happens. Ask students, "What was the difference?" and they must brainstorm an explanation of what they witnessed. Phenomena can also be shown using videos if they are too dangerous or expensive to demonstrate in class.

Another example is asking students questions and delaying the answers in order to build anticipation. In a chemistry unit, we wanted students to understand the difference between mass and weight. We developed the following three questions for students to answer in their warm-up:

1. Which is heavier: 1 kg of rock or 1 kg of feathers? How do you know?

2. Which has more atoms: one grape or one watermelon? How do you know?

3. Which has more gravity: the moon or the Earth? How do you know?

Students discuss possible answers with learning partners and document ideas in their lab notebooks. The purpose of the warm-up is to build anticipation, so we aren't concerned that they write the correct answers. This warm-up can also be used to activate prior knowledge, which we discuss in detail in Chapter 13: Strategies for Activating Prior Knowledge.

After students complete their warm-up, we continue to build anticipation by saying, "We are not going to give you the answers to the questions. It's your job today to determine if your answers are accurate." We then introduce the activity they will complete in order to learn the required information. We explain that after the activity they will have the chance to change their answers.

When we describe building anticipation in professional development classes, we remind teachers that "there's a reason why we don't want our friends to spoil the ending of a movie, book, or sporting event. We want to experience the emotional ride that accompanies the event. Learning can be this type of event too." We don't want to spoil the end of a lab for students but, instead, build anticipation so that learning is exciting.

We are strategic when thinking about using a warm-up to build anticipation. We follow this four-step process:

1. Identify the concept students should learn by the end of the lesson. In the chemistry unit example, we wanted students to differentiate between mass and weight.

2. Develop the warm-up, which may include writing questions, designing a demonstration, or identifying a video. To get students to begin thinking about mass and weight, we wrote three engaging questions that we thought most students might answer incorrectly because they had a lack of background knowledge.

3. Create an activity to teach the concept. We created a three-station lab that instructed students to weigh objects, read an article about the number of atoms in the human body, and calculate their weight on different planets.

4. Connect the cool down to the warm-up so students reflect on the accuracy of their answers. Students were instructed to use their lab results to determine if their answers were correct or need to be changed. An example of how we ended the lesson on the difference between mass and weight can be found in the section Cool Downs: Making New Connections Using the Warm-Up.

Are we this thoughtful about every warm-up we use to prompt anticipation? Of course not! Sometimes we just get a fun idea and try it. But it's safe to say, as with all classroom instruction, the more we plan ahead, the more likely our classroom instruction will be a positive learning experience for most of our students.

Warm-Ups: Teaching or Reviewing Background Knowledge

Warm-ups can also be used to teach or review background knowledge. A structured format for this type of warm-up is to use a KWL chart. This graphic organizer is a three-column chart students use to document what they *know* about a given subject, what they *want* to know about the subject, and what they *learned* about the subject. We provide examples and resources for using KWL charts in Chapter 13: Strategies for Activating Prior Knowledge.

When we want to teach or review background knowledge needed to access an upcoming lesson, we attempt to incorporate students' interests and/or connect their prior experiences. Here are a few examples:

Example 15.1

We overheard students debating in the hallways about whether or not water is wet. See Figure 15.1 for the warm-up we developed for the chemistry lesson that was going to teach students the unique characteristics of water.

Example 15.2

Before teaching students about wildlife strikes, which is when wild animals come into contact with man-made objects, the warm-up required them to watch a video of a deer that was hit by a bus. The deer's body broke the windshield and it landed inside the bus near the door. The deer popped up and tried tirelessly to get out of the bus. The bus driver finally pulled over, opened the door, and the deer ran away, unharmed. The warm-up instructions said, "Write about a time when you saw an animal hit a man-made object. If you've never seen this happen, then write about what you imagine it would be like."

Example 15.3

To teach students the concept of inertia, we took the class outside where a sledge-hammer was resting against a low-set table. Near the table we had stored half a water-melon, a dozen raw eggs, a concrete block, and two pillows. We placed one raw egg on the table, picked up the sledgehammer, and asked the class, "Talk to a partner and determine which object will win the Battle of Inertia: the sledgehammer, egg, or table?"

We quickly found out that none of the students knew what "inertia" was but they all had witnessed what happens when two or more objects come into contact with each other. After they made a prediction, we asked, "How do you know?" This question prompted students to think about what they knew prior to class and to use this knowledge to defend their hypothesis. We then swung the sledgehammer and destroyed the egg. Note that students were standing in a safe zone so they weren't hit by debris and we wore a plastic poncho. We asked, "Who was the winner of the Battle of Inertia?" Students identified the sledgehammer and table, which they had accurately guessed.

We continued this activity as we demolished two eggs at the same time and then the watermelon by itself. We repeated the process with a pillow, two pillows, and the concrete block. Afterwards, the class returned to the classroom where the warm-up question asked, "Knowing the winners and losers for the Battle of Inertia, how would you define the term 'inertia'?"

Students were encouraged to discuss their answers with learning partners. They wrote their answers in their lab notebooks, and then we reviewed the answers as a class to ensure that every student had the necessary information to be successful in the activity we had planned for them that day.

Warm-Ups: Reviewing Previous Material

Warm-ups can also be used to review previously taught material. After students complete warm-ups that are intended to review previously taught material, we review the answers as a class. We want to ensure that every student has learned the concept.

For example, the day after students had completed the three-station lab that helped them to differentiate between mass and weight, we chose to use a warm-up that would review their learning. Students were shown Figure 15.2 and asked to answer the questions asked by Person 1 and Person 2 that are in the figure.

After attempting to answer the questions individually, we provide time for students to share their responses with a learning partner. Students are encouraged to use their partner's feedback to modify their answers. This exchange is followed by a class discussion. Person 1's mass remains the same because they did not alter the number of atoms in their body, but their weight would decrease because the moon is smaller than Earth so it has less gravity. Person 2's mass and weight changed. They gained mass when they ate the pizza's atoms, which also increased their weight.

SPECIFIC IDEAS FOR COOL DOWNS

We use cool downs for three reasons:

1. to connect the warm-up to the activity that followed it;
2. to review the content from the preceding activity;
3. as a formative assessment so we know if students have learned the content.

We discuss how to use cool downs as formative assessments in Chapter 17: Strategies for Assessing Student Learning. The next sections discuss the remaining purposes for using cool downs, and we offer ideas for incorporating the NGSS crosscutting concepts into cool downs.

Cool Downs: Making New Connections Using the Warm-Up

Cool downs can wrap up the end of class by connecting the warm-up to the activity that followed it.

In the previous section Warm-Ups: Previewing New Material to Build Anticipation, we discussed a lesson beginning with a warm-up that asked these three questions:

1. Which is heavier: 1 kg of rock or 1 kg of feathers? How do you know?
2. Which has more atoms: one grape or one watermelon? How do you know?
3. Which has more gravity: the moon or the Earth? How do you know?

After the students have completed a three-station lab, they returned to their seats for a cool down. We placed the three questions back on the board and instructed students to use their lab results to analyze the accuracy of their answers.

Students benefit in two ways when they are responsible for determining the accuracy of their answers. First, students are practicing their critical thinking skills because they have to compare and contrast their answer with their lab results. Second, research has shown that when a person recognizes that he or she has answered a question incorrectly, the memory areas of the brain become activated to prepare for new learning, which can increase retention (Kang et al., 2008).

After students finalize their answers, we discuss them as a class. Our goal is to ensure that students have learned the proper definitions of mass and weight and can differentiate between the two concepts. In this sense, the cool down is a formative assessment and helps us plan for the next day. If most of the students answered the cool down questions correctly and can accurately differentiate between mass and weight, then we know that the focus for tomorrow's lesson can be the next topic. But if many students are struggling with the cool down questions, then we plan for a second activity and give them another opportunity to learn the information.

Cool Downs: Reviewing Newly Taught Material

Cool downs can also be used to answer new concept-related questions instead of those already asked in a warm-up. For example, after teaching students how to perform dimensional analysis, we developed a cool down that instructed students to complete these two practice problems:

1. If a car is traveling at 65 mph and uses 1 gal of gas every 15 miles, how many gallons of gas will the car use if it maintains its current speed for 3.5 hr?

2. If a father does four loads of laundry every week for 8 weeks and it takes 2.5 hr for every load, how many minutes did he spend doing laundry for those 8 weeks?

After students have time to work on the problems and compare them to their learning partner's answers, we randomly choose a pair of students to demonstrate the math on the board. The answer to the first question is 15.2 gal of gas and the answer to the second question is 4,800 min.

Cool downs that review newly taught material must have their answers reviewed with the class. This process ensures students have learned the new concepts they were exposed to during the lesson and reinforces that learning. This type of cool down can also be used as a formative assessment. If the majority of the students calculate incorrect answers, then we need to reteach the material in a different way.

Incorporating NGSS Crosscutting Concepts into Cool Downs

Cool downs are an effective tool for testing students' ability to use the crosscutting concepts that are required by the Next Generation Science Standards (NGSS). The crosscutting concepts are described in detail in Chapter 5: Strategies for Using Project-Based Learning. Chapter 5 also discusses how to integrate the crosscutting concepts into project-based learning. See Table 15.1: Ideas for Integrating Crosscutting Concepts into Cool Downs for topics that can quickly provide practice or assessment of students' skills using crosscutting concepts.

See the Technology Connections section for additional ideas on integrating crosscutting concepts into cool downs.

As we mentioned, we are not always strategic in planning warm-up and we have to make the same confession about cool downs. Sometimes our cool downs can consist of asking students to write about one important thing they learned that day.

Table 15.1 Ideas for Integrating Crosscutting Concepts into Cool Downs

NGSS discipline	Crosscutting concept(s) used in cool down	Cool down example: Students will...
Earth and Space Sciences: water cycle and gravity (integrates physics)	Energy and matter	...explain the energy that drives evaporation in the water cycle and the force that drives precipitation
Earth and Space Sciences: climate change and adaptation (integrates biology)	1. Stability and change 2. Cause and effect	...predict adaptations that occurred while interpreting a graph of the Earth's climate for the past 600,000 years
Physical Sciences: kinetic and potential energy	Patterns	...sort random objects into those with high kinetic energy and those with high potential energy
Physical Sciences: gravity	1. Systems and system models 2. Patterns	...predict what would occur if you drop a cup filled with water that had a hole in the bottom. Would the water come out while the cup was falling? Why or why not?
Life Sciences: predator/prey	1. Scale, proportion & quantity 2. Cause and effect 3. Patterns	...determine the relationship between predator and prey by viewing a graph showing the changes in their population densities over time
Life Sciences: evidence for evolution	1. Structure and function 2. Patterns	...explain the implications as they pertain to evolution after observing X-rays of a human hand, whale pectoral fin, bat wing, bird wing, and penguin flipper
Technology, Engineering, and Applications of Science: Coding	Systems and system models	...read a code to determine flaws and then fix them
Technology, Engineering, and Applications of Science: energy conservation (integrates physics and earth science)	Energy and Matter	...brainstorm ideas for minimizing the loss of energy of a specific technology

Other times—because life happens and perhaps our lesson went on too long—we forego the cool down, but, in this situation, we are purposeful in our planning for the following day because we need to determine if the previous lesson was successful.

DIFFERENTIATION FOR DIVERSE LEARNERS

Many warm-up and cool downs require extensive writing because students are justifying their answers. We allow students who have writing challenges or who are learning English to draw pictures representing their answers. We can also provide students with sentence starters and writing frames. Examples of sentence starters can be found in Chapter 3: Strategies for Teaching the Scientific Method and Its Components and writing frame examples are available in Chapter 9: Strategies for Teaching Writing.

Student Handouts and Examples

Figure 15.1: Is Water Wet?
Figure 15.2: Reviewing Previous Material

What Could Go Wrong?

Warm-ups and cool downs should take no more than 5 min for students to complete. If a student is struggling to finish a task quickly, we sometimes shorten it by decreasing the number of questions to answer.

Students who enter class late or who leave early often miss out on the benefits offered by warm-ups and cool downs. When students don't make it to class until after the warm-up, we have a one-on-one discussion (if possible) to catch them up so they can begin working on the day's activity. If a student leaves early, we assign the cool down as homework and follow up with them during the following day's warm-up.

Technology Connections

Several prompts for the crosscutting concepts can be found at "Prompts for Integrating Crosscutting Concepts into Assessment and Instruction" (http://stemteachingtools.org/assets/landscapes/STEM-Teaching-Tool-41-Cross-Cutting-Concepts-Prompts_Nov2016.pdf).

TeachThought lists "10 Smart Tools for Digital Exit Slips" for teachers who want to use more technology and less paper in their classrooms (https://www.teach-thought.com/technology/smart-tools-for-digital-exit-slips).

Figures

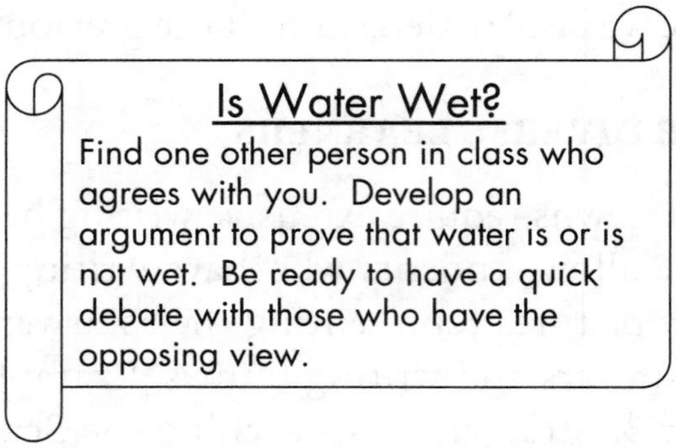

Is Water Wet?

Find one other person in class who agrees with you. Develop an argument to prove that water is or is not wet. Be ready to have a quick debate with those who have the opposing view.

Figure 15.1 Is Water Wet?

I love being on the moon! Which is different now that I'm here: my weight or mass? How do you know?

I just finished eating an entire pizza. Which is different now: my weight or mass?

Figure 15.2 Reviewing Previous Material

CHAPTER 16

Strategies for Reviewing Content

What Is It?

There are a variety of ways to review new content, ranging from quick daily review activities to longer reviews of larger amounts of information. Reviewing does not need to be a tedious task and, in fact, many of the strategies we use can be engaging and fun for students.

Continuous review of new content can increase the likelihood that students will learn and retain it. Content can also be reviewed in preparation for an upcoming assessment.

Why We Like It

In our experience, reviewing content in novel ways results in both higher student engagement and greater learning. Our review techniques incorporate the concept of "retrieval practice." Retrieval practice is an instructional strategy that involves students recalling information without using any resources (Gonzalez, J., 2017). Having students pull information from their memory and write it down leads to better long-term retention of content. Studies have shown it also can lead to better achievement (McDaniel, Agarwal, & Huelser, 2011, p. 407). Retrieval practice strategies can include flashcards and low stake quiz situations (during games in class and online resources). Both are discussed in the Application section.

Supporting Research

Research shows that the more students are required to review information, the more likely they are to make connections with their new learning. Additionally, use of retrieval practice increases the chance they will retain their learning in long-term memory (Rosenshine, 2012, p. 19).

Studies have found that science students who attend help sessions that review content perform better in exams than those who do not (Jensen & Moore, 2009, p. 60).

Some of our review activities use games. Studies have shown that academic games in the classroom can lead to increased social skills, academic performance, memory, and the ability to apply knowledge to new contexts (Sharp, 2012, p. 43). Additional research on technology-based games also shows their use can increase academic achievement for students of all ages (Shapiro, 2014).

Skills for Intentional Scholars/NGSS Connections

Our range of review activities allows for practice in all of the Skills for Intentional Scholars. Students can enhance critical thinking and creative problem-solving skills by using their knowledge in new ways. They also can improve their communication skills because they must express what they have learned and remembered during the activities.

Application

The review strategies we discuss here can be used at any time, including at the end of a unit. Daily review of concepts can also occur through the use of warm-ups at the start of class and cool downs at the end of class. Both are explained in Chapter 15: Strategies for the Beginning and Ending of Class.

BINGO

When there is a lot of vocabulary (including people, events, and places) in a particular unit, one way to review is to play BINGO as a class.

A BINGO board has 25 squares, five rows and five columns. Each column is labeled with one of the letters to the word BINGO. In the very center of the game board, in the middle of the N column, there is a free square. See Figure 16.1: Blank BINGO card.

To prepare for the game, we create a list of 24 terms we want to review with the students. We write them on separate index cards or other pieces of paper and place them in a bowl.

We also decide how to prepare the FREE square, which is the middle square of the N column. There are two different ways we use the FREE square.

1. The students write "FREE" and they all begin the game with that square covered.

2. If we have a surplus of time and energy (or, if we have a student "TA"), we create an individualized bingo card for each student by placing their photo in the FREE square and they all begin the game with that square covered. To obtain photos, we use our district's attendance application that includes individual student photos.

On the day of the game, each student is provided with 25 beads, poker chips, lima beans, or any other small trinket we can find. We also give each student a copy of Figure 16.1: Blank BINGO Card. We place the list of 24 terms on the board and instruct students to randomly write one term in each of the squares.

We then give students 3 min to walk around the room, asking their peers for definitions they don't remember or want to verify. They are allowed to write the definitions inside the square that contains the word. After 3 min, students are instructed to return to their desks.

We randomly pull one of the terms from the bowl, read its definition, and then give students time to identify the word on their BINGO card before reading the next definition. If our class includes English language learners (ELLs), we provide additional time before we pull the next term from the bowl.

When students have five in a row (a column, row, or diagonal), they scream "BINGO!" They read off the words they covered so that we can verify that they have a successful BINGO and if they do, they receive an award, such as healthy food snacks. If a student has a false BINGO, we make sure to explain the definition of the term they got incorrect and then we continue with the game.

BOX GAME

The box game is used to review quick facts. We prepare for the box game by writing 50 questions or math problems students can answer very quickly in one or two words. Each question requires students to retrieve the information without any resources. Here are some examples:

- How many centimeters are in 10 decimeters?
- Who is the father of genetics?
- How many planets are there?
- What term is defined as "the animal that is killed by a predator"?

- What is the equation for Newton's second law of motion?
- What organisms have cell walls?
- What charge does a neutron have?

Then we make the box. We make one for every class so when we work with middle and high school students, we make multiple box games.

To make the box, we begin with a small eraser in an envelope. We close the envelope and use packing or duct tape to seal it shut. We place the envelope into a box and tape the box. That box is then placed into another box that is also taped. Finally, the box is placed into the final box and taped. The time it takes to play the game is determined by the amount of tape used to tape the boxes. For a 10–15 min game, we've found we need to use about ¾ roll of packing tape or ¼ roll of duct tape.

On the day of the game, we take the class to a large open space, usually outside or in the school gym. The students make one large circle and the box goes into the middle. We explain the rules to the students:

1. The winner is the person who can open the box and find the eraser first.

2. Only one person is allowed in the middle at a time.

3. When you go into the middle to try to open the box, you can use anything except tools and your teeth.

4. I'm going to begin by randomly choosing one person to ask a question. If you answer the question quickly and in less than 3 s, then you get to go into the middle to try and open the box. If you don't answer correctly or if it takes you too long to answer, I will move to the next person in the circle.

5. While you are in the middle trying to open the box, I'm going to continue asking your peers questions. You remain in the middle, trying to open the box until the next person answers a question correctly, at which point you return to your spot in the circle and the next person goes into the middle to try and find the eraser.

6. This game does not ensure that all of you will have an opportunity to go into the middle of the circle. Be prepared that some of you may never go into the middle while some of you may go in the middle several times.

We then stand inside the circle, randomly choose the first student, and ask them a question. If they answer the question correctly and quickly, they can go into the middle to try and open the box. The students believe this is an easy task because they don't realize there are multiple layers of boxes. To engage all students the majority of the time, we allow peers in close proximity to help the student whose turn it is to answer a question. We move very quickly from student to student.

The first student who can remove the eraser from the envelope receives a prize, such as a decorated pencil, healthy food, or extra credit.

We've had students who enjoyed the box game so much that they made their own box games and brought them in for the next review day. One student varied her box in a creative way. When the students broke open the first box, there were two boxes to choose from. The entire class gasped in surprise. They enjoyed the extra challenge. It did take a bit longer to find the eraser so, when we use this variation, we plan for at least 15 min or use less tape.

ARE THE WINNERS LOSERS?

Are the Winners Losers? is a review game that doesn't require any student materials. However, if students will be completing a math review, we may allow them to use scratch paper and calculators depending on the complexity of the questions.

The only materials teachers need are a set of game cards, which are available in Figure 16.2: Are the Winners Losers? Game Cards, and a process to randomly call on students. Tara uses popsicle sticks and Mandi uses index cards, but any format is compatible with this review game.

To prepare for the game the first time, we create the game cards by laminating and cutting them into individual cards. Laminating is not required, but it does preserve them so we can use the same cards again.

We then write a list of review questions to ask students during the game. These generally relate to math or just require short answers.

We begin the game by randomly grouping students into teams of 3 or 4.

The game cards are set in a pile face down in a common area of the room, preferably near us. We assign each team a number and write those numbers across the top of the classroom board so all students can see.

We then teach the class how to play the game by reading the following directions:

1. Today you will play the Are the Winners Losers? game. Usually the winners of a game win it, but not in this game. Sometimes the winners lose the game and the losers win it instead.

2. We will ask you a series of questions.

3. We will only read a question one time, which means you need to pay attention.

4. After we read a question, you will have 30 s to discuss the answer.

5. At the end of 30 s, no one is allowed to talk. If you do, your team loses 100 points.

6. We will randomly call on one of you. The person we call on is the only person who can provide an answer. Remember, there's no talking, which means that

every one of you needs to know the answer before the 30 s ends. If you don't know the answer but your team members do, be sure to ask them. And if you know the answer, be sure your teammates all know it too.

7. If you get the answer correct, you can choose a game card. You will earn the points stated on the card. I will keep track of your score on the front board. Your card is then placed into the discard pile face up so it can't be used again.

8. If you get the answer wrong, your team is disqualified from answering this question. I will randomly choose another player from another team and ask them for the answer.

NOTE: When we play this game with students the first time, we do not tell them that some game cards will say that they "lose 100 points" or must "give points to another team." We let these cards be a surprise, which then explains why the name of the game is Are the Winners Losers?

We usually set a predetermined amount of time to play the game. For example, we'll communicate to students that the class will play for the rest of the period or for 15 min. When that time has passed, the team with the most points wins.

This game has a good chance of engaging all students most of the time because they must know the answer before we randomly call their name. Students are all actively working to retrieve information from their memories, which is enhancing their learning.

In our experience, we've played review games with students where one team earns a tremendous lead on the rest of the class or one team falls severely behind the rest of the class. When this occurs, the teams that are behind tend to give up and exhibit off-task behavior. A benefit to Are the Winners Losers? is that the game cards can equalize teams' scores at any time. For example, the majority of the game cards award 50–100 points; however, one of the game cards is worth 500 points. If a team who is behind chooses this card, they may catch up or even take the lead. And there's a card that requires one team to switch scores with another team. If a team with an extensive lead chooses this card, then they lose their lead when they switch their scores with another team. There is always a chance, even with the last question, that any one of the teams will win the game, so students are more likely to stay engaged throughout the entire activity.

ONLINE REVIEW GAMES

There are many online games available for classroom use. See the Technology Connections section for a list of them.

This section provides resources for using our favorite three online review games: Kahoot!, Quizlet (Live), and Socrative.

All three of these online review tools require the teacher to have a computer projector in order to show the questions, answers, and results on a screen. Ideally, every student uses their own device (laptop, computer, smartphone, tablet, or Chromebook), but students can be grouped into pairs if there is a shortage of devices. An exception is Socrative's Space Race review game, which requires a device for every three or four students.

We prefer these three review tools because they don't require students to set up an account or establish a password. The Kahoot!, Quizlet, and Socrative features that we use are free; however, all three platforms offer a paid upgrade that provides additional features (we don't discuss those added tools here).

See Table 16.1: Comparison of Kahoot!, Quizlet (Live), and Socrative for an analysis of how these three online review tools are similar and different (of course, tech tools are always evolving, so these comments may or may not be accurate in the future).

The process for using these three review tools is very similar. The teacher creates questions or flash cards on each site and then the review tool turns them into an interactive online interface.

Table 16.1   Kahoot! vs. Quizlet (Live) vs. Socrative

Characteristic	Kahoot!	Quizlet (Live)	Socrative
Can be used for formative assessment	Yes. Immediately after a game, the teacher is provided the top three students. After the activity teachers can download individual student reports.	Not for individual students. It provides the teacher with the most common wrong answers but the teacher doesn't know which individuals are struggling.	Yes. The results are provided real-time. Additionally, there are individual student reports that can be downloaded.
Can be done at home, without the teacher	Yes, up to 100 students.	Not Quizlet Live, but there are seven independent activities students can use independent of the teacher.	No
Can be sent to students via Google Classroom	No	Yes, Quizlet allows teachers to share their vocabulary cards.	No
Can be shared with colleagues	Yes	Yes	Yes
Can be fun and used as a classroom game	Yes. Students earn points as they answer the questions correctly. The quicker they answer, the more points they earn.	Yes. Students work together in groups of 3–5 to answer 12 questions correctly.	Yes

While we discuss Kahoot!, Quizlet (Live), and Socrative below, other resources that can be used to create similar online review games include:

- Philologus (www.philologus.co.uk/index.php)
- Class Tools (http://www.classtools.net)
- Jeopardy Labs (https://jeopardylabs.com)
- Review Game Zone (https://reviewgamezone.com)
- Quizizz (https://quizizz.com)
- Blended Play (http://www.blendedplay.com)

Kahoot! (https://kahoot.com)

To use Kahoot! as a teaching tool instead of a review tool, see Chapter 13: Strategies for Activating Prior Knowledge, which provides resources for creating and using Blind Kahoot!s.

The Kahoot! review tool provides a search feature that allows teachers to find and use Kahoot!s that have already been created. When we are making a new Kahoot!, we usually begin with another teacher's Kahoot! so we can minimize the amount of work we need to do. We make a copy and modify it to meet the needs of our students.

Students must first enter their name when playing Kahoot!. Students often use nicknames that we don't recognize. For example, the last time we played Kahoot! with a class, one student typed their name as "$y = mx + b$" and this caused some difficulty because when we looked at the report after the game, we didn't know who it was. Therefore, we ask students to enter their real names when we play Kahoot!.

Kahoot! only has multiple choice questions with two to four answer options. This does allow for true/false questions and fill-in-the-blank. Here are examples of the three possible types of questions:

Example of a True/False Question in Kahoot!

Q: The photic zone is the upper most layer of an aquatic system.

    A1: true

    A2: false

Example of a Multiple Choice Question in Kahoot!

Q: The zone through which there is no sunlight is called the

    A1: littoral zone.

    A2: hadal zone.

    A3: pelagic zone.

    A4: aphotic zone.

Example of a Fill-in-the-Blank Question in Kahoot!

Q: Estuaries are a combination of _____ and _____.

    A1: freshwater and acidic water.

    A2: tepid water and polluted water.

    A3: freshwater and saltwater.

    A4: acidic and basic water.

The teacher must project their computer screen so all students can see it because the questions and answer options only appear on the teacher's computer. Four colors that coordinate with the four answer options appear on the students' devices.

After time runs out or all of the students answer the question—whichever occurs first—the correct answer is revealed on the teacher's screen. After a question's answer is revealed, each student's screen will change color. If it's red, that indicates they answered the question incorrectly and if their screen is green, then they answered correctly.

We want to provide extra learning opportunities to the students who answer a question incorrectly. We often have a private conversation at their desk to clarify information.

As the game progresses, it celebrates students who are in the top five or who have correctly answered several questions in a row, referred to as a streak. When the game concludes, it announces the top three winners.

The biggest benefit of using a Kahoot! is its ability to engage all students most of the time. When students are using their phones to play, a text is always a temptation, as is the draw of social media sites. However, we are standing in the back of the room or walking around and encouraging students to only participate in the Kahoot! review.

There are reports available for download that provide data that teachers can use to create intervention or enrichment. For example, the report provides the number of students who answered each question correctly and lists individual student answers for every question.

One option to support ELLs and students with learning challenges is to team them up with another student. In fact, having everyone play in student teams can also work well.

Quizlet (Live) (https://quizlet.com)

Quizlet can be used to review vocabulary, events, people, and dates. To make a Quizlet, the teacher enters a term in one column and its definition in another column. Quizlet uses this information to create flashcards.

Quizlet provides a search feature that allows teachers to find and use other teachers' Quizlets. When we are making a new Quizlet, we begin here so we don't have to reinvent the wheel. After finding another teacher's Quizlet, we make a copy and modify it to meet the needs of our students.

Quizlet offers seven types of review activities for students to use independently. Here is a short description of each:

1. *Flashcards*—students are shown the word, they say the definition aloud, and then flip the card to verify their definition; this can also be done in the reverse order with the definition being shown first and the student guessing the word.

2. *Learn*—students are shown the definition and receive four options. They must choose the word that matches the definition.

3. *Write*—students are shown the definition and they must type the matching word.

4. *Spell*—students are shown the definition, the application says the word, and the student types the word they hear. This is most effective for ELLs.

5. *Test*—students are tested using the following formats: fill-in-the-blank, multiple choice, and matching.

6. *Match*—students receive several words and definitions that are randomly placed on the screen. They must click on the word and then click on its definition to make a match.

7. *Gravity*—words appear on the screen one at a time and students must type the definition.

A unique use of Quizlet is that it can be used without the teacher, which means students can make their own Quizlets and search for and use other people's Quizlets.

Sometimes we assign one of the seven independent activities as homework, as long as the students have access to the Internet at home. When students complete a project or lab but class time remains, we instruct students to make a Quizlet for the class. This assignment can be an enrichment activity or we can ask them to complete one of the seven independent activities.

Quizlet Live is a review game that involves movement. Once all of the students in a class have entered their names into their devices, the teacher begins the competition. Quizlet randomly places students into groups of three to five (although there is an option for the teacher to create the groups). Students are encouraged to leave their desks, find their group members, and sit next to them.

Each member of the same group is shown the same definition on their device. However, each member has four different terms on their device. Together, the team must determine which term is being defined and who has that term. The person whose device displays the term clicks on it. The first team to match 12 terms in a row first wins the competition.

After the Quizlet Live is complete, the most commonly missed terms are provided on the teacher's screen. We spend time reviewing these terms with students prior to playing again, which can be done with the same teams or, if we want our students moving, Quizlet offers an option to shuffle the teams before beginning the next game.

The biggest benefit of using Quizlet Live is its ability to engage all students 100% of the time. Students must talk to each other because they must determine who has the correct term on their device.

Sometimes we integrate the seven independent activities into Quizlet Live. For example, prior to beginning the Live game, we will provide 5 min for students to review content by using any of the seven independent activities. We find they are better prepared for the Live game when we provide this time. Another example is using the seven independent activities during the Live game. If the majority of the class is struggling to match the definitions and the terms, which can be determined by watching their progress on the teacher's screen, then we pause the Live game and provide independent learning time before continuing the game.

Socrative (https://socrative.com)

Socrative is a quiz tool that can be used to review and administer formative and summative assessments.

Socrative has three types of question formats: multiple choice, true/false, and short answer. These questions can be used as a quiz, an interactive game called Space Race, or an exit ticket.

Quiz

In its traditional quiz format, students independently complete a quiz, which can be student-paced or teacher-paced. As students answer questions, the teacher's screen, which should not be projected onto a common screen, displays how each student is answering each question. Socrative indicates a correct answer with the color green and an incorrect answer with red. After everyone is done with the quiz, reports are available that indicate how every student answered every question.

To use a Socrative quiz as a review tool, we launch a quiz using the teacher-paced option. We do not choose the options to shuffle the questions or answers because we want every student to receive the same experience. We do choose the option that provides students with the correct answer once they complete a question.

After all students answer the first question, we use the data on our private screen to determine an intervention plan. If only a few students missed the question, we choose a student who answered the question incorrectly to be responsible for explaining the correct answer to the class. We say, "Bobby, we need your help. Can you please be responsible for this question? I'm going to explain it to the class first and then you will explain it to the class when I'm done." We quickly reteach the information and then ask the chosen student to do so. We try to reduce the student's anxiety by giving them prior notice that they will be responsible for teaching the class. Of course, doing this kind of activity requires that there is a class culture of encouraging risk, viewing mistakes as opportunities to learn, and students viewing themselves as part of a community to support each other.

If many students missed the question, we direct them to talk with their learning partners about the correct answer, which was provided to them when they submitted their answer. Then we call on a student who answered the question incorrectly and who is partnered with a student who answered the question correctly. If no such pairing exists, then we reteach the information and randomly choose a student to explain the answer to the class. If they struggle, we offer support, such as asking them a guiding question, offering the opportunity for them to look at their notes, or providing a page number in the textbook they can read quickly. The goal is to make the student responsible for the answer, even if it requires a bit of time.

We suggest using only the multiple choice and true/false formatted questions in a review.

Socrative will grade short-answer questions; however, if the student misspells a word, etc., then Socrative marks it as "incorrect."

Space Race

Another way to use Socrative as a review tool is to use the Space Race option. We begin by grouping our students into teams of two, three, or four, depending on the number of devices that are available. We make the groups as small as we can so that every student has the opportunity to participate during the entire game.

We then launch a quiz using the Space Race option. Student groups create a team name and then answer the questions. For every correct answer, their rocket inches toward the finish line. We project our private screen on the board so students can compare their team's progress with others.

When the game is over, we review the reports to identify which questions were difficult for most of the teams. We reteach that content and then play the game again to see if the students' performance increases.

Unfortunately, Space Race doesn't provide data about individual students.

Exit Ticket

Socrative also offers an exit ticket activity that we use to review at the end of a lesson. By launching an exit ticket, students automatically receive these three questions:

1. How well did you understand today's material? (Multiple choice: students have four options to choose from)
2. What did you learn today? (Short answer)
3. Please answer your teacher's question. (Short answer)

When we assign an exit ticket to students, we write a content-specific question on the front board and instruct students to answer that question when they get to number three on Socrative's exit ticket activity.

Socrative lists individual student answers in a report, which we use to determine the review we'll conduct the following day at the beginning of the class. For review strategies that occur at the beginning of class, see Chapter 15: Strategies for the Beginning and Ending of Class.

Socrative does not have a search feature, so to access other teachers' quizzes we must obtain the other teacher's share code. Each quiz has a unique share code so quizzes aren't shared without the author's permission.

DIFFERENTIATION FOR DIVERSE LEARNERS

A differentiation strategy we use for some review games is to allow students to use their class notes during the review. In our experience, many students feel more confident when they have access to their notes, regardless of whether or not they use them. Usually, if we allow one student to use their notes, we allow all students to do so because we want to conceal who is receiving extra support.

Students with physical challenges may find it difficult to play the box game so we allow them to use tools. For example, we've allowed students to use their walkers and wheelchairs to break open the box. The goal is that no one is left out, so we bend the rules if that's what it takes to involve every student.

When students with walking aids play Quizlet Live, we give them the option to remain in their seat and call their group members to them. This is especially useful when we choose to shuffle the teams every time we play a series of games.

As we mentioned earlier, we also sometimes allow ELLs and those with learning challenges to partner up with a peer during online quiz games.

While playing Are the Winners Losers?, we read the question twice, instead of once, in order to support ELLs. We also provide more than 30 seconds for students to discuss their answers.

Student Handouts and Examples

Figure 16.1: Blank BINGO Card (Student Handout)
Figure 16.2: Are the Winners Losers? Game Cards

What Could Go Wrong?

Obviously, when a class review incorporates games, there may be issues with students who are competitive. Students may take winning and losing very seriously, which could lead to conflict. To prevent this as much as we can, we remind students these are friendly games and they should remain respectful throughout the activity. If we know of specific students who typically have issues with being overly competitive, we may pull them aside to have a private conversation to ward off any problems with that student prior to the start of the game.

There will be learning curves when students first start using new technological platforms. Sometimes we assume students are more tech savvy than they may actually be and forget they need time to adjust to new programs. One big point to keep in mind when utilizing new technology is patience. Things may not go smoothly the first time as students log on and figure out how to interact with the new technology. We need to remember to take a breath and remind ourselves that the review activity will be more successful as students become familiar with the platform.

Another issue with technology is that it may not work. If students are prepared to play a game and the Internet goes offline, one option is to quickly convert to a non-online game format. Having multiple mini whiteboards can make this change an easy one. Instead of answering machine-generated questions by keyboard, students can work in small groups to write responses to questions asked by the teacher.

When students participate in a Quizlet Live or Kahoot! review activity, the name they enter will appear on the teacher's screen. Sometimes students enter inappropriate words or names. To minimize this behavior, we don't project our computer's

Table 16.2 Student Interface Videos

Kahoot!	Quizlet Live	Socrative
"5 Minute Guide to Kahoot!" (https://www.youtube.com/watch?v=rZUew1wIQts)	"Quizlet Live Tutorial" (https://www.youtube.com/watch?v)	"Socrative—Space Race" (https://www.youtube.com/watch?v=0RnsdGm-oek)
"Kahoot! Demo for Teachers" (https://www.youtube.com/watch?v=5mRzrjbM6aw)	"Quizlet Live: Beginning to End" (https://www.youtube.com/watch?v=JuvJ0OYpeV4)	"Socrative Space Race" (https://www.youtube.com/watch?v=unPli-qZ7jk)

screen onto the classroom screen until every student has entered their name. We then review the names, remove any that are inappropriate, and ask those students to log in again with an appropriate name. We display our computer screen on the classroom screen once we've verified that all of the names are school-friendly.

Technology Connections

Larry Ferlazzo provides a list of many different web-based games in his blog entitled, "The Best Websites for Creating Online Games," which is available at http://larryferlazzo.edublogs.org/2008/04/21/the-best-websites-for-creating-online-learning-games.

The student and teacher interfaces for Kahoot!, Quizlet Live, and Socrative are different. We've found that it's beneficial to know what the students are looking at while they participate in these review activities. There are many online videos that show the student interface. See Table 16.2: Student Interface Videos for links to videos that show the student version of these three online review tools.

Figures

BINGO Card

B	I	N	G	O

Figure 16.1 Blank BINGO Card (Student Handout)

Lose 50 points	Gain 50 points	Lose your next turn	Gain 25 points and go again!
Gain 100 points	Lose 10 points	Steal 50 points from another team (the team of your choice)	Give 50 points to the team with the least number of points
Gain 500 points	Gain 5 points	Gain 10 points	Gain 150 points
Gain 100 points	Gain 100 points	Gain 100 points	Gain 100 points
Keep this card! REVERSE!!! When the other team is allowed to steal from you, tell them no and reverse it so you are allowed to steal from them!	Steal 100 points from another team (the team of your choice)	Steal 50 points from another team (the team of your choice)	Steal 10 points from another team (the team of your choice)
Gain 100 points	Gain 100 points	Gain 100 points	Gain 100 points
Gain 100 points	Lose 100 points	Lose 100 points	Gain 100 points and go again!
Steal a player from another team. It's your choice who you want to steal.	Gain 100 points	Gain 100 points	Gain 1 point

Figure 16.2 Are the Winners Losers? Game Cards

Lose 50 points	Gain 50 points	Lose your next turn	Gain 50 points and go again!
Gain 100 points	Lose 10 points	Steal 50 points from another team (the team of your choice)	Give 50 points to the team with the least number of points
Gain 500 points	Gain 5 points	Gain 10 points	Gain 150 points
Gain 100 points	Gain 100 points	Gain 100 points	Gain 100 points
Exchange scores with another team. You have to choose one! Hopefully you don't currently have the highest score right now.	Steal 100 points from another team (the team of your choice)	Steal 50 points from another team (the team of your choice)	Steal 10 points from another team (the team of your choice)
Gain 100 points	Gain 100 points	Gain 100 points	Gain 100 points
Gain 100 points	Lose 100 points	Lose 100 points	Gain 100 points and go again!
Steal a player from another team. It's your choice who you want to steal.	Gain 100 points	Gain 100 points	Gain 1 point

Figure 16.2 (Continued)

CHAPTER 17

Strategies for Assessing Student Learning

What Is It?

Researchers and educators typically identify three types of assessments: diagnostic, formative, and summative (Swearingen, 2002). Diagnostic assessments determine students' background knowledge and identify misconceptions. However, we are not going to discuss diagnostic assessments in this chapter because we have covered them in Chapter 13: Strategies for Activating Prior Knowledge.

Formative assessments are non-graded activities that provide data for teachers and students. Teachers can use them to provide feedback to students so they can reflect on their learning progression and plan for future learning. Teachers can use formative assessments to help them plan for re-teaching, intervention, and enrichment. Ultimately, formative assessments can improve a student's learning and a teacher's teaching (Carnegie Mellon University, n.d.).

Summative assessments occur at the end of a unit. They can indicate a student's progress in learning the standards and can be used by students, parents, teachers, administrators, and state officials (Woods, 2017, p. 1).

Effective assessments require students to show an understanding of the content they've learned and demonstrate acquired skills. On the first day of school, we announce to students, "This is a *thinking class*, not a memorization class. You will need to memorize some things, which has been expected of you in the past, like when you learned to tie your shoe or spell your name. However, we will require you to also understand the information we teach you, which requires you to *think*."

To help students differentiate between memorization and understanding, we ask them to raise their hands if they can recite the Pledge of Allegiance (or some other commonly memorized verse, such as one from a popular song to which students are currently listening). Most students raise their hands to indicate they know the Pledge. We instruct these students to keep their hands raised if they can explain what it means to "pledge your allegiance to a country." Most hands are lowered, at which time we continue, "Although you may have memorized the Pledge of Allegiance, you may not understand it. Our goal is that you understand what we teach you in this class."

In the book, *Understanding by Design*, authors Grant Wiggins and Jay McTighe (2005) describe how to plan units so students understand content. They explain that, "Understanding thus involves meeting a challenge for thought. We encounter a mental problem, an experience with puzzling or no meaning. We use judgment to draw upon our repertoire of skill and knowledge to solve it" (Wiggins & McTighe, 2005, p. 39). To assess students on their understanding, tests and activities they complete must include a challenge that requires them to use their learned knowledge in a novel situation.

Assessing students on their learning can occur in a variety of ways in the science classroom. Student understanding of content can be assessed using diverse testing methods, such as performance-based or traditional paper-and-pencil tests. Performance-based assessments are "the demonstration and application of knowledge, skills, and work habits" (Association for Supervision and Curriculum Development, 2011, p. 1). Assessments can also include a list of choices where students choose how to demonstrate their learning.

Why We Like It

Formative assessments can provide the data we need to determine if our current lessons are effectively teaching content. When the majority of students perform well on a formative assessment, this can be an indicator that they are learning and are ready to move to the next concept. However, when most students struggle on a formative assessment, we know we need to develop a different approach.

Formative assessments can also identify individual student needs, such as their misconceptions and misunderstandings. We can use this data to support individual students, which is often referred to as "intervention" (Hooper, n.d.). While some students receive intervention, others can receive an enrichment activity that allows them to dig deeper into the content (Taylor, 2019).

Another reason we use formative assessments is because they can provide an opportunity for students to self-reflect on their learning and learning efforts. We use a structured format called "learning goals and scales," which provides students with feedback every few days so they can determine if they're learning and what may need to change to make them more successful.

Summative assessments can be used for teacher and student reflection. By analyzing and interpreting summative data, sometimes patterns emerge that reveal areas of opportunity. For example, while working with teachers in a professional development class, one of our colleagues recognized that the majority of her students who were seated in the back of the classroom scored lower on assessments than those who sat in the front of the room. These students weren't failing, but she knew they were not reaching their full potential. She knew she needed to ensure she was monitoring and providing feedback to all students, regardless of their seat location in her classroom.

We also like to give students options when we assess their learning. Giving students choice in how they are assessed can allow for more creativity and provide additional opportunities for them to apply information instead of just regurgitating facts for a test (Davenport, 2018).

Supporting Research

A meta-analysis of the effects of formative assessment was completed by educational researchers Paul Black and Dylan Wiliam. After analyzing more than 250 publications, they concluded that, "While formative assessment can help all pupils, it yields particularly good results for low achievers by concentrating on specific problems with their work and giving them a clear understanding of what is wrong and how to put it right" (Black & Wiliam, 1998).

Researchers have found that learning goals and self-reflection can have a positive impact on intrinsic motivation and overall student performance (Grant & Dweck, 2003, p. 550; Alesch & Niblack-Rickard, 2018, p. 25).

Studies also show self-reflection can lead to deeper learning, growth, and students taking more ownership over their learning (JISC, 2015; Eisenbach, 2016).

Research indicates that students can demonstrate learning at higher levels when they are assessed with a performance-based assessment, particularly one that interests them (Bae & Kokka, 2016, p. 13).

Skills for Intentional Scholars/NGSS Connections

Effective assessments create opportunities for all three of the Skills for Intentional Scholars to be demonstrated. Students must use critical thinking and creative problem solving to apply the knowledge they have learned in all assessment types that test for their understanding of the content. Students must also be able to effectively communicate in order to demonstrate their learning.

The Science and Engineering Practices in the Next Generation Science Standards require that students develop and use models; construct explanations and design solutions; and obtain, evaluate, and communicate information, all of which can be accomplished while assessing student learning (National Science Teaching Association, 2014).

Application

Formative and summative assessments have different purposes and may often have different formats. We begin by discussing how to use cool downs as formative assessments. Then we provide a very detailed description of how to develop and use learning goals and scales to identify students who require intervention or enrichment prior to the summative assessment. And, finally, we discuss the process for developing summative assessments, including performance-based assessments. Although there are many differences between formative and summative assessments, both should test for student understanding and not solely focus on memorization.

FORMATIVE ASSESSMENTS

Formative assessments are non-graded activities that provide data to both students and teachers. Students can use them to identify the concepts they are finding difficult to understand and what are—and aren't—effective learning strategies. Teachers can use formative assessments to plan for individual student needs, such as intervention and enrichment.

We usually administer formative assessments at the beginning or end of the class period. If they occur at the end, we refer to them as "cool downs." In this section we will discuss various types of cool downs and how to use learning goals and scales as a structured form of formative assessment. See Chapter 15: Strategies for the Beginning and Ending of Class for a further discussion of warm-ups and cool downs.

COOL DOWNS: PROCEDURES

After students complete the day's primary lesson activity, they are instructed to return to their seats to complete the day's cool down. We place the cool down on the board or project it onto a screen (see examples in the next section). Because we want to determine the needs of individual students, we ask that students complete their cool downs independently. Students can document their answers on an index card, sticky note, or scrap piece of paper.

Once all students are done with their cool down, students exchange their papers. We then share the answer key with the class and ask students to correct their partner's paper. Once the feedback is complete, we provide a few minutes for partners to provide a verbal explanation of the corrections so students know how they can improve their answers.

We often collect cool downs because they provide us with important data about student learning (or the lack of it). Cool downs can act as a formative assessment that indicates if the majority of the class is ready for the next concept or if we need to reteach the lesson. This kind of analysis can help us more immediately support students who need it.

COOL DOWNS: EXAMPLES

Cool downs can be quick formative assessments that require no more than 10 min: 3–5 min for students to answer the questions and 3–5 min to review their answers with a learning partner and participate in a class discussion.

The following are a few examples of cool downs we've used:

Example 17.1

After teaching students the concept of *species*, the cool down asked three questions, which reviewed the content we had hoped they had learned in that day's activity. Here are the three questions we asked:

1. Design an experiment that would determine if Disney's Goofy is a dog.
2. Why do species have common names and scientific names?
3. Why is it beneficial that every species has its own unique scientific name?

This cool down requires that students apply their knowledge of species to a novel situation, such as designing an experiment. It also asks them to justify nomenclature rules. All three questions provide the opportunity for students to demonstrate their understanding of content because none of these questions were directly asked during the lesson.

Example 17.2

We generally spend several days teaching significant digits in chemistry. At the end of every day, students complete a cool down that asks them to calculate the answer to a math problem and present their answer using the correct number of significant digits. Then on the last day of the unit, the cool down asks students to connect the importance of significant figures with Isaac Asimov's quote that is in Figure 17.1.

Although we teach how to determine and use significant figures, we never mention Isaac Asimov or his quote during the lessons. With this cool down, students are required to apply their new knowledge (significant digits) to explain a novel situation (Issac Asimov's quote).

Example 17.3

After completing an activity that taught students the significance of the sun's angle of incidence, we asked the following question:

On Planet A, the angle of incidence is 35° during one season and 84° during a different season. During which season does Planet A experience an angle of incidence of 84°? Explain your answer.

This cool down is another example of students applying their learning to an unfamiliar situation. During the lesson, we discussed how the angle of incidence affects Earth's temperature. The cool down requires that students apply their knowledge of Earth to another planet that has a different axial tilt.

Example 17.4

A more general cool down can be completed using an online tool called Socrative, which can be accessed at https://socrative.com. This tool has an option called *Exit Ticket*, which asks students these "canned" (pre-set) questions:

1. How well did you understand today's material? (Multiple choice: students have four options to choose from)

2. What did you learn today? (Short-answer)

3. Please answer your teacher's question. (Short-answer)

For further information regarding how to use Socrative's Exit Ticket, see Chapter 16: Strategies for Reviewing Content.

LEARNING GOALS AND SCALES

A specific tool that we use for both warm-ups and cool downs is learning goals and scales (LG&S), which engages students in a review of previously taught content and a time of reflection. When we begin planning a unit, we first write a standards-based learning goal. Then we break the goal into increments that are written as a scale of 0–4, where a 0 rating indicates that the students don't know any of the learning goal's content and a 4 rating indicates the students have accomplished the goal and completed an enrichment activity.

When we plan a unit, we use the backward design format, which dictates that teachers first write learning goals, then the unit assessment, and finally the daily lessons (Culatta, 2019). We begin our planning by starting with the chosen standard(s). We use the standard(s) to develop a learning goal and its scale, which is used to create the summative assessment. Then we write daily lesson plans to support student understanding of content.

NOTE: We also include a section on a "Lower-Prep Version of Learning Goals and Scales" for teachers who might want to experiment with this strategy first prior to making it a major part of their instructional routine.

Learning Goal Development

Learning goals state what students should know and be able to do at the end of a unit. They generally take several weeks for students to accomplish. They differ from daily targets, daily objectives, and learning objectives because these focus on what should be accomplished at the end of a lesson (Marzano, 2013).

There are many learning goals and scales available online for every subject and grade level; however, we prefer to write our own because they drive our planning and we can customize them to our specific state standards, available resources, and student needs.

Before we begin writing a learning goal, we decide the standard(s) that will be taught. To model this process, we share an example of a lab safety and scientific method learning goal, along with explaining the process we used to arrive at it.

We begin every school year, regardless of the grade level and subject we are teaching, with the state standard that says students should be able to design, safely conduct, and communicate controlled investigations. When we unpacked this standard for an eighth grade general science class, we determined that it included the following skills that students should be able to do at the end of the unit:

1. Exercise lab safety procedures.
2. Develop a testable hypothesis and design a controlled experiment.
3. Communicate the experiment's results.

We used the standard and its components to write the learning goal, which is written in student-friendly language by starting with "I can." The goal reads, "I can demonstrate lab safety procedures, set up an experiment, and communicate an experiment's results." Notice that the learning goal has three parts. This is intentional. We've found that having three specific parts helps to write the goal's scale, which we discuss in the next section.

The biggest difficulty in writing learning goals is determining the necessary background knowledge students must have before they can accomplish each of the three parts of the goal. We specifically write the goal so that the first part is required background knowledge for the second part, which is then required background knowledge for the third part. For our example learning goal, "I can demonstrate lab safety procedures, set up an experiment, and communicate an experiment's results," we require students to pass lab safety tests with a minimum grade of 80% before they can participate in labs. This means students need to be able to demonstrate lab safety procedures prior to setting up their experiment, which is also necessary prior to communicating the experiment's results.

Scale Development

After writing the learning goal, we develop a scale from 0–4. Scales are similar to rubrics. They indicate to students how much of the learning goal they've accomplished and what learning must still occur prior to the summative assessment. Figure 17.2: Example Scale is the scale we wrote for the learning goal, "I can demonstrate lab safety procedures, set up an experiment, and communicate an experiment's results."

When we write a scale, we keep in mind Carol Dweck's research about students who have a growth mindset, which—among other elements—states that if they believe they can learn, they are likely to apply more effort (Mindset Works, 2017). To provide students with the encouragement they may need to put forth effort, we use the word "yet" and emphasize it by writing it using all capital letters. See Chapter 6: Strategies for Teaching the Engineering Process for additional information regarding the cultivation of growth mindsets.

We use the three succinct parts of the learning goal to develop the scale. A rating of a 0 indicates the student has not yet learned any of the three parts. A 1 rating indicates that a student has learned the first part but not parts 2 or 3. This pattern continues until rating 4, which is intended for students who enjoy challenges, require an enrichment lesson, or have a passion for the subject and want to learn more. We provide a detailed discussion about the 4 rating in the section titled Enrichment Ideas.

Learning Goals and Scales in the Classroom

LG&S are intended to help both students and teachers. Students can benefit from LG&S because they know what they are expected to learn or do, how much of the expectation they've met, and how much more they must learn (Marzano, 2007, p. 23).

LG&S can benefit teachers because as students complete formative assessments, it's easy to identify which students require intervention and which would benefit from an enrichment activity. The next four sections of this chapter discuss: how to introduce a new LG&S to students; how to use LG&S to motivate students to learn; how to use LG&S for student reflection; and when to assess students.

Introducing a New Learning Goal and Scale

We begin every unit with a formative assessment to determine every student's background knowledge and how much of the learning goal they already know. To prevent students from feeling anxious about their assessment scores, we purposely use the term "practice test" and explain that they are not graded. Throughout the unit, students frequently complete formative assessments so we can identify their learning progression and move them along the scale.

We use the practice test data to determine each student's initial rating on the scale. One lesson we quickly learned is that students should never decide their own ratings. When we facilitate professional development classes, we explain that, "Students, like most of us, often don't know what they don't know." We equate this to the first year we taught astronomy. We thought we had an immense grasp on the subject until we began planning the first unit. We realized very quickly that we had a lot to learn! We didn't know how much we didn't know.

We purposefully write the unit's first practice test to be very difficult. Our goal is that nearly every student is assigned a 0 rating because it "levels the playing field," meaning that no one student is rated higher than another. We don't want students to feel negatively when they discover their first rating is a 0 so we remind them that the content has not yet been taught and there is no expectation that they know it YET. When we are teaching secondary students, we explain that we expect them to "fail" the practice test because they should be taking a different class if they already know the information.

We test only for the first part of the learning goal, which, using our example, is that students can demonstrate lab safety. Our aim with the initial practice test is to determine a student's background knowledge regarding the first part of the learning goal. We don't test for the remaining parts because practice tests should require only a few minutes of class time. Their purpose is to determine if a student will be assigned a rating of 0 or 1. Students who answer all of the questions accurately and thoroughly are assigned a rating of 1 while students who don't meet these high expectations are assigned a rating of 0.

A variation is to assign students a half rating, which is used for students who answer most, but not all, of the questions on the practice test correctly. We rarely use this variation for the first practice test because we hope nearly all students earn the same rating. However, using half ratings in subsequent practice tests can be one way to differentiate struggling students. For further differentiation strategies, see the Differentiation for Diverse Learners section.

Figure 17.3: Example of a Unit's First Practice Test is the practice test we use to determine students' initial ratings on the scale for our example learning goal regarding lab safety and the scientific method. Although we haven't taught the material yet, we ask questions that will not require students to regurgitate facts but instead to apply their knowledge. Our aim is always to test for an understanding of content, including background knowledge.

After students receive the results of their first practice test, they each receive a copy of Figure 17.4: Reflecting on My Learning—Blank. We provide students with the unit's learning goal and the upcoming date of the summative assessment, which they document on their Reflecting on My Learning worksheet.

Students then document the goal they set for themselves. We ask, "Do you want to earn a 3, which indicates that you accomplished the entire learning goal or do you prefer to challenge yourself and aim for a 4 rating?" In our experience, some students don't believe they can accomplish the required work for a 4 rating, so they never try. To encourage students to push themselves outside of their comfort zone, we announce the work they must do to achieve a 4 rating. For example, using our lab safety and scientific method learning goal, we tell students to achieve a 3 rating, they will conduct an experiment that leaves a gummy bear in water overnight. To earn a 4 rating, they will be required to design an extension of the experiment. They don't have to actually perform the experiment, they only need to design it, which includes writing a hypothesis, identifying variables, etc. In our experience, once students know what is expected of them, it seems less intimidating and they tend to push themselves further up the scale.

We hope all students attempt a rating of at least a 3 because achieving it indicates that they have accomplished the minimum learning goal. But we realize that depending on the content, some students may struggle just to obtain a 2 rating. There have been numerous times when a student achieves a 2 rating on one learning goal but then achieves a 3 on the subsequent learning goal. In our experience, background knowledge can heavily influence how much students learn. This is one reason why we place so much emphasis on activating background knowledge in Chapter 13: Strategies for Activating Prior Knowledge.

Figure 17.4 also asks students to commit to one specific action *they* can take to increase the likelihood that they will accomplish their goal. When learning goals and scales are first introduced, students most commonly write, "study more," "review my notes," or "pay attention in class." To avoid these ambiguous statements, we provide examples of nine specific things to which students can commit. Here are the nine commitments:

1. Using online game sites, such as Quizlet, Kahoot, and/or Quizizz, search for a lesson that pertains to the content.
2. Watch a YouTube video about the content we are learning.
3. Complete your homework on time.
4. Ask one question every day, either to your teacher or to your learning partner.

5. Make flash cards from your vocabulary sheet (index cards or in Quizlet).

6. Review your vocabulary 5 min every night.

7. When you are absent, create a plan for learning the material you missed.

8. If you tend to daydream or sleep, ask to stand in the back of the classroom or during an activity.

9. Create your own idea! How do you best learn/study? What has worked for you in other classes?

Students then graph their practice test rating on the bar graph in Figure 17.4. In the first column, they graph the rating they were assigned based on their practice test results. They also title the first column with the date of the practice test.

We then collect their Reflecting on My Learning worksheets until the next formative assessment.

See Figure 17.5: Reflecting on My Learning—Completed Example for an example of how the reflection worksheet looks at the end of a unit. At this point, on the first day of the unit, they will only have the top half completed with one data point on the graph.

We, as teachers, need to know which students aren't moving along the scale. These are the students who would benefit from intervention before the summative test. See the section Intervention Ideas for a list of possible interventions.

Using a Learning Goal and Scale to Motivate Learning

We introduce our first lesson of the unit. We start by telling students, "Most of you are on a zero rating, which is okay because we haven't *yet* taught the information to you. If you already knew all of this material, then we would wonder, 'why are you in this class?' You simply haven't learned this *yet*, which is important to remember. We are going to start teaching you now."

To use the example of the lab safety and scientific method learning goal, we continue, "To move to a rating of a 1 on the scale, you must be able to demonstrate lab safety." This statement provides purpose for student learning. They know what they need to do to move on the scale, which provides them with direction and motivation. Now we begin to teach the lesson.

As we teach lab safety, we continually use warm-ups and cool downs to determine if students are learning. Once we have formative assessment data indicating students are ready to move to a 1 rating, we give another practice test. In some cases, we can give the same practice test we gave on the first day of the unit because that practice test only tested for their knowledge of the first part of the learning goal. This practice test is in lieu of a warm-up or cool down.

We collect the practice tests, provide feedback, and assign a rating on the scale. If students answer all of the questions correctly, their new rating is a 1. If they answer at least half of them correctly, we assign a 0.5 rating because we want to honor students for their efforts and learning. If a student doesn't answer any of the questions correctly, they remain at a rating of 0. When we return the practice tests to students, we remind them that the practice test scores will not be entered into the gradebook.

Using a Learning Goal and Scale to Help Students Reflect on Their Efforts

After returning the completed practice tests, we review the answers as a class. Then we return students' Reflecting on My Learning worksheets that they began on the first day of the unit. They are instructed to graph the results of their practice test.

Do learning goals and scales motivate all students? We surveyed our students by asking, "How did you feel when you accomplished your goal?" Here are some students' answers:

DARRIUS: I felt good. I felt like I was actually learning and growing.

KHADIJA: I pushed myself more.

SAMUEL: I was proud of the hard work I put into class.

HAYDEN: I felt more accomplished because I had accomplished my goals and it makes me more excited to learn.

Not everyone moves on the scale at the same time as their peers. Sometimes it's obvious why a student doesn't move and it's an easy fix. For example, some students may have been absent, in which case we explain they will soon take a practice test so they can move, too.

Other times, it's not obvious why a student didn't move on the scale. We pull these students aside and have a private conversation. We explain, "We were surprised when we reviewed your practice test. We thought you were ready. Did you feel the same way?" We've had students share personal stories, such as how their test anxiety gets in the way of their performance or how a challenge at home is a distraction right now. Regardless of their situation, we assure them that these practice tests are not graded so it's okay if they didn't do well the first time. They will always have a chance to test again and move on the scale.

Some students tell us that they studied and then express frustration because they don't know why they didn't do well on the practice test. We help them problem-solve by asking them how they studied, with whom did they study, and for long did they study. We also asked our students, "How did you feel when you didn't accomplish your goal?" Here are some students' responses:

ZAHARA: I was bummed. But I felt encouraged to work harder.

AZAMI: I was really upset. But after discussing it with you, I felt better and found that I wasn't studying effectively. Now I study differently for all of my classes.

KIM: It was disappointing and I wanted to do better.

MALIK: I felt OK, I just know that I will have to push harder, and change how I am studying.

LULU: It made me develop different study strategies and showed me I needed to try harder.

When we talk with students who haven't moved on the learning scale, it's another opportunity to provide them with an example of how to use a growth mindset. We stress that although they haven't learned the information *yet*, we will continue to work with them so they eventually learn it. For examples of how we support students who aren't moving on the scale, see the section Intervention Ideas.

The bottom of Figure 17.4 allows for students to record their reflection from one practice test to the next. They first write down the date of the practice test. Then, if they moved up to a 1 rating, they document what actions they took that resulted in the improvement. If they didn't move to a 1 rating, they explain what they will do differently to improve the next time we take a practice test.

In our experience, students of every grade level struggle to identify a change they can make that will increase their learning so they are better prepared for the next practice test. We remind them to read what they wrote near the top of their Figure 17.4: Reflecting on My Learning worksheet where it states, "One specific thing I will commit to doing to improve my learning is. . ." If they haven't been exercising that commitment, then they recommit to it or make a different commitment. Because we collect their Reflecting on My Learning worksheets, we encourage them to write their commitment in their science notebooks or phones.

See Figure 17.5: Reflecting on My Learning—Completed Example for an example of how the reflection looks at the end of a unit. At this point students should have two data points graphed on the top half and #1 should be done on the bottom half.

When to Assess Students Who Didn't Move on the Scale

If a student doesn't move on the scale, regardless of the reason, we always provide additional opportunities for them to demonstrate their learning. Once we've intervened to provide differentiated instruction and the student feels confident they will perform well on a practice test, we offer them the following options for taking another practice test:

1. Retake the written practice test before or after school or at lunch

    Because we review the answers to the practice test in class, we create a second version of it that students complete in their own time.

2. Take the practice test orally before or after school or at lunch

    We've found oral practice tests can often provide support for students who are English language learners or who have learning challenges. It takes the form of a discussion because we ask students for clarification or ask them to provide an example so their answers include more evidence of their understanding and not just their memorization.

3. Wait until the next time we take a practice test

    When we wrote the learning goal, we ensured that the first part was required background knowledge for the second part, etc. Therefore, if a student waits until the next practice test, they can demonstrate their learning of the first part by using this knowledge to answer the questions that will test for the second part.

There are times we use classroom activities to assess every student's learning. See the Other Forms of Formative Assessment to Move Students on a Scale section for examples.

Lower-Prep Version of Learning Goals and Scales

We recognize that creating LG&S and then assessing for them can be time-consuming. When we first began implementing LG&S, it was daunting. It can take several hours to write learning goals, the scales, and the practice tests for one unit. And class time must be dedicated to students taking and reviewing the practice tests, which are generally given to students once each week, requiring about 25 min.

When we first began using LG&S, we started off small. We created a one-part learning goal that was very specific and could be assessed with our current set of lessons, which avoided the creation of practice tests. For example, the learning goal, "I can demonstrate lab safety procedures, set up an experiment, and communicate an experiment's results," was shortened to "I can follow the steps of the scientific method." Students then received a checklist that listed the scientific method steps:

1. Ask a question.
2. Perform research.
3. Write a hypothesis.

4. Set up and perform an experiment.

5. Analyze results.

6. Write a conclusion.

7. Publish results.

As students completed classroom activities, such as asking an experimental question, they highlighted the associated step to indicate they had accomplished it. We didn't have to create a unique assessment to determine if they could ask an experimental question because we were already doing so in our lesson.

For resources that support the teaching of the scientific method, see Chapter 3: Strategies for Teaching the Scientific Method and Its Components.

Other Forms of Formative Assessment to Move Students on a Scale

Any ungraded activity can be used as a formative assessment so teachers can identify students who are struggling. See Chapter 15: Strategies for the Beginning and Ending of Class for additional resources pertaining to formative assessments.

In addition to a practice test, we've also used strategies and tools discussed in other chapters such as lab reports, individual and class discussions, warm-ups, cool downs, and classroom activities to assess student learning. For example, when students are learning about lab safety, they complete an activity entitled, Identifying Broken Lab Safety Rules, which is shared in Chapter 1: Strategies for Teaching Lab Safety. The activity is Figure 1.2: Identifying Broken Lab Safety Rules and its answer key is available in Figure 1.3: Identifying Broken Lab Safety Rules—Answer Key.

These types of formative assessments can easily be used outside of Learning Goals and Scales. They can also be used to demonstrate evidence of student competency of some of those goals.

It's Time for the Summative Assessment

When the majority of the class has reached the rating of a 3, we know it's time to give the summative test. Of course, if you are not using the scales, you will have your own measure for determining when it's time for this kind of end-of-unit assessment and the Summative Assessment section later in this chapter offers ideas for developing effective ones.

By now we've assessed student learning multiple times, provided intervention, and provided enrichment (see the Intervention Ideas and Enrichment Ideas sections for this discussion). In our experience, the rating that students have at this point is highly indicative of how they will do on the summative test. We've found that students at a 3 rating generally earn an A or B on the test, students with a 2 rating earn a C, students at a 1 rating score a D, and students with a 0 rating fail the test.

After students take the summative, we return their Reflecting on My Learning worksheets so they can add their test score to the graph and document how they studied for the test. On the second page of the worksheet, it asks students if they met their goal and then instructs them to reflect on their efforts. They can use the answers to these questions to plan their learning for the next unit. For example, if a student achieved their goal, then they answer the question that asks, "If you reached your goal, what did you do to achieve it? Be very specific." Students usually document their study strategy. Because they know this study strategy works for them, they can transfer it to the next unit's Reflecting on My Learning where it states, "One specific thing I will commit to doing to learn and accomplish my goal is. . ."

Intervention Ideas

Interventions are "specific, formalized steps to address a particular need" that a student has (Lee, n.d.). For example, if a student is struggling to identify dependent and independent variables, an intervention would be providing the student a learning partner who can act as a peer tutor. The pair work together, attempting to identify the variables in example experiments.

Here is a list of the most commonly used interventions in our science classes:

1. Pairing struggling students with strong peers who will guide them through the work and not do the work for them.
2. Working with students in small groups so the teacher-to-student ratio is smaller.
3. Checking in with struggling students more often.
4. Asking struggling students to explain why their answers are correct.
5. Providing students with more examples.
6. Modeling how to study.
7. Using the strategy of corrective instruction to reteach content that students didn't learn the first time. Corrective instruction involves teaching the same content in a different way because the first strategy that was used was ineffective (PowerSchool, 2016). An example of corrective instruction occurred after analyzing a formative assessment. We realized a handful of our students thought that batteries have electricity inside of them. We developed a new lesson to help them better understand batteries. We began by showing them a video of a potato being used as a battery and then asked them to touch a potato. Students observed that they weren't electrocuted when they held the potato, cut into the potato, or bit the potato. This led to a discussion about what electricity is and how batteries work. After repeating the formative assessment, the data revealed that students had a better understanding of how batteries produce electrical currents. By presenting the same

information in a different way than in our original lesson, students increased their understanding of the content.

8. Providing a visual representation of the content, such as a model. One of the science and engineering practices in the NGSS requires that students develop and use models because they can increase student comprehension, especially for intangible concepts, such as valence electrons. To help students understand where valence electrons are located in relation to the nucleus, they can create, analyze, and interpret Bohr diagrams.

See the Technology Connections for more resources regarding interventions.

Enrichment Ideas

While some students are receiving interventions, what do the remaining students do?

Our goal, although not always achieved, is that every student is working diligently every minute of every class period. So while some students are receiving the interventions they need, the rest of the class participates in an enrichment activity.

This is the purpose of the 4 rating on a scale. To earn a 4 rating, students must complete the work to earn a 3 on the scale, earn an A on the summative assessment, and complete an additional activity. Students don't receive a grade for the activity so we do not provide rubrics or scoring guides.

At this point in the professional development class we teach, teachers often ask why students would choose to complete extra work without receiving a grade. In our experience, some students are driven by challenges, others find the activity engaging, and others do it because we have instructed them to do so. We also entice students by explaining that we will contact their parents when their enrichment activity is complete.

See the Technology Connections section for ideas about enrichment activities.

What Do Students Say About Learning Goals and Scales?

At the end of every school year, we survey students to obtain their feedback regarding the use of learning goals and scales. One of the survey's questions asked, "How did learning goals and scales help you in class?" Here are some of the students' answers:

JUAN: Having a learning goal and scales to follow in class helped me find the best way to study, get homework done, and just enjoy the class. I found that when I did my homework, and paid attention in class, even if it was just listening for vocab words, I retained more knowledge to achieve the grade and understanding I needed for the next test and the final test.

ELIZAVETA: They helped me understand what I needed to focus on during that point in time and how much I needed to improve to reach my goal!

MALIA: Learning goals helped me by telling me what I needed to understand in the lesson. Scales showed me what I already understood and what I needed to improve on.

We also asked, "How did you use learning goals and scales?" Here are two students' answers:

ANDREW: The learning goals and the scales did help me a lot understanding where I was at with the learning goal of each unit we were in and knowing what I did know and knowing what I didn't understand, so when I had my own time that I was able to go in depth into what I didn't understand and practice it and study even more so for the next time I am able to understand the learning goal in class.

VERONICA: Having the scales gave me a chance to remember what I needed to and know what I'm going to be learning. Learning goals helped me too because they let me know how my day/class will go and what I needed to succeed that day.

Not all of our students answered positively but, depending on the class, we found 77–86% of students found that learning goals and scales improved their learning and made them better students. Although our data is anecdotal, research supports our findings. A powerful motivation tool is goal setting and when students' goals are to learn (not "get an A"), then motivation is heightened even more (Latham & Seijts, 2006).

SUMMATIVE ASSESSMENTS

Unlike formative assessments, summative assessments indicate the end of a learning unit or period. Their purpose is to inform students, teachers, administrators, parents, and state officials of the amount of learning that was accomplished.

In this section, we will discuss how to create tests that assess student understanding (which we refer to as "thinking tests") instead of just assessing memorization. In addition, we will provide examples of the various formats that can be used when creating summative assessments, such as performance-based assessments.

Thinking Tests

We were inspired to coin the term "thinking test" after taking a course that teaches how to keep the end in mind when planning units. The course focused on the order in which teachers plan units. Instead of beginning with the daily lessons and then developing the summative assessment, the course teaches the backward design model, which begins by writing learning goals, then creating the unit test, and, finally, choosing the daily lessons that will best support the learning goals (University of Arizona, Office of Instruction & Assessment, n.d.). The idea of backwards design is not a new one. In 1950, Ralph Tyler participated in an ambitious educational research project called the Eight-Year Study where he asked, "How can we assume that purposes are being obtained?" (Tyler, 1950, p. 1). He further explained that academic achievement is synonymous with the attainment of knowledge so the assessment teachers use should be the driving force of their daily instruction (Tyler, 1950).

Another version of backwards design is called outcome-based education (OBE). One of the best-known proponents of OBE is Dr. William Spady. Spady includes two approaches to OBE: traditional/transitional and transformational. The traditional/transitional approach focuses on teaching students content whereas the transformational approach emphasizes the skills students need to be successful post-high school, such as our Skills for Intentional Scholars (Nicholson, 2011).

Thinking tests require students to use both of Spady's OBE approaches. Thinking tests are written in a way that expose students to unique data, phenomenon, or events, which requires them to use their newly acquired content knowledge to solve a problem, communicate the meaning of data, and interpret a situation.

Developing Thinking Tests: Types of Questions

Thinking tests are traditional paper-and-pencil tests that are comprised of open-ended questions. We prefer open-ended (short-answer) over close-ended questions (multiple-choice, true/false, matching) because we can grant students partial credit. Close-ended questions are either 0% or 100% correct. They can't indicate if a student has learned part of the learning goal, which means partial credit can't be earned. But open-ended questions can provide the opportunity to give a student partial credit. When students are required to explain their answer, we can give them credit for the portion of the concept they did learn.

In addition, open-ended test questions allow students to explain their thinking, which can be another way to earn credit. When we develop thinking tests, we create an answer key but, sometimes we discover a question has a possible answer that we didn't include in the answer key. Open-ended questions allow students to explain their thinking and justify their response, which may provide an alternate correct answer.

We work with secondary students who have learning challenges and it's not uncommon that they feel defeated when it's testing time. They may have difficulty motivating themselves to work hard, study, and ask questions. We believe that one reason for this problem could be that these students have received failing grades in many of their previous science classes and they may have given up on themselves. By using open-ended questions, they can earn partial credit for the learning they did accomplish. This drives up their test scores, which, in our experience, increases their self-esteem and they may begin to work harder, participate more, and ask for help more often.

Education and sociology professors at Stanford University, including Sean F. Reardon, a Professor of Poverty and Inequality in Education, analyzed 8 million fourth and eighth grade students' test data to determine if there was a difference in how they performed on open-ended and closed-ended questions. They concluded that 25% of the "achievement gap" (which is probably more correctly called the "Opportunity Gap"; Ferlazzo, 2011) between males and females on state assessments is explained by the question format. Females tend to answer open-ended questions with more accuracy than they do close-ended questions (Reardon, Kalogrides, Fahle, & Zárate, 2018). Using this data, it has been suggested that math and science teachers should place more emphasis on open-ended questions (Berwick, 2019).

We do acknowledge that there are drawbacks to using open-ended questions on a summative test. They take longer to grade and a teacher can't ask as many questions as they can when they use close-ended questions (University of Washington, Center for Teaching and Learning, 2019). However, we believe these are teacher-centric disadvantages and that the advantages of receiving partial credit for what students have learned and being able to explain an answer are student-centric.

Developing Thinking Tests: Testing for Understanding

Before a student can perform well on a thinking test, they must know more than just content. They must also be able to use their Intentional Scholar Skills. Our teaching methods must match our assessments methods. If we want students to understand material, then we must teach them how to understand it and then how to demonstrate their understanding.

Wiggins and McTighe describe six facets of understanding, which are, "the kinds of performance evidence we need to successfully distinguish factual knowledge from an understanding of the facts" (Wiggins & McTighe, 2005, p. 161). We use the six facets of understanding to create thinking tests. Not all six facets are included in every test; however, Wiggins and McTighe state that the first facet of *explanation* must be included in every assessment because we need to know what the students think their answers mean and the justifications they provide for them (2005, p. 167).

Here are the six facets and a description, in addition to an example of each:

1. Explanation: explain an answer, make connections, or develop a theory using data analysis

   Question: One of the largest diamonds known to man is a white dwarf star known as Lucy. It's located in the Centaurus constellation, about 50 light years away from Earth, which means to see it you need to use a telescope. The diamond weighs 2,270,000,000,000,000,000,000,000,000 tons! Some people say geologists should study Lucy and others say astronomers should study her. Explain why both people are correct.

   Answer: Lucy is a diamond, which is a mineral and geologists study naturally forming minerals. Astronomers study space and Lucy is located not here on Earth but 50 light years away in space.

2. Interpretation: interpret stories, art pieces, musical works, situations, claims, or data; can also be an interpretation of ideas and feelings from one medium to another

   Question: In the movie, *The Wizard of Oz*, the witch is splashed with water and begins to melt to her death. While she shrinks, she screams, "I'm melting" in a very irritating high pitched voice. If the witch was educated about moon phases, what else could she have said instead of "I'm melting"?

   Answer: "I'm waning!"

3. Application: use of knowledge in a different skill or situation; can be using knowledge in a different content area

   Question: In June and July of 2013, a fire burned 8,400 acres of land near Prescott, Arizona, in a town called Yarnell. There was a huge loss of habitat for both humans and animals, which will take a very long time to recover without help. Create a habitat restoration project for the Yarnell area. Hint: Yarnell is in the Chaparral biome.

   Answer: I would begin by planting trees and bushes to begin succession. Once these started to grow and bud, the first-level consumers would naturally be drawn to return to the forest. And then the second-level and finally the third-level consumers would make their way back home. To expedite the process, I would manually reintroduce some native species of plants and small animals.

4. Perspective: explain a different point of view or the other side of a debated topic, make connections to explain the "big picture," identify underlying assumptions and their effects, or critique with explanation and evidence

Question: In 2010, a ship collided with the Great Barrier Reef in Australia. In an attempt to clean up the resulting oil spill, chemical dispersants that break down oil were dumped into the ocean. These dispersants have a hydrophilic end and a hydrophobic tail. Some scientists argue that it's best to let the oil disperse naturally. Our instinct is to clean up the oil spill. Explain the point of view of the scientists who believe the oil should disperse naturally. According to them, what might be one drawback of adding hydrophilic and hydrophobic chemicals to the ocean and why does this drawback outweigh the benefits?

Answer: Because the dispersants are both hydrophilic and hydrophobic, they have opposing forces so they cause the oil to break up into smaller droplets. These smaller oil drops can easily be spread farther and deeper than the larger, heavier oil. This oil spreading affects the wildlife in more distant locations and on the floor of the ocean that would not otherwise be affected. It's best to contain the oil on the surface so only the surface creatures are affected.

5. Empathy: appreciate another person's thoughts and feelings, especially when they are in contrast to our own

    Question: You are a conservation biologist who has been asked to speak at the annual conference of Traditional Medicine. You recently learned that rhinoceroses are being hunted and killed because the people who practice traditional medicine believe that rhinoceroses' horns cure cancer. Write a short speech (one paragraph) that would help them to understand why they must not collect horns. Your speech must be respectful of their belief system and culture; after all, if you are rude, you will alienate your audience and they won't want to listen to your very important message. HINT: It helps to put yourself in their shoes as you write your speech.

    Answer: "Thank you for having me today. I'm excited to tour your beautiful city and share in your delicious food. As a conservation biologist, it is my job to help species who are about to go extinct. I've chosen to focus on the rhinoceros. I know you too must be worried that it is near extinction; after all, you harvest the horns for very important medicine. I'm here today to discuss a solution to our common problem. How can we slow down the killing of the rhinoceros so that you have horns in the future and the world has a hefty rhinoceros population?"

6. Self-Knowledge: self-assess learning

    Question: While your teacher was passing out the test, she also returned the practice test you took at the beginning of the unit. Choose two questions that you got wrong and correct the answers. Explain why your new answers are the correct answers.

Answer: On my practice test, I said that 23,459.1 mm = 0.234591 km but I was wrong. The correct answer is 0.0234591 km. When I originally converted the millimeters, I forgot about the base level of the metric system and only moved the decimal point five times. I should have moved the decimal point six times.

When we develop a thinking test, we look at the learning goal and decide what students should be able to do if they have complete understanding of the goal. For example, if students should be able to analyze and interpret data on a graph, then we write a test question that presents students with a graph and asks them to interpret the data.

Thinking tests have fewer than 10 questions because our class periods are only one-hour long and we want students to complete the test in that time period. Each question is usually worth a minimum of two points: one point for the correct answer and one point for the explanation, justification, or evidence. For an example of a thinking test we wrote for a toxicology unit, see Figure 17.6: Toxicology Unit Thinking Test.

Performance-Based Summative Assessments

At the end of each of our units, students complete two types of assessments: a thinking test and a performance-based test. Performance-based assessments can be lab reports, research reports, websites, skits, posters, or slideshows, as shown in previous chapters of the book. Performance-based assessments can demonstrate what students have learned and how they can apply it, which is an example of Wiggins and McTighe's third facet of understanding: Application (2005, p. 165). Another method of performance-based assessment is models, which we will discuss further in this section.

Developing Performance-Based Assessments

Wiggins and McTighe's six facets of understanding can also be used to develop performance-based assessments, which are, "the kinds of performance evidence we need to successfully distinguish factual knowledge from an understanding of the facts" (2005, p. 161). Similar to thinking tests, not all six facets are included in every test. However, Wiggins and McTighe state that the first facet of *explanation* must be included in every performance-based assessment because, as with thinking tests, we need to know how students interpret their knowledge and how they justify their answers (2005, p. 167).

Here are the six facets and a description, in addition to an example of a performance-based assessment for each:

1. Explanation: explain an answer, make connections, or develop a theory using data analysis

    Given an unknown chemical, students perform multiple tests to determine its identity and then use the test results as evidence of their conclusion.

2. Interpretation: interpret stories, art pieces, musical works, situations, claims, or data; can also be an interpretation of ideas and feelings from one medium to another

    Students collect the daily relative humidity using a sling psychrometer for two weeks. They graph their data and interpret its meaning. Then they compare their data with the relative humidity data of a different biome in a different country. They explain why the two biomes have similar or different relative humidities.

3. Application: use of knowledge in a different skill or situation; can be using knowledge in a different content area

    Students design a complex circuit that includes a minimum of five different electrical devices that must run using a 12 or 15 V DC power supply. The design must operate at 4, 8, and 12 or 15 V. The design must include resistors (Performance Assessment Resource Bank, n.d.). Students must explain how they designed the circuit and the role of the resistors.

4. Perspective: explain a different point of view or the other side of a debated topic, make connections to explain the "big picture," identify underlying assumptions and their effects, or critique with explanation and evidence

    Students research fracking, focusing on its benefits and drawbacks. They write two letters. One letter is from a citizen of a town where fracking is occurring. The letter explains the citizen's point of view. Students then write a response to the citizen as a representative of the fracking company and explain the company's stance.

5. Empathy: appreciate another person's thoughts and feelings, especially when they are in contrast to our own

    Students answer situational questions that require them to role play. For example, while teaching biology, students took on the role of a physician to address specific patient case studies. Here is an example of one question: Tycho Brahe (1546–1601) was a wealthy Danish astronomer. In October 1601, he attended a banquet in Prague. During the party, he had the urge to urinate but thought it would be poor manners to excuse himself so he held his urine in until after the party, at which time he was surprised to find out he couldn't urinate. Eleven days later he died. The theory is that his cause of death was uremia, which is urine in the blood. Write an explanation of why some people choose to ignore their body's messages. If you were a doctor, how would you motivate a patient who was ignoring a homeostatic message from his body?

6. Self-Knowledge: self-assess learning

   Students choose any lab report they wrote during the current unit. They edit the report by correcting their errors and improve the report by integrating their newly acquired vocabulary from the unit. They then design a new experiment that would further their learning on the subject.

Offering Choice in Performance-Based Assessments

We also use choices for performance-based assessments. Assessments that allow for student choice differentiate for students with different interests and strengths. Some students may prefer to write a response, while others prefer to prove their learning through a piece of art or video. We have found that students are often more engaged and perform better when they are given the opportunity to decide how to demonstrate their learning.

When we introduce a summative assessment that includes student choice, we give each student a copy of Figure 17.8: Student-Choice Performance-Based Assessment, which is an example from a seventh grade ecology unit. Students are instructed to choose any combination of activities listed but the total points of their chosen activities must be a minimum sum of 50 points. We allow students to complete more than 50 points worth of activities but they do not receive extra credit for doing so.

The more points assigned to an activity, the more work that is required. Some students choose an activity based on the amount of work they perceive it will require. Other students choose activities they find interesting; for example, students who are artistic and enjoy drawing tend to choose the A2, which requires them to create a comic strip and B3, which engages a student by drawing a scene of biotic and abiotic factors in a given environment.

We provide students with three 1-hour periods to complete their activities. We walk around as they work and provide immediate feedback so students know when they are doing well and when they can improve. They are permitted to use any resources they need, such as class notes, online videos, their learning partner, and the Internet.

Models as Performance-Based Assessments

One of the Science and Engineering Practices required by the Next Generation Science Standards is modeling, which includes computer simulations, diagrams, analogies, physical replicas, and mathematical representations (National Science Teaching Association, 2014). For a model to be used as a summative assessment, it should require students to explain their design and justify their ideas. For example, an analogy we use in biology class is called, "Cell Analogy." Students choose an object they have an interest in that has multiple components, such as a concert hall, movie theater, skateboard, or basketball game. Students compare the function of a cell's organelles to the function of a component in their chosen object. One example is that the solar panels on a house (a student's chosen object) have the same function as the chloroplast in a plant cell.

The assessment students turn in for a grade is a model of their chosen object (a house, for example) with the analogous components labeled and described, indicating how it's similar to a cell's specific organelle. They must include the shared 11 organelles and 2 plant organelles (the cell wall and chloroplasts). Student model examples are available in Figure 17.9: Cell City Models—Student Examples, which includes a model entitled, "A Cell Is Like a Pizza" and "A Cell Is Like a Bookstore." The checklist we use for this assessment is Figure 17.10: Checklist for Cell City Models.

See the Technology Connections section for additional performance-based assessment ideas.

DIFFERENTIATION FOR DIVERSE LEARNERS

When students are initially filling out Figure 17.4: Reflecting on My Learning, we've found that some students benefit from receiving the handout with the learning goal already completed. Some students find it difficult to transfer information from the board to their paper so we complete as much of the handout for them as we can.

When using learning goals and scales, we sometimes choose to move students half a point on the scale instead of a full point. We've found that students who remain on the same rating can feel defeated and lose their motivation to work hard, regardless of our best efforts. We find one reason, even if it's minor, to move them that half point. This change is often enough to "jump start" their efforts again, especially if we also celebrate by making contact with their parents. We explain to a parent that their child found a specific concept especially challenging, but they never gave up, and persevered! Students (and parents) appreciate the personal connection and love that the call from the teacher was positive, not negative.

English language learners and other students who have reading comprehension difficulties may have difficulty reading and understanding the questions in thinking tests, though for obviously different reasons. These test questions include many scenarios or stories so students who struggle to read or who are learning the language require a lot of support. To help them, we remove unnecessary information from the test questions and add hints. We also offer to read them test questions aloud.

In addition, we tell students that they can ask us for the definition of any word on the test that is not bolded and underlined, which are the vocabulary words that we taught them during the unit and those that are part of the assessment. We instruct students to raise their hand and when we come over, they only have to point to the word they don't know. We will kneel down near them and whisper the definition to them. We also provide an example and, if necessary, we draw a picture. They are welcome to ask us questions and request additional examples and pictures.

The goal is that their reading skills aren't being tested but, instead, their understanding of the content. Some students choose to draw their answers instead of writing in paragraph form, which we also accept. See Figure 17.11: Toxicology Unit Thinking Test Modified for an example of how we modified the test in Figure 17.6. The modified test has the same answer key, which is Figure 17.7.

Student Handouts and Examples

Figure 17.1: Final Day Cool Down Activity

Figure 17.2: Example Scale

Figure 17.3: Example of a Unit's First Practice Test (Student Handout)

Figure 17.4: Reflecting on My Learning—Blank (Student Handout)

Figure 17.5: Reflecting on My Learning—Completed Example

Figure 17.6: Toxicology Unit Thinking Test (Student Handout)

Figure 17.7: Toxicology Unit Thinking Test—Answer Key

Figure 17.8: Student-Choice Performance-Based Assessment (Student Handout)

Figure 17.9: Cell City Models—Student Examples

Figure 17.10: Checklist for Cell City Models (Student Handout)

Figure 17.11: Toxicology Unit Thinking Tests Modified (Student Handout)

What Could Go Wrong?

The first time students take a thinking test, it is typical for teachers to discover an "implementation dip," a concept studied by Michael Fullan, a change management expert. He defines an implementation dip as the phenomenon that occurs, "as one encounters an innovation that requires new skills and new understandings" (Burnside, 2018).

Mandi documented an implementation dip when she tested her students on their vocabulary skills. She "taught" students vocabulary words by requiring them to memorize their definitions. Then she tested them for their memorization, resulting in an average test score of 88%. But she realized they didn't truly learn the words because they couldn't correctly use them in their writing. She changed her teaching style by incorporating the three Skills for Intentional Scholars. She taught them another set of vocabulary words and tested them for their understanding. Her students' average test score was 78%, which is 10% less than when she required them to only memorize the words' definitions. This is explained by the implementation dip.

For the next set of vocabulary words, Mandi continued to use lesson plans that required students to use their Skills for Intentional Scholars. She again tested them at the end of the unit for their understanding of the words. Their average test score was 90%, which is 2% higher than when she tested them for their memorization. More importantly, students were correctly using their new vocabulary words in their writing.

After returning students' first thinking tests, we explain to them what the implementation dip is. We assure them that as we practice our thinking, communicating, and problem-solving skills, their test scores will increase. We remind them to have a growth mindset. It's okay that they haven't honed these skills *yet* and with more practice we know they will excel.

Another difficulty that students encounter when they first prepare for thinking tests is that they don't know how to study. If they have only been exposed to tests that require memorization, then they study by memorizing. But memorizing doesn't help students on thinking tests; they need to study differently. Prior to the first test, we offer the following study suggestions for students:

- Have someone who is not taking this class ask you "why," "how," and "what if" questions about your vocabulary terms. For example, "What if the Earth was tilted 90° on its axis?" and "How do molecules break in a covalent bond?" The less the person knows about the content, the better their questions will be and the more you will have to explain to them. This is great practice for a thinking test!

- Write a story that uses all of the vocabulary terms in a meaningful way. If you can use the terms correctly in your writing, then you understand their definitions. If you write your story two days before the test, I will look at it and give you feedback.

- Look over all of your classwork during the unit. Make a list of the terms that caused you confusion on those assignments. Draw pictures representing the terms.

- Watch online videos about the unit. Stop the video every few minutes and summarize the content of the video in your own words.

Technology Connections

We use the following resources for intervention ideas:

- STEM Learning offers free online resources for interventions that are the most effective in a science classroom (www.stem.org.uk/triplescience/intervention).

- Achievement for All describes six strategies that can be used for interventions (https://afaeducation.org/free-dt-resources/explore-our-resources/interventions-in-the-classroom).
- SaintA, a child-welfare and advocate agency, lists 101 Classroom Interventions (https://sainta.org/101-classroom-interventions).

We use these resources for enrichment activity ideas:

- Fourth and fifth grade hands-on activities can be found at http://Education.com (https://www.education.com/activity/science).
- Science Buddies offers free lesson plans that support hands-on enrichment activities for students fourth–twelfth grade (https://www.sciencebuddies.org/teacher-resources/lesson-plans).
- PTOToday lists 36 art and science enrichment ideas (https://www.ptotoday.com/pto-today-articles/article/9-36-ideas-for-arts-and-science-enrichment).

We use the following resources for performance-based assessment ideas:

- The book, *Performance Assessments in Science,* is available for free online. It includes ideas that pertain to fifth through tenth grade (https://www.rand.org/content/dam/rand/pubs/monograph_reports/2006/MR660.pdf).
- The Wisconsin Department of Public Instruction created performance-based assessments that support the Next Generation Science Standards for fourth through twelfth grade (https://dpi.wi.gov/science/assessment/examples).
- Stanford University has developed performance-based assessments for life, earth, and physical sciences that pertain to fifth grade through middle school (https://snapgse.stanford.edu/snap-assessments/short-performance-assessments).

Attributions

Thank you to Jason Prichard, the original author of Figure 17.8: Student-Choice Performance-Based Assessment, which provides an example of an ecology unit.

Thank you to Athena Loya and Jadin Hughes for allowing us to include their bookstore cell city model. And thank you to Lucas Peterson and Treven Lucas for allowing us to include their pizza cell city model.

Figures

Isaac Asimov was quoted as saying, "Almost right is no better than wrong," Use his quote to explain why significant digits are important to use.

The quote from Isaac Asimov was obtained on July 20, 2019 at https://todayinsci.com/QuotationsCategories/W_Cat/Wrong-Quotations.htm.

Figure 17.1 Final Day Cool Down Activity

4 = I learned everything I needed for a 3 rating plus I designed an experiment that is an extension of the experiment we conducted in class.

3 = I can demonstrate lab safety procedures, set up an experiment, and communicate an experiment's results.

2 = I can demonstrate lab safety procedures and set up an experiment but I cannot YET communicate an experiment's results.

1 = I can demonstrate lab safety procedures but I cannot YET set up an experiment or communicate an experiment's results.

0 = I can't YET demonstrate lab safety procedures, set-up an experiment, or communicate an experiment's results.

Figure 17.2 Example Scale

Name: _____

Practice test for Learning Goal 1: I can demonstrate lab safety procedures, set up an experiment, and communicate an experiment's results.

Directions: Answer the following questions as best you can. Because this information has not yet been taught to you, it's okay to respond, "I don't know," but this is the only time this response is allowed in science class.

1. What is the definition of science?

2. Why is science a required course in school?

3. Provide an example of how an adult who does not work in a science-related field would use science.

Figure 17.3 Example of a Unit's First Practice Test

Name: _____

Reflecting on My Learning

This unit's learning goal states _____

_____

_____ .

The test for this unit is scheduled for _____ and my goal is to earn a ____ rating by then.

One specific thing I will commit to doing to improve my learning is _____

_____ .

Scale Rating vs.
Date of Pre-Test or Activity

Directions: Below, write the dates from your graph and then document one specific thing you did to learn or one specific thing you need to do to improve your learning.

1. Date: _____   One thing I did or need to do: _____
2. Date: _____   One thing I did or need to do: _____
3. Date: _____   One thing I did or need to do: _____
4. Date: _____   One thing I did or need to do: _____
5. Date: _____   One thing I did or need to do: _____

Figure 17.4   Reflecting on My Learning—Blank (Student Handout)

6.   Date: _____   One thing I did or need to do: _____

7.   Date: _____   One thing I did or need to do: _____

8.   Date: _____   One thing I did or need to do: _____

Now that we have completed the unit test, did you meet your goal?

If you reached your goal, what did you do to reach your goal? Be very specific.

If you did not reach your goal, what will you do differently next time to reach your goal? Be very specific.

Figure 17.4   (Continued)

Reflecting on My Learning

This unit's learning goal states _I can provide evidence to explain why_
science is important, demonstrate lab safety procedures, and
perform the steps to the scientific method.

The test for this unit is scheduled for _Sept 3_ and my goal is to earn a _3_ rating by then.

One specific thing I will commit to doing to learn and accomplish my goal is _completing_
my homework on time

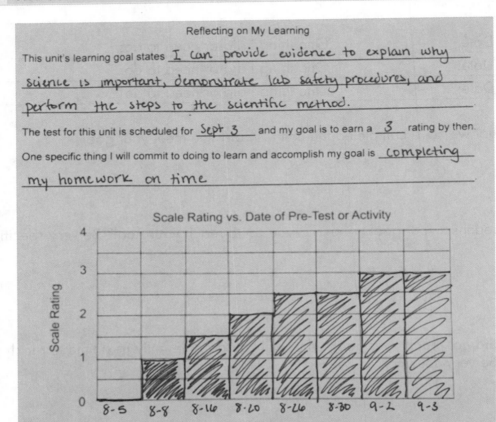

Scale Rating vs. Date of Pre-Test or Activity

Date of Pre-Test or Activity

Directions: Below, write the dates from your graph and then document one specific thing you did to learn or one specific thing you need to do to improve your learning.

1. Date: 8-8   One thing I did ~~or need to do~~: I did my homework!
2. Date: 8-16 One thing ~~I did or~~ need to do: I was absent and didn't make-up wo
3. Date: 8-20 One thing I did ~~or need to do~~: studied rules for 30 minutes
4. Date: 8-26 One thing I did ~~or need to do~~: paid attention, worked with my par-
5. Date: 8-30 One thing ~~I did or~~ need to do: write in complete sentences
6. Date: 9-2   One thing I did ~~or need to do~~: wrote in complete sentences
7. Date: 9-3   One thing I did or need to do: studied for 20 minutes
8. Date: One thing I did or need to do:

Now that we completed the unit test, did you meet your goal?

        Yes!

If you reached your goal, what did you do to reach your goal? Be very specific.

When I answered the questions, I used complete sentences.
I also studied with my mom for 20 minutes. She asked
me "why" and "how" questions.

If you did not reach your goal, what will you do differently next time to reach your goal? Be very specific.

Figure 17.5   Reflecting on My Learning—Completed Example

Name: _____

Toxicology Unit End Thinking Test

Directions: Answer the questions correctly and thoroughly. Remember to explain your answers!

1. Southampton and the Adirondacks in New York are far from major cities but they are receiving acid deposition. This worries me because if we do not address the pollution quickly, these places might become so contaminated we may never have the chance to go back to the clean environments that we once treasured. A great example is the sugar maples, which are the trees that give us maple syrup. These trees are dying because the air and soil pollution is so potent.

    Explain how this scenario is an example of toxicology.

2. Provide a possible explanation for how Southampton and the Adirondacks have acid deposition if they are far from major cities.

3. The *Exxon Valdez* oil spill is considered to be one of the worst in our nation's history, dramatically decreasing the local bird population. Use what you know about the definition and theme of ecology to describe three other changes that would have occurred in the ocean after the bird population plummeted.

4. Fentanyl: The Powerful Opioid that Killed Prince (the artist who sang "Purple Rain")

    The famous musician, Prince, died on April 21, 2016, due to an accidental drug overdose. He died because he consumed a counterfeit pain pill that was laced with fentanyl (https://www.nbcnews.com/news/us-news/no-criminal-charges-prince-s-overdose-death-prosecutor-announces-n867491). The pills in his home were labeled as "Watson 385," which is a combination of hydrocodone and acetaminophen. But, according to the autopsy report, he died of fentanyl toxicity.

Figure 17.6 Toxicology Unit Thinking Test (Student Handout)

It's becoming more popular for drug dealers to include fentanyl in other street drugs. This is a problem because people may be taking fentanyl without knowing it and it's a very potent drug. Fentanyl is 100 times stronger than morphine and 50 times stronger than heroin.

Below is a dose-response curve for morphine. Add a curve for heroin and label it. Add a curve for fentanyl and label it.

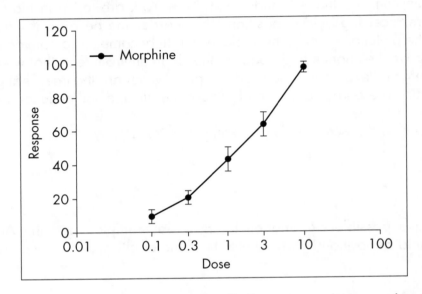

5. A father who works at an e-waste recycling company has two daughters, ages 1 and 2 years old. He recently learned that his girls' blood lead levels are 18 micrograms per deciliter. There is no safe blood lead level but medical professionals suggest that parents should take action once their children's blood lead levels exceed 5 micrograms per deciliter.

   His daughters have never visited him at work. Describe how the lead may have been transferred from his company to his house.

6. What are two changes the father could make to minimize the amount of lead that is transferred from his work to his home?

Figure 17.6 (Continued)

7. Factory workers tend to be exposed to higher levels of chemicals and are sometimes unwittingly poisoned at rates higher than the general population. Asbestos is an example of a chemical that factory workers are often exposed to because it is used in textiles, building materials, insulation, and brake linings. Capable of causing severe lung damage, including asbestosis and mesothelioma, asbestos is now strictly regulated. Today, we are not only concerned about workers exposed to traditional industrial chemicals, but also to those used in the electronics industry, as well as bio- and nano-engineered products.

You are the manager of a factory. The Environmental Protection Agency has asked for a list of the 10 employees in your factory who are most likely to have asbestosis or mesothelioma. According to the dose-response principle, what would be the optimum indicator for employees who would be in the top 10?

Figure 17.6 (Continued)

Name: _____ *Answer Key*_____

Toxicology Unit End Thinking Test

Directions: Answer the questions correctly and thoroughly. Remember to explain your answers!

1. Southampton and the Adirondacks in New York are far from major cities but they are receiving acid deposition. This worries me because if we do not address the pollution quickly, these places might become so contaminated we may never have the chance to go back to the clean environments that we once treasured. A great example is the sugar maples, which are the trees that give us maple syrup. These trees are dying because the air and soil pollution is so potent.

Explain how this scenario is an example of toxicology.

Toxicology is the science that studies the effects and detection of contaminants. The above paragraph is an example of toxicology because it talks about how the pollution (a contaminant) is affecting the forests (the sugar maples).

2. Provide a possible explanation for how Southampton and the Adirondacks have acid deposition if they are far from major cities.

The pollution is being blown in from other major cities. The wind can carry air particulates around the world in two weeks; for example, when Mount St. Helens erupted in 1980, its ash was blown in from the east about two weeks after the eruption.

3. The *Exxon Valdez* oil spill is considered to be one of the worst in our nation's history, dramatically decreasing the local bird population. Use what you know about the definition and theme of ecology to describe three other changes that would have occurred in the ocean after the bird population plummeted.

The decreased number of birds would cause a lack of food for their predators, causing the predator population to decrease. Without the local bird population, their prey population would increase. Bird species that don't spend time on the water's surface would experience an increase in their population because they don't have to compete with the birds who died from the oil spill.

4. Fentanyl: The Powerful Opioid that Killed Prince (the artist who sang Purple Rain)

The famous musician, Prince, died on April 21, 2016, due to an accidental drug overdose. He died because he consumed a counterfeit pain pill that was

Figure 17.7 Toxicology Unit Thinking Test—Answer Key

laced with fentanyl (https://www.nbcnews.com/news/us-news/no-criminal-charges-prince-s-overdose-death-prosecutor-announces-n867491). The pills in his home were labeled as "Watson 385," which is a combination of hydrocodone and acetaminophen. But, according to the autopsy report, he died of fentanyl toxicity.

It's becoming more popular for drug dealers to include fentanyl in other street drugs. This is a problem because people may be taking fentanyl without knowing it and it's a very potent drug. Fentanyl is 100 times stronger than morphine and 50 times stronger than heroin.

Below is a dose-response curve for morphine. Add a curve for heroin and label it. Add a curve for fentanyl and label it.

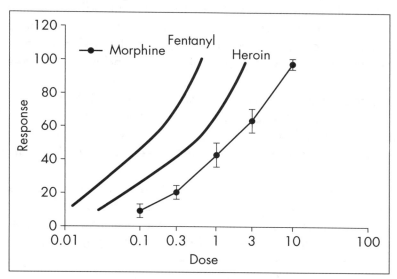

5. A father who works at an e-waste recycling company has two daughters, ages 1 and 2 years old. He recently learned that his girls' blood lead levels are 18 micrograms per deciliter. There is no safe blood lead level but medical professionals suggest that parents should take action once their children's blood lead levels exceed 5 micrograms per deciliter.

His daughters have never visited him at work. Describe how the lead may have been transferred from his company to his house.

When the father leaves work at the end of his shift, he is bringing home the lead on his skin, in his hair, and on his clothes and shoes.

Figure 17.7 (Continued)

6. What are two changes the father could make to minimize the amount of lead that is transferred from his work to his home?

The father could change his clothes at his company, place them in a plastic bag, and wash them as soon as takes them out of the bag. If showers are available at his work, he could shower there. He could have one pair of dedicated shoes for work and keep them in a locker or in his car in a plastic bag. He could change jobs.

7. Factory workers tend to be exposed to higher levels of chemicals and are sometimes unwittingly poisoned at rates higher than the general population. Asbestos is an example of a chemical that factory workers are often exposed to because it is used in textiles, building materials, insulation, and brake linings. Capable of causing severe lung damage, including asbestosis and mesothelioma, asbestos is now strictly regulated. Today, we are not only concerned about workers exposed to traditional industrial chemicals, but also to those used in the electronics industry, as well as bio- and nano-engineered products.

You are the manager of a factory. The Environmental Protection Agency has asked for a list of the 10 employees in your factory who are most likely to have asbestosis or mesothelioma. According to the dose-response principle, what would be the optimum indicator for employees who would be in the top 10?

The dose response principle says that the more dose you receive, the more response that occurs. Therefore, the 10 employees most likely to have asbestosis or mesothelioma (the response) are those employees who have worked in the factory the longest (the dose).

Figure 17.7 (Continued)

Ecology Activities

Select from the activities below. Each category of activities has a different point value. You must complete activities that add up to at least 50 points. Your final grade will be determined by the accuracy of the information and the thoroughness of your activity. Have fun!

A = 20	**A = 20**	**B = 30**
1. Describe your **ecosystem, community, population, and species.** (1/2 page) 2. Make a comic strip that shows the relationship between a **predator and its prey** (6–8 panels in color). 3. Use two or more examples to explain **why decomposers** are good (1/2 page). 4. Create an experiment that would test if a population of birds **migrate or immigrate.** Include your **hypothesis** in the correct format.	5. Write a rap song about **Rachel Carson, Barry Commoner,** and/or **John Muir.** 6. Describe what the city of Chandler would be like if only **native plants** were present. (1/2 page) Include a sketch and two examples. 7. Choose an organism. Have your organism write a letter to his cousin that lives in the same biome but in a different part of the world. The letter must describe the **organism's habitat.** (1/2 page)	1. Create a superhero that prevents **species** from going **extinct.** Draw a picture of your superhero and write a story about how your superhero has saved species. (one-page story in addition to the drawing). 2. Create a crossword puzzle using at least 15 ecology-related words. Clues must be in your own words. Must include key. 3. Draw a scene showing a total of 15 **biotic and abiotic** examples. List each of the examples on a separate sheet of paper indicating which is **biotic** and which is **abiotic.**
C = 40	**D = 50**	**D = 50**
1. Write a creative story that describes how an **ecologist** affects the **environment.** (at least one page). 2. Find an article from the newspaper and write about how it relates to the **study of ecology.** (one page). 3. Survey at least three of your family members. How are their **niches** different from one another? (at least one paragraph response for each person interviewed and a fourth paragraph comparing/contrasting their niches).	1. Write a script for a play about **habitat destruction** and **habitat restoration.** Include cast, stage directions, settings, character descriptions, and narration. 2. Write a puppet show that demonstrates the difference between **consumers** and **producers.** Must have at least two different characters and two scenes.	3. Create a newspaper that specializes in **Environmental Science,** including the causes and effects of **pollution, acid rain,** and **clear** vs **selective cutting** (At least three stories and two ads). Must be in color. 4. Research the career of a **conservation biologist** and explain the importance of **biodiversity.** (one page, two sources with bibliography). 5. Create a game about **Competition,** including **limiting factors, predators,** and **prey.** Must include all necessary materials and instructions.

Figure 17.8 Student-Choice Performance-Based Assessment (Student Handout)

A Cell Is Like a Pizza

Student's answer on the left says, "Cell wall is structure of bread like crust for protection." Student's answer on the right says, "Nucleus controls cell like bread of pizza makes up the entire pizza."

Figure 17.9   Cell City Models—Student Examples

A Cell Is Like a Bookstore

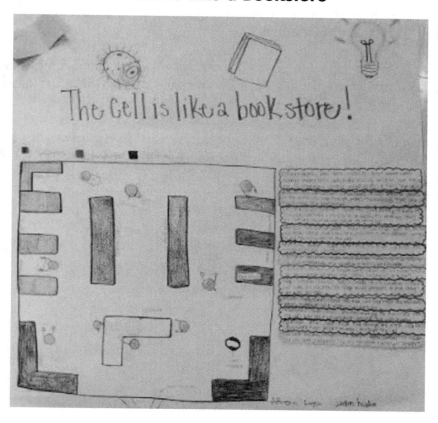

Here is a close-up of the student's writing on the right side of "The Cell Is Like a Bookstore" project:

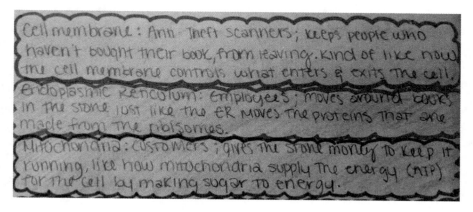

Figure 17.9 (Continued)

The student's first answer says, "Cell membrane: Anti-theft scanners; keeps people who haven't bought their book from leaving. Kind of like how the cell membrane controls what enters & exits the cell."

The student's second answer says, "Endoplasmic reticulum: Employees; moves around books in the store just like the ER moves the proteins that are made from the ribosomes."

The student's third answer says, "Mitochondria: Customers; gives the store money to keep it running, like how mitochondria supply the energy (ATP) for the cell by making sugar to energy."

Figure 17.9 (Continued)

Name_____

Cell Analogy Checklist

As we learned in class, there are 11 structures that plant and animal cells have in common, in addition to two organelles that only plants have. Your job is to create a cell analogy and then design a model that depicts the comparisons between a cell and your model.

For example, if I chose to compare a cell to a house, then I would construct a model of a house. Then I would compare components of the house with structures in a cell. As an example, I would compare the house's solar panels to chloroplasts because they both collect sunlight that is used for energy.

Below are the 13 cell structures that you must have in your model:

- ❏ nucleus
- ❏ mitochondria
- ❏ chromosomes
- ❏ vacuole
- ❏ cell membrane
- ❏ cell wall
- ❏ ribosomes
- ❏ lysosomes
- ❏ endoplasmic reticulum
- ❏ cytoplasm
- ❏ golgi
- ❏ nucleolus
- ❏ chloroplast

Your model must include labels that explain how each of its components is similar to a specific structure in a cell. There are examples available in the front of the classroom so you can see what previous students have created. You may not use my idea of a house or the other students' ideas. You need to do your own thinking.

As you complete a comparison, mark it off the list so you know it's done.

Figure 17.10 Checklist for Cell City Models (Student Handout)

Name: _____

Toxicology Unit End Thinking Test

Directions: Answer the questions correctly and thoroughly. Remember to explain your answers!

1. Two towns in New York are far from big cities but they have a lot of **acid deposition**. This worries me because if we do not decrease the **pollution** levels, these towns might become very contaminated. A great example is the sugar maples, which are the trees that give us maple syrup. These trees are dying because the air and soil **pollution** is so strong.

   Explain how this story is an example of **toxicology**. HINT: Define **toxicology**.

2. How could these two towns have **acid deposition** if they are far from major cities?

3. The Exxon Valdez **oil spill** is one of the worst. It decreased the local bird **population**. What are three other changes that would occur after the bird **population** went down? HINT: Write **ecology's** theme.

4. Fentanyl: A strong drug that kills a lot of people

   The famous musician, Prince, died on April 21, 2016, due to an accidental drug overdose. He died because he consumed a counterfeit pain pill that was laced with fentanyl (https://www.nbcnews.com/news/us-news/no-criminal-charges-prince-s-overdose-death-prosecutor-announces-n867491). The pills in his home were labeled

Figure 17.11 Toxicology Unit Thinking Test Modified (Student Handout)

as "Watson 385," which is a combination of hydrocodone and acetaminophen. But, according to the autopsy report, he died of fentanyl **toxicity**.

It's becoming more popular for drug dealers to include fentanyl in other street drugs. This is a problem because fentanyl is 100 times stronger than morphine and 50 times stronger than heroin.

Below is a **dose-response curve** for morphine. Add a **curve** for heroin and label it. Add a **curve** for fentanyl and label it.

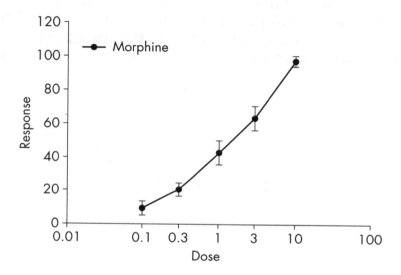

5. A father who works at an **e-waste recycling company** has two daughters, ages 1 and 2 years old. He recently learned that his girls; **blood lead levels** are 18 micrograms per deciliter. There is no safe **blood lead level** but medical professionals suggest that parents should take action once their children's **blood lead levels** exceed 5 micrograms per deciliter.

   His daughters have never visited him at work. Describe how the **lead** may have been transferred from his company to his house.

6. What are two changes the father could make to decrease the amount of **lead** that is transferred from his work to his home?

Figure 17.11   (Continued)

7. Factory workers tend to be exposed to higher levels of **chemicals** and are sometimes poisoned. Asbestos is an example of a **chemical** that factory workers often touch and breathe in. Asbestos is found in textiles, building materials, insulation, and brake linings. Capable of causing severe lung damage, including asbestosis and mesothelioma, asbestos is now strictly regulated. Today, we are not only concerned about workers exposed to traditional industrial chemicals, but also to those used in the electronics industry, as well as bio- and nano-engineered products.

You are the manager of a factory. The Environmental Protection Agency has asked for a list of 10 employees in your factory who are most likely to have asbestosis or mesothelioma. According to the **dose-response principle**, what would be the optimum indicator for employees who would be in the top 10?

Figure 17.11   (Continued)

CHAPTER 18

Strategies for Co-Teaching

What Is It?

Many schools have classrooms that contain two teachers within a room working with one group of students. These may be teachers trained to work with students who have learning challenges and/or English language learners. It is likely that most science teachers will experience a teacher coming into their room during instructional time or working with shared students at some point in their career.

Why We Like It

If done effectively, co-teaching offers many benefits to *all* students. Mandi started her career as a special education resource teacher before switching to a general education teacher. This move allowed her to see both sides of a co-teaching situation: going into another teacher's classroom as a co-teacher and having co-teachers come into her classroom. She realized there are certain qualities of co-teaching that lead to higher effectiveness.

Tara has had a full-time special education teacher in her science classroom for several years. She is an advocate for co-teaching because students generally benefit from two professionals being available to answer questions, explain concepts, and support labs and other classwork. In addition, having two adults available to develop rapport with students enhances the learning environment for everyone.

There are various models for setting up the classroom, which we will discuss below. We also provide tips that we have discovered can lead to more successful co-teaching situations.

Supporting Research

Research has found co-teaching environments can lead to increases in language arts and reading, as well as decreases in referrals and absences (Solis, Vaughn, Swanson, & McCulley, 2012).

Studies have also found that while some co-teaching models can be more successful than others, all co-teaching environments can help meet the needs of all learners and lead to significant academic gains (Cermele, 2017, p. 90). The research focused on three co-teaching models: interventionist, specialist, and departmentalized. The interventionist model consistently produced statistically significant student outcomes. This model assigns a special education teacher with four certified seventh–twelfth grade content teachers (social studies, math, English, and science). The special education teacher attends all four classes with the students and then provides further support in a smaller self-contained class later in the school day.

The other two models are called specialist and departmentalized. They, too, can improve student outcomes, though to a lesser extent (Cermele, 2017, p. 90). In the specialist model, the special education teacher who is certified in the content area co-teaches with the content teacher. The departmentalized model pairs a certified science teacher with a certified math teacher. They work together to teach both science and math. Then a certified English teacher is paired with a certified social studies teacher so they can teach both content areas together.

Skills for Intentional Scholars/NGSS Connections

In successful co-teaching classrooms, all of the Skills for Intentional Scholars can take place. Students can take part in joint lessons that promote critical thinking, creative problem solving, and effective communication.

Application

This section outlines a variety of co-teaching models and offers tips to support an effective co-teaching classroom.

CO-TEACHING MODELS

There are six main approaches to co-teaching that are most widely used (Friend & Cook, 2004, p.15). In an ideal world, these methods are applied in class with two content area teachers. Practically speaking, some can work well with a competent student teacher, and others with an "intervention" teacher (for English language learners or students with learning challenges). The six strategies are:

1. *One Teach, One Observe:* During this strategy one teacher is providing instruction while the other teacher is observing the lesson. This strategy is beneficial for collecting data on students. It can also be used to collect data on the efficacy of a lesson, such as how well students understood the given directions.

   An example of One Teach, One Observe is when students have behavior goals, such as "remaining on task" or "not disrupting." While one teacher is leading students through the lesson, the other teacher observes the class, specifically to keep track of how many times a student calls out and is prompted to get back on task. During this time the second teacher is not actively assisting students, but instead gathering data for an upcoming parent meeting, an updated IEP (Individualized Education Program) meeting, or for internal reflection and discussion among the two co-teachers.

   We use this strategy most often at the beginning of the year while we are getting to know our students. We assign students a shoebox challenge, which requires the class to be divided into groups of three or four students. Each group is provided a shoebox of identical supplies, such as 5 index cards, a rubber band, 10 straws, tape, and 20 paper clips. Students are challenged to create the tallest structure. There are a variety of shoebox challenges; we've provided links to our favorite shoebox challenges in the Technology Connections section.

   While one teacher leads the class through the challenge and monitors for on-task behavior, the other teacher documents observations regarding how students interact in their groups. In our experience, these initial observations can help us plan for group work throughout the year. It is important, though, to avoid making generalized judgments based on one observation! Obviously, we make adjustments as we learn more about our students and they change throughout the year.

2. *One Teach, One Assist:* This model is similar to the One Teach, One Observe, but instead of the second teacher observing students, they are assisting students throughout the lesson. The second teacher can offer assistance to all students in the class, not only those who have identified learning challenges.

   One Teach, One Assist is used most often during whole group lessons. While one teacher is instructing, the other teacher is walking around to help with any questions and ensure students are on task. The second teacher can also identify parts of a lesson that many students find difficult. That teacher then stops the instructing teacher by saying something like, "It seems we are struggling with problem number four. I think we may need to review it as a class." This process helps identify concepts that may need further instruction and allows for reteaching during the lesson.

3. *Parallel Teaching:* Parallel Teaching is when both teachers are covering the same lesson at the same time, but the class is broken into two smaller groups. This arrangement allows teachers to provide more supervision and guidance throughout the lesson since they are each working with fewer students.

We prefer Parallel Teaching when we teach students to use new lab equipment, such as a microscope, Vernier probes and software, or triple beam balances. We begin by splitting the class in half. One of us might show half the class how to calibrate a probe, electronic scale, or balance while the other teacher is giving the same instruction to the second half of the class. Afterwards, students practice their new skill, which can cut instruction time in half and provide every student with practice and immediate feedback. This type of lesson is difficult to execute when there is only one teacher and a full classroom of students. See Chapter 19: Strategies for Using Scientific Tools and Technology for resources to teach students how to use microscopes, Vernier probes, and balances.

4. *Station Teaching:* In this model, the lesson's content is divided into three stations: two teacher-led and one independent-student work station. Each teacher instructs at his or her station and repeats it while students rotate through all three stations. This process also offers the benefit of teachers working with smaller groups of students.

We use Station Teaching when we teach concepts that require two steps. For example, many labs require students to make a graph. After students attempt to make their graph independently or with a partner, they go to Station 1 where one of us checks the quality of their graph. Then students go to Station 2 where the other teacher helps them to interpret the meaning of their data. Station 3 is located at each student's desk where they work with the student sitting next to them to answer reflection questions about the lab and data.

Station Teaching can also be used when students perform dangerous or unfamiliar tasks in one activity. For example, when students are first learning how to test the minerals in a rock, one of us sits at Station 1 to help students safely drop hydrochloric acid on their rock. The other teacher sits at Station 2 to help students perform a streak test because this is the first time they've performed this activity. Station 3 includes the remaining tests (color, luster, transparency, hardness, light refraction), which students can safely and easily perform by reading step-by-step directions.

5. *Alternative Teaching:* In Alternative Teaching, one teacher instructs a larger group of students, while the other takes a smaller group to provide them with

more intensive instruction on the same topic. This model is helpful when there are small groups of specific students who require a differentiated lesson plan.

We sometimes use this method when we divide into ability-based groups (see Chapter 2: Strategies for Teaching Lab Procedures where we discuss when to make this division and when not to make it, along with research supporting those decisions) to read an article. As we discussed in Chapter 8: Strategies for Teaching Reading Comprehension, we believe in generally "amplifying" text and not "simplifying," but there are times when it makes more sense pedagogically and timewise to offer different groups the "same" text at different lexile levels. In those situations, one group may read an article with a higher lexile rating than the other group.

Another time to use this co-teaching method is when, for whatever reason (including the fact that we might not have taught a topic well), a number of students have not fully grasped an important concept. In those situations, one teacher can pull the students together to re-teach the lesson in a *different* way, which is called corrective instruction. One mistake we have made is not understanding that if a student hasn't learned from our original lesson, it doesn't often make sense for us to just repeat it. While the first teacher is instructing those students who need further assistance, the other teacher provides an enrichment opportunity for the remaining students who have accomplished the learning goal. See Chapter 17: Strategies for Assessing Student Learning for resources that assess student needs and provide intervention opportunities, including corrective instruction, and enrichment lessons.

6. *Team Teaching:* This strategy is probably the most challenging because it requires teachers to provide instruction together. It requires a lot of planning, but both teachers benefit by having a shared control of the classroom.

Our best use of Team Teaching is when we teach our students especially difficult concepts and creatively use our differences. For example, Tara is not an athlete and doesn't have a basic knowledge of sports, whereas Mandi is an athlete and coach and possesses great appreciation for sports. Tara teaches the science concept, using the metaphors and similes she is familiar with, and then Mandi teaches the concept a second time but using sports metaphors and similes. We've found that all students are more likely to comprehend scientific concepts because they've been taught using two different explanations.

Another way to use Team Teaching is when there are two (or more) ways to accomplish one goal. For example, when we teach students how to identify independent and dependent variables, Tara teaches the strategy of using the letters of the alphabet. She explains to students that, "*I*, the scientist, have control over the *Independent* variable, both of which begin with the letter *I*. And the *Dependent* variable is the *Data* that is gathered *During* the experiment and recorded in the *Data* table. They all start with the letter *D*."

Mandi then identifies the variables using a different "trick." She teaches the students that: "The independent variable comes first in the experiment. It's the one thing the scientist is altering when setting up the experiment. And the independent variable is the first variable mentioned in the hypothesis. But the dependent variable occurs after the independent variable, just like it appears in a hypothesis after the independent variable." Students then have the choice to use Tara or Mandi's strategy. See Chapter 3: Strategies for Teaching the Scientific Method and Its Components for resources to teach variables and hypotheses.

CO-TEACHING TIPS

Take Time to Plan Together

Successful co-teaching occurs when there is successful co-planning. In an ideal world, co-teachers have a shared prep period so they can plan instruction together, but we know this is not always the case. If teachers do not have common prep time, some ideas to co-plan include asking school administration for class coverage to allow both teachers shared time to work together or creating an online document to share lessons and adaptations for all learners. Regardless of how it is done, finding the time to plan with one another is critical to providing effective instruction.

Be Open-Minded

While taking the time to plan together, it is important to remain open-minded. Every teacher has a unique expertise within their fields. While a strategy may not be one we've used before, it may be what is best for kids. Tara was always open to suggestions when Mandi proposed instructional strategies that would help students who were receiving special education services. Mandi also benefited because she learned many new strategies that were beneficial to all students.

Communication Is Key

Just like any relationship, communication is key within a co-teaching situation. Teachers must talk often about lessons and students when they work together daily. If one teacher observes a problem (in a lesson, regarding a student, etc.), it needs to be communicated so both teachers can work together to solve it.

Get to Know Each Other

Getting to know a co-teacher is important not only to build a relationship, but also to learn each other's strengths. Our best co-teaching experiences were ones where we took the time to learn about each other's experiences, strengths, and challenges. Having a good relationship with a co-teacher leads to more cooperation in planning and interacting with students.

Stay United

Working with adolescents and parents can be challenging at times and co-teachers need to stay united and "have each other's backs." We've had many times where students have tried to "play us" off against each other. Of course, there were times when we didn't agree but we worked out our disagreements in private.

This is not to say that co-teachers should remain silent in the face of obvious unfair or inappropriate classroom practices. We all have bad days. Co-teachers must have the kind of relationship that allows one to be able to signal to the other that it might be time to step outside and take a breath. They must also have the type of candid relationship of mutual accountability where they can discuss ways to correct mistakes in a restorative fashion.

To help parents and students perceive us as a united front, we place both of our names on our class syllabus. And when we email parents, we add each other to the distribution list, use first-person plural pronouns such as "we" and "our," and include both of our names in the closing.

Share Responsibility

When co-teaching, every student in the class should be considered both teachers' students. We always have to remember it is not *your* or *my* students, but *OUR* students. This philosophy means that both teachers share responsibility for planning, instruction, parent outreach, grading, and classroom management.

DIFFERENTIATION FOR DIVERSE LEARNERS

One advantage of a co-teaching classroom is that students have two professional educators in the room to both identify and intervene when they need assistance. Planning and implementing differentiation strategies are more feasible when you have the benefit of two teachers present—it creates opportunities for individualized and small group instruction.

Of course, just having two teachers in the room doesn't automatically mean this kind of differentiation will happen. It takes a collegial, reflective, and mutually accountable co-teaching relationship to ensure that students gain these benefits.

What Could Go Wrong?

While research and experience show co-teaching can lead to more success for all students, it is not always an easy process to work with other teachers. There will be times when teachers have personality conflicts, disagreements, or difficulties working together. However, one way to overcome these challenges is to always keep the needs of students at the forefront of all discussions. When times get tough with co-teaching, keep this in mind and always keep trying!

Technology Connections

A list of resources for co-teaching can be found at "Selected Resources Related to Co-Teaching" (http://www.ascd.org/publications/books/110029/chapters/Selected_Resources_Related_to_Co-Teaching.aspx).

Information on co-teaching with ELLs can be found at "The Best Resources for Co-Teaching with ELLs" (http://larryferlazzo.edublogs.org/2017/07/07/the-best-resources-on-co-teaching-with-ells-please-suggest-more).

We have two favorite shoebox challenge resources. Frugal Fun for Boys and Girls offers more than 30 shoebox engineering challenges for students of all ages. Their website is called "30+ Awesome Stem Challenges for Kids (with Inexpensive or Recycled Materials)" (https://frugalfun4boys.com/awesome-stem-challenges). The Scottish Council for Development and Industry created a PDF of eight shoebox challenges that can easily be altered for use in any country. The PDF can be downloaded for free at "Stem in a Shoebox on a Shoestring" (www.yecscotland.co.uk/LiteratureRetrieve.aspx?ID=137398).

References

AAUW (American Association of University Women). (n.d.). Who we are. Retrieved from https://www.aauw.org/who-we-are

Achieve, Inc. (2017a). Next Generation Science Standards: DCI Arrangements of the Next Generation Science Standards. Retrieved from https://www.nextgenscience.org/sites/default/files/AllDCI.pdf

Achieve, Inc. (2017b). Topic arrangementt of the Next Generation Science Standards. Retrieved from https://www.nextgenscience.org/sites/default/files/AllTopic.pdf

Ackoff, R., & Greenberg, D. (2008). *Turning learning right side up: Putting education back on track*. Upper Saddle River, NJ: Pearson Prentice Hall.

ACT, Inc. (2019). Preparing for the ACT test. Retrieved from http://www.act.org/content/dam/act/unsecured/documents/Preparing-for-the-ACT.pdf

Alesch, K. E., & Niblack-Rickard, F. E. (2018). The effect of goal setting and student self-reflection on motivation and on task behavior in the upper elementary public Montessori environment. Retrieved from Sophia, the St. Catherine University repository website: https://sophia.stkate.edu/cgi/viewcontent.cgi?article=1282&context=maed

Allday, R., Bush, M., Ticknor, N., & Walker, L. (2011). Using teacher greetings to increase speed to task engagement. *Journal of Applied Behavior Analysis, 44*, 393–393. Retrieved from https://www.researchgate.net/publication/51254238_Using_teacher_greetings_to_increase_speed_to_task_engagement

Allday, R. A. (2011). Responsive management: Practical strategies for avoiding overreaction to minor misbehavior. *Intervention in School and Clinic, 46*(5), 292–298. Retrieved from http://citeseerx.ist.psu.edu/viewdoc/download?doi=10.1.1.838.1619&rep=rep1&type=pdf

Allday, R. A., & Pakurar, K. (2007). Effects of teacher greetings on student on-task behavior. *Journal of Applied Behavior Analysis, 40*(2), 317–320. doi:10.1901/jaba.2007.86-06

Alrashidi, O., Phan, H. P., & Ngu, B. H. (2016). Academic engagement: An overview of its definitions, dimensions, and major conceptualisations. *International Education Studies, 9*(12), 41–52. Retrieved from https://files.eric.ed.gov/fulltext/EJ1121524.pdf

Andrade, H. G. (2001). The effects of instructional rubrics on learning to write. *Current Issues in Education, 4*(4), 1–22. Retrieved from https://scholarsarchive.library.albany.edu/cgi/viewcontent.cgi?referer=http://scholar.google.com/&httpsredir=1&article=1005&context=etap_fac_scholar

Archaeological Institute of America. (n.d.). Lesson plans. Retrieved from https://www.archaeological.org/programs/educators/lesson-plans

Asari, S., Ma'Rifah, U., & Arifani, Y. (2017). The use of cooperative round robin discussion model to improve students' holistic ability in TEFL class. *International Education Studies, 10*(2), 139–147. Retrieved from https://files.eric.ed.gov/fulltext/EJ1130616.pdf

Association for Supervision and Curriculum Development. (2011). What is performance assessment? Retrieved from https://pdo.ascd.org/lmscourses/PD11OC108/media/Designing_Performance_Assessment_M2_Reading_Assessment.pdf

Bae, S., & Kokka, K. (2016). Student engagement in assessments: What students and teachers find engaging. Stanford, CA: Stanford Center for Opportunity Policy in Education and Stanford Center for Assessment, Learning, and Equity. Retrieved from https://edpolicy.stanford.edu/sites/default/files/publications/student-engagement-assessments-final.pdf

Bauernfeind, N. M. (2016). The impact of movement on student learning and engagement. Doctoral dissertation. Retrieved from https://digitalcommons.hamline.edu/cgi/viewcontent.cgi?article=5174&context=hse_all

Bayraktar, A. (2013). Nature of interactions during teacher-student writing conferences: Revisiting the potential effects of self-efficacy beliefs. *Eurasian Journal of Educational Research, 50*, 63–86. Retrieved from https://files.eric.ed.gov/fulltext/EJ1059851.pdf

Beach, E. (2018). Hydro power vs solar power advantages. Retrieved from https://sciencing.com/hydro-power-vs-solar-power-advantages-6513.html

Beck, I., McKeown, M. G., & Kucan, L. (2002). *Bringing words to life: Robust vocabulary instruction.* New York, NY: Guilford Press.

Berwick, C. (2019, March 12). Keeping girls in STEM: 3 barriers, 3 solutions. Edutopia. Retrieved from https://www.edutopia.org/article/keeping-girls-stem-3-barriers-3-solutions

Biddle, S. (2012). The 10 greatest (accidental) inventions of all time. NBC News. Retrieved from http://www.nbcnews.com/id/38870091/ns/technology_and_science-innovation/t/greatest-accidental-inventions-all-time/#.XA2vxWhKhPY

Bigelow, K. E. (2012). Designing for success: Developing engineers who consider universal design principles. *Journal of Postsecondary Education and Disability, 25*(3), 211–225. Retrieved from https://files.eric.ed.gov/fulltext/EJ994287.pdf

Billings, E., & Walqui, A. (n.d.). Topic Brief 3: De-mystifying complex texts: What are "complex" texts and how can we ensure ELLs/MLLs can access them? New York, NY: New York State Education Department. Retrieved from http://www.nysed.gov/bilingual-ed/topic-brief-3-de-mystifying-complex-texts-what-are-complex-texts-and-how-can-we-ensure

Black, P., & Wiliam, D. (1998). Inside the black box: Raising standards through classroom assessment. *Phi Delta Kappa, October*, 1–13. Retrieved from https://www.rdc.udel.edu/wp-content/uploads/2015/04/InsideBlackBox.pdf

Blackburn, B. (2008). *Rigor is NOT a four letter word.* Larchmont, NY: Eye on Education.

Blazar, D., & Kraft, M. A. (2017). Teacher and teaching effects on students' attitudes and behaviors. *Educational Evaluation and Policy Analysis, 39*(1), 146–170. doi:10.3102/0162373716670260

Blumenfeld, P. C., Soloway, E., Marx, R. W., Krajcik, J. S., Guzdial, M., & Palincsar, A. (1991). Motivating project-based learning: Sustaining the doing, supporting the learning. *Educational Psychologist, 26*(3–4), 369–398. doi:10.1080/00461520.1991.9653139

Bogaert, N. (n.d.). 4 golden rules of ideation. Retrieved from https://www.boardofinnovation.com/blog/golden-rules-of-ideation

Brownstein, M. (2019). Implicit bias. In *Stanford Encyclopedia of Philosophy*. Stanford, CA: Stanford University Press. Retrieved from https://plato.stanford.edu/entries/implicit-bias

BSCS Science Learning. (n.d.). BSCA 5E instructional mode. Retrieved from https://bscs.org/bscs-5e-instructional-model

Burgstahler, S. (2015). Universal design: Process, principles, and applications. Retrieved from https://www.washington.edu/doit/universal-design-process-principles-and-applications

Burnside, O. (2018, May 10). Success in action series: Surviving the implementation dip. Retrieved from https://www.naspa.org/rpi/posts/success-in-action-series-surviving-the-implementation-dip

Byrd, C. M. (2016). Does culturally relevant teaching work? An examination from student perspectives. *SAGE Open*, 1–10. Online. Retrieved from. doi:10.1177/2158244016660744

Callaway, R. F. (2017). A correlational study of teacher efficacy and culturally responsive teaching techniques in a southeastern urban school district. *Journal of Organizational & Educational Leadership, 2*(2), 1–27. Retrieved from https://files. eric.ed.gov/fulltext/EJ1144813.pdf

Carnegie Mellon University. (n.d.). What is the difference between formative and summative assessment? Retrieved from https://www.cmu.edu/teaching/ assessment/basics/formative-summative.html

Carson, R. (1962). *Silent spring.* Boston, MA: Houghton Mifflin.

Castro, J. (2011, May 24). The learning brain gets bigger – then smaller. Scientific American. Retrieved from https://www.scientificamerican.com/article/the-learning-brain-gets-bigger-then-smaller

Cermele, A. M. (2017). Measuring the impact of three different co-teaching models on student test results in ninth-grade Algebra I. Doctoral dissertation. St. John Fisher College Fisher Digital Publications. (Fisher Paper 300)

Chadiha, K. (2019). State of science on unconscious bias. San Francisco: University of California San Francisco, Office of Diversity and Outreach. Retrieved from https://diversity.ucsf.edu/resources/state-science-unconscious-bias

City University of New York. (n.d.). Engaging students through writing: The case of a science class. Retrieved from https://www.csi.cuny.edu/faculty-staff/resources/ writing-resources/science-class

Coley, J. D., Vitkin, A. Z., Seaton, C. E., & Yopchick, J. E. (2005). Effects of experience on relational influences in children: The case of folk biology. *Proceedings of the Annual Meeting of the Cognitive Science Society, 46*, 471–475. Retrieved from http://citeseerx.ist.psu.edu/viewdoc/download?doi=10.1.1.102.9747&rep= rep1&type=pdf

College Board. (n.d.). Test dates and deadlines. Retrieved from https:// collegereadiness.collegeboard.org/sat-subject-tests/register/test-dates-deadlines

Collins, C. (2019, January 25). Why "both sides" of a story aren't enough. Teaching Tolerance. Retrieved from https://www.tolerance.org/magazine/ why-both-sides-of-a-story-arent-enough

Common Core State Standards. (n.d.). Common Core State Standards for English Language Arts & Literacy in History/Social Studies, Science, and Technical Subjects. Retrieved from http://www.corestandards.org/wp-content/uploads/ ELA_Standards1.pdf

Common Core State Standards Initiative. (2010). Common Core State Standards for English Language Arts & Literacy in History/Social Studies, Science, and Technical Subjects. Retrieved from http://www.corestandards.org/wp-content/ uploads/ELA_Standards1.pdf

Common Core State Standards Initiative. (2019a). English Language Arts standards. Standard 10: Range, quality, & complexity. Measuring text complexity: Three factors. Retrieved from http://www.corestandards.org/ELA-Literacy/ standard-10-range-quality-complexity/measuring-text-complexity-three-factors

Common Core State Standards Initiative. (2019b). Math: Standards for Mathematical Practice. Retrieved from http://www.corestandards.org/Math/Content

Common Core State Standards Initiative. (2019c). Measurement: Measurement & data. Retrieved from http://www.corestandards.org/Math/Content/MD

Concordia University. (2016). Concordia University welcomes John Maeda. Retrieved from https://www.cu-portland.edu/giving/concordia-university-welcomes-john-maeda

Cook, C. R., Fiat, A., Larson, M., Daikos, C., Slamrod, T., Holland, E. A., et al. (2018). Positive greetings at the door: Evaluation of a low-cost, high-yield proactive classroom management strategy. *Journal of Positive Behavior Interventions, 20*(3), 149–159. doi:10.1177/1098300717753831

Costley, K. C. (2014, October 30). The positive effects of technology on teaching and student learning. Retrieved from https://files.eric.ed.gov/fulltext/ED554557.pdf

Cowan, A. (2013). New science standards emphasize the engineering design process. Retrieved from https://www.sciencebuddies.org/blog/new-science-standards-emphasize-the-engineering-design-process?from=Blog

Culatta, R. (2019). Backward design. Retrieved from https://www.instructionaldesign.org/models/backward_design

Dakin, C. (2013). The effects of comprehension through close reading. Master's thesis. St. John Fisher College, Fisher Digital Publications (237). Retrieved from https://fisherpub.sjfc.edu/cgi/viewcontent.cgi?article=1238&context=education_ETD_masters

Darwin, C. (1859). *On the origin of the species*. London, UK: John Murray.

Dasgupta, N. (2013). Implicit attitudes and beliefs adapt to situations: A decade of research on the malleability of implicit prejudice, stereotypes, and the self-concept. *Advances in Experimental Psychology, 47*, 233–279. Retrieved from https://www.researchgate.net/publication/285905888_Implicit_Attitudes_and_Beliefs_Adapt_to_Situations_A_Decade_of_Research_on_the_Malleability_of_Implicit_Prejudice_Stereotypes_and_the_Self-Concept

Davenport, K. (2018). The benefits of offering students choice in assessment. Retrieved from https://medium.com/its-literacy/the-benefits-of-offering-students-choice-in-assessment-b7458fa54b8c

Deady, K. (2017, August 11). 5 steps to becoming a culturally responsive teacher. Retrieved from https://www.teachaway.com/blog/5-steps-becoming-culturally-responsive-teacher

Dhanapal, S., & Shan, E. W. Z. (2014). A study on the effectiveness of hands-on experiments in learning science among year 4 students. *International Online Journal of Primary Education, 3*(1), 29–40. Retrieved from https://umexpert.um.edu.my/file/publication/00001089_139130.pdf

Doggart, S. (2011). Twinkle twinkle little rip-off: The dark secrets of the world's most recognizable tune. *The Telegraph.* (14 November). Retrieved from www.telegraph.co.uk/expat/expatlife/8877033/Twinkle-twinkle-little-rip-off-the-dark-secrets-of-the-worlds-most-recognisable-tune.html

Dweck, C. S. (2006). *Mindset: The new psychology of success.* New York, NY: Random House.

Dweck, C. S. (2014). On the difference between a fixed and growth mindset. Retrieved from https://www.youtube.com/watch?v=hXyesVD4EJI

Dyer, F. L., & Martin, T. C. (1910). *Edison: His life and inventions.* Whitefish, MT: Kessinger Publishing LLC.

Dyer, K. (2013, August 26). Formative assessment is not for grading. Retrieved from https://www.nwea.org/blog/2013/formative-assessment-is-not-for-grading

The Education Alliance, Brown University. (n.d.). Student-centered instruction. Retrieved from https://www.brown.edu/academics/education-alliance/teaching-diverse-learners/student-centered-instruction

Education Endowment Foundation. 2017. Science: Improving the teaching and learning of science. Retrieved from https://educationendowmentfoundation.org.uk/school-themes/science/

Eisenbach, B. B. (2016, February). Student reflection: A tool for growth and development. Weekly reflections guide teaching and learning. *AMLE Magazine.* Retrieved from https://www.amle.org/BrowsebyTopic/WhatsNew/WNDet/TabId/270/ArtMID/888/ArticleID/586/Student-Reflection-A-Tool-for-Growth-and-Development.aspx

Engineering and Technology History Wiki. (2015). Early light bulbs. Retrieved from https://ethw.org/Early_Light_Bulbs

EurekAlert!. (2015, August 13). New information is easier to learn when composed of familiar elements. Retrieved from https://www.eurekalert.org/pub_releases/2015-08/cmu-nii081315.php

EurekAlert!. (2019). "Doing science" rather than "being scientists," more encouraging to those underrepresented in the field. Retrieved from https://www.eurekalert.org/pub_releases/2019-05/nyu-sr051319.php

Famous Scientists. (2014). Robert Bunsen. Retrieved from https://www.famousscientists.org/robert-bunsen/

Ferlazzo, L. (2011, April 27). The best resources for learning about the "achievement gap" (or "opportunity gap"). Retrieved from http://larryferlazzo.edublogs.org/2011/04/27/the-best-resources-for-learning-about-the-achievement-gap

Ferlazzo, L. (2015, September 14). Strategies for helping students motivate themselves. Edutopia. Retrieved from https://www.edutopia.org/blog/strategies-helping-students-motivate-themselves-larry-ferlazzo

Ferlazzo, L. (2016, May 17). Response: Culturally sustaining pedagogy "increases student engagement & learning." Education Week. Retrieved from http://blogs.edweek.org/teachers/classroom_qa_with_larry_ferlazzo/2016/05/response_culturally_sustaining_pedagogy_increases_student_engagement_learning.html

Ferlazzo, L. (2019, March 21). New study says student self-assessment effective & it makes one particular useful point. Retrieved from http://larryferlazzo.edublogs.org/2019/03/21/new-study-says-student-self-assessment-effective-it-makes-one-particular-useful-point

Ferlazzo, L., & Hull Sypnieski, K. (2018, March 29). Activating prior knowledge with English Language Learners. Edutopia. Retrieved from https://www.edutopia.org/article/activating-prior-knowledge-english-language-learners

Feynman, R. (1973). *Take the world from another point of view*. Boston, MA: WGBH Public Broadcasting System.

Fisher, D., & Frey, N. (2013). Annotation: Noting evidence for later use. Principal Leadership. Retrieved from https://s3-us-west-1.amazonaws.com/fisher-and-frey/documents/annotation.pdf

Flaherty, C. (2019, June 7). (More) bias in science hiring. Inside Higher Ed. Retrieved from https://www.insidehighered.com/news/2019/06/07/new-study-finds-discrimination-against-women-and-racial-minorities-hiring-sciences

Frey, N., & Fisher, D. (2013). Close reading. Principal Leadership. Retrieved from https://s3-us-west-1.amazonaws.com/fisher-and-frey/documents/close_read.pdf

Friend, M., & Cook, L. (2004). Co-teaching: Principles, practices, and pragmatics. Workshop. Albuquerque: New Mexico Public Education Department, Quarterly Special Education Meeting. Retrieved from https://files.eric.ed.gov/fulltext/ED486454.pdf

Garcia, N. (2019). What is dimensional analysis? Retrieved from https://study.com/academy/lesson/what-is-dimensional-analysis-definition-examples.html

Gimbel, E. (2019, June 10). The resurgence of 3D printers in modern learning environment. EdTech. Retrieved from https://edtechmagazine.com/k12/article/2019/06/resurgence-3d-printers-modern-learning-environments-perfcon

Ginsburg, D. (2014, February 28). Bell to bell learning: Students' right, teachers' duty. Education Week. Retrieved from http://blogs.edweek.org/teachers/coach_gs_teaching_tips/2014/02/bell_to_bell_teaching_and_learning_students_right_teachers_duty.html

Girotra, K., Terwiesch, C., & Ulrich, K. T. (2010). Idea generation and the quality of the best idea. *Management Science, 56*(4). Retrieved from). doi:10.1287/mnsc.1090.1144

Gonzalez, J. (2017, September 24). Retrieval practice: The most powerful learning strategy you're not using. Retrieved from https://www.cultofpedagogy.com/retrieval-practice/?utm_source=feedburner&utm_medium=twitter&utm_campaign=Feed%3A+CultOfPedagogy+%28Cult+of+Pedagogy%29

González, N., Moll, L. C., & Amanti, C. (Eds.) (2005). *Funds of knowledge: Theorizing practices in households, communities, and classrooms.* Mahwah, NJ: Lawrence Erlbaum Associates Publishers.

Gonzalez, V. (2017, June 28). My first year as an ESL teacher. . .it wasn't all roses. Retrieved from https://elementaryenglishlanguagelearners.weebly.com/blog/are-you-practicing-culturally-responsive-teaching

Good, J. J., Woodzicka, J. A., & Wingfield, L. C. (2010). The effects of gender stereotypic and counter-stereotypic textbook images on science performance. *Journal of Social Psychology, 150*(2), 132–147. Retrieved from https://www.ncbi.nlm.nih.gov/pubmed/20397590

Grant, H., & Dweck, C. S. (2003). Clarifying achievement goals and their impact. *Journal of Personality and Social Psychology, 85*(3), 541–553. Retrieved from https://www.researchgate.net/profile/Heidi_Grant/publication/5995271_Clarifying_Achievement_Goals_and_Their_Impact/links/0c96051afa203385ff000000.pdf

Green Action for Health & Environmental Justice. (n.d.). Environmental justice and environmental racism. Retrieved from http://greenaction.org/what-is-environmental-justice

Green, V. N. (2012). Effects of classroom discussions on student performance and confidene in the science classroom. Master's paper. Montana State University. Retrieved from https://scholarworks.montana.edu/xmlui/bitstream/handle/1/1383/GreenV0812.pdf;jsessionid=7CDAC5D78AA1616E6112479CC95B79E3?sequence=1

Greenfield, S., Whelan, B., & Cohn, E. (2006). Use of dimensional analysis to reduce medication errors. *Journal of Nursing Education, 45*(2), 91–94. Retrieved from https://www.healio.com/journals/jne/2006-2-45-2/%7Bec640cd5-1c72-48d6-8aec-5752a183d166%7D/use-of-dimensional-analysis-to-reduce-medication-errors

Gregory, A., Hafen, C. A., Ruzek, E., Mikami, A. Y., Allen, J. P., & Pianta, R. C. (2016). Closing the racial discipline gap in classrooms by changing teacher practice. *School Psychology Review, 45*(2), 171–191. Retrieved from https://www.ncbi.nlm.nih.gov/pmc/articles/PMC5302858

Griss, S. (2013, March 20). The power of movement in teaching and learning. Education Week. Retrieved from https://www.edweek.org/tm/articles/2013/03/19/fp_griss.html

Gunn, J. (2017, November 3). The evolution of STEM and STEAM in the U.S. Retrieved from https://education.cu-portland.edu/blog/classroom-resources/evolution-of-stem-and-steam-in-the-united-states

Hammond, Z. (2013, March 6). Five things not to do during Black History Month. Teaching Tolerance. Retrieved from https://www.tolerance.org/magazine/five-things-not-to-do-during-black-history-month

Hammond, Z. (2015). Culturally responsive teaching & the brain: About. Retrieved from https://crtandthebrain.com/about

Hammond, Z. (2018). Culturally responsive teaching puts rigor at the center. The Learning Professional, 39 (5), 40–43. Retrieved from https://learningforward.org/wp-content/uploads/2018/10/culturally-responsive-teaching-puts-rigor-at-the-center.pdf

Hardiman, M. M., JohnBull, R. M., Carran, D. T., & Shelton, A. (2019). The effects of arts-integrated instruction on memory for science content. *Trends in Neuroscience and Education, 14,* 25–32. Retrieved from https://www.sciencedirect.com/science/article/pii/S2211949317300558

Harmon, J. M., Hedrick, W. B., & Wood, K. D. (2005). Research on vocabulary instruction in the content areas: Implications for struggling readers. *Reading & Writing Quarterly, 21*(3), 261–280. Retrieved from https://www.tandfonline.com/doi/full/10.1080/10573560590949377?scroll=top&needAccess=true

Harris, W. (n.d.). How the scientific method works. Retrieved from https://science.howstuffworks.com/innovation/scientific-experiments/scientific-method9.htm

Hattersley, L. (2016, September 16). Microsoft Excel vs Apple Numbers vs Google Sheets (for iOS). Macworld. Retrieved from www.macworld.co.uk/review/business/microsoft-excel-vs-apple-numbers-vs-google-sheets-3510107

Hattie, J., & Timperley, H. (2007). The power of feedback. *Review of Educational Research, 77*(1), 81–112. doi:10.3102/003465430298487

Hawking, S. W. (1988). *A brief history of time: From the big bang to black holes.* London, UK: Bantam.

Helmenstine, A. M. (2019, October 3). What chemistry is and what chemists do. Retrieved from https://www.thoughtco.com/what-is-chemistry-p2-604135

Hill, C. (2010). *Why so few? Women in science, technology, engineering, and mathematics.* Washington, DC: AAUW. Retrieved from https://www.aauw.org/research/why-so-few

Hooper, L. (n.d.).Formative assessment and instructional intervention. Retrieved from https://www.mailman.columbia.edu/sites/default/files/legacy/Formative-Assessment-and-Instructional-Intervention.pdf

Hopson, M. H., Simms, R. L., & Knezek, G. A. (2014). Using a technology-enriched environment to improve higher-order thinking skills. *Journal of Research on Technology in Education, 34*(2), 109–119. Retrieved from. doi:10.1080/15391523.2001.10782338

Hunter, R. (2004). *Madeline Hunter's mastery teaching.* Thousand Oaks, CA: Corwin.

International Institute for Restorative Practices. (n.d.). Defining restorative: 5.2 circles. Retrieved from https://www.iirp.edu/defining-restorative/5-2-circles

Irons, A. (2010). An investigation into the impact of formative feedback on the student learning experience. PhD thesis. University of Durham. Retrieved from http://etheses.dur.ac.uk/890

Janzen, J., & Stoller, F. L. (1998). Integrating strategic reading into L2 instruction. *Reading in a Foreign Language, 12*(1), 251–269. Retrieved from http://nflrc.hawaii.edu/rfl/PastIssues/rfl121janzen.pdf

Jensen, P. A., & Moore, R. (2009). What do help sessions accomplish in introductory science courses? *Journal of College Science Teaching, 38*(5), 60–64. Retrieved from https://www.questia.com/library/journal/1G1-219656756/what-do-help-sessions-accomplish-in-introductory-science

JISC. (2015). Student self-reflection. Retrieved from www.jisc.ac.uk/guides/transforming-assessment-and-feedback/self-reflection#

Jordan, L. (2018, January 17). Women report high levels of gender discrimination in STEM fields. Seeker. Retrieved from https://www.seeker.com/culture/women-report-high-levels-of-gender-discrimination-in-stem-fields

Kamehameha Schools. (2007). The writing process: An overview of research on teaching writing as a process. Retrieved from http://www.ksbe.edu/_assets/spi/pdfs/reports/WritingProcessreport.pdf

Kang, M. J., Hsu, M., Krajbich, I., Loewenstein, G., McClure, S. M., Wang, J. T.-Y., et al. (2008). The hunger for knowledge: Neural correlates of curiosity, Semantic Scholar. Retrieved from https://www.semanticscholar.org/paper/The-Hunger-for-Knowledge-%3A-Neural-Correlates-of-Kang-Hsu/43b06df4bcef7435a12e22dc8bbfb9891e3e3bf7

Kang, M. J., Hsu, M., Krajbich, I., Loewenstein, G., McClure, S. M., Wang, J. T.-Y., et al. (2009). The wick in the candle of learning: Epistemic curiosity activates reward circuitry and enhances memory. *Psychological Science, 20*(8), 263–273. Retrieved from https://www.cmu.edu/dietrich/sds/docs/loewenstein/WickCandleLearning.pdf

Khoii, R., & Poorafshari, B. (2018). The impact of cooperative performance on the cloze test on the development of vocabulary knowledge. Paper presented at International Conference "ICT for Language Learning." Retrieved from https://www.academia.edu/2083046/The_Impact_of_Cooperative_Performance_on_the_Cloze_Test_on_the

Kilic, D., Sezen, N., & Sari Uzun, M. (2012). A study of pre-service science teacher's graphing skills. *Procedia – Social and Behavioral Sciences, 46*, 2937–2941. Retrieved from https://www.sciencedirect.com/science/article/pii/S1877042812017223

Knobloch, J. (1994). *Xunzi: A translation and study of the complete works* (Vol. 3, Books 7–16). Redwood City, CA: Stanford University Press.

Kozleski, E. B. (2010). Culturally responsive teaching matters! Retrieved from http://www.equityallianceatasu.org/sites/default/files/Website_files/CulturallyResponsiveTeaching-Matters.pdf

Krueger, A. (2010, November 16). 15 life-changing inventions that were created by mistake. Business Insider. Retrieved from https://www.businessinsider.com/these-10-inventions-were-made-by-mistake-2010-11

Ladson-Billings, G. (1994). *The dreamkeepers: Successful teachers of African American children.* San Francisco, CA: Jossey-Bass.

Lai, M., Luong, D., & Young, G. (2015). A study of kinesthetic learning activities effectiveness in teaching computer algorithms within an academic term. In *Proceedings of international conference on Frontiers in Education: Computer Science and Computer Engineering* (pp. 44–50). Las Vegas, Nevada, USA (July 27–30). Retrieved from http://worldcomp-proceedings.com/proc/p2015/FEC2400.pdf

Larson, L., Dixon, T., & Townsend, D. (2013). How can teachers increase classroom use of academic vocabulary? *Voices from the Middle, 20*(4), 16–21. Retrieved from https://www.bhamcityschools.org/cms/lib5/AL01001646/Centricity/Domain/131/Classroom%20Use%20of%20Academic%20Vocabulary.pdf

Latham, G. P., & Seijts, G. (2006). Learning goals or performance goals: Is it the journey or the destination? Ivey Business Journal. Online. Retrieved from https://iveybusinessjournal.com/publication/learning-goals-or-performance-goals-is-it-the-journey-or-the-destination

Lee, A. M. I. (n.d.). Instructional intervention: What you need to know. Retrieved from https://www.understood.org/en/learning-attention-issues/treatments-approaches/educational-strategies/instructional-intervention-what-you-need-to-know

Lemov, D. (2015a, August 10). Dylan Wiliam advises: Forget the rubric; use work samples instead. Retrieved from https://teachlikeachampion.com/blog/dylan-wiliam-advises-forget-rubric-use-work-samples-instead

Lemov, D. (2015b, December 10). What is "breaking the plane"? Retrieved from http://teachlikeachampion.com/blog/what-is-breaking-the-plane

Lewis, V. (2017). Veroniiiica: Veronica with four eyes. Retrieved from https://veroniiiica.com/2017/08/07/photosensitivity-in-the-classroom

Libarkin, J., & Ording, G. (2012). The utility of writing assignments in undergraduate bioscience. *CBE Life Sciences Education, 11*(1), 39–46. doi:10.1187/cbe.11-07-0058

Liou, D. D.-Y. (2011). Students of color and their teachers' expectations for academic success. Doctoral dissertation. Retrieved from ProQuest Dissertations Publishing. (ProQuest 3486571)

Literary Devices. (n.d.). Definitions and examples of literary terms. Retrieved from https://literarydevices.net/narrative#

Lloyd, R. (1999, September 30). Metric mishap caused loss of NASA orbiter. Retrieved from http://www.cnn.com/TECH/space/9909/30/mars.metric.02

Ludwig, M. J., Boyle, A., & Lindsay, J. (2017, November 7). Review of evidence: Arts integration research through the lens of the Every Student Succeeds Act. Retrieved from https://www.wallacefoundation.org/knowledge-center/Documents/Arts-Integration-Research-Every-Student-Succeeds-Act-ESSA.pdf

Lyman, F. (1981). The responsive classroom discussion. In A. S. Anderson (Ed.), *Mainstreaming digest* (pp. 109–113). College Park, MD: University of Maryland College of Education.

Lynch, M. (2015, November 8). Culturally responsive teaching starts with students. Retrieved from https://www.teachthought.com/pedagogy/culturally-responsive-teaching-starts-with-students

Manoli, P., & Papadopoulou, M. (2012). Graphic organizers as a reading strategy: Research findings and issues. *Creative Education, 3*(3), 348–356. Retrieved from https://file.scirp.org/pdf/CE20120300011_69910750.pdf

Martinez, M. (2016, January 28). Flint, Michigan: Did race and poverty factor into water crisis? Retrieved from https://www.cnn.com/2016/01/26/us/flint-michigan-water-crisis-race-poverty

Marzano, R. J. (2004). The importance of background knowledge. In R. J. Marzano (Ed.), *Building background knowledge for academic achievement.* Alexandria, VA: ASCD. Retrieved from http://www.ascd.org/publications/books/104017/chapters/The-Importance-of-Background-Knowledge.aspx

Marzano, R. J. (2007). *The art and science of teaching: A comprehensive framework for effective instruction.* Alexandria, VA: Association for Supervision and Curriculum Development.

Marzano, R. J. (2010). The art and science of teaching/summarizing to comprehend. *Educational Leadership, 67*(6), 83–84. Retrieved from http://www.ascd.org/publications/educational-leadership/mar10/vol67/num06/Summarizing-to-Comprehend.aspx

Marzano, R. J. (2013). Art and science of teaching/targets, objectives, standards: How do they fit? *Educational Leadership, 70*(8), 82–83. Retrieved from http://www.ascd.org/publications/educational-leadership/may13/vol70/num08/Targets,-Objectives,-Standards@-How-Do-They-Fit%C2%A2.aspx

Marzano, R. J. (n.d.). *Tips from Dr. Marzano: The highly engaged classroom.* Alexandria, VA: ASCD. Retrieved from https://www.marzanoresearch.com/resources/tips/hec_tips_archive#tip25

Marzano, R. J., Carbaugh, B., Rutherford, A., & Toth, D. (2013). Marzano Center observation protocol for the 2014 Marzano teacher evaluation model. Retrieved from https://www.learningsciences.com/wp/wp-content/uploads/2017/06/2014-Protocol.pdf

Mastromonaco, A. (2015). Exit tickets' effect on engagement and concept attainment in high school science. Master's thesis. Dominican University of California Graduate Master's Theses, Capstones, and Culminating Projects, 184. Retrieved from https://scholar.dominican.edu/cgi/viewcontent.cgi?article=1185&context=masters-theses

Mathes, J. C. (2017). History of the University of Michigan College of Engineering 1940–1970. In *The University of Michigan, an encyclopedic survey supplement* (pp. 123–136). Ann Arbor, MI: University of Michigan Press. Retrieved from http://um2017.org/History_of_Engineering_1940-1970.html

Matulka, R., & Wood, D. (2013). *History of the light bulb.* Washington, DC: U.S. Department of Energy. Retrieved from https://www.energy.gov/articles/history-light-bulb

McDaniel, M. A., Agarwal, P. K., & Huelser, B. J. (2011). Test-enhanced learning in a middle school science classroom: The effects of quiz frequency and placement. *Journal of Educational Psychology, 103*(2), 399–414. Retrieved from https://pdfs.semanticscholar.org/780e/e39bcd30d72dd4702eee9245f725922838d9.pdf

Mercer, N., Dawes, L., Wegerif, R., & Sams, C. (2004). Reasoning as a scientist: Ways of helping children to use language to learn science. *British Educational Research Journal, 30*(3), 359–378. Retrieved from https://thinkingtogether.educ.cam.ac.uk/publications/journals/Mercer_Dawes_WegerifandSams2004.pdf

Miller, A. (2011, December 15). Courageous conversation: Formative assessment and grading. Edutopia. Retrieved from https://www.edutopia.org/blog/courageous-conversation-andrew-miller

Miller, D. I., Nolla, K. M., Eagly, A. H., & Uttal, D. H. (2018). The development of children's gender-science stereotypes: A meta-analysis of 5 decades of U.S. draw-a-scientist studies. *Child Development, 89*(6), 1943–1955 Retrieved from. doi:10.1111/cdev.13039

Minahan, J. (2017). Helping anxious students move forward. *Educational Leadership, 75*(4), 44–50. Retrieved from https://jessicaminahan.com/wp-content/uploads/Helping-Anxious-Students-Move-Forward-Red-Work-Avoidance-Minahan_EL_1218.pdf

Mindset Scholars Network. (2015). Learning mindsets: Purpose and relevance. Retrieved from https://mindsetscholarsnetwork.org/learning-mindsets/purpose-relevance#

Mindset Works. (2017). Decades of scientific research that started a growth mindset revolution. Retrieved from https://www.mindsetworks.com/science

Mitchell, K. (2018, January 10). Women in STEM experience discrimination more than women in non-STEM fields & here are ways to fix that. Bustle. Retrieved from https://www.bustle.com/p/women-in-stem-experience-discrimination-more-than-women-in-non-stem-fields-here-are-ways-to-fix-that-7845715

Naidu, B., Briewin, M., & Embi, M. A. (2013). Reading strategy: Tackling reading through topic and main ideas. *English Language Teaching, 6*(11), 60–64. Retrieved from http://www.ccsenet.org/journal/index.php/elt/article/view/31108

National Aeronautics and Space Administration (NASA). (2014). *International system of units: The metric measurement system.* Retrieved from https://www.nasa.gov/offices/oce/functions/standards/isu.html

National Center for Educational Statistics (NCES). (2018). *Characteristics of public school teachers.* Washington, DC: U.S. Department of Education. Retrieved from https://nces.ed.gov/programs/coe/indicator_clr.asp

National Center for Educational Statistics (NCES). (2019). *Projections of education statistics to 2027* (46th ed.). Washington, DC: U.S. Department of Education. Retrieved from https://nces.ed.gov/pubs2019/2019001.pdf

National Council of Teachers of Mathematics. (2015). The metric system. Retrieved from https://www.nctm.org/Standards-and-Positions/Position-Statements/The-Metric-System

National Education Association (NEA) Foundation. (n.d.). Writing tutorial. Retrieved from https://www.neafoundation.org/for-educators/grant-resources/writing-tutorial

National Research Council. (1996). *National science education standards.* Washington, DC: National Academy Press.

National Research Council. (1997). Misconceptions as barriers to understanding science. In National Research Council, *Science teaching reconsidered: A handbook* (Chapter 5). Washington, DC: National Academies Press. Retrieved from https://www.nap.edu/read/5287/chapter/5

National Research Council. (2012). *A framework for K-12 science education: Practices, crosscutting concepts, and core ideas.* Washington, DC: The National Academies Press. Retrieved from https://www.nap.edu/catalog/13165/a-framework-for-k-12-science-education-practices-crosscutting-concepts

National Science Teaching Association. (2014). Science and engineering practices. Retrieved from https://ngss.nsta.org/PracticesFull.aspx

National Science Teaching Association. (2015). NSTA position statement: Safety and school science instruction. Retrieved from https://www.nsta.org/about/positions/safety.aspx

National Science Teaching Association. (n.d.). Crosscutting concepts. Retrieved from https://ngss.nsta.org/crosscuttingconceptsfull.aspx

Nevid, J. S., Pastva, A., & McClelland, N. (2012). Writing-to-Learn assignments in introductory psychology: Is there a learning benefit? *Teaching of Psychology, 39*(4), 272–275. doi:10.1177/0098628312456622

Next Generation Science Standards. (2017). DCI arrangements. Retrieved from https://www.nextgenscience.org/sites/default/files/AllDCI.pdf

NGSS. (2013a). "All standards, all students": Making the next generation science standards accessible to all students. In National Research Council. (Ed.), *Next generation science standards: For states, by states (contents and research background of the standards)*. Washington, DC: National Academies Press. Retrieved from https://www.nextgenscience.org/sites/default/files/Appendix%20D%20Diversity%20and%20Equity%206-14-13.pdf

NGSS. (2013b). Science and engineering practices in the next generation science standards. In National Research Council. (Ed.), *Next generation science standards: For states, by states*. Washington, DC: The National Academies Press. Retrieved from https://www.nap.edu/read/18290/chapter/12

NGSS. (2013c). Crosscutting concepts. In National Research Council. (Ed.), *Next generation science standards: For states, by states*. Washington, DC: The National Academies Press. Retrieved from https://www.nextgenscience.org/sites/default/files/Appendix%20G%20-%20Crosscutting%20Concepts%20FINAL%20edited%204.10.13.pdf

NGSS. (2013d). Engineering design in the NGSS. In National Research Council. (Ed.), *Next generation science standards: For states, by states*. Washington, DC: The National Academies Press. Retrieved from https://www.nextgenscience.org/sites/default/files/Appendix%20I%20-%20Engineering%20Design%20in%20NGSS%20-%20FINAL_V2.pdf

NGSS. (2013e). Connections to the common core state standards for mathematics. In National Research Council. (Ed.), *Next generation science standards: For states, by states*. Washington, DC: The National Academies Press. Retrieved from https://www.nextgenscience.org/sites/default/files/Appendix-L_CCSS%20Math%20Connections%2006_03_13.pdf

NGSS. (2013f). Case study 1: Economically disadvantaged students and the next generation science standards. In National Research Council. (Ed.), *Next generation science standards: For states, by states (contents and research background of the standards)*. Washington, DC: The National Academies Press. Retrieved from https://www.nextgenscience.org/sites/default/files/%281%29%20Economically%20Disadvantaged%206-14-13_0.pdf

NGSS. (2013g). Three-dimensional learning. In National Research Council. (Ed.), *Next generation science standards: For states, by states*. Washington, DC: The National Academies Press. Retrieved from https://www.nextgenscience.org/three-dimensions

NGSS. (2013h). MS-PS2 motion and stability: Forces and interactions. In National Research Council. (Ed.), *Next generation science standards: For states, by states*. Washington, DC: The National Academies Press. Retrieved from https://www.nextgenscience.org/dci-arrangement/ms-ps2-motion-and-stability-forces-and-interactions

NGSS. (2013i). HS energy. In National Research Council. (Ed.), *Next generation science standards: For states, by states*. Washington, DC: The National Academies Press. Retrieved from https://www.nextgenscience.org/topic-arrangement/hsenergy

NGSS. (n.d.). FAQs. In National Research Council. (Ed.), *Next generation science standards: For states, by states (contents and research background of the standards).* Washington, DC: The National Academies Press. Retrieved from https://www.nextgenscience.org/faqs##Contents1

NGSS Life Sciences. (2018). Classroom procedures. Retrieved from https://www.ngsslifescience.com/science.php/science/classroom_management_procedures

Nicholson, K. (2011, January 3). Brief #4: Outcome-based education. Retrieved from http://www.archive.jfn.ac.lk/OBESCL/MOHE/OBE-Articles/Academic-documents-articles/4.OBE-Brief-4.pdf

Novak, M. A. (2017). Case studies listening to students using kinesthetic movement while learning to graph linear functions. Doctoral dissertation. Ohio LINK Electronic Theses & Dissertations Center. Retrieved from https://etd.ohiolink.edu/!etd.send_file?accession=kent1498162366548228&disposition=inline

Okonofua, J. A., & Eberhardt, J. L. (2015). Two strikes: Race and the disciplining of young students. *Psychological Science, 26*(5), 1–8. Retrieved from https://www.americanbar.org/content/dam/aba/events/youth_at_risk/Okonofua%20%20Eberhardt%20-%20Two%20Strikes%20-%20Race%20and%20the%20Disciplining%20of%20Young%20Students%20(1).authcheckdam.pdf

Organisation for Economic Co-operation and Development (OECD). (2015). New approach needed to deliver on technology's potential in schools. Paris, France: OECD .Retrieved from https://www.oecd.org/education/new-approach-needed-to-deliver-on-technologys-potential-in-schools.htm

Pare, D. (2017). Grouping students by ability: Homogeneous versus heterogeneous classrooms. Doctoral dissertation. Retrieved from ProQuest Dissertations Publishing. (ProQuest 10618052)

Patall, E. A., Cooper, H., & Wynn, S. R. (2010). The effectiveness and relative importance of choice in the classroom. *Journal of Educational Psychology, 102*(4), 896–915. doi:10.1037/a0019545

PBLWorks. (2019). Project-based learning. Retrieved from https://www.pblworks.org/what-is-pbl

Performance Assessment Resource Bank. (n.d.). Physics. Retrieved from https://www.performanceassessmentresourcebank.org/tags/physics

Phillips, K. W. (2014). How diversity makes us smarter. *Scientific American, 311*(4), 42–47. doi:10.1038/scientificamerican1014-42

Pious, S. (n.d.). The psychology of prejudice: An overview. Retrieved from https://secure.understandingprejudice.org/apa/english/page24.htm

Pope, D., Brown, M., & Miles, S. (2015). *Overloaded and underprepared: Strategies for stronger schools and healthy, successful kids.* Hoboken, NJ: Wiley.

PowerSchool. (2016). How to isolate skill gaps for corrective instruction. Retrieved from https://www.powerschool.com/resources/blog/how-to-isolate-skill-gaps-for-corrective-instruction

Prince, J. M., & Felder, M. R. (2006). Inductive teaching and learning methods: Definitions, comparisons, and research bases. *Journal of Engineering Education, 95,* 123–138. doi:10.1002/j.2168-9830.2006.tb00884.x

Pritchard, R. J., & Honeycutt, R. L. (2005). The process approach to writing instruction: Examining its effectiveness. Retrieved from https://www.nwp.org/cs/public/download/nwp_file/8500/Writing_Research_-_Chapter_19_-_Reduced.pdf?x-r=pcfile_d

Quote Investigator. (n.d.). I have gotten a lot of results! I know several thousand things that won't work. Retrieved from https://quoteinvestigator.com/2012/07/31/edison-lot-results/#more-4181

Rasinski, T., Padak, N., & Newton, J. (2017). The roots of comprehension. *Educational Leadership, 74*(5), 41–45. Retrieved from http://www.ascd.org/publications/educational-leadership/feb17/vol74/num05/The-Roots-of-Comprehension.aspx

Rea, S. (2015, June 8). Researchers find everyone has a bias blind spot. Retrieved from https://www.cmu.edu/news/stories/archives/2015/june/bias-blind-spot.html

Reardon, S. F., Kalogrides, D., Fahle, E. M., & Zárate, R. C. (2018). The relationship between test item format and gender achievement gaps on math and ELA tests in 4th and 8th grade. *Educational Researcher, 47*(5), 284–294. Retrieved from https://cepa.stanford.edu/content/relationship-between-test-item-format-and-gender-achievement-gaps-math-and-ela-tests-4th-and-8th-grade

Reichelova, M., & Teleki, A. (2013). The role of dimensional analysis in teaching physics. Retrieved from https://www.researchgate.net/publication/256187138_The_Role_of_Dimensional_Analysis_in_Teaching_Physics

Robb, L., & Lewis, J. P. (2007). *Poems for teaching in the content areas: 75 powerful poems to enhance your history, geography, science, and math lessons.* New York, NY: Scholastic.

Rosenshine, B. (2012). Principles of instruction: Research-based strategies that all teachers should know. *American Educator, 36*(1), 12–19. Retrieved from https://www.aft.org/sites/default/files/periodicals/Rosenshine.pdf

Rosenthal, R., & Jacobson, L. (1968). Pygmalion in the classroom. *The Urban Review, 3*(1), 16–20. Retrieved from https://link.springer.com/article/10.1007/BF02322211

Rossiter, M. J., Abbott, M. L., & Kushnir, A. (2016). L2 vocabulary research and instructional practices: Where are the gaps? *The Electronic Journal for English as a Second Language, 20*(1), 1–25.

Rowe, M. B. (1986). Wait time: Slowing down may be a way of speeding up! *Journal of Teacher Education, 37,* 43–50. Retrieved from https://www.scoe.org/blog_files/Budd%20Rowe.pdf

Salustri, F. A. (2003). An extremely abbreviated history of engineering design. Retrieved from http://deseng.ryerson.ca/~fil/t/history0.html

Sample, K. (2019). Central American farmers head to the U.S., fleeing climate change. *New York Times*, April 13. Retrieved from https://www.nytimes.com/2019/04/13/world/americas/coffee-climate-change-migration.html

Settles, I. H. (2014). *Women in STEM: Challenges and determinants of success and well-being.* Washington, DC: American Psychological Association. Retrieved from https://www.apa.org/science/about/psa/2014/10/women-stem

Shapiro, J. (2014, June 27). Games in the classroom: What the research says. KQED News. Retrieved from https://www.kqed.org/mindshift/36482/games-in-the-classroom-what-the-research-says

Sharp, L. (2012). Stealth learning: Unexpected learning opportunities through games. *Journal of Instructional Research, 1,* 42–48. Retrieved from https://files.eric.ed.gov/fulltext/EJ1127609.pdf

Silverstein, S. (1974). *Where the sidewalk ends.* New York, NY: HarperCollins.

Silverstein, S. (1981). *A light in the attic.* New York, NY: HarperCollins.

Society of Women Engineers. (2016). What drives female attrition in STEM professions? Highlights from the Society of Women Engineers' National Gender Culture Study. Retrieved from https://research.swe.org/wp-content/uploads/sites/2/2016/08/16-SWE-029-Culture-Study-10_27_16-Final-CP.pdf

Society of Women Engineers. (2019). 2019 research update: Percentage of female engineers and college graduates broken down by state. Retrieved from https://alltogether.swe.org/2019/02/2019-research-update-percentage-of-female-engineers-and-college-graduates-broken-down-by-state/

Solis, M., Vaughn, S., Swanson, E., & McCulley, L. (2012). Collaborative models of instruction: The empirical foundations of inclusion and co-teaching. *Psychology in the Schools, 49*(5), 498–510. doi:10.1002/pits.21606

Sparks, S. D. (2015, March 31). Middle students find success tutoring peers, in N.Y.C. Study. *Education Week, 34*(9). Retrieved from https://www.edweek.org/ew/articles/2015/04/01/middle-students-find-success-tutoring-peers-in.html?cmp=ENL-EU-NEWS2-RM

Staats, C. (2015–2016). Understanding implicit bias: What educators should know. *American Educator, 39*(4), 29–33. Retrieved from https://www.aft.org/ae/winter2015-2016/staats

Stacho, T. J. (2013). My students have trouble with transitions. . .What can I do? Retrieved from http://www.behaviorinschools.com/My_Students_Have_a_Hard_Time_with_Transitions.pdf

Stembridge, Y. (2017, April 14). 3 lessons learned when bringing to life culturally responsive practices. Retrieved from http://www.myreflectionmatters.org/3-lessons-learned-when-bringing-to-life-culturally-responsive-practices/

Stroessner, S., & Good, C. (n.d.). Stereotype threat: An overview. Excerpts and adaptions from Reducing Stereotype Threat.org. Retrieved from https://diversity.arizona.edu/sites/default/files/stereotype_threat_overview.pdf

Swearingen, R. (2002). A primer: Diagnostic, formative, & summative assessment. Retrieved from http://www.ewcupdate.com/userfiles/assessmentnetwork_net/file/A%20Primer_%20Diagnostic,%20Formative,%20&%20Summative%20Assessment.pdf

Tarasawa, B. (2018, September 27). Three research-based culturally responsive teaching strategies. Retrieved from https://www.nwea.org/blog/2018/three-research-based-culturally-responsive-teaching-strategies/

Taylor, A. (2017). Guest post: How to help students overcome misconceptions. Retrieved from http://www.learningscientists.org/blog/2017/7/25-1

Taylor, M. A., Wirth, O., Olvina, M., & Alvero, A. M. (2016). Experimental analysis of using examples and non-examples in safety training. *Journal of Safety Research*, *59*, 97–104. doi:10.1016/j.jsr.2016.10.002

Taylor, W. (2019, January 10). Enrichment in the classroom. Retrieved from https://learningessentialsedu.com/enrichment-in-the-classroom/

The Teacher Toolkit. (n.d.). Exit ticket. Retrieved from http://www.theteachertoolkit.com/index.php/tool/exit-ticket

Teaching Science as Inquiry. (2019). Exploring our fluid Earth: Scale, proportion, and quantity. Retrieved from https://manoa.hawaii.edu/exploringourfluidearth/standards-alignment/next-generation-science-standards-ngss/crosscutting-concepts/scale-proportion-and-quantity

Terada, Y. (2019, May 22). 50 years of children drawing scientists. Edutopia. Retrieved from https://www.edutopia.org/article/50-years-children-drawing-scientists

Tewksbury, B. (n.d.). What are jigsaws? Retrieved from https://serc.carleton.edu/NAGTWorkshops/teaching_methods/jigsaws/why.html

Thompson, A. G., Philipp, R. A., Thompson, P. W., & Boyd, B. A. (1994). Calculational and conceptual orientations in teaching mathematics. In D. B. Aichele & A. F. Coxford (Eds.), *Professional development of teachers of mathematics* (pp. 79–92). Reston, VA: National Council of Teachers of Mathematics.

To, J., & Carless, D. (2015). Making productive use of exemplars: Peer discussion and teacher guidance for positive transfer of strategies. *Journal of Further and Higher Education*, *40*(6), 746–764. doi:10.1080/0309877x.2015.101431

Torres, T. (2016, February 4). Why brainstorming doesn't work (and what to do instead). Retrieved from https://www.inc.com/teresa-torres/why-brainstorming-doesnt-work-and-what-to-do-instead.html

Tyler, R. W. (1950). *Basic principles of curriculum and instruction*. Chicago, IL: University of Chicago Press.

UCD Neuropsychology Lab. (2018). Why is the prefrontal cortex so important? Retrieved from https://ucdneuropsychologylab.wordpress.com/2018/12/17/why-is-the-prefrontal-cortex-so-important/

The Understood Team. (2019). The difference between accommodations and modifications. Retrieved from https://www.understood.org/en/learning-attention-issues/treatments-approaches/educational-strategies/the-difference-between-accommodations-and-modifications

University of Arizona, Office of Instruction & Assessment. (n.d.). Backward design. Retrieved from https://oia.arizona.edu/content/290

University of Leicester. (2010, October 28). Two's company but three's a crowd: Two people can learn to cooperate intuitively, but larger groups need to communicate. Science Daily. Retrieved from https://www.sciencedaily.com/releases/2010/10/101027202505.htm

University of Washington, Center for Teaching and Learning. (n.d.). Constructing tests. Retrieved from http://www.washington.edu/teaching/teaching-resources/preparing-to-teach/constructing-tests

von Stumm, S., Hell, B., & Chamorro-Premuzic, T. (2011). The hungry mind: Intellectual curiosity is the third pillar of academic performance. *Perspectives on Psychological Science, 6*(6), 574–588. Retrieved from https://www.hungrymindlab.com/wp-content/uploads/2015/10/von-Stumm-et-al-2011.pdf

Wade-Leeuwen, B., Vovers, J., & Silk, M. (2018, June 10). Explainer: What's the difference between STEM and STEAM? The Conversation, online. Retrieved from https://theconversation.com/explainer-whats-the-difference-between-stem-and-steam-95713

Wenglinsky, H. (2005). *Using technology wisely: The keys to success in schools.* New York, NY: Teachers College Press.

Wenglinsky, H., & Silverstein, S. C. (2006–2007). The science training. *Educational Leadership, Dec.–Jan.,* 24–29. Retrieved from http://web.nmsu.edu/~susanbro/educ451/docs/The_science_training_of_teachers.pdf

Wieman, C. E. (2014). Large-scale commentary of science teaching methods sends clear message. *Proceedings of the National Academy of Sciences of the United States, 111*(23), 8319–8320.

Wiggins, G., & McTighe, J. (2005). *Understanding by design.* Alexandria, VA: Association for Supervision and Curriculum Development.

Williams, D. H., & Shipley, G. P. (2018). Cultural taboos as a factor in the participation rate of native Americans in STEM. *International Journal of STEM Education, 5*(17), 1–8. Retrieved from https://link.springer.com/article/10.1186/s40594-018-0114-7#citeas

Witkin, R. (1983). Jet's fuel ran out after metric conversion errors. *New York Times* (July 30). Retrieved from https://www.nytimes.com/1983/07/30/us/jet-s-fuel-ran-out-after-metric-conversion-errors.html

Wong, H. K., & Wong, R. T. (2018). *The first days of school: How to be an effective teacher* (5th ed.). Mountain View, CA: Harry K. Wong Publications.

Wong, H. K., Wong, R. T., & Jondahl, S. F. (2014). *The classroom management book.* Mountain View, CA: Harry K. Wong Publications.

Woods, J. (2017). Assessments 101: A policymaker's guide to K-12 assessments. Education Commission of the States. Retrieved from https://www.ecs.org/wp-content/uploads/Assessments-101_A-policymakers-guide-to-K-12-assessments.pdf

World Meteorological Organization. (n.d.). Frequently asked questions. Retrieved from http://www.wmo.int/pages/prog/wcp/ccl/faq/faq_doc_en.html

Wormeli, R. (2007). *Differentiation: From planning to practice, grades 6–12.* Portsmouth, NH: Stenhouse Publishers.

Wormeli, R. (2016). Teaching students responsibility. Association for Middle Level Education. Retrieved from http://www.amle.org/BrowsebyTopic/WhatsNew/WNDet/TabId/270/artmid/888/articleid/639/Teaching-Students-Responsibility.aspx

The Writing Center. (2019). Argument. Retrieved from https://writingcenter.unc.edu/tips-and-tools/argument/

Your Dictionary. (n.d.). Examples of informative essays. Retrieved from https://examples.yourdictionary.com/examples-of-informative-essays.html

Zupko, R., & Chisholm, L. J. (2019). Measurement system. In *Encyclopedia Britannica.* Retrieved from https://www.britannica.com/science/measurement-system

Index

organizers for, 381; grouping strategies for, 29; high school, 48–49; hypothesis writing by, 48; IEPs for, 406; inquiry process for, 97–98; math teaching for, 282; moving students, 26–27; PBL for, 126; reading comprehension of, 191–192; research and, 47; reviewing content for, 447–448; scientific method and, 47–49; student attention, 27; student monitoring and, 29; teaching writing to, 219–220; time management for, 27–29; vocabulary teaching for, 170

Diversity: creativity and, 26; enrichment and, 396

Documentaries, 98

Donne, John, 339

Drafting, 207

Drama, 342–345

Drawing, 163–164

Drawing the Atmospheric Layers - Answer Key, 187

Drawing the Atmospheric Layers - Elementary and Junior High, 201

The Dreamkeepers (Ladson-Billings), 395

Dress Code, Science Safety Contract, 8–9

DRY MIX, 260

Dua Lipa, 341

Dweck, Carol, 138

Dyer, F. L., 137

E

Earth and Space Science: astronomy topics, 164, 211, 377, 461; Crosscutting Concepts for, 432; debate topics for, 250; diverse contributors to, 410; ecology topics, 217, 264, 409, 477; environmental science topics, 47; geology topics, 117–118; kinesthetic movement and, 351; measurement in, 277; NGSS and, 337; PBL for, 125; storytelling in, 345; website design and, 350

Earthquakes, 91, 93, 167, 350

Eclipses, 166, 350

Ecology: units, 217, 264, 409, 477; vocabulary, 163

Ecology Essential Questions Argument Essay, 233–234

Ecology Example Argument Essay Organizer, 236

Edison (Dyer & Martin, T. C.), 137

Edison, Thomas, 136–138

EDpuzzle, 28

Edublog, 52

Education World, 127

Effective communication: for activating prior knowledge, 374; beginning and ending of class, 424; for classroom procedures, 19; in cleaning procedures, 21; in co-teaching, 502; cultural responsiveness and, 397; in discussions, 240; of engineering process results, 134, 147; of information, 88; in inquiry process, 89; in math teaching, 259; in time management, 23; for vocabulary teaching, 162; for writing teaching, 206

Egg drop challenge, 139, 151

Eight-Year Study, 471

Elementary and middle school: graphs for, 259–261; humanities studies in, 336–337

ELLs. *See* English language learners

Emdin, Christopher, 408

Empathy, 474

Encyclopedia Brittanica, 269

Ending of class: application, 424–433; classroom management during, 425; common problems with, 433; creative problem solving for, 424; critical thinking, 424; diverse learners during, 433; effective

communication for, 162; ELLs and, 168; Excel, 279; Fast Facts, 169–170; hypothesized definitions in, 163; interdisciplinary examples, 164–165; NGSS standards on, 161; prefixes, 162–164; research on, 161; roots, 162–164; skills for intentional scholars on, 161; student handouts and examples, 170–171; suffixes, 162–164; teacher-for-a-day, 168; technology connections for, 171; word exposure and, 164
Vocabulary Definition Worksheet, 174
von Stumm, S., 89

W
Wait time, discussion strategies and, 251
Wakefield, Ruth, 51
Walker, C. J., 410
Warm-ups, 423–425; background knowledge and, 428; common problems with, 433; ideas for, 426–430; previewing material for, 426–428; previous material review, 430
Washington, George, 269
Water Cycle, 187
Water Cycle Concept Map, 197
Water recycling, 246

Watson, James, 346
We Are Teachers website, 284, 355
Webquests, 28
Website design, 350
West, Gladys, 410
Where the Sidewalk Ends (Silverstein), 337
Which Type of Graph Should I Use?, 291
Which Type of Graph Should I Use? - Answer Key, 293–294
White, Mandi, 20, 117, 167, 209, 217, 222, 241, 242, 479, 501, 506
Wiggins, Grant, 454, 472
Wildlife Strike Data Analysis and Interpretation, 265, 295–296
Wildlife Strike Data Analysis and Interpretation - Answer Key, 265, 297–298
Wildlife strikes, 429
William, Dylan, 455
Wind farms and turbines, 127, 131, 382
Women, in science, 346, 411–412
Women's History Month, 409–410
Wong, Harry, 19, 30, 404
Wong, Rosemary, 30, 404
Woody, Caroline, 387, 390
Word banks, 6, 170
Word Wall Challenge, 165–169

Word Wall Challenge Rubric, 166, 175
Word Wall Examples, 176
Word Wall Wall, 165, 167
Words in a Sentence, 165, 171
Writing: bad, 208; CER structure, 215–217; effective, 208; essays, 122, 124, 217; frames, 219, 433; grants, 23; ICE structure, 215–217; informative/explanatory, 211–215; journal/learning log, 218; narrative, 209–211; quickwrites, 219; summaries, 219
Writing, teaching: application of, 206–220; argument in, 215–218; benefits of, 205; checklists in, 207; climax, 210; common problems in, 220–221; critical thinking for, 206; daily writing activities in, 218; defining, 205; for diverse learners, 219–220; drafting in, 207; essay topic ideas in, 215–218; exposition, 210; falling action, 210; feedback in, 214; models, 208; NGSS for, 206; prewriting in, 206–207; process of, 206–207; publishing in, 207; research for, 206;